Statecraft and security

In this book a group of influential and distinguished scholars analyse some of the key questions in contemporary international relations. The book is in three parts. In the first, the lessons and legacies of Cold War are examined, including debates about its rise and fall, and the implications of the superpower nuclear confrontation. Part Two asks questions about powers and politics in the post-Cold War world: about the USA's potential as a world leader, Russia's troubled future, Japan's potential power, the China syndrome and Africa's problems. The final part looks further into the future, discussing international organisation, life politics and the potentialities for human society under the conditions of globalisation. The book shows how different countries and different groups of countries are confronting urgent issues of statecraft in a period of radical global transformation.

KEN BOOTH is Professor in the Department of International Politics at the University of Wales, Aberystwyth. His books include *Strategy and Ethnocentrism* (1979), *Law, Force and Diplomacy* (1985), *International Relations Theory Today* (co-edited, 1995), and *International Theory: Positivism and Beyond* (co-edited, 1996).

Statecraft and security

The Cold War and beyond

Edited by

Ken Booth

CAMBRIDGE
UNIVERSITY PRESS

PUBLISHED BY THE PRESS SYNDICATE OF THE UNIVERSITY OF CAMBRIDGE
The Pitt Building, Trumpington Street, Cambridge CB2 1RP, United Kingdom

CAMBRIDGE UNIVERSITY PRESS
The Edinburgh Building, Cambridge, CB2 2RU, United Kingdom
http://www.cup.cam.ac.uk
40 West 20th Street, New York, NY 10011–4211, USA   http://www.cup.org
10 Stamford Road, Oakleigh, Melbourne 3166, Australia

First published 1998

Printed in the United Kingdom at the University Press, Cambridge

Typeset in Plantin 10/12pt [CE]

A catalogue record for this book is available from the British Library

Library of Congress cataloguing in publication data

Statecraft and security: the Cold War and beyond / edited by Ken Booth.
    p.   cm.
Includes index.
ISBN 0 521 47453 1 (hardback) – ISBN 0 521 47977 0 (paperback)
1. World politics – 1989 – 2. Cold War – Influence. I. Booth, Ken.
D860.S75   1998
909.82 – dc21 97–40985 CIP

ISBN 0 521 47453 1 hardback
ISBN 0 521 47977 0 paperback

This book is in honour of Michael MccGwire

Contents

Part three   Beyond: resistances and reinventions

Contributors

PHILIP ALLOTT is Reader in International Public Law in Cambridge University and has been a Fellow of Trinity College since 1973. From 1960 to 1973 he was a legal adviser in the British Foreign Office. He is the author of *Eunomia – New Order for a New World* (1990).

BARRY M. BLECHMAN is co-founder and Chairman of the Henry L. Stimson Center, a non-profit research and educational organisation in Washington DC. He has worked on international security issues for more than thirty years and is currently examining ways to strengthen the UN collective security system.

KEN BOOTH is Professor of International Politics, University of Wales, Aberystwyth, and a former Chair of the British International Studies Association. His most recent book, edited with Steve Smith, is *International Relations Theory Today* (1995).

MICHAEL CLARKE is Professor of Defence Studies at King's College, London and Executive Director of the Centre for Defence Studies. He has previously taught at the universities of Newcastle upon Tyne, Manchester and Wales. He has been a Fellow at The Brookings Institution, Washington DC, and the Royal Institute of International Affairs, London.

MICHAEL COX is Professor of International Politics, University of Wales, Aberystwyth, and an Associate Research Fellow at the Royal Institute of International Affairs, London. His latest book is *US Foreign Policy after the Cold War* (1995).

DONALD C. F. DANIEL is Professor and Director of the Strategic Research Department, Center for Naval Warfare Studies, Naval War College, Newport, RI. His most recent book co-edited with Bradd C. Hayes, is *Beyond Traditional Peacekeeping* (1995).

CORI DAUBER teaches Communication Studies at the University of North Carolina. Her research focuses on argument and rhetorical structures in the debate over Western defence policy. She is the author of *Cold War Analytical Structures and the Post War World* (1993).

KAREN DAWISHA is Professor of Government at the University of Maryland, College Park. Her most recent books are (with Bruce Parrott) (*Russia and the New States of Eurasia: The Politics of Upheaval* (1994) and *Eastern Europe, Gorbachev, and Reform: The Great Challenge* (1989: 2nd edn, 1990).

RAYMOND L. GARTHOFF is a Senior Fellow in Foreign Policy Studies at the Brookings Institution, Washington DC, and is a retired US ambassador. He is the author of many works relating to the Cold War, including *The Great Transition: American–Soviet Relations and the End of the Cold War* (1994), and *Detente and Confrontation: American–Soviet Relations from Nixon to Reagan* (1985; rev. edn, 1994).

ANTHONY GIDDENS is Director of the London School of Economics and Political Science. He was formerly Professor of Sociology and Fellow of King's College, Cambridge. His most recent books include *The Transformation of Intimacy* (1993) and *Beyond Left and Right* (1994).

GEOFFREY HAWTHORN teaches Sociology and Politics in the Faculty of Social and Political Sciences at Cambridge University. His most recent book is *Plausible Worlds: Possibility and Understanding in History and the Social Sciences* (1991). He works in particular on the politics, national and international, of the South.

MICHAEL HERMAN was for thirty-five years a British civil servant in the Government Communications Headquarters, the Cabinet Office and the Defence Intelligence Staff. He has been a Research Fellow at Nuffield College, Oxford and Keele University, and teaches intelligence at King's College London. He writes on intelligence and international relations.

IAN HOPWOOD works for UNICEF in New York. He has recently undertaken research on social policy in Africa, with special reference to the health sector and the social consequences of economic reform. He has been UNICEF Representative in Zambia and Guinea and has also worked in Zaire, Cameroon and the Congo.

CATHERINE MCARDLE KELLEHER is currently serving at NATO as the personal representative of US Secretary of Defense and the Defense Advisor to the US Ambassador. She was previously a Senior Fellow at the Brookings Institution, Washington DC. She has taught at Maryland, Denver, Michigan and Columbia universities.

RICHARD NED LEBOW is Professor in the Graduate School of Public and International Affairs and Department of Political Science at the University of Pittsburg. His most recent book (with Janice Gross Stein) is *We All Lost the Cold War* (1994).

JOHN MCDONNELL is a Russian military affairs analyst with the US Central Intelligence Agency. He was at the Centre for Foreign Policy Studies, Dalhousie University, Halifax, Canada, during the 1970s and co-edited (with Michael MccGwire and Ken Booth) *Soviet Naval Policy* (1975) and (with Michael MccGwire) *Soviet Naval Influence* (1977).

ROBERT O'NEILL is the Chichele Professor of the History of War and a Fellow of All Souls College, Oxford. He was formerly Director of the International Institute for Strategic Studies, London and Head of the Strategic and Defence Studies Centre, Australian National University, Canberra.

OLES M. SMOLANSKY is Professor of International Relations at Leighigh University. His most recent books are *The USSR and Iraq: The Soviet Quest for Influence* (1991), and co-edited (with George Ginsburgs and Alvin Z. Rubinstein), *Russia and America: From Rivalry to Reconciliation* (1993).

DENIS STAIRS is Professor of Political Science at Dalhousie University in Halifax, Canada. He was formerly University Vice-President (Academic and Research) and President of the Canadian Political Science Association. He is a Fellow of the Royal Society of Canada, and author of *The Diplomacy of Constraint: Canada, the Korean War, and the United States* (1974).

JANICE GROSS STEIN is Harrowston Professor of Conflict Management and Negotiation at the University of Toronto. Her most recent book (with Richard Ned Lebow) is *We All Lost the Cold War* (1994).

JOHN D. STEINBRUNER has been Director of Foreign Policy Studies at the Brookings Institution in Washington since 1978. Before that he taught at Yale and Harvard Universities. Recent publications include (with Ashton B. Carter and William J. Perry) *A New Concept of Cooperative Security* (1992), and (with William Kaufmann) *Decisions for Defense: Prospects for a New Order* (1991).

Preface

We live in an era of question-marks. We thought that we knew what was happening during the Cold War: but did we? We assume we are asking the right questions today: but are we? Is history at an end, or only at a beginning? Can we possibly know the future, when we are so divided about the meaning of the past? Are we justified in feeling so anxious about the twenty-first century, or is it merely end-of-millennial *angst*? Having survived the Cold War, why are governments so confused and seemingly unable to do a better job? What are we to think?

The chapters below attempt to give students of world affairs a range of ideas and information to help them think about such questions in relation to some of the major issues in international relations. They span the debate over the origins and nuclear lessons of the Cold War to philosophical speculation about the so-called human condition. I asked a group of influential and distinguished scholars to write short and accessible think-pieces on major themes, with minimal academic paraphenalia, and a high ratio of ideas and argument to descriptive detail. As such, I trust that these essays will be plundered by students and appreciated by general readers in their own attempts to understand the complex pressures which have shaped, and are shaping all our lives.

In the course of preparing this book I have incurred several debts. The chief one is to the contributors themselves, for their exceptional degree of cooperation. This is clearly the result of their commitment to their friend and colleague to whom this book is dedicated. I wish also to thank, once again, Louise Barham, Donna Griffin, Vicki Jones and Elaine Lowe for their customary efficiency, cheerfulness and word-processing skills and Mark Smith for proof-reading and compiling the index. Finally, it gives me pleasure to record that any royalties made from this book will be devoted to an annual Michael MccGwire prize for mature students in the Department of International Politics at the University of Wales, Aberystwyth, an inspired idea of Eurwen Booth.

KEN BOOTH
Aberystwyth

Introduction

Ken Booth

This is a crucial time to reflect on the recent past and long-term future of international relations. During the Cold War there was an Iron Curtain in all our heads (to a lesser or greater extent), but no sooner had it been dismantled than we become burdened by fresh disquiets. The West, and the rest of the industrialised world, slipped from Cold War pressures to post-Cold War preoccupations almost without drawing breath. For the others it was simply dependency as usual. It was therefore easy to move towards the future on the basis of traditionalist axioms and half-digested lessons about the present. For Western policy-making elites in particular, as the ostensible 'winners' of the Cold War, the aims and assumptions of international politics remain shaped to some degree by the experiences of the half-century of Cold War. But what exactly were those experiences? And what conclusions should be drawn from them? The problem has been pithily expressed by Michael MccGwire as follows: 'To be sure "we" won and "they" lost, and to that extent the Soviet Union was proved "wrong": but were "we" therefore right?' By identifying a set of key issue-areas, the essays below attempt to step back from the headlines and outside the intellectual inertia of Cold War ideas, and so nudge thinking in directions which will help readers chart their own courses through this era of question marks, in terms of rethinking the past and reinventing the future, pragmatically managing the transition from where we are to where we might want to be in terms of international security.

Overview

The structure of the book is simple. Its three parts are divided on the basis of the recent past (the Cold War), the present (post-Cold War), and the longer term future ('beyond'). However, I will argue later that the three concepts are always practically linked by a critical synergy, since we live, simultaneously, in our pasts, presents and futures. What

1

we do is always shaped by the collision or collusion of memory and moment, hope and fear.

This introductory chapter gives a summary of the individual essays, with a linking commentary showing how they fit together in a coherent whole. To begin, the chapters in Part One discuss key lessons and legacies of the Cold War. The first chapter attempts to provide a context for thinking about the next stage in international relations – Cold War mindsets and models of the post-Cold War. The Cold War and its endings (to use Cynthia Enloe's insightful plural) represent the starting point of the book, the Cold War being the experience that warped human history, by turning a relatively straightforward contestation of states into a potential species catastrophe as a result of any breakdown in the superpower strategy of Mutual Assured Destruction (MAD). The next three chapters discuss central questions about this period: why did the Cold War begin and develop the way it did? What brought it to an end? How should we think about the roles played by nuclear weapons in the global superpower confrontation? The chapters in Part Two ask – and seek to answer – big questions about the problems and prospects facing various actors and regions. The focus at the start is on the Cold War superpowers, since it was their relationship which structured much of international politics for nearly half a century, and the United States and Russia will obviously remain key actors for the indefinite future. (The book cannot provide coverage of every actor and region. Chapters follow on China and Japan, Africa and the multi-state periphery of Russia, and the roles of 'medium' powers; these provide perspectives on East Asia, states under strain, and secure but globally weak powers. Space constraints demand choice, and this has led to a 'northern' and 'developed world' focus, because it is here where the potential for agency in the post-Cold War world is greatest.) The four chapters in Part Three take a variety of longer term perspectives, looking at recent trends as they affect people, societies and international society as a whole. The chapters share the assumption that the Cold War was not an act of nature, like a storm; it was a human phenomenon, created and sustained by structures of thought. Likewise, what lies beyond the Cold War will be shaped by the structures of thought, conceived and reconceived, and made material, by individuals and the political units they constitute and reconstitute. The final chapters discuss where we think we are in human history – as individuals, as societies and as humans – and where we might be. They are informed by a sense that humanity has arrived at a decisive evolutionary crossroads, in this the first truly global era.

The prominence of 'statecraft' in this book's title testifies to the continuing roles of states in setting the agendas and conducting the business of global politics, while the broadened conception of 'security' used throughout underlines the challenges that foreign and defence ministries face in determining the character of those agendas and the outcomes of their actions. The 'beyond' in the title refers both to chronology, in the sense that every chapter, in one way or another, is concerned with the period after the Cold War, and to the belief that the limits of Cold War thinking about international relations need to be breached; in particular, the desirability of broadening the theory and practice of statecraft, escaping the constraints of unilateral conceptions of international security, recognising the breakdown of statist norms in the face of globalisation and interdependence, and rethinking the past in re-imagining the future.

Lessons and legacies

Rethinking the past is a highly political activity, and in the first chapter I attempt to set what follows in context by arguing that the memory of the Cold War is a political prize over which there has been and will continue to be a serious struggle. Equally, there is a major debate about how to characterise the post-Cold War situation. It has largely polarised around the 'New Pessimists' and the 'Old Optimists'. The inadequacies of both positions are discussed, as are the various models which have been proffered as best describing the present state of world politics. This is not merely an academic exercise. The dominating images of reality will shape how we behave.

The relationship between images (often distorted) and behaviour (often counter-productive) is a theme of Raymond Garthoff's overview of the origins, course and ending of the Cold War. His chapter rejects the comforting simplicities of Cold War clichés about blame and instead points to the historical conjunction of international structures and human agents in the complex dynamics of the aftermath of a world war. He shows that particular decisions could be blamed on one government or leader or other, but that the general pattern was one of shared (if not necessarily equal) blame. The behaviour and attitudes of the US:SU constituted a mirror image. Both reshaped the political structures of the territories they occupied according to their own interest; both regarded their own actions as completely justified; both thought it proper to exclude the other from its own sphere; both blamed the other for the situation; and both adopted double standards.

In the light of his general theme, Garthoff emphasises the importance for scholars and policymakers to take the opportunity to learn from this experience, so as not to repeat the same errors. A major assumption in his argument – contra the neo-realist fatalists who have been so influential in the theory and practice of foreign policy – is that the Cold War was not inevitable. Outcomes were avoidable. Garthoff argues that, in the decisive 1946–50 period, a series of interlocking decisions led to the escalation and militarisation of the confrontation between the United States and the Soviet Union, but no less significant was the disappearance of efforts at cooperation and the resolution of conflicts. This surrender to the logic of conflict and pessimism offers powerful lessons to human relations at all levels.

Garthoff describes the Cold War's defining feature as the ideological worldviews of communism and anti-communism. Thus the power of ideas was central to the Cold War. The superpowers lined up as opposites, globally and in all spheres, and other aims and values were subordinated to what they saw as the necessities of the confrontation. Military considerations in particular rose in significance. A major element in Garthoff's analysis is his critique of Western nuclear deterrence policy, with its apolitical and mechanistic character. Risks were raised unnecessarily by the excessive militarisation of the super-power rivalry, faith in fallible technologies and the advancement of technical requirements over true strategic thinking. When political differences are converted into military currency in this way, a different and dangerous logic takes over. Garthoff questions whether various US interventions in the name of containment – notably Korea and Vietnam – were necessary. Some will say that it is easy to argue this now, after the struggle is over. The fact is that some said it at the time.

Turning to the end of the Cold War, Garthoff asks whether it could have been brought about sooner. He does not regard the occasional periods of superpower détente as having been decisive opportunities in this regard, because of the strength of the underlying ideological confrontation. Détente was simply a way of cushioning the risks of the global confrontation, not a set of policies to end it. Given the centrality of ideology in his analysis, the Cold War could only have ended for Garthoff when one side abandoned its position, and could persuade the other of the change. It was Mikhail Gorbachev's historical role to do this. According to Garthoff, any reasonably objective reading of the origins and development of the Cold War must lead to the conclusion that both sides contributed to its development, and hence both share the blame: but when it comes to the end of the Cold War, the role of Gorbachev must be seen as decisive. In Garthoff's judgement, the end came not because of Western pressure (the victory of geopolitical containment and the nuclear arms race) but in spite of it. The historic turning-point came about as a result of the recognition by Gorbachev of the growing contradictions in the Soviet system. The world view which had sustained one side of the Cold War was altered by political intellect, not extravagant military threats. If Garthoff is right – and remember that the Soviet Union was an 'advanced' country by most global indicators in the second half of the 1980s (not a typical 'defeated' country) – then this suggests that the ending as well as the rise of the Cold War was not the inevitable product of a structural confrontation between the first and second powers in the system, as neo-realist theory would demand. Both events were the outcome of the political choices of the participants.

In the first chapter, I will ask whether the 'real' Cold War will ever get into our books. For me this real Cold War must include a comprehensive counting of costs, actual and potential. Some historians and commentators overlook its costs in their desire to inflate the success of their own side, but a comprehensive balance sheet must be part of any attempt to draw lessons. In this respect the Cold War can be described as history's Great Escape. Never before was so much nightmarish destruction threatened to so many, so instantaneously, for so long, without it actually going off. But this obvious historical fact is now accompanied by widespread denial – an escape from memory. There is a continued and profound unwillingness to remember and internalise the potential costs of superpower Armageddon. This nuclear amnesia, common among scholars and general public alike, is typical of today's Cold War ethnic cleansing.

The attitudes just described are of considerable importance since nowhere is the infrastructural relationship between the Cold War and the post-Cold War more crucial than in the area of nuclear weapons, while what is considered to be the Cold War's nuclear commonsense feeds directly into the issue of nuclear proliferation. Consequently, sophisticated attempts to draw lessons from the nuclear dimension of the Cold War, as in the chapter by Richard Ned Lebow and Janice Stein, are urgent. Their theme is that the record of the Cold War suggests that nuclear deterrence should be viewed as a very dangerous medicine, and one on which the superpowers overdosed. While the authors are cautious about drawing wider lessons, their diagnosis points to the conclusion that nuclear weapons did not confer real security benefits during the Cold War. The message is that those states contemplating nuclear proliferation ought to look carefully at the history of the US–Soviet nuclear relationship; the chapter shows that their nuclear postures led to reckless behaviour and proved self-defeating. These lessons should also be heeded by the existing nuclear powers, whose own continuing nuclearism legitimises the self-defeating momentum of nuclear proliferation.

The Cold War nuclear rivalry will remain a controversial issue among historians, strategists and political observers for the foreseeable future; did nuclear weapons 'restrain' the SU/US from expansion/roll-back? Was MAD the great international pacifier, or was it an autonomous threat to peace? Did the nuclear arms race hasten the end of the Cold War, or did its infrastructure and rationalisation prolong it? Lebow and Stein have things to say which are relevant to these questions, but their chapter is primarily focused on issues of strategy, and the distinction between 'general' and 'immediate' deterrence. In the case of the Cuban missile crisis of 1962, immediate deterrence on the part of both superpowers proved to be provocative rather than preventive; it helped bring about just the kind of confrontation they were trying to avoid. Once the crisis erupted, however, general deterrence played a moderating role, and both sides blinked (not just the Soviet Union). As in Cuba in 1962, so general deterrence failed to avert a crisis in the Middle East in 1973. However, as in 1962 it contributed to the resolution of the crisis. Immediate deterrence failed in 1962, but was not tried in 1973.

The chapter argues that the role of nuclear weapons can be clarified by distinguishing between the strategy and reality of Cold War nuclear deterrence. The former refers to the manipulation of risk, which aggravated tensions and increased costs, whereas the 'reality' of the nuclear confrontation was the mutual realisation that superpower war would be an unprecedented catastrophe. Fortunately, the moderation induced by the reality of nuclear deterrence helped curtail the tensions associated with the dynamics of nuclear strategy. Lebow and Stein clarify other contradictory consequences of nuclear deterrence, and they challenge Cold War conventional wisdom about nuclear threats, such as the view that US nuclear strategy disciplined an aggressive and opportunity-driven USSR. In their view it was self-deterrence by the superpowers, resulting from a combination of fear of war and relative satisfaction with the status quo, that prevented catastrophe.

From their analysis of Cold War nuclear strategy, Lebow and Stein draw a number of conclusions that are at odds with those of the nuclear-use theorists of the 1980s and earlier. Their nuclear lessons point to the illusion of exploiting real or imaginary nuclear advantages, the difficulty and risk involved in trying to make credible nuclear threats, the provocative rather than restraining consequences of strategic build-ups, and the general robustness of nuclear deterrence when leaders on both sides are mutually aware of each other's fear of war. However, in practice, they argue that there was a mutual fear among Cold War opponents that nuclear deterrence was less robust than it was, and that this both increased the dangers of and prolonged the mistrust underlying the Cold War. The paradox of Cold War nuclear history is that superpower nuclear strategies undercut much of the political stability which should have been brought about by the reality of nuclear deterrence.

The final chapter in Part One looks at the Cold War and beyond in relation to one person's life and work – Michael MccGwire, to whom this book is dedicated. What he wrote in and about the Cold War, and is writing in and about what 'beyond' might mean, is the focus of the collaborative chapter by Michael Herman, Donald Daniel, John McDonnell, Michael Clarke and Cori Dauber. MccGwire's multidimensional contribution to thinking about the Cold War is analysed in such areas as naval intelligence, Soviet naval strategy, the relationship between Soviet military objectives and foreign policy, the superpower maritime confrontation, nuclear deterrence, international security and global futures. These analyses offer important insights into issues of individual choice, structures, resistances and reinventions – subjects returned to in Part Three. In this chapter will be found lessons for all of us, as it attempts to begin to bridge the gap between distant matters of statecraft and what we as scholars and the interested public might do. People are acted upon by the structures in which they find themselves, as a result of the forces of history and contingent circumstances, but we all have some space, however little, to change and challenge. Even so, human agency is frequently sucked out of the story of International Relations by the passive language we choose. The Berlin Wall did not 'fall': it was *pushed*. And the Cold War did not 'end': it was *ended*. Rewriting the future of international relations in the human interest requires rejecting language that ignores human agency. In short, if future world politics are to be an improvement over those in the past, then individuals and collectivities must decide to change their assumptions, axioms and actions. The Berlin Wall had first to be torn down in the head, and the Cold War had first to be wound down in the mind.

Powers and policies

Part Two opens its discussion of the contemporary international environment by looking at the United States, the country for which learning the lessons of the Cold War is the most urgent. The United States has the most power to shape the post-Cold War order, but at the same time it is also the country for which 'objective' learning is probably the most difficult, since it supposedly won the Cold War, and winners tend to be conservative. Consequently, uncertainty pervades much US thinking about both its own domestic situation and its international responsibilities. The United States has lost an enemy and not yet found a role. It emerged from being first-among-equals during the Cold War to being the only post-Cold War superpower. But can it lead, and if so for what purpose? What price superpower when the agenda shifts from military to economic and other instruments? What are the strengths and weaknesses of US diplomacy in the new international environment? What has been learned? These are some of the questions addressed by John Steinbruner in Chapter 5.

Between the 'declinist' and 'triumphalist' arguments about the US future in world affairs, Steinbruner adopts a nuanced stance, arguing that the United States does clearly lead the world in important ways, but that it is not clear that it can rise to the task of redesigning the post-Cold War international political order. A major constraint here is the continuing grip of Cold War thinking and habits evident in the current US military posture, economic arrangements, and ways of thinking about the world – all the result of the inertia of Cold War success. Steinbruner believes that a decisive redirection of US policy is necessary because there are changes taking place that are altering the basic conditions of international politics. He addresses two in particular: the revolution in information technology and the surge in world population, both of which are historically novel and which dramatically challenge entrenched attitudes.

In the post-Cold War era Steinbruner is certain that economic performance will be an overriding priority for governments, and that they will have to evolve more effective patterns of collaboration. In turn, economic benefits will have to be shared more widely among surging populations if civil order is to be maintained, and civil order has to be maintained if the global economy is to develop. Civil order and the global economy both require the absorption of labour. In this way a state's employment strategy is now, potentially, an international security issue. In the future international order the primary source of threat for Steinbruner is not imperialism or irredentism, but the danger of the internal disintegration of societies. Statecraft must begin at home.

Military power will remain important, but the chapter suggests that its role is moving from being central to being residual. Classic inter-state aggression is 'infeasibly expensive' and states cannot be kept together these days by force. Nevertheless, complex issues exist, where economic integration and military stabilisation converge, and which present the United States (or any aspiring world leader) with pressing tasks. These are, primarily, the creation of a stable security environment for Russia, the development of an effective international system to restore legal order when it breaks down, and the need to redesign arrangements for controlling weapons proliferation. In dealing with such problems – which involve systematic cooperation with the military establishments of former adversaries, redesigning structures of international collaboration, and overcoming the isolation of some economies – habits of thought derived from the Cold War will be influential, but not always in positive directions. The need for international collaboration in the military and economic fields therefore emerges strongly from Steinbruner's analysis. The preoccupation with meeting demands for economic satisfaction will mean that governments must relinquish their instincts for preserving independent control, and, instead, design common methods. Likewise, in the military field, he endorses the view that the only security is common security in an era of proliferating long-range destructive capabilities.

In answer to the question 'can the United States lead?' Steinbruner concludes that the record so far in the 1990s offers reasons for both optimism and pessimism. On the negative side, the United States has inherited some adverse legacies, and faces enormous contingent problems: on the positive side, the culture of the United States has proved itself to be inventive, historically, and the United States as a whole is better positioned to lead the world than any other existing polity.

Nowhere will the problem of overcoming Cold War legacies be more difficult than in the case of US relations with (the successor state to) its erstwhile superpower adversary. Russia is one of the great enigmas in the contemporary international situation. There have been a series of remarkable changes since the late 1980s, with Russia's transition to a form of democracy and a market economy, and, on the whole, Russian society has accepted the changes with remarkable equanimity. As ever, the 'loser' in a confrontation believes it has most to learn, and urgently, from its supposed mistakes; at the same time there has been great sensitivity among the Russians – a mixture of hurt pride and dented confidence – about what has been lost in terms of international status and power. In such circumstances nationalism is a significant element in the outlook of political parties across the Russian political spectrum. An isolated and ignored Russia – pressed by NATO expansion eastwards, for example – will not become a relaxed member of international society. History here is a guide, as is evident from the continuing difficulties and historical traditions discussed by Oles Smolansky in his account of Russia and its past. This chapter is followed by Karen Dawisha's exploration of the area where any future Russian ambition might first be evident, namely that political space formerly occupied by Soviet power and now dubbed the 'near abroad'.

In seeking an answer to the perennial question 'can Russia escape its past?' Smolansky emphasises the importance of geography as well as history. As a result of the centuries of expansionist success by imperial Russia, and then the Soviet Union, the present leaders in Moscow have inherited numerous problems deriving from the very extent and diversity contained within the new Russia.

The past exercises a grip on contemporary Russia through political culture. The 'old Russia' was not destroyed in 1917. It lived on in the Soviet system's authoritarianism, the sway of the Orthodox church, the secret police, the bureaucracy, corruption and nationalism. Today's Russia has strong ties – in culture and nostalgia – to both its immediate (communist) and more distant past. However, Smolansky does not paint a picture of the new Russia being entirely in the grip of history. Although Russian political culture has no roots in Western-style democracy, he believes that the seeds of a new political system have been planted, and he questions the assumption that a return to authoritarianism is simply a matter of time. Authoritarianism in Russia is not historically pre-ordained, and the apparent popularity of some extreme politicians today may rest on a fragile foundation. As ever, the economy is crucial, and Smolansky believes that the problem – a historical one – lies not with the outlook of the Russian people but with the ability and vision of those who rule them.

The legacy of the past, but also the potentiality for change, is also evident in foreign policy. In contrast with the universalist and revolutionary aspirations of the former Soviet Union, Smolansky argues that the new Russia is dramatically less interested in the 'far abroad'. Though many Russians resent the decline in their country's international prestige and power, he does not foresee a return to previous ambitions, even if extreme nationalist politicians were to achieve power. But he believes the situation is very different regarding Russia's 'near abroad'. Here, Moscow has made clear its determination to remain involved, and this is one (rare) matter on which all Russian political groups agree. In the pursuit of its goals in these neighbouring areas, Russia holds a number of material assets, notably oil, gas and military power, which it could use to political effect.

It is precisely the issue of the future relationship between Russia and different parts of its near abroad that is the theme of Karen Dawisha's wide-ranging chapter. What unites this with the previous chapter is the belief in the significance of the Russian question for future international security, and the centrality in this question of what happens in the

Eurasian political space adjacent to a possibly insecure Russia. At the heart of Dawisha's analysis is the continuing phenomenon of imperialism. She identifies two models: traditional imperialism, which is an impulse from the metropole itself, and what she calls 'autocolonialism', which results from factors within the potential colonised space.

For traditional imperialism to reassert itself in Russia it would require both a motive and a capability. She believes there is no lack of motive in some Russian political circles, nor are the capabilities absent. But the picture is complex. There are competing and distracting pressures internally, while there is a mixture of constraints as well as opportunities in the neighbouring territories. Russian public opinion, for example, has been mixed about military intervention; simultaneous with nationalist feelings seeming to demand a more assertive foreign policy, actual public support was not strongly in favour of Moscow's military adventure in Chechnya. On balance, Dawisha concludes that for the immediate future at least, the Russian state has neither the capability nor the unified will to engage in a sustained policy of imperial expansion on traditional lines. Even so, this does not mean that Russia will not dominate Eurasian political space; this is where the concept of auto-colonialism comes in.

There are two main motives for autocolonialism, security and economics, and both exist today. The economic problems of the former Soviet republics are considerable, and in comparison Russia is at a substantial advantage; the former Soviet territories now look to Moscow for subsidies, for example. There is also instability in a number of areas, and in some cases the Russian military are seen as potential helpers – not their usual image in the West. So, the new weaker states need Russia, there are traditional ties between them and Moscow, and the Kremlin is not necessarily seen as untrustworthy. At the same time as there are pressures for autocolonialism, Dawisha argues that the new Russia has moved from an inchoate policy towards its neighbours to one marking out the area as one of vital interest, and in the latter regard there is a consensus within Russia that the former Soviet area constitutes a natural Russophone zone. She argues that the international community would oppose by various means any renewed and concerted Russian drive to recreate its former empire, but she believes that it is not clear that it would condemn all Russian attempts to increase its influence and activities in what is recognised to be its 'national security zone'. Unlike the case with other collapsed empires in the twentieth century, the proximity of the metropole and the newly independent states is bound to lead to a more intense relationship. The most realistic course, according to Dawisha, is for the new states to resist the pressures for autocolonialism, and instead to promote, against all the obstacles, a policy of interdependence, with both Russia and the wider world.

One of the key actors in that wider world will be Western Europe, in whatever political and economic shape it eventually emerges. The next two chapters examine a Western Europe that is in the process of negotiating between its history and its future in both its internal development and external relations. Western Europe, historically the cockpit of inter-state rivalry, now offers the world a fascinating experiment with regard to many of the key issues of our time: inter- as well as intra-state democracy and legitimacy, the meaning of security, the evolutionary potential of trans-boundary and trans-cultural identities, the utility of war, the interplay of local and distant interests, community-building and, last but not least, the ability of societies to learn from history. Such issues are touched upon in relation to Western Europe's internal development by Catherine Kelleher and in relation to its wider challenges by Robert O'Neill.

In the debate about the future of the European Union Kelleher presents an encouraging picture. In her opinion the neo-realist theory which predicts a bleak future for Western Europe, in which traditional power politics and old rivalries will re-emerge, is too pessimistic. Evidence for this, in the short run, can be seen in the efforts towards closer monetary cooperation within the EU in the 1990s, despite all the evident difficulties. Kelleher argues that the neo-realist viewpoint is based on three false assumptions. First, it assumes that European unity was essentially a product of the Cold War. She argues that this is mistaken; its origins lay in the attempt by Europeans to find a cure for the endemic rivalry of France and Germany, and to deal comprehensively with the historic 'German problem'. Thus the impetus for European unity lay in reactions to the horror of the Second World War, and earlier historical experiences, not the Soviet threat in the Cold War. The second false assumption is the neo-realist belief that the United States will gradually abandon the European continent as a result of the disappearance of Cold War imperatives. Kelleher argues that while there is some domestic pressure within the United States for reduced involvement, policymakers have learned the powerful lessons of history; as a result, the United States is likely to remain actively engaged in Western Europe for the foreseeable future. (Its role in NATO's eastern expansion is one token of this.) In addition, key Western European governments want that engagement, and she believes that the actual post-Cold War situation demands it. Finally, there is the mistaken neo-realist assumption that contemporary Western European governments will revert to 'balance of power' politics. Again, Kelleher argues that the major players have learned from history. They fully understand that the traditional axioms of international politics led to catastrophe. National self-interest itself now tells the societies of Western Europe that there is more to gain – in a globally interdependent international system dominated by economic relations – from European cooperation rather than from disunity and competition.

Despite the weaknesses of neo-realist analysis, Kelleher accepts that it does raise legitimate concerns about the future of Western Europe, because the end of the Cold War has radically changed the framework for the development of cooperation. These concerns are examined in relation to the crucial issues of 'deepening', 'widening' and the 'German Question'. 'Deepening' refers to the problem of addressing the EU's internal relations, and is of particular importance to 'Europeanist' states such as France and Germany, and to the EU establishment in Brussels. The challenge of 'widening' membership (and at the same time re-defining the transatlantic relationship) is one of the most far-reaching issues facing the EU in its external relations. The problems involved in expanding into Central and Eastern Europe, and possibly beyond, are enormous because of the relatively underdeveloped economies of the countries in the region, and in some cases the potential for instability in their internal politics. Yet Kelleher believes that expansion is necessary if the EU is to survive, as this is the most direct way to promote democracy, economic development and security to its east, and so avoid a major division on the European continent comparable with the divide between the United States and Latin America. With respect to the future of transatlantic relations, there may be less emphasis on the need to show a common front than during the Cold War, but it is likely that transatlantic ties will continue to hold fast when really serious issues are at stake. Several post-Cold War crises have underlined the need for continued cooperation. Finally, and central to all these issues, is the 'German Question'. What will be (and should be) the role for a unified and economically dominant Germany within Western Europe? Kelleher's argument is cautiously hopeful, noting German prominence in the move towards deepening, yet the importance to Germany of widening. Many delicate issues remain, particularly regarding Germany's future security role, but in each case the solution appears to be in strengthening the *European* dimension.

Although she argues that neo-realist predictions are based on mis-apprehensions, Kelleher fears that there is a danger that people might believe them, and so they will become self-fulfilling. How Western Europe responds to its challenges will depend on how well it learns the lessons of its past. If it learns the right lessons, and has a broad vision,

then Kelleher sees the basis for unprecedented intra-European cooperation. If its thinking and statecraft are determined by the misapprehen-
sions and dark predictions of neo-realist theory, then the future will be
uncertain.

'Widening' is also a theme of Robert O'Neill's chapter, but in this
case what is at issue is Western Europe's ability to think about security
more broadly than was the case in the Cold War. The basic thrust of the
chapter is that Western Europe is not an actor of dominating global
importance in international security, but that it has considerable security
interests across the world and can make significant contributions in the
shape of forces, expertise and economic resources. O'Neill expects that
Western Europe's long-term security role will be played in partnership
with the United States and Japan, not alone.

An important theme of the chapter is that future security challenges
will be of a quite different character from those of the past. The principal
security threat for Western Europe is no longer major international war
but a possible 'avalanche of chaos'. The latter has many causes, and
some of their manifestations will have a military dimension, but in
general a wider range of responses to challenges must be conceived than
was the case in the Cold War. This is already evident in conflict
prevention, an area in which the countries of Western Europe have the
skills, but at present lack an appropriate organisation. O'Neill discusses
the existing organisations acting in the security field, and concludes that
none of them comprehensively address the security problems of the
post-Cold War era. He sketches the outline of an alternative, which he
calls *The Alliance for Development in Europe*. He hopes such an alliance
would develop the appropriate strategic thinking to help Europe avoid
the dangers of drifting along in traditional ways, giving yesterday's
answers to tomorrow's problems.

O'Neill believes that there is now an almost unanimous view that
major inter-state wars in Europe belong to history, though some security
issues remain, especially in the East. Beyond its own continent, Western
Europe has a range of security interests, such as the development of
international law, the control of weapons of mass destruction and the
promotion of human rights and democracy. A basic task here is less fire-
fighting in a traditional (military) sense than working to strengthen the
fabric of peace and international order. In this respect, O'Neill believes
the potentiality of public opinion must be stressed; for him it is
ultimately the dominant force in both national and international politics.

Japan, like Western Europe, is more an economic than a military
factor in global politics. It also fears the prospect of major inter-state

war less than the tearing apart of the fabric of international order. As a result, Japan also needs to conceive international security broadly and to look far beyond its physical horizon. But for Japan history entails sensitive legacies, both globally and regionally, and this is one of the themes of Geoffrey Hawthorn's chapter. Hawthorn contrasts the economic future of Japan, which seems clear, with its political future, which appears opaque. The different predictions about the latter range from 'realists' who believe that Japan must translate its economic power into military power, to 'idealists' who believe Japan can and will deploy its power in a civilian manner. The range of views is not surprising, given Japan's history and the complexity of the present. Nowhere is the legacy of the past more sensitive for Japan than in its relations with other countries in Asia. Japanese corporations have increasingly been investing in Asia, as well as in the West, and these investments have benefited other countries in addition to Japan; this helps mitigate the mistrust arising from history, especially when Japanese policymakers are able to handle issues sensitively. As a result, Japan has been able to develop closer ties with ASEAN, and even construct more positive relationships with China and Russia. In these cases politeness and economic power have worked together. These factors have not been similarly employed in Japan's relations with the two Koreas, however, which presently confront its policymakers with their most immediate regional problems.

After 1945 Japan developed a reputation for the quality of its decisionmaking at home and abroad. Today questions are being asked about the country's political culture and political system. The post-war experiment is under strain, and it remains to be seen whether Japan can adapt to the new circumstances. In the area of foreign policy Hawthorn argues that the consensus is unlikely to change. Although some believe that Japan will seek to become a traditional great power, possibly with nuclear weapons, Hawthorn argues that both the successes of past policies and recognition of the benefits of continuity will result in the country steering a more modest course. Hostility in Asia and elsewhere would be generated by a more assertive policy, though in future Japan will be expected to play a role with a higher profile in those areas the West construes as significant for international security. During the Cold War the foundation for Japanese security policy was the Mutual Security Treaty with the United States. Some thought its rationale might have ended when the Soviet threat disappeared, particularly against the background of the strains it had to endure during the 1980s; nevertheless, because of the mutual advantages it brings, for the present neither partner shows signs of wanting to revoke the Treaty.

For the foreseeable future Japan will not follow the road predicted by traditional realists. What matters to Japan, like other East Asian states, is economic success, and this requires cooperation rather than conflict. Prudence will also dictate East Asia following the direction in which the West wants to take the world in the next century. But East Asia, including Japan, will not regard cooperation as entailing cultural convergence. Asian states will assert their difference, both from the West and from each other. Hawthorn concludes with a view that embraces neither Fukuyama's 'end of history' nor Huntington's 'clash of civilisations'. He foresees a Japan in which pride will replace deference, an East Asia which will follow the West, and an Asia which is not one civilisation. Such a future would be infinitely more complex than some assume, but also more realistic in the best sense of the word.

Japan will be one of the key actors in shaping an answer to the question: is the future Asian? Some in the West believe that Western ascendancy in world affairs has peaked, that Asian political power will grow alongside its economic growth, that Asia rather than the West will be the real winner of the Cold War, and that the time has come for the ascendancy of 'Asian values'. As a result, there is some expectation that the West might discover its next major enemy in Asia. Against these fears, others doubt whether Asian countries can maintain their recent levels of economic growth, note the widespread internal problems and constraints within Asian countries, and wonder what exactly are *Asian* values (*whose* Asian values?) in a diverse region, rich with cultures. Together with Japan, the country towards which observers look for answers to the key questions about Asia's future is China, the historic sleeping dragon of international politics. As the century closes, with spectacular growth rates in China, the old question arises: will China finally translate its size and ambition into political and military power, or will it yet again be thwarted by the gigantism and disparity of its population, the limitations of its ideology and its infrastructural weaknesses? This is the subject of Michael Cox's chapter on the next claimant for world power out of Asia.

The historical significance of the Chinese revolution of 1949 is difficult to exaggerate, but Cox argues that we are liable to forget how threatening (to some) and appealing (to others) Mao's China once seemed to be. Every bit as significant as the 1949 revolution itself, however, has been China's growing impact on world affairs in recent decades, such that some now argue that China will come to dominate the international system within the next half century in a way comparable to the leadership of the United States in the second half of the twentieth century, and before that Great Britain.

The basis of China's emergence as a world power has been Deng's reform programme and its economic consequences – a modernising process whose origins, Cox insists, lay further back (in Mao's time) than is usually credited. Yet alongside the country's spectacular economic growth there remains the smouldering problem of the country's social and political development – a problem magnified by the fact that China contains about one quarter of the world's population. The challenges are enormous, from some political pressure to reduce the democratic deficit at home, to external pressures from the US 'democratic hegemon' on issues such as China's human rights. Given all the historic problems of governing China, Cox argues that there appears to be very little chance that Deng's immediate successors will relax their grip on power or allow freer expression for their people. The lessons of what happened to the apparently invincible Soviet Union, leading up to the capitulation in Eastern Europe in 1989 and then the final collapse of the Soviet state in 1991 seem all too apparent.

If business-as-usual is the general projection for Chinese internal politics, the same is broadly true for the country's external policy. Cox rejects the worst-case predictions being advanced about a violent Chinese will-to-power in the Asia-Pacific region. The reasons have less to do with the Chinese leadership's intentions – though these play a part – than with the complexities of and constraints on China's relations with its neighbours and the rest of the world, and with its limited economic and military capabilities through the first decade of the twenty-first century. In short, Cox believes that the worst-case predictions about China's external behaviour are based upon an exaggerated conception of the nation's real capabilities: for the foreseeable future China can only be a 'very incomplete superpower'. The danger of alarmism in the West and in the rest of Asia about China's intentions and capabilities in the aftermath of the ending of the Cold War is that it might provoke a replay of the origins of the US–Soviet Cold War, which escalated in the aftermath of the ending of the Second World War. A future US–Chinese Cold War cannot be ruled out, if the main actors repeat the mistakes of the 1940s and 1950s (see Chapters 1–4) but there are powerful factors which can and should push in the opposite direction.

While analysts of international security look towards East Asia and contemplate its economic dynamism and potential great powers, they look at Africa and see a continent that has been marginalised and in which every state and society is under strain. Hence, from most African perspectives, 'international society' at the end of the twentieth century does not look in the good shape that it does for many in the West. Cold War bipolarity has disappeared, with its ideological dividing line and threat of East–West nuclear catastrophe, but for countless millions across the globe this only serves to expose a much older bifurcation, that between the world's haves and have-nots. In these circumstances, whose post-Cold War will dominate our books – that defined by Northern neo-realists or that defined by women refugees from famine and war on the Horn of Africa? The answer is as obvious as it is old, based on the close relationship between power and agenda-setting potential. However, until we can be more confident of giving voice to marginalised voices in the standard texts of our subject, can the academic study of International Relations claim to confront 'the real' in world affairs?

In many parts of the world severe political, economic and environmental problems exist, and in none more so than Africa, the chosen focus for the chapter on the non-industrialised world. Africa is the continent out of which we all came, and on which I believe international society should be judged. Ian Hopwood's essay shows that 'Afro-pessimism' is the order of the day, but he nevertheless argues that it is not a continent without hope. Africa is both the bloodbath of Rwanda and South Africa's liberation from apartheid.

Africa south of the Sahara is suffering a widespread economic crisis. There are losses in exports and investments; the pro-Africa pro-development coalitions in many industrialised countries are not influential; and the outside world as a whole has lost interest in Africa in favour of other continents. How one interprets the causes of Africa's economic crisis shapes one's ideas for reform. One view is that the problem is essentially domestic – this is the conviction of the World Bank – and so domestic reform within African countries has been stressed. The resultant Structural Adjustment Programmes (SAPs) have sparked great controversy, and much of Hopwood's chapter is concerned with assessing the debate about their effectiveness and appropriateness. Three main weaknesses are identified: the hostile global economic environment, the design of the SAP packages, and the problems in the relationships between aid agencies and recipient governments. Among the implications of Hopwood's analysis, two are of general significance in terms of statecraft and security. First, the interconnectedness of security issues (such as the interplay between political stability, economic collapse and military dangers); and second, the tendency for governments to become involved in local crises not because of human need, but because of political expediency. The economic crises in Africa, that can have massive (in)security consequences, have political as well as economic causes, and Hopwood argues that a crisis of governance underlies Africa's development problems. As in other parts of the world, political reform in Africa has seen a rise in 'democracies', but whether imported models can survive in societies with little or no democratic tradition is a major imponderable. The task facing African societies is enormous, having simultaneously to try to consolidate new democratic institutions and bring about urgent economic reforms. Weak state institutions, vested interests, uncertain legitimacy, traditionalism and fragile civil society all have to be dealt with, and the record is so far mixed. Africa is not an undifferentiated whole, and some regions contain factors that offer more promise of success than others. But there are no quick fixes, anywhere.

Despite – even *because of* – the depth of Africa's crisis, Hopwood argues that there is reason for hope. There is learning by doing; crises stimulate invention and opportunity; space has been opened up for new definitions of development; the failure of imported models is leading to the exploration of Africa's own unique ways, and the example of Africa's reformers should inspire the outside world to become involved with Africa, but with more creative attitudes than in the past. In the working out of a new framework for partnership between Africa and the rest of the world Hopwood emphasises the importance of a commitment to a global ethic, in which the discourse of human rights should be prominent. He believes that focusing on children, and their rights and needs, might be an effective and relatively uncontroversial way ahead. There is the need to redefine development away from its economic connotation rooted in consumerist materialist values. By responding to Africa's crisis in a broader spirit, Hopwood believes that the international community could help not only to support African governments and peoples, but also rekindle a sense of common purpose and shared humanity essential for planetary survival.

One of the consequences of the decline of geopolitical interest in Africa, with the passing of the Cold War's great game, has been the space it has opened up for the initiatives of middle-level countries. This is also the case elsewhere: the multipolar system into which the post-Cold War world seems to be evolving at the state level creates more opportunities than hitherto for a positive role for so-called middle powers. Multipolarity opens up space, disorder creates incentives, and there are numerous flashpoints in which middle-power conflict resolution skills could be beneficial. To name but the most obvious: the Kurdish situation and the continuing tensions between Israel and its neighbours in the Middle East, the conflict over Kashmir and in Afghanistan in South Asia, and the possible escalation of the generation-long eyeball to eyeball confrontation on the Korean peninsula. Improving regional security must be an integral part of putting together the jigsaw of international security, and it is the potential significance of middle powers in this process which is the theme of the chapter by

Denis Stairs. He asks two main questions: what can middle powers do? And what should they do? His answers are complicated, and begin with a discussion of the problems of defining a 'middle power' and of identifying commonalities in attitudes and behaviour. Arguing that some earlier attempts to categorise middle powers have been idiosyncratic, Stairs himself comes to the conclusion that having 'middling' capabilities does not determine what middle powers will do, but only what in principle they can do. That is, middling power is a necessary but not sufficient condition for certain roles; other factors will shape what those roles might be (for example, whether a particular 'middle' power will aim to become a regional 'great' power).

Having problematised the significance of *middling* power as a determinant of the behaviour of the states that possess it, Stairs asks the normative question: what role should they play? This is a question, he recognises, implicitly rooted in the assumption that middle powers can generally be counted upon to promote the goals and policies of what he describes as the international public good. From this perspective, the key roles for middle powers are familiar: mediation, multilateralism, conflict prevention and resolution, and pluralism. Middle powers are in the middle, politically as well as in terms of resources. Stairs then goes on to examine the 'facilitating attributes' that lead a particular middle power to pursue internationalist objectives and pragmatically pluralistic policies. Importantly, Stairs debunks the assumption that middle powers are necessarily guided by virtuous motivation; he prefers to note the occasional convergence of national interest and international service. As a result, he does not feel able to deliver a neat list of middle powers. Stairs shows, for example, the prominence of *small* powers in peacekeeping – ostensibly the classical middle power role. The picture that he uncovers is one of middle powers behaving in a variety of ways; his conclusion is that the concept of 'middle power' is less a scientific category than an ideology of foreign policy.

Despite the debunking, Stairs wants to retain something of the concept of 'middle power', and so he identifies certain states of secondary rank with similar capabilities and outlooks. The containment and resolution of conflict is a common feature of their statecraft. Building on this, the chapter explores whether such states can act more effectively than in the past in the areas of peacekeeping and peacebuilding, especially in association with the United Nations, and consistent with the Charter. Stairs identifies the advantages for international security of a group of countries developing a standing capacity to work together, efficiently, in the interests of international public service. The recommended approach is pragmatic, building slowly on what exists, rather than directly confronting the big issues of the reform of the United Nations. Such an approach, he believes, might give strength and encouragement to the process of international community building.

Resistances and reinventions

In Part Three of the book, the chapters look beyond the immediate post-Cold War world, and contemplate what needs to be changed, if people are to live in security. The spectrum covered extends from individuals through states to the whole species. Four main conclusions emerge from these chapters: first, the desirability in academic International Relations of breaking away from the constraints of the statist-defined 'international' level, and conceiving world politics more holistically; second, the centrality of ideas as well as material factors in shaping human security, and the urgent need to change the theories by which we structure our global lives; third, the increasing significance of globalising forces – positive and negative – in the daily lives of everybody on the planet; and, finally, the growing utility of community – the densification of obligation and identification – as the ruling idea for human governance at different levels, and especially the all-inclusive level of humankind.

While community-building is a long-term feature of some proposals and policies to enhance international security, regionally and globally, who, in the meantime, is to keep the peace when it breaks down? A clear answer is not forthcoming when governments seem so concerned to direct their attention and energies into domestic issues, and keep away from risky external entanglements. What constitutes statecraft when bullets begin to fly in faraway failed states, with no oil in the ground to energise the national security interests of distant potential helpers? During the Cold War it was expected that the superpowers would attempt to contain local outbreaks of violence aided by their friendly neighbourhood strongmen. In the paradigm-less geopolitics of the post-Cold War world, there is less certainty about what should be done and who will do what, given the preoccupations of the one remaining superpower, the variable reputation of regional organisations, the possible threat of regional powers tempted by hegemony rather than peace, the limited capabilities and interests of middle powers and the weak leverage of global civil society. In such circumstances many people look hopefully, and not for the first time, towards some notion of collective security, and the United Nations, international society's controversial but only multipurpose, almost universal organisation. This hope figures centrally in Barry Blechman's chapter on international peace and security in the next century.

In the twentieth century, according to Blechman, the leaders of the world had three opportunities to advance the cause of collective security; they have failed twice, and even now, with the third opportunity, they are not responding in a manner designed to meet the needs of the future. In Blechman's chapter, as in others, there is a strong sense that traditionalist attitudes and behaviour with respect to the definition and operationalising of security policy will have to change radically if the predictable – let alone the unpredictable – problems of future international politics are to be addressed. Old habits and outlooks must be resisted and security on a global scale must be reinvented. Despite the lack of vision so far exhibited by most governments since the late 1980s, Blechman nevertheless believes there is reason for confidence about the future of international security. The root of this confidence is his belief that fundamental changes are taking place in the structures of global society in ways that create the potentiality for a truly global community and international peace and security. The achievement of these goals depends upon the positive interplay between the growth of shared (global community) values and powerful international institutions.

Blechman suggests that identifiable trends are fundamentally transforming the international system. Above all, the basic fabric of international relations, especially among the industrialised nations, clearly points in the direction of a more peaceful world. The key trends are economic interdependence, the diffusion of technology, a global network of shared knowledge, value convergence, and the erosion of sovereignty. Together, these are helping to produce routine cooperative behaviour, and it is Blechman's expectation that technical and economic coordination will spill over into the areas of security and statecraft.

The future envisaged by Blechman is not based on simple optimistic assumptions. The chapter gives realistic recognition to potential sources of conflict, such as overpopulation, underdevelopment, extreme nationalism, and the ambition of regional hegemons. The resultant dangers from these mean that a working collective security system is desirable. Blechman believes that the UN should be the focus of such a system, and the chapter discusses what is needed to make it workable. To begin with, most of the leading countries in the UN – especially the United States – need to change their ambivalence about the organisation. Were such attitudes to be overcome then the UN could begin to reform itself in areas that presently hamper its contribution to international security, notably the anachronistic composition of the Security Council, financial arrangements and constraints on its military operations.

Many governments are uneasy about substantial reform of the UN;

they fear that it would lead to giving too much power to the Secretary General and/or the Security Council, which in turn might lead to too great a propensity to interventionism. The present opposition of the United States to such changes means that no such reforms will happen soon. Nevertheless, Blechman thinks that a start could be made to help overcome some of the problems evident, for example, in the US response to the war in former Yugoslavia in the early 1990s. Even if far-reaching reform in the UN is unlikely in the short term, thinking about it for the longer term will help when and if conditions make it more feasible. According to Blechman, at the heart of the UN's contribution to a more effective collective security system will be greater professionalisation and a reformed Security Council; together these will give key states more confidence in the organisation, which in turn will make the UN a more effective pillar of international security.

Although the framework of most chapters is set by the international dimension, all the authors, in different ways, point to the inter-relationships between domestic contexts and international outcomes. For example, the tensions between the haves and have-nots within as well as between countries can lead to stresses and strains that impact on regional instability and the global economy. What is increasingly clear is that the autonomy of the 'international' level of world politics – as posited by 'realist' International Relations – is not sustainable in this era of globalisation, if it ever was. Throughout the social sciences there has been a collapsing of the levels of analysis and the interpenetration of old disciplinary boundaries; so we have seen the growth of world politics, world sociology, new geography and so on. Simultaneously, the human sciences also reflect a sense of change, flow, flux and uncertainty. These matters of interconnectedness, surprise, lack of control, and choice are the themes of the chapter by Anthony Giddens. His starting point is that the world has taken us by surprise, both as individuals and as collectivities. It has been an assumption of the human sciences in the West over the past 200 years that knowledge would yield progressive mastery over the world, yet the world has not increasingly fallen under human control. The problem is not ignorance, but human interventions in the physical world and in our own history.

According to Giddens, we face different sorts of risk, and 'manufactured uncertainty' from our own efforts to control our destiny has increasingly come to dominate 'external risks'. The change can be seen in the physical world, where 'nature' is no longer real nature. The increased dominance of manufactured risk in the social realm is marked by globalisation (the increased ease and density of communication creates novel local experiences and institutions), detraditionalisation (one of whose outcomes is fundamentalism) and social reflexivity (the necessity of reflecting on the conditions of life in circumstances where knowledge is from multiple sources and contested). In such circumstances, all social institutions come under strain. Political legitimacy is threatened and the welfare state is challenged. The key shift for Giddens is in policy orientation away from emancipatory politics to life politics (life decisions not life chances).

In the changing social conditions described by Giddens, the environment in which political bargaining takes place changes, and he believes this can have positive implications for dealing with poverty and inequality. Instead of thinking only in terms of income transfers, for example, people can think of life-style bargaining. Reinventing work is one way by which redistribution can take place. Early retirement, as conceived by 'time pioneers', is one illustration of such possibilities, but few things are more significant worldwide than a new social contract between men and women. Giddens rejects the implication that the idea of a social contract that would be redistributive downwards is necessarily utopian in face of domestic and global pressures towards inequality, division and fragmentation. He argues that there is always a choice and that life policy mechanisms offer some possibility of defending values which otherwise might lose their purchase.

While the bulk of his argument refers to industrialised societies, Giddens insists that it has global relevance. We live in a 'decentred' world. Globalisation used to be synonymous with Westernisation, but he believes this is no longer the case. We are faced by global risks, but also emergent global systems. There is a relationship between life-style bargaining and global security, and between life politics and emancipatory politics on a global scale. The chapter concludes that we all have to face a more radically open future, but a future in which the poorest might teach us most.

The power of ideas, and the potential openness of the future, is also stressed in Philip Allott's chapter. His first paragraph gets to the heart of the matter, declaring that human nature, the human condition and human history are 'self-forged chains', which exist nowhere but in the mind, and that humanity will only achieve its potential when it frees itself from deformed ideas about what it is. These deformed ideas have their effects in all aspects of life, but for present purposes they are most importantly enacted on the 'grandest stage of all' in the 'tragi-comedy of the state-system'.

Allott argues that the myth of human nature is one of the most ancient and most powerful ideas. But it is also intellectually fragile. It has performed a basic function in the history of 'human self-constituting', including furnishing regressive ideas about the universal self. In the debate about the nature of human nature – whether it is biologically given or a human invention – Allott believes that it should be seen as the latter, though it has invariably been seen as the former. One result has been the institutionalising of human alienation. Allott considers the so-called human condition to be yet another myth, like human nature, which has also led to self-alienation, thereby helping us to evade the responsibility of becoming human. Our central myths have internalised fear, hate and shame. Humans have also internalised conflict as a foundational myth. We have constituted ourselves in conflict, from the class struggle to Mutual Assured Destruction. One reason why humanity persists with so dismal a view of its own potentiality is history, the story we tell about our past. War has exercised a particular fascination and domination in all our histories. According to Allott, the obsession with war is the other face of the obsession with the state, 'the coldest of cold monsters'.

For Allott, humanity is its own creation. Humans cannot think beyond their own thinking, but we have made ourselves what we need not have been. The images we have of ourselves in the form of human nature, the human condition and human history, are 'phantom symptoms' of a 'suicidal soul-system'. We could choose another way.

Choice – resistance and reinvention are versions of it – is the theme of Part Three. Together, the first three chapters cover international organisation, life politics, and human nature, human history and the human condition. The Conclusion attempts to set the earlier discussion about lessons and legacies, powers and policies, and resistances and reinventions in the context of living in the first truly global age, and the challenge this brings for students of and practitioners in international relations. Three aspects of global transformation are discussed: globalisation, global governance and global moral science. The discussion of globalisation concentrates on the step-change being brought about in human affairs as a result of living in a wired world under the conditions of global capitalism. The issue of global governance points to the need to rethink how world politics might be organised in an era in which increasing numbers of people are coming to have radically different relationships to time, space, distance, economics, identity, work and so on. Finally, global moral science asks whether the ruling (political and ethical) ideas of the past can answer the future's searching questions. As we attempt to rethink the big pictures of security, and address immediate problems of statecraft, our political and intellectual challenges proliferate: working out the relationships between identities and cultures, agencies and structures, interests and instruments, ethics and referents. Our era of question-marks deepens. Whose answers triumph will determine whom the twenty-first century will be for.

Part One

Cold War: lessons and legacies

1 Cold Wars of the mind

Ken Booth

The Cold War was the *déja-là* of the end of human civilisation.[1] For nearly fifty years an international 'system' or 'society' which had become dysfunctional – explicitly MAD – daily practised the genocidal routines, and accepted the ethical and other implications involved in destroying (at the least) what passed for civilised life in the northern hemisphere. The horrifying scale and manner of the threatened slaughter was beyond the margins of the nightmares and fantasies of previous centuries. The infrastructure of this Armageddon, and its mindsets, have not been eliminated; they have only been pushed from the centre. The Cold War is not over. It exists as our living recent past, and it exerts a powerful presence by being both remembered and forgotten in complex ways. As a particular historical period the Cold War has come to an end, of course, but in various guises it continues as an important political reality.

Cold Wars

The Cold War is not over in two senses. It is not over because the experience, lessons, remembrances and forgettings of the four and a half decades after 1945 remain important political factors in international relations today, and it is not over because the Cold War of modern memory can be seen as an instance of a particular culture of global conflict which long predated recent history and which shows few signs of being dead. The Cold War is memory, mindset and prize.

The memory of the Cold War is a prize to struggle over. The apparently 'academic' debate over what the Cold War *was* is part of the politics of deciding what the post-Cold War *is*. The very dates by which we define the Cold War are also sites for politics: *when* it was is a way of defining *what* it was.

In terms of the conventional Western memory the Cold War was a confrontation, which became global, between the Soviet and Western systems. In all sectors of relations – military, ideological, diplomatic, economic and propaganda – there was conflict, but open war was always avoided between the major protagonists. There were however several extremely dangerous crises, and a number of brutal wars took place between their proxies. The historical origins of the confrontation lay in the traditional suspicion between Western liberalism and Russian authoritarianism, which had led to the Russian empire never being fully welcomed into the Western great power club in the nineteenth century. In the twentieth century a new round in the confrontation was sparked in 1917 by the Bolshevik revolution and Wilsonian crusading. It reached its culmination following the breakdown of the anti-Axis allies between 1944 and 1947 and the emergence of the United States and the Soviet Union as the world's leading military powers. In brutal and insinuating ways, this Cold War came to dominate the pattern and character of international relations across the globe. From such a perspective the recent Cold War describes only one stage in a *historical* adversarial relationship between the West and Russian power on the Eurasian landmass – a confrontation which (as a result of NATO expansion and Russian fears and hopes) may not yet have run its course.

Another viewpoint – less historical and more ideological – focuses on the period between 1917 and 1991, from the Bolshevik revolution to the decision to wind up the Soviet state. This might be called the *long* Cold War. Here the emphasis is on the political clash between the rival ideologies, communism and capitalism. Typically, this characterisation puts the blame for the start of the confrontation on the Bolsheviks, and only sees its end with the collapse of the Soviet state. What might be called the *short* Cold War was marked by the consolidation of the Western and Soviet systems at the end of the Second World War. This period, 1947–53, was dominated by the leaderships of Harry Truman and Josef Stalin, and marked out post-war international relations in terms of a highly militarised US–Soviet global rivalry. Yet another version prefers to see an original – the *first* – Cold War, between 1944 and 1962, and a *second* or new Cold War, between 1979 and 1987. The first Cold War began before the Axis powers had been defeated, as the manoeuvring started for favourable post-war positions; it then escalated dangerously into a militarised confrontation which was not ameliorated until the Cuban missile crisis brought home to decisionmakers the narrowness of the divide between Cold War and catastrophe in the era of intercontinental delivery systems and nuclear weapons. Thereafter, a 'limited adversarial relationship' developed, characteristic of other great power rivalries in the past, until the convergence of the Reagan and Brezhnev leaderships, when both superpowers reverted to fundamentalist types, and escalating words and deeds again led to fears of war.

This period ended with the emergence of Mikhail Gorbachev as the leader of the Soviet Union and his determination (which proved more successful than anyone could have reasonably imagined) to change the character of the Soviet–US rivalry. The Cold War was publicly brought to a close by the former protagonists in 1990. By this definition the ending of the Cold War was not synonymous with the ending of the Soviet state. Probably the widest usage of the term 'Cold War' refers to the *systemic* struggle which always managed to fall just short of hot war, between the Soviet Union and its allies and the United States and its allies, that developed alongside the defeat of Hitler in 1944–5, passed through various stages of intense confrontation and détente, and ended with the decision to wind up the Soviet state in 1991.

These different Cold Wars – the *historical*, the *long*, the *short*, the *first* and the *second*, and the *systemic* – are the familiar Cold Wars, and they form the starting point of this book. But I also want to introduce the concept of Cold War in another guise, what might be called the Cold War of the mind. This Cold War long predated the historical episodes just mentioned. If it manifests itself in the years ahead, it will mean that the current label for our times, 'the post-Cold War world', will have proved to be a historical oxymoron. The 'Clash of Civilisations' thesis (Huntington, 1993) already reveals a bipolar mindset that characterises the Cold War of the mind.

What I am calling the Cold War of the mind began about 700 years ago and by the 1970s/1980s had reached its apogee and cosmically destructive potential in the 50,000 nuclear-warhead confrontation between the United States and Soviet Union. As we are reminded in Philip Allott's chapter, later, the phrase *guerra-fria* originated in the thirteenth century, to describe the confrontation between Islam and Christianity in Spain. The Cold War which is the starting point of this book is the (so far) ultimate manifestation of the same international political culture of conflict. The Cold War of the mind is exhibited when a confrontation between nations or states ceases to be simply a matter of a political clash of interests and instead takes on the character – the depth, the pervasiveness, the semi-permanence, the identity and the commitment – of an eschatological political culture. This was the meaning of the words at the start of the Introduction suggesting that the Iron Curtain imprisoned us all. Both sides embraced an eschatological culture about the games nations play.[2]

As the Middle Ages evolved into the modern period, the axioms of international security crystallised into Machiavellian ethics, the Clausewitzian philosophy of war, and the Westphalian state system. It was the converging logics of these positions which released the bomb at

Hiroshima, with all it implied in terms of equating security with massive destructive power. The rational strategy to terminate world war seamlessly became the rational strategic threat to deter world war. Bernard Brodie wrote the basic tract of nuclear deterrence a month after Hiroshima. Previously, I have seen this as essentially a token of Brodie's prescience (Booth, 1991a) but now would prefer to interpret it simply as evidence of the essential continuity of strategic thought, between war and post-war. (There is a warning here for those who may be imagining that the strategists of the Cold War's victors have undertaken a radical strategic rethink for the 1990s and beyond. What they believed terminated the Cold War will inform their strategising about the post-Cold War.)

If it was sovereign states in Clausewitzian collision that led to Hiroshima, it was a sovereign state exercising Westphalian jurisdiction that led to Auschwitz. The form *cuius regio, eius religio* could be interpreted in the mid-seventeenth century as an expression of a degree of religious toleration, but now it can be read as *who the ruler? whom the exterminated?* These twin Holocausts, both revealed to the world in 1945, are sometimes seen as the dark sides of the Enlightenment. This is mistaken. The logics, the emotions and the cultures which produced them lay much further back in human history. What was 'modern', was the science and technology. Hiroshima and Auschwitz showed the terrible convergence of Enlightenment science and pre-Enlightenment solipsist massacre.

The extremism – 'exterminism' was E. P. Thompson's word – embodied in Cold War genocidal strategies is characteristic of an eschatological outlook on world affairs. Such a mindset is fuelled by ethnocentrism, political realism, ideological fundamentalism and strategic reductionism (Booth, 1987: 39–45). Ethnocentrism, meaning 'culture-bound', is the inability of an individual or group to see the world through the eyes of others, the possession of attitudes of national superiority, and the interpretation of the thoughts and behaviour of those from other cultures in terms of one's own. 'Realism' is an ideology which criticises those who believe that there is significant scope for reason, law and morality in human relations. Instead, realists fatalistically emphasise the role of interests, power and selfish human nature. Ideological fundamentalists are those who are drawn to the most basic beliefs, doctrines, analyses and programmes upon which their particular ideology rests. Such outlooks establish boundaries on thought and action and simplify the *kto-kovo?* (who–whom?) in world politics – Lenin's fundamental political question (Bell, 1958). Finally, strategic reductionists are those who see international politics as a rather crude and mechanistic process of power politics. Security comes only through military strength, since we are assumed to inhabit a zero-sum social universe.

The mindsets just identified informed much superpower behaviour during the Cold War. They helped perpetuate and intensify the confrontation, and frequently proved counter-productive. Ethnocentrism, for example, was evident in the way each superpower created weapons of mass destruction which threatened to destroy civilisation in the northern hemisphere (at least) in furtherance of their own 'national security policy'; and it was evident in the tendency in the West to use phrases such as the 'long peace' (because *we* lived in peace, the cries of those paying the costs of the hot Cold War in the Third World could be ignored). The crude mindset of realism was nicely captured in Stalin's famous question: 'How many divisions has the Pope?' Power, seen only in simple terms, can become an addiction, and what William Fox called 'doctrinaire realism' (1985: 12) comes to replace true *realpolitik*. Ideological fundamentalism, with its demand for authority and loyalty, was evident in Brezhnev's doctrine of the 'Socialist Commonwealth' following the invasion of Czechoslovakia in 1968, and in the Reagan administration's insistence on policy as a loyalty test (in its relations with its Western European allies on issues such as Star Wars in the mid-1980s). Finally, strategic reductionism was evident in the obsession of the planners of both superpowers with the military balance, state-of-the-art technology, parity and 'windows-of-vulnerability'. Together, these mindsets helped to create a situation in which a confrontation between two states, one representing a version of welfare capitalism and the other a version of state socialism, threatened humanity with unprecedented catastrophe. The Cold War was history's Great Escape and we need urgently to learn from it. We need to learn not only technical lessons about the elements of statecraft – strategy and diplomacy – but also take to heart the cultural warnings about the mindsets that intensified and perpetuated the potential catastrophe.

The immediate focus of US–Soviet rivalry was the clash of interests, ambitions and fear in the unsettled situations created by the end of the Second World War. But the Cold War of the mind turned this confrontation into a morality play. A 'just deterrent' was created by those who believed in the morality and rationality of trying to save themselves by threatening to destroy the whole of civilisation. World affairs shifted, overnight, from a total World War to total Cold War, and from a 'just war' to a 'just deterrent'. And the worse the enemy was made to appear, the better one believed oneself to be. Since its thirteenth-century origins, the Cold War of the mind has involved the demonisation of the adversary. If, in the aftermath of the Second World War, which A. J. P. Taylor called the 'good war' (1976: 274), it did not prove possible to have a 'good peace', then at least the adversaries were determined it be a good Cold War. And that needed demons. But when eschatological philosophies become locked in confrontation, their advocates tend to become mirror-images of each other. If one fights demons, one's own demonic behaviour seems justified. Some allied strategies in the Second World War, such as massive terror bombing, are testimonies to this. Likewise, in the Cold War, McCarthyism was a mirror-image of the Kremlin's intolerance, not the true opposite of Soviet totalitarianism. This is a warning that is relevant today. Tina Rosenberg has expressed it clearly in relation to dealing with the past in today's Eastern Europe. She writes:

When the state does not grant its citizens the right to defend themselves from its power, when it withholds from citizens information that concerns them, when it declares itself lord and master of the truth, when it twists the legal system to suit political ends, democracy is threatened. The opposite of communism is not anti-communism, which at times resembles it greatly. The opposite is tolerance and the rule of law. (Rosenberg, 1995: 406–7)

Total confrontations are concerned, among other things, with the defence of one's own identity, but the paradoxical result of Cold Wars of the mind is that one increasingly takes on the appearance of what one is supposedly confronting.

At its height the Cold War was simply portrayed as a confrontation between totalitarianism and the free world, but the reality was much more complex. Stephen J. Whitfield has shown in detail how the United States in the 1950s took on characteristics of its adversary (1991). If not to the same extent, or in exactly the same manner, both superpowers engaged in the suppressing of nationalism in countries in their own 'back-yard', both suppressed dissent at home, both conducted policy in secret, both skewed their economies in the interests of the military-industrial complex, both elites exhibited paranoia, ideology became extreme and both states wanted loyalty rather than rationality from their allies. The Cold War imprisoned US culture and politics, as well as those of Soviet Russia. While the Soviet Union was crushed under the orthodoxies of the *Zhdanovschina*, Whitfield has described how the United States in the 1950s lurched to the right ideologically and imposed unprecedented cultural constraints; how 'left-wing' activities were closely and vigorously monitored by the FBI; how Congressional hearings ruined careers with innuendo and the blacklist; how a 'boxed-in' press and television stood aside when the CIA arranged the over-throw of the government of Guatemala; how paranoia led to and was fed by nuclear air-raid drills and high-publicity spy trials. In these circumstances comfort was found in familiar refuges; these included the cornucopia of US technological consumerism, evangelising Christianity (judiciously mixing a redemptive cocktail of fear of god, fear of communism and fear of Armageddon), and a popular culture which demonised and brutalised the 'Reds', made 'squealing' mandatory and showed that the gun-slinger in the white hat always wins in the end.

An eschatological enemy is a threat, but also a promise. What enmity promises is the clarification of one's own identity. Enemies in a Cold War are undoubtedly real – they pose a material threat and have hostile intent – but enemy images can also be an effective resource in domestic and foreign policy. For individuals and groups, identifiable villains ('diabolical enemy images') perform psychological, sociological and political functions (Finlay, Holsti and Fagen, 1967: 6–24). Psychologically, enemy imaging serves several possible functions: it may help sublimate frustration, justify improper behaviour, serve to focus aggressiveness, divert attention from other problems, and provide a contrast by which to measure or inflate one's own worth or value. Sociologically, enemy images may help foster solidarity and cohesion, improve the definition of objectives and make it easier for individuals to accept training and socialisation in group norms. Politically, enemy images can assist in the identification of interests, the definition of goals, the planning of programmes, the socialisation of citizens, the maintenance of an ideology, and, by polarising good and evil, can intensify orthodoxy and dogmatism and so help create heightened nationalism and consensus. In short, enemies can be useful.

Under Cold War pressures crude enemy images often serve better than sophisticated ones. Such images are helped by what T. E. Lawrence called 'a fundamental crippling incuriousness' about adversaries (quoted in Booth, 1979: 26). Various pressures acting on individuals resist any inclination to overcome the incuriosity; a satisfying illusion is often preferable to a complicated reality. Consequently, one of the differences between a Cold War and a hot war is the role played by imaginary forces rather than brute force.

Mary Kaldor has argued that the dynamics of the Cold War and the nuclear arms race were not simply to be found in the international arena, in the interaction of mutual threat systems, but more importantly in the domestic political and socio-economic ambitions and fears of the major protagonists. From this perspective the Cold War can be seen as a mechanism for managing domestic problems. Because of this, Kaldor argues that the East–West confrontation was an 'imaginary war' (1990). This imaginary war imposed a kind of East–West symmetry, with

Atlanticism and Stalinism being mutually reinforcing. If there is an element of truth in this argument, it underlines the appropriateness of the old phrase about the 'games nations play'. When one looks at the games being played today, there is plenty of evidence of the mindsets discussed earlier. However, they have not (yet) converged, and created their global demon (though several candidates have been lined up for inspection).

Finally, having looked at the Cold War as memory and mindset, there is the issue of Cold War history as post-Cold War politics. 'The memory of the past is a prize worth struggling for' is one of the themes of Tina Rosenberg's *The Haunted Land* (1995: xviii). Her book is an account of the lives caught up in the political changes in Eastern Europe after 1989, when official orthodoxies gave way overnight to different orthodoxies. Politics, in part, becomes a struggle for the control over and manipulation of memory: the latter is an important political prize. In the 1920s and 1930s this was fully understood by the Nazis, who used the 'stab in the back' legend and other stories to gain power, and then used a romanticised version of Germany's heroic past to sustain their position. The future – in part – belongs to those who can make the present appear a 'natural' extension of the past. Memory matters, and there is little reason to suppose that the future of the Cold War's past will be any different. This would have been the view of George Orwell, who said 'Whoever controls the past controls the future' (quoted by Rosenberg, 1995: xviii). What is true for post-communist societies is also true for international society, in terms of the politics of memory and struggle with respect to the Cold War. To some degree, whoever controls the international history of the Cold War controls the international politics of the post-Cold War.

The international history of the Cold War has been and will remain a contested area. In his book *Wartime*, Paul Fussell relates how Walt Whitman, after scrutinising the facts of the American Civil War, and seeing and listening to hundreds of wounded soldiers, declared: 'the real war will never get in the books' (1989: 290). By this he meant that many aspects of the 'real' war would remain locked up in the heads of those who fought; and they would die with these memories, unrecorded. Nearly fifty years after the Second World War finished, Fussell tried to rectify Whitman's warning in relation to the war in which he himself had been a young soldier. He did not think he had succeeded, although critical approval was given to the book; the problem was and is the impossibility of revealing any war satisfactorily on paper. Can we say the same about the Cold War? Will the real Cold War ever get in the books? Such questions obviously themselves beg two more fundamental questions. First, what was the *real* Cold War? And second, and most politically pertinent, *whose* real Cold War will get in the books (and dominate them)?

Unless Western historiography of the period changes dramatically, the Cold War of the books will remain in the hands of those for whom the dominant memory will be that of a managed confrontation between ideological enemies in which Right triumphed. The conventional account will not dwell on the secret or hidden Cold War. Locked up in individual and institutional memories are many terrible acts, from radio-activity testing on individuals, to state terrorism against nationalist and other opponents in superpower backyards, to the expertise invested in planning a nuclear holocaust. Costs will be overlooked, silenced or marginalised: these include the casualties in proxy wars, minds manipulated in hospitals, the secrecy that undermined democracy, the degradation of culture, the cult of force, and the missilemen ready at a moment's notice to turn the keys that would unleash a nuclear hell on *very* far away places about which they knew nothing. Nor is there likely to be space in the conventional accounts for the 'silent genocides' in the Third World. The costs of the Second World War were direct and obvious. The true costs of the Cold War have been hidden away, ignored, denied, forgotten, rationalised or consigned to a convenient political amnesia.

The main difference between the Cold War of the mind in the second half of the twentieth century and previous cases of eschatological bipolarity was that the costs of getting the former wrong threatened to be particularly catastrophic and potentially universal. In this important sense the Cold War as an *event* cannot be classified in Braudelian terms as 'dust', because it had the very power to reduce history to dust. As a result, statist power structures had, and continue to have, incentives to prevent the real Cold War getting in the books. To do otherwise would be to expose the extent to which they placed the security of their own sovereignty before human security. The power and pervasiveness of Cold War common-sense mean that it will be a long time before the great mass of people will be receptive to radical critiques of the Cold War, and accept that it was a truly MAD system (even if rational according to its lights). But in time people will surely want to ask: why was so much threatened for so little? Future historians will no doubt have the critical distance to be able to persuade their readers to look back on the potential global holocaust of the US–Soviet confrontation – history's Great Escape – with all the curiosity and disdain we now feel about strange, brutal, and extremist practices such as the burning of 'witches' or the mass torture of 'heretics'.

None of the above is intended to deny the heroism and good sense demonstrated on all sides in relation to some aspects of the Cold War; nor is it to suggest that important issues were not at stake or that everywhere there were moral equivalencies. What it does suggest is that what passes in the books for the 'Cold War' in the contemporary Western mind is far from that which will become commonplace in the far future – separated from the late twentieth century with critical distance and historical imagination. For the moment, however, complacency rules in Cold War studies. Perhaps we will never know how close the world came to suffering the war to end all wars, because those who participated did not know at the time, and still less so with hindsight do they know how they would have reacted if their adversary had taken the next escalatory step in a particular crisis. We are now learning that there were many more risks than was assumed in the power-serving strategic studies literature of the time; we are now clearer about the malfunctions in the C^3 (command, control and communications) systems of the strategic forces of both superpowers, the possibility of inadvertent war, and the mistakes in crisis mismanagement (MccGwire, 1991: 387–92; Blair, 1993; Sagan, 1993; Scott and Smith, 1994). Clearly, there were positive sides to the Cold War for the West – no world war, no communist expansion westwards, unprecedented prosperity and so on – but nobody is served by ignoring the dark side. What if it had all gone horribly wrong, as the record is now showing was far from impossible? We have not yet made a full accounting of the costs of the Cold War, either as individual societies or as a potential global community of victims.

It is a major task for scholars to try to expose the costs and dangers of the Cold War before a heavy snowfall of political convenience is allowed to pile up and cover worrying contours. Part of history's Great Escape consists of an escape from memory, including that of what might have been. Forgetting and denial include the catastrophic possibilities of nuclearism, the millions of deaths in proxy wars or wars legitimised or excused by supposed bipolar strategic necessities, the roles played by the superpowers in impairing the development of so many countries and in stoking today's civil wars by profligate weapons transfers, propaganda and the imposing of global strategic templates on complex local situations, the opportunity costs in terms of diminished and wasted lives, and the historic distraction from the more fundamental issues confronting the human race. The Cold War bequeathed a material infrastructure and a particular mindset, and with them continuing costs and dangers. It is easier to forget – or forget selectively – a Cold War rather than a real war. Real wars demand more intrusive post-mortems. The Cold War of the mind is encouraged by convenient rememberings and forgettings, and the story of all wars is told, at least in the first instance, by the victors. The victors of the Cold War have been primed to conceive politics on a global scale according to the assumptions and axioms of the MAD era of strategic history. For the time being, the inability of many people – but not all – to face the past and expose and accept the Cold War in all its guises, is one of the 'morbid symptoms' that characterise the 'interregnum' in world politics which began with the winding down of the Cold War and will continue for the indefinite future (see Booth, 1991b: 1–28). This interregnum is the context for many of the chapters in this book – a confusing time whose meaning and label have yet to be agreed.

The nameless nineties

Having tried in the previous section to contextualise some of the discussion in Part One about the Cold War, the present section attempts to situate the chapters (especially in Part Two) in relation to a wide variety of viewpoints about the character of the post-Cold War world: the predictions of the 'new pessimists', the visions of the old (liberal) optimists, and finally, the structural features isolated by contending models of contemporary world order/disorder.

The phrase 'New Pessimism' was coined by Charles William Maynes (1995). In the immediate aftermath of the ending(s) of the Cold War, at the turn of the 1980s/90s, there was widespread confidence about the international future and optimism about the benefits of a peace dividend. In contrast, as the mid-1990s approached, Maynes identified 'a growing sense that the future will be worse than the past' both at home and abroad; and for intellectuals 'the future seems increasingly sombre while the past acquires an artificial glow' (pp. 35–6). Americans and Europeans have entered 'a new age of pessimism' he argued (p. 33). Behind the attitudes he identified – the search for a simple big picture, with clear enemies and a bifurcated world – can be seen elements of the Cold War of the mind.

The harbingers of the new pessimism, according to Maynes, were Robert Kaplan's 'The Coming Anarchy', Matthew Connelly and Paul Kennedy's 'Must It Be The West Against the Rest', and John Mearsheimer's 'Why We Will Soon Miss The Cold War' – all of which appeared in the *Atlantic* – 'America's premier intellectual and cultural monthly' – and Samuel Huntington's 'The Clash of Civilizations', which appeared in *Foreign Affairs*. 'The Coming Anarchy' warns of a world splitting apart – a 'bifurcated world' – with the West inhabiting islands of comfort being threatened by a tidal wave of criminal anarchy on the part of the masses of alien races and cultures. The future threatens to be a regression to a violent state of nature in which it is doubtful whether the United States, and the West in general, can survive in their present form. Being overwhelmed by an alien tide is also the theme of 'Must It Be The West Against The Rest'. Here the threat is illegal immigrants. In his influential article 'The Clash of Civilizations', Samuel Huntington portrays a post-Cold War world in which the Soviet threat to the West has been replaced not by a challenging superpower, but by civilisational fault-lines and confrontations. Accordingly, the future is one in which Western interests, values and power will be increasingly threatened by Islamic fundamentalism and the rising power of nations in East Asia. In 'Why We Will Soon Miss The Cold War' (better known in its longer version, 'Back To The Future') Mearsheimer argues that the Cold War represented a period of unprecedented stability in Europe, resulting from the US–Soviet stand-off and NATO–WTO alliance discipline. With these constraints gone, replaced by less calculable multipolarity, historic features of the international system – anarchy, self-help, the drive for power and security – will lead to the revival of historic forms of international conflict.

Maynes himself does not share the pessimism of these sombre US intellectuals, and instead argues a case for 'cautious optimism' for four main reasons (pp. 40–4). First, he believes that the pessimism they are reflecting is that of the well-to-do who fear change to the status quo. Their arguments grow out of the pessimism of the privileged, not a full analysis of the actual situation. Second, while there is much that is alarming in contemporary world affairs, it seems worse because of the excessively high hopes entertained by many as a result of the events of 1989. Furthermore, when set against a more realistic picture of the history of the Cold War than the 'very rosy' one that tended to be projected in its aftermath, the current period 'seems peaceful indeed'. Third, while the end of the Cold War did give space for the reopening of some ethnic conflicts, Maynes emphasises that it also closed a half-century when the world faced global nuclear terror. Finally, while attitudes vary in different parts of the world, he believes that there are signs that there is a growing recognition of the disutility of war, that the age of hegemony might be over, and that the 'cult of power' is being challenged by the realisation that internal development rather than external expansion is the way ahead. In sum, Maynes concludes that despite increased surface turbulence, the international system is 'structurally sound', and that belief in the future and a willingness to undergo the pain necessary to make a better future are the keys to overcoming the possibilities forecast by the new pessimists (pp. 44–9).

There is something more to the new pessimism, according to Maynes, than mere political 'analysis'. These influential articles were 'profoundly flawed' he believes, but the fact that people continue to be drawn to them 'says more about us than about the arguments' (p. 36). He suggests that Kaplan's article, for example, fed fears whose roots lay deep in the minds of white America, which in turn lay far back in US history. The Connelly and Kennedy article, and that of Huntington, tap into a pervasive fear of the 'yellow peril'. Maynes believes that the power of suggestion is so strong in these matters that evidence is not required: readers just 'know' they are true (p. 39). Furthermore, many feel uncomfortable without an enemy, and so there is a search to find one. Maynes concludes: 'So much follows politically and diplomatically if one accepts such a sombre picture of mankind's fate' (p. 36).

It is possible to see in the new pessimism elements of the Cold War of the mind: the preference for simple oppositions, self-identity through other-ness, embattled righteousness, fatalism, ethnocentrism and crude realism. Many in the West are primed for new definitions of 'us' and 'them', with the simplifications and gratifications of a *guerra fria*. To the extent it has influence, the new pessimism is important because of the important inter-relationships between our images of the world we inhabit and our behaviour in it. These inter-relationships are at the heart of what has been described as the main metatheoretical issue facing international theory today, namely: do theories offer explanatory accounts of international reality, or is theory constitutive of that reality? (Smith, 1995: 26). In terms of the earlier discussion this metatheoretical issue can be expressed as follows: is the new pessimism of the 1990s a reflection of a darkening international reality, or is it a theory which is constructing that reality? Since I believe it is the latter – dominating theories construct situations and then operate as self-fulfilling explanations – I believe it is important to challenge the pessimistic accounts on their own ground, that is, their claim to describe the world 'as it is'. I want therefore to address four assertions about the contemporary international situation which have already hardened into 'post-Cold War' political clichés. Each of the inter-related clichés rests on a dubious reading/forgetting/rewriting/nostalgia/manipulation of the Cold War. They are: first, the view that the world is now a more dangerous place; second, the assertion that there has been an increase in conflict in the world; third, the fear that the collapse of the Soviet Union has created unprecedented instabilities; and, finally, the belief that we are seeing levels of ethnic conflict and rising nationalism which make for un-paralleled disorder. There are strong arguments against each of these accounts.

First, it is not easy to determine the criteria for measuring danger, especially on a global scale, and so how can we calibrate whether the world has become a more dangerous place? How do we balance the small risks of the ultimate global catastrophe with rather more likely smaller conflicts? Assessing the balance of danger is difficult, but nevertheless some things can be said with confidence. For the immediate future the world is significantly less threatened by the possibility of a nuclear war between any of the major nuclear states; there has been an evident turn against nuclear weapons in strategic planning and political legitimacy. That said, the dangers of nuclear proliferation remain, and may have increased, while some strategists in the existing nuclear states continue to trust the utility of nuclear weapons. Overall, and for the present, the worst nuclear case has shrunk from the threat of global catastrophe to that of regional disaster. Nor is the picture one of increasing danger in terms of conventional war. We must not forget that the Cold War was characterised by a bipolar confrontation that was so intrusive that most local and regional conflicts were fanned by superpower support and supplies. Against the argument that the ending of the Cold War has lifted the constraints on some historic conflicts, history suggests that the dynamics of the Cold War escalated the hot wars in Korea and Vietnam, as well as in numerous local nationalist and anticolonial wars in the Third World. Overall, it is therefore impossible to sustain the view that the *world* has become a more dangerous place in the 1990s in military terms than it was during the Cold War. Some places (for example, the Trans-Caucasus) are more dangerous, because there is fighting where previously there was none, but in other parts (for example, southern Africa) endemic wars appear to have stopped. In terms of the highest levels of destructive power, it seems that the nuclear factor is now only an element rather than a preoccupation in relations between the major nuclear states, while the fear of regional proliferation, though still justifiably real, only repeats expectations about spreading capabilities dating from the 1960s (Beaton, 1966; Buchan, 1966). None of this is to say that things cannot deteriorate; it is only to assert that they have not. One litmus test of the prevalence of order over disorder in the contemporary situation is the confidence of shopkeepers, who, in increasingly far-flung locations, eschew immediate cash transactions for all the complexities and delayed gratifications required in a credit-carded world.

Proponents of the verdict that the 1990s have been characterised by a 'New World Disorder' – that there has been an actual increase in political violence – reveal more anxiety than analysis. Since 1945 the number of wars in each decade has been quite stable, though it obviously depends how one defines a 'war'. Of the thirty-five wars taking place in the mid-1990s, according to one source, all were within single states, though there was external intervention in a significant number (Regehr, 1994: 14–15). Of these thirty-five only eight broke out after 1989. The other twenty-seven began during the Cold War, were exacerbated by it, and have been prolonged by the weaponry and support given to one side or the other. The struggles in Angola and Afghanistan are testimonies to the Cold War fanning conflict rather than dampening it down, even beyond the end of the East–West conflict. Certainly there have been new wars, in the Balkans, the Gulf and the Caucasus, but none of these brutal conflicts matched the scale of violence seen during the Cold War on the Korean peninsula, in Vietnam or in the Iran–Iraq meatgrinder. Alongside the assertion of the new pessimists that there has been an increase in war is the argument that there has been a significant trend away from inter-state to intra-state violence. But such a view was already commonplace to students of international relations by the late 1960s. In 1966 Robert MacNamara, then US Secretary of Defense, stated that in the previous eight years only 15 out of 164 internationally significant outbreaks of violence had been military conflicts between states; and in 1971 Samuel Huntington claimed that between 1961 and 1968 114 out of the world's 121 major political units had endured some form of violent civil conflict (the figures are quoted in Garnett, 1975: 62).

One appalling aspect of intra-state warfare which has attracted attention in the 1990s has been 'ethnic cleansing'. This ugly phenomenon, which comes in different styles and dimensions, is not unique to the present. In 1945, Churchill and Stalin agreed that Germans be expelled from their eastern lands to make space for the geopolitical shift westwards of Poland and the USSR; in this ethnic cleansing an estimated 2 million people died. More recently, Charles Maynes has drawn attention to the Turkish (Islamic) 'cleansing' of (Orthodox) Greeks, notably in Cyprus (1995: 42). Such violence has not been uncommon in modern history, from the ethnic cleansing of the Indian nations in north America four generations ago to the destruction of the aboriginals in Australia, to the butchery in Rwanda in 1994. In addition to making its contribution to this terrible pattern of ethnic violence, the post-Cold War period has also seen major steps towards the settling of apparently intractable conflicts in some parts of the world: after decades of confrontation the 1990s have seen remarkable if very fragile steps in a 'peace process' between Israel and the Palestinian people; after a quarter-century of blood-letting in Northern Ireland, democratic politics have attempted to replace the power of the gunmen; and in contrast to the Cold War, which saw governments in South Africa create a system of institutionalised racism at home and brutal destabilisation wars against its neighbours, the 1990s witnessed a miraculous transformation in both respects, with apartheid rejected and the country's first black president, Nelson Mandela, emerging with a claim to be the Man of the Century. In all three cases it would have been unrealistic to have expected peace to have evolved seamlessly and speedily out of what appeared to be intractable conflicts. Today's violence takes place within the framework of a peace process in each case, whereas formerly calls for peaceful settlement struggled to be heard within the dominant context of violence. Within the space of a few years, these represent remarkable transformations in intractable conflicts. Overall, therefore, such comparisons suggest that there are no grounds for the claim that we are living in a New World Disorder in the 1990s, following the 'long peace' of the Cold War.

Typical of the poor history which can easily lead to poor politics have been the expressions of anxiety surrounding the collapse of the Soviet empire. Somehow, because the Soviet state is seen as a failure, so must the collapse of its empire be seen as less controlled and more threatening that the retreat from empire of other powers. Without doubt there has been serious instability in parts of the former Soviet bloc, but to date the scale and extent of violence have been contained. The achievement has been remarkable, in comparison with the prolonged conflicts and bloodletting which accompanied (and will continue to accompany until the Irish question is settled) the British retreat from empire, which is often projected as a model of imperial withdrawal. None of the Soviet withdrawals has (yet?) led to the mass outbreak of violence which followed the British withdrawal from the Indian subcontinent. Furthermore, despite the major dislocations in Central and Eastern Europe resulting from the transition from Soviet empire to hopeful capitalist democracies, considerable social and political tolerance has been evident; there has not been the explosion of ethnic tension and nationalist ambition that many feared. The ethnic mistrust and accompanying violence which scarred the breakup of Yugoslavia has not been typical of eastern Europe: it has been a terrible exception.

One of the commonest arguments used to justify the image of disorder in the post-Cold War world is the claim that there has been a 'rise' or 'increase' in nationalism. This argument is both historically unsound and over-general. It is unsound because it overlooks the world-wide nationalist upsurge that took place in the decades following the end of the Second World War, which brought an end to centuries of European colonial power. It is over-general because it fails to recognise the real character of much contemporary nationalism. For the most part, in the North, contemporary nationalism has not been 'extremist' nationalism. Rather, it has been the nationalism of groups wanting to escape from alien empire (for example, Poland from the Soviet empire) or of national groups wanting to leave multination states (for example, Slovenia from Yugoslavia or Scotland from the United Kingdom). In such cases, old empires or what are misleadingly called 'nation states' have been threatened by fragmentation, but in each case a major aim of the aspiring national unit has been to integrate into the structures of 'Europe'. Nationalists have sought to free themselves of alien rule in order to create a 'normal country' (in the Western sense). In this way wider (regional) integration is pursued through a policy of (state or bloc) fragmentation. Nationalism in the South in recent years has been conservative on the whole, a force for social cohesion against outside pressures. It has been used as social cement in the face of rapid change and the intrusions of globalisation. In both the developing and developed world, therefore, with a handful of notable exceptions, contemporary nationalism is characterised by long-term integrationist and stabilising tendencies rather than expansionist ambitions. Finally, if nationalism's character is multifaceted, in the manner just suggested, on what basis can we calculate whether it is 'increasing' or not? And even if we were to decide it is on the 'rise', is order served by its suppression or its accommodation?

Nothing in these points comparing the Cold War/post-Cold War worlds should be read as minimising the conflicts and dangers which have been in evidence. The argument is simply that the cliché about a New World Disorder does not stand up to scrutiny. In the Cold War tens of millions were killed in war, and hundreds if not thousands of millions were threatened by the superpower nuclear confrontation, and we called it the 'long peace'; in the post-Cold War hundreds of thousands have been killed, and we call it the new world disorder. There is no reason to feel nostalgic for the Cold War. It was cosmically threatening and locally dangerous. The post-Cold War world is distressing and dangerous, but not in the same way. Some might dismiss this conclusion as optimistic, but it would be wrong to do so. It is merely a statement that, amid the change and morbid symptoms, there is reason for hope.

For some observers of the international scene there is more than cause for hope: genuine optimism is thought to be justified. This viewpoint is that of the new (liberal) optimists. The most prominent exponent of this school has been Francis Fukuyama, who, if he had not existed, would have had to have been invented. Although Fukuyama's arguments have attracted scorn from some academic quarters, his grand assessment of what was happening in world politics at the end of the Cold War – 'The End of History' (1989, 1992) – provided us with an important bench-mark from which to establish our bearings. Some aspects of his work are flawed, as will be discussed below, but it nevertheless offers a comprehensive and important account of the Cold War, and beyond.

Fukuyama's three main conclusions, which have had wide currency, are: first, liberal democracy has triumphed over other twentieth-century 'systemic' challengers, notably communism; second, the spread of liberal democracy is a sure recipe for peace, since liberal democracies do not fight each other; and third, liberal democracy represents the height of political rationality, and a system which brings comfort and satisfaction to its citizens. There are problems with each of these arguments (Booth, 1993: 354–64).

First, are we at the end of history, in Fukuyama's sense? That is, have all the fundamental questions of political and social organisation been settled, so that there will be no more conflict over major issues of ideology? Without doubt, liberal democracy has seen off its present challengers: but this is likely to be a short-term rather than a long-term achievement, and even in the short term liberal democracy remains, globally speaking, a minority preference. Furthermore, the fertile soil that once helped the spread of communism still exists; the world is witness to unjustifiable inequalities, wretched poverty and violent oppression. And the material circumstances of world politics – the environment, science and technology, population growth – are changing. Given this combination of factors, challenges to Western-style liberal democracy, and capitalism, are not only feasible, they are predictable. There are challengers today, in the shape of some varieties of Islam and various traditional political cultures, but these are not potential systemic challengers. Further, it is not even evident that liberal democracy is the most effective way to run a capitalist economy, and Fukuyama himself shows some admiration for the more authoritarian societies of East Asia and the successful way they have welded the disciplines of their traditional societies to the demands of capitalism. Capitalism and liberal democracy may have triumphed over Soviet-style communism, but the major issues of ideology are not settled for the rest of history.

The idea that the triumph of liberal democracy marks the end of history represents astonishing historical parochialism, in the sense that it regards contemporary Western society as the culmination of history, and a universal model for the future. It remains to be seen whether liberal democracy can set down roots beyond its existing areas, in other types of political culture. It is certainly the case that liberal democracy has not been a popular idea, historically; and it flies against the record of history to think that history might have an ideological end-point. Having said that, the combination of liberal democracy and capitalism at the end of the twentieth century is undoubtedly a very powerful force.

A second pillar of the end of history thesis is the alleged congruence of liberal democracy and peace. There has been an extensive debate about the 'democratic peace' thesis. The argument in favour rests on some empirical evidence ('democracies' do not fight each other), shared values (notably the mutual recognition of legitimacy between demo-cratic societies), the ostensible peaceful inclination of democratic foreign policies, and the common interest in peace which is said to be the consequence of commercial interdependence. This is the classic nineteenth-century liberal harmony of interests thesis, which flies in the face of realist thinking about international relations (see Carr's critique, 1946). Against such criticisms, neo-liberal institutionalists argue that societies can learn from experience, and that the liberal democracies have learned from their self-destructive behaviour in the past. It is safest to say that the jury must be out on the democratic peace hypothesis. There have been too few rigorously definable liberal democracies, and their historical circumstances have made peace between them an imperative (the combination of US hegemony in the West and the Soviet threat from the East in the aftermath of a very destructive war). In short, the sample is too small, and their situation is too special. Furthermore, if John Mueller is right, there has been in any case a clear secular trend in history working against the institution of major war (1990). In the mid-1960s Klaus Knorr argued that territorial conquest had lost its utility; the cost of war had gone up and the benefits had gone down (1966). One implication of these arguments is that peace between major powers is increasingly predictable *regardless* of the ideological com-plexion of the states concerned; democracy simply strengthens the trend. So, while there are some strong arguments in support of the democratic peace thesis, it is too soon to say that liberal democracies will not fight each other. And even if they have not fought each other over the significant period of time since the Second World War, there is scope for asking whether this is because of their liberal democratic character or other circumstantial factors.

The third of the ostensible triumphs for the liberal optimists is in the area of values. Fukuyama sees liberal democracy as the height of political rationality; it offers a system which brings the good life to its citizens, and tries to do the same to others through the spread, for example, of human rights. There is an obvious element of truth in these arguments, especially when liberal democracy's achievements are compared with those of other political systems. However, there is also a downside, both at home and abroad. The combination of 'possessive individualism', 'consumer democracy', 'the capitalist world economy' and 'unconstrained science and technology' – all of which are part of the contemporary West – creates problems in terms of the effects of complacent and inward-looking policies at home, the destruction of the global environment and some tough policies externally which result in an unequal distribution of the world's wealth. Western societies can provide considerable material satisfaction for many of those who live in them, but these societies are unfriendly to those who cannot successfully compete, or who do not want to, while the emphasis on consumption and individualism is demonstrably ill-adjusted to the predictable problems of an increasingly densely populated and environmentally challenged planet. A fundamental factor in all this is what J. K. Galbraith calls the 'culture of contentment' (1992). The consumer appetites of Western societies began to be whetted in the eighteenth century, and they have now gathered an apparently irresistible momentum. Protecting the well-off (now the majority) in Western societies has become the essential business of elections and most aspects of public policy. If this means further domestic introspection and further tax cutting, so much the worse for the disadvantaged at home and in the rest of the world.

Even if we think the 'West is best', the best will not be good enough, except for those who believe that an individual's only responsibility is to meet his or her own needs and wants. Lasting security will not be forthcoming without the extension of political and moral obligations – the politics of inclusiveness – at all levels. In domestic politics, if a group's dignity is offended too much, a riot may result; when ethnic or national groups are deprived of justice, within or across borders, then terrorism may be the outcome. If countries are pushed too far these days, the consequence may be the proliferation of weapons of mass destruction. The privileged within the 'culture of contentment' should not forget that within the culture of discontentment the risking of punishment or death may not be the worst thing. Lasting security will grow not out of the selfish exercise of power, but out of the creation of community and the processes of emancipation.

Neither rightist pessimism nor liberal optimism satisfactorily define the nameless nineties, and beyond. They represent only two sets of viewpoints about the state of the post-Cold War world. At this point it is useful to offer a snapshot of the nine main images or models which have been circulating about the emerging global order since the late

1980s. They are not mutually exclusive, but it is helpful to separate them:

1. *Global order through collective security.* This idea briefly (re)surfaced with the revival of the UN in the late 1980s, when the United States and Soviet Union started cooperating in ways that had been hoped for by some of the founders of the UN, but had not been achieved. Progress towards settlement was made in several regional conflicts. However, the collapse of the Soviet Union and its transformation into non-communist Russia (both less powerful and less predictable than its predecessor) put a halt to this. In any case, further progress would have confronted the inherent problems of operating any collective security organisation in an inter-state system with states of unequal power, traditional amities and enmities and ambiguous rather than clear-cut sources of conflict (Claude, 1964: ch. 12 is the classic critique of collective security).

2. *The 'New World Order'.* The New World Order (NWO) was a mixture of US primacy, liberal triumphalism and Western propaganda dressed in the banner of international order; its main features were straight out of the Cold War. The 1990–1 Gulf War was described by President Bush as the 'first test' of his NWO, and he proclaimed it a victory. But the energy behind the policy quickly faded, even though the label lived on. To the extent the concept had a strategy, it was the idea that the 'international community' in the shape of the members of the United Nations, led by the United States, would try and maintain peace and security. The United States would be the policeman of international law (not to mention judge and jury) while the rest of the West would provide the posse (notably Britain) and the financial support (notably Germany and Japan). The liberal optimism of Fukuyama fed primarily into this model.

3. *Pax Americana.* This third model is a more conspiratorial version of the one preceding. In this case, NWO means the New World (gives out the) Orders. The image is one of traditional US imperialism, boosted by victory in the Cold War, exercising its power in a 'one superpower world'. A situation is envisaged of the United States acting ruthlessly to further its interests, regardless of whether it has the backing of the 'international community'. Policy is dominated by the military-industrial complex and a compliant media (Chomsky, 1991, 1994), with the aim of ever-more complete US domination of the politics and economics of world affairs. The critics of this viewpoint see a United States preoccupied with its domestic problems and lacking the power and will to be the global interventionist of old.

4. *Old World Disorder.* This model, which reflects a strong sense of nostalgia for the supposed stability of the Cold War, sees comparisons

between the present era of world politics and the nationalism and instability of the periods before the two world wars. Consequently, it is thought to be only a matter of time before there is a dangerous rise in the ambition of the old major powers. Particular fears have been focused on Germany and Japan. The image is of a competitive multipolar world, in which even the United States no longer has the power to play the role of a (benevolent) hegemonial leader (Mearsheimer, 1990). This is an inter-Cold War or even pre-war world: international politics are never so bad that they cannot get worse.

5. *A world of continental-sized regions.* The emergence of a simple bipolar world, in the manner of the Cold War, does not seem to be an immediate possibility. However, that there could be another single super-power challenger to the United States cannot be entirely ruled out: Russia could rebuild to achieve global status on the ruins of the Soviet Union, China may yet translate its numbers into world power, Japan might become a military and political giant to match its economic strength, and the European Union's metamorphosis into a powerful unitary actor is not impossible. While a bipolar arrangement based on two pre-eminent powers is not unthinkable, the current consensus favours a multipolar pattern rather than the pattern that characterised the US–Soviet Union Cold War. Of the multipolar models suggested, the most prominent is that of tripolar regionalisation, based on the trading areas dominated by the United States, the European Union and Japan. This is not envisaged as a simple 'balance of power' model, however, dominated by what George Kennan once called the 'military mathematics' that characterised the Cold War superpowers. Instead it will be an order shaped by the power of the dollar, the Eurocurrency and the yen. The trend towards continental-sized trading areas has been apparent for some time, and is not a cause for worry unless the continental regions turn into mutually antagonistic protectionist blocs, ideological camps and military alliances. The fear is that international politics may be on a slippery tripolar slope. Against this must be set all the pressures favouring interdependence, even in a situation of powerful regionalisation. The following model is a cultural variant of the regional one.

6. *The clash of civilisations.* Among the world views of the new pessimists, the one that seems to be attracting most independent influence and attention, positive and negative, is Huntington's prediction that the twenty-first century will, like the rest of history before it, be shaped by civilisations (1993). Civilisations, which Huntington describes as the largest unit of human identity, are the sites of human self-definition in terms of ancestry, language, religion and culture. In an attempt to define the post-Cold War in a similar manner to George

Kennan's historic 'containment' article at the start of the Cold War, Huntington argued that clashes between civilisations now represent the greatest threat to world peace. Culture has replaced ideology as the geopolitical indicator, and the danger points of world politics are the 'fault lines' between civilisations, as in Bosnia, the Transcaucasus, Kashmir, Sudan and elsewhere. What is driving the clash at this point in history is the population explosion in the Islamic world and the rising economic power of East Asia. These developments are fuelling the challenge to the West's world dominance, including its pretention to universal values. The model is one of intensifying inter-civilisational conflict over issues such as nuclear proliferation, immigration, human rights and democracy. The ultimate threat is a global war of civilisations. After the alarmism, Huntington offers some thoughts about the way in which clashing civilisations can learn to coexist.

7. The seventh model, *New World Disorder*, is a variant of the previous one. It is not a world going 'back to the future', to use Mearsheimer's phrase (1990), but is rather one in which old problems have an overlay of 'new' ones, resulting from the pressures of globalisation, economic problems, population growth, environmental stress, the spread of crime and disease, and the proliferation of weapons of mass destruction and so on. The characteristic feature of this new world disorder is system-overload: no significant referent object – individuals, families, societies, states, ecosystems – can cope. The symptoms include crime, social distress, collapsed states, refugees, fundamentalism, desertification and genocide.

8. *North/South*. A number of the models just discussed had a major North/South (or core-periphery) component, in terms of sites of order/disorder, zones of peace/war, and states of development/underdevelopment. One theory explaining this picture has been prominent in academic International Relations since the 1970s, namely 'structuralism' or 'globalism' (see, in particular, Wallerstein, 1979 and 1991, and, for a general overview, Viotti and Kauppi, 1990: 399–518). The key features of this model are the historic development, spread, and structural dominance of the capitalist world economy, the necessary relationship of exploitation and dependency between unequally developed states, the relative insignificance in historical terms of the Cold War, and the likelihood of increased friction in future between the most highly industrialised states over resources and markets. This is therefore a model in which the core exploits the periphery, but with the new twist that the ending of the Cold War has opened up the prospect of increased intra-core economic competition, now that the disciplining factor of the Soviet Union has gone.

9. Finally, there is a *World Society* image of global order. This comes in a variety of forms, but essentially it is a 'bottom up' rather than 'top down' view of progress in global governance. It looks towards a more secure world as a result of the spread of progressive 'world order' values such as humane governance, non-violence, a human rights culture, economic justice and policies committed to a sustainable environment (Falk, 1992). Behind such ideas, as spread by progressive trans-national social movements, are notions of a developing global civic culture, species identity and human community. Statism – the concentration of all loyalty and decision-making power at the level of the sovereign state – is seen to be the problem not the solution to global order and human development. The political forms of such a future are sometimes labelled a 'new medievalism', to imply a multilayered, patchwork system of governance, with overlapping and mutually balancing authority structures and identities. Sovereignty will be limited and functional, not all-embracing and statist, as in the Westphalian model. 'States' as they exist territorially today would remain administrative and political units, but order would lie not in state sovereignty but in more inclusive ideas about common human identity and global community. To realists, such a picture is 'unrealistic'. It has always been thus for realists with regard to big ideas, though history testifies that 'impossible' ideas in one era can overturn notions of what constitutes a people's identity and community; and these ideas can overturn world politics. In feudal times ideas about a 'national' identity and a 'national' community would have appeared 'unrealistic', as would democracy in the era of the Divine Right of Kings. For realists, politics is the art of the possible, but for emancipationists who do not believe that we ever live in the best of all possible worlds, the heart of politics *is* possible worlds.

Each of the models just discussed attempts to give meaning to the complex pattern of contemporary events. The 1900s conform to none of them, exactly, though it is possible to find some evidence to support each of them. There is disorder, of both 'old' and 'new' varieties, but there is also plenty of order, and the expectation of more with the qualified triumph of democracy and the global grip of the capitalist world economy. In the South, there is a swathe of dictatorship, debt, decay, disease, deforestation and death, while in the West the decade is characterised by economic struggle, domestic strain, consumerism, contentment, introspection, anxieties about the world at large and reducing confidence about the future. Without doubt, there are region-alising tendencies, but there is also rampant globalisation. We certainly live in a world of states, but alongside states there are alternative foci of power, authority and loyalty. In some parts of the world there is a tribalisation of politics, but elsewhere progress has been made towards resolving some intractable conflicts and global social movements grow in numbers and influence, aided by easier communications. The world is becoming smaller, which promises advantages in terms of the prospects for humane global governance, but the shrinkage also threatens more vulnerability as environmental decay and population expansion proceed apace (though both these issues are now on the international agenda). In such confused and confusing contextual circumstances, the pressure for Cold-War-like simplicities and certainties are enormous. In the face of all this, the great questions of international relations take on a new urgency and complexity. It was always thought to be so, but at the end of the twentieth century there are grounds for thinking that the need to confront the so-called human condition on a global scale is truly unique. The chapters below attempt to deal with specific aspects of the urgent challenges this situation raises for statecraft and security.

NOTES

1 This idea is stimulated by Michel Foucault's discussion of the link between madness and death, and his image of madness as the 'already-there' of death. For Foucault it was as if the person who is mad must repeat incessantly the drama of dying: 'The head that will become a skull is already empty' (quoted in Miller, 1995: 99).
2 An eschatological conception of international politics derives from Anatol Rapoport's categorisation of philosophies of war ('Introduction', 1968).

REFERENCES

Beaton, Leonard (1966) *Must the Bomb Spread?* (Harmondsworth: Penguin).
Bell, Daniel (1958) 'Ten Theories in Search of Reality: The Prediction of Soviet Behavior', *World Politics* (April), 315–53.
Blair, Bruce G. (1993) *The Logic of Accidental Nuclear War* (Washington, DC: The Brookings Institution).
Booth, Ken (1979) *Strategy and Ethnocentrism* (London: Croom Helm).
　(1987) 'New Challenges and Old Mindsets: Ten Rules for Empirical Realists', in Carl G. Jacobsen (ed.), *The Uncertain Course. New Weapons, Strategies and Mindsets* (Oxford: Oxford University Press), pp. 39–66.
　(1991a) 'Bernard Brodie', in John Baylis and John Garnett (eds.), *Makers of Nuclear Strategy* (London: Pinter Publishers), pp. 19–56.
　(1991b) *New Thinking About Strategy and International Security* (London: HarperCollins Academic).
　(1993) 'Liberal Democracy, Global Order and the Future of Transatlantic Relations', in *Brassey's Defence Year Book 1993* (London: Brassey's), pp. 356–66.

Buchan, Alistair (1966) *A World of Nuclear Powers?* (Englewood Cliffs, NJ: Prentice-Hall).

Carr, E. H. (1946) *The Twenty Years' Crisis: 1919–1939* (London: Macmillan).

Chomsky, Noam (1991) *Deterring Democracy* (London: Verso).

(1994) *World Orders, Old and New* (London: Pluto Press).

Claude, Inis L. (1964) *Swords into Ploughshares. The Problems and Progress of International Organization* (London: University of London Press).

Falk, Richard (1992) *Explorations at the Edge of Time. The Prospects for World Order* (Philadelphia: Temple University Press).

Finlay, David, Holsti, Ole, Fagen, Richard (1976) *Enemies in Politics* (Chicago: Rand McNally).

Fox, W. R. T. (1985) 'E. H. Carr and Political Vision: Vision and Revision', *Review of International Studies*, vol. 11, pp. 1–16.

Fukuyama, Francis (1989) 'The End of History', *The National Interest*, vol. 16(1), 3–18.

(1992) *The End of History and the Last Man* (London: Hamish Hamilton).

Fussell, Paul (1989) *Wartime* (New York: Oxford University Press).

Galbraith, J. K. (1992) *The Culture of Contentment* (London: Sinclair-Stevenson).

Garnett, John (1975) 'The Role of Military Power', in John Baylis et al., *Contemporary Strategy. Theories and Policies* (London: Croom Helm), pp. 50–64.

Huntington, S. (1993) 'The Clash of Civilisations?', *Foreign Affairs*, vol. 72(3), 22–49.

Kaldor, Mary (1990) *The Imaginary War* (Oxford: Blackwell).

Knorr, Klaus (1966) *On the Uses of Military Power in the Nuclear Age* (Princeton, NJ: Princeton University Press).

Maynes, Charles William (1995) 'The New Pessimism', *Foreign Policy*, 33–49.

MccGwire, Michael (1991) *Perestroika and Soviet National Security* (Washington, DC: Brookings Institution).

Mearsheimer, J. J. (1990) 'Back to the Future: Instability in Europe after the Cold War', *International Security*, vol. 15(1), 5–52.

Miller, James (1995) *The Passion of Michel Foucault* (London: HarperCollins Publishers).

Mueller, John (1990) *Retreat From Doomsday* (New York: Basic Books).

Rapoport, Anatol (ed.) (1968) *Clausewitz On War* (Harmondsworth: Penguin Books).

Regehr, Ernie (1994) 'Warfare's New Face', *World Press Review*, vol. 41(4) April, 14–15.

Rosenberg, Tina (1995) *The Haunted Land. Facing Europe's Ghosts after Communism* (London: Vintage).

Sagan, Scott D. (1993) *The Limits of Safety: Organisations, Accidents, and Nuclear Weapons* (Princeton, NJ: Princeton University Press).

Scott, Len and Smith, Steve (1994) 'Lessons of October: Historians, Political Scientists, Policy-makers and the Cuban Missile Crisis', *International Affairs*, vol. 70(4), 659–84.

Smith, Steve (1995) 'The Self-Images of a Discipline: A Genealogy of

International Relations Theory', in Ken Booth and Steve Smith (eds.), *International Relations Theory Today* (Cambridge: Polity Press), pp. 1–37.

Taylor, A. J. P. (1976) *The Second World War. An Illustrated History* (Harmondsworth: Penguin).

Viotti, P. R. and Kauppi, M. V. (1990) *International Relations Theory: Realism, Pluralism and Globalism* (New York: Macmillan).

Wallerstein, I. (1979) *The Capitalist World Economy* (Cambridge: Cambridge University Press).

(1991) *Geopolitics and Geoculture: Essays on the Changing World System* (Cambridge: Cambridge University Press).

Whitfield, Stephen J. (1991) *The Culture of the Cold War* (Baltimore: The Johns Hopkins University Press).

Raymond L. Garthoff

Some readers may express surprise that the question is even posed. After all, the Soviet Union lost the Cold War and even collapsed under its burden; surely its failure bears witness to its blame. Moreover, being accustomed to believing both that 'Right will prevail' and that we are on the side of Right, the outcome is the one that had been expected as well as desired. Possibly others, more cynical, would still assume that since the victors write history, as the adage has it, why bother to raise the question? By now, yet other readers will be preparing themselves for an unexpected conclusion; why introduce the subject this way (or, indeed, at all) unless the author intends to conclude that we (the West) won, but none the less we were to blame? I would, however, hope that readers will avoid prejudgements and bear with me in a fresh look at the question.

By posing the issue as 'who is to blame?', rather than 'what caused the Cold War?', we are assuming the answer to be certain people – political leaders – and not faceless elemental abstractions incapable of blame, such as a geopolitical contest,[1] a political duel or an ideological confrontation. (I use the editorial 'we' in this instance because it was the editor who suggested this title for my contribution, although I take responsibility for accepting it and drawing the inferences from it noted above. By speaking of blame, we are also prejudging that the Cold War *would* better have been avoided, and we are implying that perhaps it *could* have been avoided.) The Cold War arose on the foundation of all three of the objective factors, as we shall see, but it was also the product of subjective perceptions of such factors and their significance. And this was of crucial importance.

The Cold War is now established as a specific episode in history. Although there is room to debate precisely when the Cold War began and ended (and to a certain extent value in doing so), there is a general consensus that it began in 1946–7 and ended in 1989–90. Only for the purpose of establishing a more precise illustrative landmark, I would suggest that the advent of the Cold War was signalled by Winston Churchill's address at Fulton College, Missouri, on 5 March 1946, vividly describing the descent of an Iron Curtain dividing Europe. And by the same token, the end of the Cold War can be dated to the breaching of the Berlin Wall on 9 November 1989, again symbolising the end of the division of Europe and of the world.

Other events, given somewhat different weight by various historians, identify other steps in the unleashing of the Cold War between 1945 and 1948, and in its conclusion between the sudden collapse of the Soviet empire in Eastern Europe in late 1989, the reunification of Germany, and celebration of the reunification of Europe in the Paris Charter in November 1990. But by the time of the communist takeover of Czechoslovakia and of the Berlin Blockade in 1948 no one doubted we were in what had already (in 1947) been dubbed 'the Cold War', and by the end of 1990 virtually no one disputed that the Cold War was over. This was a full year before the end of reform communist rule in the Soviet Union, and of the Soviet Union itself, be it noted. The collapse of the Soviet Union in 1991 confirmed the irreversibility of the end of the Cold War, but was not required to accomplish that result.

Beginnings of the Cold War

The seeds of the Cold War, it could well be argued, had been present even with the creation of the wartime alliance coalition of the Big Three powers against the Axis powers in 1941. They shared a common interest in defeating the Axis powers, but once that had been achieved the common interest dissolved and was promptly succeeded by a sharp split over filling the political vacuum left by the total defeat of Germany, Italy and Japan and the wide swathe of Axis satellite and occupied territories covering most of Europe. The wartime leaders at Yalta made a first cut at dealing with the problem, although they created more illusion of agreement than resolution of the issues.

There was a political and economic vacuum in much of Europe, but there was no military vacuum; the armed forces of the victorious allies had occupied it all, up to a line where they now faced each other, soon no longer as allies. Apart from a few adjustments to meet earlier agreements (in particular, Western troops moving to occupy West Berlin, and Soviet troops to occupy portions of south central Germany), the military division of Europe was a consequence of the end of the war, rather than of postwar decisions of the Allied powers.[2] Early postwar decisions from 1945 to 1948, mostly in 1945–6, did however establish the pattern of a sharper division of Germany (and Berlin), and of exclusion of the Western powers from effective sharing of occupation power in Eastern Europe – and a parallel exclusion of the Soviet Union from sharing in occupation power in Japan and Italy. These decisions, by both sides, contributed to a pattern of non-cooperation of the former allies.

The not dissimilar actions of the two sides in reshaping the political structures of occupied enemies in their own images and as their own new allies also gave rise to another pattern to become familiar in the Cold War. Each saw its own actions as fully justified and proper, including exclusion of the other, and yet each blamed the other side for pursuing a similar parallel path. A double standard was applied by both sides.

The rapid retreat from wartime cooperation of the three principal allies to a split between Britain and the United States on the one hand, and the Soviet Union on the other, in managing the occupation of former enemy (and some formerly enemy-occupied) territories was thus one strand in the weaving of the Cold War. One can identify particular decisions in which the blame was on one side or the other, but the general pattern in this process, while not so perceived by either side, was shared blame by both sides.

By 1947 the pattern of a split between two sides not only replaced the wartime and immediate postwar tripartite pattern, but within the Western side the shared British–US roles had shifted by spring 1947 to one of a dominant American position, albeit with a continuing close relationship. The British transfer of responsibility for support (and in effect protection) of Greece and Turkey to the United States reflected this change, as well as giving rise to the first US pronouncement of a policy of containment of potential geopolitical advance by the Soviet Union (and by non-Soviet communists, as in Greece). From 1947 on, the leading protagonists of the Cold War were clearly the United States and the Soviet Union, reflecting the real power position of the United States through the whole of the postwar period. In the formative years of the Cold War, however, Britain played an important role along with the United States, again as exemplified in the leading role played by Churchill's Iron Curtain call to arms in 1946.

Joseph Stalin, in an 'electoral' address in Moscow on 9 February 1946, had sounded a call on the Soviet people to gear up for a long struggle, and this speech was taken in the West as an ominous sign. By coincidence, at this general juncture three important long dispatches on the Soviet–Western relationship were sent to their home capitals by the US chargé d'affaires in Moscow, George Kennan (on 22 February), by the British chargé in Moscow, Frank Roberts (on 14 March), and somewhat later by the Soviet ambassador in Washington, Nikolai Novikov (on 27 September).[3] Also on 24 September 1946, Clark Clifford of the White House staff submitted to President Truman a report on Soviet objectives based on a survey made at his direction (by Clifford and his colleague George Elsey), collating the views of interested senior officials in the US government (including Kennan and Charles Bohlen), but without the burden of inter-agency 'clearance'. Truman was impressed by the sobering negative prognosis of the memorandum in its evaluation of Soviet aggressive aims. He decided not to circulate or publish it even at a highly classified level, but it had a substantial impact on his thinking.[4] It reinforced the message of Kennan's 'Long Telegram' and called for containment ('restraint') of the Soviet threat.

The policy of containment received its public articulation in the 'Truman Doctrine', set forth on 12 March 1947, with specific application to Greece and Turkey but explicitly couched in global terms. The Marshall Plan for economic recovery of Western Europe, launched on 5 June, was open also to the countries of Eastern Europe and the Soviet Union, but it would have tied those countries to the West and Stalin saw it as a scheme to isolate and weaken the Soviet Union. In July, Kennan's rationale of a containment policy, first presented a year earlier in his 'Long Telegram', was elaborated in an article in *Foreign Affairs* under the pseudonym 'X' – although his authorship was quickly unmasked, drawing far greater public attention to the article than would an official policy statement or an article attributed to Kennan. The X article was somewhat less philosophical and more hard-toned than had been the Long Telegram, but the message was the same (as it had been in the Clifford–Elsey memorandum as well). The Marxist–Leninist ideological foundation for unremitting if measured confrontation of the two systems was taken as the basis for a US-led Western counter-policy of containment.

In late September 1947 the Soviet leadership tightened the controls of the Eastern 'camp', and clearly reaffirmed the struggle of two contending camps in a speech by Politburo member Andrei Zhdanov, representing Stalin at the foundation of the Cominform, a new coordinating organisation for leading Western as well as satellite Eastern European communist parties. In concrete actions tightening – and extending – the Soviet-led camp, the Communist Party of Czechoslovakia in a political manoeuvre seized power in Prague in February 1948. (In the same month efforts by the Finnish communists to gain power were quashed.) Finally, Western moves to consolidate the western occupation zones of Germany led in June to a Soviet counter-move to place pressure on West Berlin through a blockade of land transit – which the United States effectively countered with an imaginative airlift of supplies to the beleaguered city.

In April 1949 the North Atlantic Treaty was signed and the North Atlantic Treaty Organization (NATO) came into being – over strong Soviet protests. Also during 1949 the United States and Britain stepped up covert efforts to subvert communist rule in several countries of Eastern Europe and the western USSR (Albania, Poland, the Baltic states and Ukraine in particular).

By June 1950, when North Korea invaded the south and the United States (and United Nations) intervened militarily, the Cold War was in full sway and the militarisation of the confrontation proceeded apace. NATO, now led by General Dwight Eisenhower, and soon encompassing the beginnings of West German rearmament, shifted into high gear. The US 'charter' of the Cold War, NSC-68, approved by President Truman in April, now came to provide a rationale for a global American military buildup, not only to wage the war in Korea, but also to provide muscle to NATO, to expand the network of US military bases, to shift to a large quantitative buildup of nuclear weapons, and to create other regional alliances in the Middle East and South East Asia as well as bilateral US alliances with key countries around the world, including Japan.

This quick sketch of a few of the salient developments from 1946 through 1950 is intended merely to note some of the key events. There were of course many steps taken by both sides that contributed to the growth of confrontation, and no less significant was the decline and virtual disappearance of efforts at cooperation and resolution of differing and conflicting interests.

The nature of the Cold War

The real record of the Cold War has still to be compiled. The sharply divergent accounts of events on the two sides not only differed over responsibility for growing hostility, but over the facts. Even identification of relevant events was divergent or disputed. Increasingly, the logic of the struggle led to attention only to actions of the other side that were hostile (or at least depicted as hostile), and with no recognition that many such actions – on both sides – were reactions to actions earlier taken by the other side.

Throughout the Cold War, neither side was as blameless as it saw itself – and far less blameless than it depicted itself. Similarly, neither side was as guilty as it was depicted, or even as it was seen, by the other side. But the logic of confrontation made it politically (and psychologically) useful to demonise the adversary and to see God (or History) as on one's own side. Dean Acheson, who had first realised at the time of rallying congressional support for the Truman Doctrine the need for simplified black versus white categories in order to mobilise political acceptance, later commented in a telling phrase that there was a political necessity to depict the Western–Soviet confrontation starkly in terms 'clearer than the truth'. Yet this process of oversimplified exaggeration came to influence not only publics but policy-makers themselves as well.

The reality of the competition provided each side with ample grounds not only to confirm its own judgement that it was right, and on the side of Right, but also to have genuine suspicions and fears of the other. It is important to realise that not only did this process feed vicious propaganda and public perceptions, but also that it influenced and sometimes dominated actual assessments and beliefs of the leaders. This was the most insidious aspect of the process of reciprocal prejudgement and projection of blame. Moreover, while reality could be interpreted (sometimes easily, sometimes only by feats of unconscious legerdemain) as supporting the image of the enemy and of permanent conflict, there was an underlying ideological conception that established the essential foundation for the whole Cold War – the Marxist–Leninist conception of world class struggle as an objective phenomenon, rendering inevitable and inescapable a global geopolitical conflict. That such a Marxist–Leninist world-view underlay Soviet thinking and policy was, if sometimes misunderstood in terms of its operational role, obviously recognised by Western leaders, who tirelessly drew attention to communism as the enemy. What was not reflected upon, although it would not have been denied, was that the attribution of this world-view to the leaders of the Soviet Union and 'world communism' *also underlay the Western policy of anti-communism*. Containment of Soviet and communist expansion was seen as necessary because that was seen as the driving force behind the concrete adversary: the leaders of the Soviet Union, and all at their command.

Acts of state policy that might have been taken even if the communist ideology had never existed were none the less taken by both sides in the belief that they were sanctioned, respectively, by communism and by anti-communist containment. Moreover, while Western policy (in alternating phases of confrontation and détente) remained essentially one of containment, many in the West went an important step further. Why, was their argument, should the West continue a policy of mere containment that could, even if successful, last indefinitely, and moreover might some time fail. Why not extirpate communism, defeat and destroy the Soviet empire and the Soviet Union, not merely contain its further expansion. Why not roll back and defeat and destroy communism? Although sometimes rhetorically powerful in domestic political propaganda, especially in the United States, and sometimes inhibiting palliatives such as détente, this logical embrace of ultra anti-communism never became state policy in the West. But the Manichaean ideological underpinning was there for the containment version of Western policy that *was* the heart of operative ideology and policy from the late 1940s to the late 1980s.

If only briefly, note must also be taken of the fact that the ideologically-driven dynamic of the Cold War also had serious repercussions and impact on the internal life of each country, more pervasively in the case of the Soviet Union (above all in Stalin's day), but reaching far beyond obvious excesses such as McCarthyism in the United States as well. Some have characterised the result as the rise of the 'national security state'.

In the final analysis, the shared ideological world-view of communism/anti-communism, imputing an ineluctable contest, was the distinguishing feature defining the Cold War. In Western analytical terms, the Cold War was a zero-sum game in which the gains of one side were automatically losses to the other, ruling out genuine compromise, reconciliation, shared interests and conflict resolution by any means but prevailing over the other. In Marxist–Leninist terms, this was encapsulated in the phrase *Kto kogo?* Who will prevail over whom? In analytical terms, the communist version posited a 'correlation of forces' between adversaries, a version of the balance of power with the important distinction that while the given relationship at any moment would be in flux, the ultimate objective and result would be not an equilibrium balance, but victory for the side that prevailed when the correlation ultimately tipped decisively. This conception was rarely recognised in the West, and when it was it was almost always interpreted in terms of the military balance of forces, which was *not* the Marxist–Leninist conception (military power being an important factor, one crucially important not to neglect, but neither the driving force of history nor the ultimate arbiter, and hence not the foundation of Soviet policy).

The shared view of the ideology of 'communism/anti-communism' was an amalgam of myth and reality. Neither side was set on 'world domination' with the clarity, intensity, consistency or malevolence imputed by the adversary. Yet leaders on both sides did foresee and seek to counter efforts of their adversaries in the belief that the enemy was foreordained (or believed he was foreordained) to carry the struggle to the end. Moreover, leaders on both sides *did* hold ideologies that foresaw and sought to further global hegemony of their own system. Although the Marxist–Leninist ideology was most explicit, the US-led counter-communist ideology was not guided only by containment of communism. There was a strong belief in the Wilsonian and Roosevel-tian themes of 'making the world safe for democracy' and assumptions about the nature of democracy that excluded any place for an ideology opposed to pluralism, human rights and other attributes of a 'world community' (moreover, as *Time* magazine had dubbed it, the world was now living in 'The American Century').

The global rivalry spanned by the communist–anti-communist shared world-view also means that other aims and values were perforce subordinated 'for the duration' to the supreme task of waging and winning the Cold War. This meant, as earlier noted, even certain curbs on normal freedoms at home in the interests of security. It also meant subordinating other considerations in relationships with other countries, overlooking some rather large anomalies in depicting the anti-commu-nist coalition as 'the Free World'. Many of its members lacked human and political rights no less or even more than did citizens of communist countries.

This was one major distinction of the ideologically undergirded Cold War that distinguished it from earlier geopolitical rivalries such as the 'Great Game' played between Great Britain and Russia over south-west and central Asia in the nineteenth century. But there were others. It was altogether more dangerous, and the ideologically based zero-sum game approach to global rivalry in a bipolar world also subordinated the leavening influences of the balance of great powers in the eighteenth and nineteenth centuries.

Paradoxically, the effect of an all-consuming ideological world-view (and its antithesis) between camps led by two superpowers in a quite different way cultivated a sense of a 'great game'. Western nuclear deterrence, the military arm of containment,[5] degenerated into an apolitical, mechanistic exercise based on game theory. 'Scenarios' of second and third 'strategic' nuclear strikes after thousands of thermo-nuclear detonations across the northern hemisphere replaced political analysis and undermined *any* ideological rationale. To be sure, sanity in political judgement was not lost and we survived the Cold War. But the risks were raised unnecessarily by excessive militarisation of the rivalry, excessive reliance on fallible technologies of warning and communi-cation, and substitution of technical 'requirements' of deterrence in such coin as missile 'throw-weight' for strategic thinking.

Containment and deterrence led to vast arrays of arms and political-military alliances. In addition to the deployment of military assets, this process of political militarisation also generated its own additional 'requirements' buttressing those of military power. Seeking to maintain a favourable military balance, even if nominally only 'parity', set high requirements for military competition. Maintaining the military (and deterrent) balance was demanding, especially because there always existed a margin of uncertainty that each side wanted to assure to itself and deny to the opponent. But the reality of the military-deterrent balance was not deemed enough. Perceptions of the military balance and of the power relationship were also seen as crucial. Deterrence, of course, is predicated on an adversary's recognition of capability for retaliation. Reassurance to one's allies as well depends on their perceptions of both strength and will to use it on their behalf (the latter feature again pressing for a margin of superiority). Thus in addition to meeting requirements for assuring a real military deterrent power, the perceptions of that power by both friend and foe must also be assured in order to maintain credibility, and effectiveness, of deterrence of the enemy and reassurance of one's allies. Yet capabilities sufficient to survive an enemy attack and retaliate in similar measure are, perforce, so powerful as to be threatening if used in a first strike.

Although the nuclear deterrent relationship was central to the containment policy, it was far from encompassing it. Military, political and economic power was also engaged around the world. The same factors were at work. For example, credibility of the will of the United States to deter or contain a Soviet challenge in Europe was instrumental in leading the United States into the two large wars in Korea and Vietnam. To reassure allies, as well as to deter even 'proxy' communist expansion, it was deemed essential for the United States to commit its own conventional military power.

The US intervention in the Korean War was successful, not only in denying the North occupation of the South, but in putting into motion a major American and NATO military buildup. Yet it is increasingly clear that the assumption at the time, that Stalin was testing the resolve of the United States and that a US failure to intervene would have encouraged the Soviet Union to move militarily in Europe (or anywhere else), was almost certainly wrong. Similarly, neither allies or adversaries would have seen US resolve on containment or deterrence weak if Indochina had been let slip under local communist rule in the 1950s or 1960s.

If my judgement on these two examples is correct, it suggests that many lesser battles of the Cold War were also unnecessary, even given the fact of the Cold War contest. Still more, it raises questions as to whether there may not have been earlier opportunities to bring the Cold War to a close. On the other hand, there remain many indications that until the mid-1980s Soviet leaders continued to see the world through an ideological prism that precluded their ability to envisage a real end to the Cold War. Similarly, when a Soviet leader *did* see the world differently and seek to end the Cold War, it was only after repeated and significant unilateral actions and concessions that the Western leaders were prepared to accept that fact.

It is only with the end of the Cold War that it has become clear that this underlying ideological foundation mandating an adversarial relationship was what prevented any of the periods of détente from becoming a stepping-stone to a post-Cold War world. Détente was a way of cushioning the risks to permit continued competition and the workings of the historical forces that would ultimately determine the outcome of the struggle. And it did perform that historic service. But détente was still a means of the class struggle, as the Soviets openly avowed during the détente of the 1970s, and a veiled form of containment, as the record of US policy in the 1970s closely observed clearly shows (and as Kissinger and Brzezinski boast in their memoirs).

The ending of the Cold War

The Cold War could end only when two things occurred: first, when a *Soviet* leader abandoned the Marxist–Leninist conception of the world, as Mikhail Gorbachev did in 1986, and demonstrated in many actions from 1986 to 1991; and second, when *the West* would come to recognise that fact and abandon its no longer relevant image of an ideologically committed permanent adversary and the derived foundation for its containment policy (as the West gradually came to realise in the late 1980s, and suddenly concluded in 1989–90, the year from the fall of the Berlin Wall to the Paris Charter for the new reunified Europe). In the interests of history, it is important to realise that the Cold War came to an end, and an acknowledged end, while modified communist rule still prevailed in the Soviet Union. To be sure, the end of communist rule and of the Soviet Union itself at the close of 1991 closed the books on an era, but the Cold War had already ended when the ideological underpinnings of a world view based on an adversarial relationship were abandoned in word and deed by the protagonist and the antagonist.

The end of the Cold War, and an assessment of responsibility for that achievement, does not fully answer our question as to 'who is to blame' for the Cold War. But it does strongly argue that the Marxist–Leninist ideology played a crucial role in both launching and ending the Cold War. It is not possible to ascribe blame to an idea, so one must assign responsibility for the impact of that idea to those who held the conception, or perhaps to those who originated it and inculcated it. Joseph Stalin conveniently bridges those two categories to the extent that he had been part of the leadership of the Bolshevik party under Lenin that refined and developed the conception, as well as the Soviet leader responsible for its reassertion at the time the Cold War began.

I do not believe the Cold War would have occurred without Stalin (or an equivalent convinced Marxist–Leninist Soviet leader in the late 1940s). On the other hand, a later Soviet leader, Mikhail Gorbachev, deliberately abandoned that same Marxist–Leninist conception and, more than any one else, ended the Cold War. Yet the Cold War outlived Stalin by some thirty-five years. Is Stalin (and Lenin) to blame for that?

Notwithstanding the absolutely crucial role of the ideological under-pinning to the geopolitical contest, the history of that Cold War itself, from its origins to its demise, must also be addressed to determine who was to blame for more than forty years of Cold War. Who waged the Cold War, and how, to keep it alive all that time? How was the ideological foundation kept alive so long – particularly since it is now universally accepted to have been faulty? Could Western leaders with a different *form* of containment have withheld communist (Soviet) expansion without also long sustaining Soviet views of the validity of their false ideology? Could Soviet leaders have waged the Cold War in ways that need not have sustained it for so long (and, on reflection, did they)? In short, we need to ask not only who was to blame for starting the Cold War, but who was to blame for waging it in such a way that it lasted for over four decades. Which leaders, which policies and which decisions were to blame for that? And what assumptions, perceptions and other considerations underlay those decisions and policies?

Among those who have been wrestling with these questions for years is Michael MccGwire. Always prepared to pursue the quest for the truth relentlessly, he has contributed much through published studies of the importance of threat perception and analysis of military requirements as factors contributing to the dynamics of the Cold War, and to seeing the Soviet perspective on these matters. He has also written a number of unpublished papers on this subject which I hope he will now complete and publish.[6]

Any reasonably objective reading of the record of the Cold War can only lead to the conclusion that both sides contributed, and both sides share the blame. The next steps, however, are not easy: (1) what policies and actions could have been decided upon that would have been preferable? (2) who, on each side, and not just the leaders responsible (sometimes nominally) for final decisions, were to blame for faulty or inferior policies and actions? and, finally (3) in the end, which side bore most of the blame for keeping the Cold War going? Any attempt to answer these questions requires judgements, and objective assessments can only be sought, not assured. But they should be sought. (In my view, the third question above, although probably the question of greatest interest to most readers – at least when they first read it – is the most difficult compound of subjective assessments, the most difficult to answer, but in the final analysis also the least important. There were enough errors and misjudgements made on both sides from which we all can learn.)

The extraordinarily role of Mikhail Gorbachev in taking the lead to bring the Cold War to an end requires its own more extended analysis.[7] In the present context, however, a few observations are appropriate and necessary. First is the fact that the 'new political thinking' that Gorbachev embraced had been developing for a long time within the Soviet system as the discrepancies between Marxist–Leninist doctrine and reality became more obvious. What was new was that Gorbachev was the first leader prepared to acknowledge those discrepancies, to change authoritative doctrine, and above all to act on the basis of necessary changes in policy and behaviour. The failures of Marxism–Leninism pertained both to the vision of the outside world and Soviet life. Gorbachev was initially disposed to believe that internal change required only reform and 'restructuring', and although he was prepared ultimately to dethrone the Communist Party and undertake radical political and economic reform, he failed in his attempt to effect a controlled internal revolution. By contrast, from the very outset he recognised that the Bolshevik world view was not only wrong, but contributed fundamentally to the Cold War. And although he initially overestimated possibilities for 'restructuring' international relations (especially with respect to Eastern Europe), he recognised from the outset that there was but one integral world, not two worlds in inevitable conflict. He set out to dismantle not only the military and geopolitical confrontation between East and West but also the underlying ideological, political and psychological underpinnings of the Cold War – and in that he succeeded. Moreover, he succeeded not because of Western pressure, but despite it.

One of the important lessons of the ending of the Cold War was that it came about not by a victory for geopolitical containment and nuclear deterrence but by the recognised failure of the Marxist–Leninist ideology. It was that fact that led Gorbachev to make drastic concessions to end the military confrontation in Europe and with the United States. The Soviet Union did not lose the arms race; Gorbachev called it off. The Soviet Union was not forced out of Eastern Europe by a Western 'crusade' or by internal rebellion; it decided to withdraw in order to end the division of Europe that lay at the heart of the Cold War.

By the time of the Charter of Paris in November 1990 the Cold War was over, and that fact was acknowledged virtually universally. Since then we have been wrestling with the post-Cold War world. But we also still need to come to terms with the Cold War as the point of our departure into this new era.

The history of the Cold War, or more precisely the Western historiography of the Cold War, is now entering a fourth phase. First, in the 1950s and early 1960s, came the establishment orthodoxy, presenting a clear case of Soviet aggression and threat, and Western defensive response. This was followed, especially in the 1960s, by a revisionist interpretation pointing out the many examples of Western initiative and ambition, and generally blaming the West for the Cold War. Third, in the 1970s and 1980s, a synthesis developed in post-revisionist recognition of shared responsibility by both sides, although usually seeing a somewhat greater Soviet responsibility.

Today, in the 1990s with the Cold War behind us, a fourth phase is opening, with the conjunction of three important elements. First, we now have the benefit of being able to see the Cold War as a whole and as an episode in recent history. Second, a wealth of formerly secret documentation, not only from Western archives, but from Russia as well, is becoming available. And third, we now have at least the potential benefit of working along with the Russians (and others) in assessing our common past experiences. (Moreover, there is a valuable but diminishing group of former Soviet officials who are knowledgeable sources and resources for this work.) Soviet historiography had never really advanced beyond the stage of a rigidly controlled orthodoxy blaming the West for the Cold War, although by the late 1980s the first steps were being taken to establish balance. Now there is opportunity for much more free discovery, not only of what has been known in the West, but of much we do not yet know about the Soviet side of the experience. Yet today there is in Russia one school of revisionism uncritically blaming the Soviet leaders for everything, while another rides a nationalist-communist backlash still blaming the West. Balance is usually neither sought nor achieved. I would not suggest that responsibility for the excesses (or even the necessities) of the Cold War was evenly shared; there are too many cases where evidently one side or the other bears the principal responsibility. But we have the common task, and opportunity, to explore more fully than ever before the full history of the Cold War and to answer, if not the question posed in the title of this chapter, at least a modified version of it: which side is to blame, and why, for each of the many turns of the Cold War over nearly half a century; what processes of action provided the dynamics of the Cold War; and above all, what can we learn from the history of the Cold War that will permit us not to repeat the errors of the past as we move into the future?

NOTES

1   Throughout the discussion of the waging of the Cold War I shall be using the term 'geopolitical' according to the prevailing fashion, referring to the exercise of *realpolitik*, rather than the imperatives of *geopolitik*. In terms of the situation giving rise to the Cold War, however, it may also be appropriate to note (without necessarily accepting either Karl Haushofer's or Sir Halford Mackinder's variants of classical geopolitics) that the objective geostrategic situation which generated the Cold War did bear a remarkable resemblance to the conception of a counter-position of a Rimland coalition versus a Eurasian Heartland, joined for the first time from central Germany through Russia into northern China, under the rule of a single centre of power in Moscow, posing Mackinder's ominous challenge, 'Who rules the Heartland, rules the World'.

2   There had been some wartime disagreements between leaders of Great Britain and the United States over wartime strategy, with greater British attention given to affecting the military situation at the end of the war and the postwar political situation. There were also some wartime – and second-thought postwar – criticisms of some of General Dwight Eisenhower's decisions on how far to advance into Germany and Czechoslovakia from the same perspective. But different wartime decisions on these matters would only have affected the basic outcome on the margin, with the partial exception of the agreement to establish Western zones in Berlin surrounded by Soviet occupied territory, a situation that contributed to later difficulties.

    The Soviet leaders nursed a conviction that the Anglo-American powers had intentionally held back from launching a second front in Western Europe until mid-1944 in order that the Soviet Union would bear the brunt of the struggle and be bled dry by the war. On the other hand, while the Western allied armies did not drive all-out for Berlin, the Red Army certainly did, for symbolic reasons and with an eye to the postwar situation, as well as to defeat the German forces.

    It is a Western Cold War myth that Stalin imposed communist rule and Soviet domination wherever Soviet troops had reached. Soviet forces were soon withdrawn from northern Norway, occupied parts of Finland, Danish Bornholm Island in the Baltic, Czechoslovakia, Manchuria and northern Iran (with a little delay and an attempt to use their presence for leverage in negotiations with Iran).

3   All were secret at the time and for many years. For the texts and commentary, see US Institute of Peace (1993).

4   Clifford has discussed the memorandum in his memoir (1991: 109–29). The full text of the memorandum, 'American Relations with the Soviet Union', was made available by Clifford years later to Arthur Krock, and is appended to Krock (1968: 419–32).

5   By a fluke of translation, the same Russian word, *sderzhivaniye*, meaning external restraint, was used to render both 'containment' and 'deterrence', causing some confusion, although inadvertently reflecting a real link. One consequence was to encourage Soviet writers to use another term for deterrence (in describing Western policy), *ustrasheniye*, meaning intimida-

tion, which had the added advantage in the Cold War context of being pejorative.

One incidental but not inconsequential result was that whenever Soviet leaders were given the texts of statements by Western leaders reaffirming their policy of deterrence, the Soviet leaders believed they were encountering open avowal of a policy of intimidation, because of course they received such texts only in translation.

6   Part of one such paper has been published: see MccGwire (1994).
7   I have sought to contribute to this endeavour in Garthoff (1994).

REFERENCES

Clifford, Clark M. with Richard Holbrooke (1991) *Counsel to the President: A Memoir* (New York: Random House).
Garthoff, Raymond L. (1994) *The Great Transition: American–Soviet Relations and the End of the Cold War* (Washington, DC: Brookings Institution).
Krock, Arthur (1968) *Memoirs: Sixty Years on the Firing Line* (New York: Funk and Wagnalls).
MccGwire, Michael K. (1994) 'National Security and Soviet Foreign Policy', in Mervyn P. Heffler and David S. Painter (eds.) *Origins of the Cold War* (London: Routledge), pp. 53–76.
US Institute of Peace (1993) *Origins of the Cold War: The Novikov, Kennan and Roberts 'Long Telegrams' of 1946* (Washington: USIP, rev. edn).

3 Nuclear lessons of the Cold War

Richard Ned Lebow and Janice Gross Stein

The role of nuclear weapons in Soviet–US relations has been hotly debated. Politicians, generals and most academic strategists believe that the United States' nuclear arsenal restrained the Soviet Union throughout the Cold War. Critics maintain that nuclear weapons were a root cause of superpower conflict and a threat to peace. Controversy also surrounds the number and kinds of weapons necessary to deter, the political implications of the strategic balance, and the role of nuclear deterrence in hastening the collapse of the Soviet imperium.

Careful analysts were alert to the difficulty of making definitive judgements about deterrence in the absence of valid and reliable information about Soviet and Chinese objectives and calculations (MccGwire, 1985/6; Betta, 1987; Bundy, 1988). Newly declassified documents and extensive interviews with Soviet and US officials permit a reconstuction of the deliberations of leaders of both superpowers before, during and after the two most serious nuclear crises of the last thirty years: the Cuban missile crisis of 1962 and the superpower crisis arising out of the 1973 Middle East war. This evidence sheds new light on some of the controversies at the centre of the nuclear debate (Lebow and Stein, 1994). Needless to say, definitive judgements must await the opening of archives and more complete information about the calculations of Soviet and US leaders in other crises, as well as those of other nuclear powers.

Restraining, provocative or irrelevant?

Students of nuclear deterrence distinguish between general and immediate deterrence (Morgan, 1977). General deterrence relies on the existing power balance to prevent an adversary from seriously considering a military challenge because of its expected adverse consequences. It is often a country's first line of defence against attack. Leaders resort to the strategy of immediate deterrence only after general deterrence has failed, or when they believe that a more explicit expression of their

71

intent to defend their interests is necessary to buttress general deterrence. If immediate deterrence fails, leaders will find themselves in a crisis, as President Kennedy did when US intelligence discovered Soviet missiles in Cuba, or at war, as Israel's leaders did in 1973. General and immediate deterrence represent a progression from a diffuse if real concern about an adversary's intentions to the expectation that a specific interest or commitment is about to be challenged.

Both forms of deterrence assume that adversaries are most likely to resort to force or threatening military deployments when they judge the military balance favourable and question the defender's resolve. General deterrence pays particular importance to the military dimension; it tries to discourage challenges by developing the capability to defend national commitments or inflict unacceptable punishment on an adversary. General deterrence is a long-term strategy. Five-year lead times and normally longer are common between a decision to develop a weapon and its deployment.

Immediate deterrence is a short-term strategy. Its purpose is to discourage an imminent attack or challenge of a specific commitment. The military component of immediate deterrence must rely on forces in being. To buttress their defensive capability and display resolve, leaders may deploy forces when they anticipate an attack or challenge, as Kennedy did in the aftermath of the Vienna summit meeting with Soviet Premier Nikita Khrushchev in June 1961. In response to Khrushchev's ultimatum on Berlin, he sent additional ground and air forces to Germany and strengthened the US garrison in Berlin. These reinforcements were designed to communicate the administration's will to resist any encroachment against West Berlin or Western access routes to the city.

General deterrence: The origins of the Cuban missile crisis indicate that general deterrence, as practised by both superpowers, was provocative rather than preventive. Soviet officials testified that US strategic buildup, deployment of missiles in Turkey and assertions of nuclear superiority, made them increasingly insecure. The president viewed all of these measures as prudent, defensive precautions. His actions had the unanticipated consequence of convincing Khrushchev of the need to protect the Soviet Union and Cuba from US military and political challenges.

Khrushchev was hardly the innocent victim of US paranoia. His unfounded claims of nuclear superiority and nuclear threats were the catalyst for Kennedy's decision to increase the scope and pace of the US strategic buildup. The new US programmes and the Strategic Air Command's higher state of strategic readiness exacerbated Soviet perceptions of threat and contributed to Khrushchev's decision to send missiles to Cuba. In attempting to intimidate their adversaries, both leaders helped to bring about the kind of confrontation they were trying to avoid.

Kennedy later speculated, and Soviet officials have since confirmed, that his efforts to reinforce deterrence also encouraged Khrushchev to stiffen his position on Berlin (Schlesinger, 1965: 347–8; see also George and Smoke, 1974: 429, 579). The action and reaction that linked Berlin and Cuba were part of a larger cycle of insecurity and escalation that reached well back into the 1950s, if not to the beginning of the Cold War. The Soviet challenge to the Western position in Berlin in 1959–61 was motivated by Soviet concern about the viability of East Germany and secondarily by Soviet vulnerability to US nuclear-tipped missiles stationed in Western Europe. The US missiles had been deployed to assuage NATO fears about the conventional military balance on the central front, made more acute by the creation of the Warsaw Pact in 1955. The Warsaw Pact itself was an attempt by Moscow to consolidate its political and physical control over an increasingly restive Eastern Europe (Remmington, 1967; Jones, 1981; Holloway and Sharp, 1984).

Once the Cuban missile crisis erupted, general deterrence played an important moderating role. Kennedy and Khrushchev moved away from confrontation and towards compromise because they both feared war. Kennedy worried that escalation would set in motion a chain of events that could lead to nuclear war. Khrushchev's decision to withdraw the missiles indicated that he too was prepared to make sacrifices to avoid war. His capitulation in the face of US military pressure was a humiliating defeat for the Soviet Union and its leader. Soviet officials confirm that it was a crucial factor in his removal from power a year later.[1] For many years, Americans portrayed the crisis as an unalloyed US triumph. Kennedy's secret promise to remove the Jupiter missiles from Turkey within six months of the end of the missile crisis, and his willingness on Saturday night, 27 October, to consider making that concession public, indicate that when the superpower leaders were 'eyeball to eyeball' both sides blinked. One reason they did so was their fear of nuclear war and its consequences.

General deterrence also failed to prevent an Egyptian decision to use force in 1973. President Sadat and his military staff openly acknowledged Egyptian military inferiority. They also had no doubt about Israel's resolve to defend itself if attacked. Egyptian President Anwar el-Sadat still chose to fight a limited war. He decided to attack Israel because of intense domestic political pressures to regain the Sinai. He had lost all hope in diplomacy after the failure of the peace missions in the early 1970s of Secretary William Rogers and although he recognised that the military balance was unfavourable, he expected it to get even worse in the future.

Israel's practice of general deterrence – it had acquired a new generation of fighters and bombers – convinced Sadat to initiate military action sooner rather than later. Egyptian military planners devised a strategy intended to compensate for their military inferiority. Egyptian officers sought to capitalise on surprise, occupy the east bank of the Suez Canal, defend against Israeli counter-attacks with a mobile missile screen, and press for an internationally imposed cease-fire before their limited gains could be reversed by a fully mobilised Israel. The parallels between 1962 and 1973 are striking. In both cases, attempts to reinforce general deterrence against vulnerable and hard-pressed opponents provoked rather than prevented unwanted challenges.

General deterrence had contradictory implications in the crisis that erupted between the United States and the Soviet Union at the end of the October War. Leaders of both superpowers were confident that the other feared war; general deterrence was robust. This confidence allowed the United States to alert its forces world-wide without fear of escalation. Soviet Premier Leonid Brezhnev and some of his colleagues, on the other hand, worried about escalation if Soviet forces were deployed in positions in Egypt where they were likely to encounter advancing Israelis. The Politburo agreed that they did not want to be drawn into a military conflict that could escalate. Fear of war restrained the Soviet Union and contributed to the resolution of the crisis.

Immediate deterrence is intended to forestall a specific military deployment or use of force. For immediate deterrence to succeed, the defender's threats must convince adversaries that the likely costs of a challenge will more than offset any possible gains.[2] Immediate deterrence did not prevent the missile crisis. After Khrushchev had decided to send missiles to Cuba, Kennedy warned that he would not tolerate the introduction of Soviet missiles in Cuba. The president issued his threat in the belief that Khrushchev had no intention of establishing missile bases in Cuba. Despite the president's warnings, Khrushchev nevertheless proceeded with the secret deployment; he was convinced that they were necessary to protect Cuba from invasion, redress the strategic balance and establish psychological equality with the United States (Lebow and Stein, 1994: 19–66).

Students of the crisis disagree about why deterrence failed. Some contend that the strategy could not have worked while others insist that Kennedy attempted deterrence too late (Lebow, 1983). Whatever the cause, the failure of deterrence exacerbated the most acute crisis of the

Cold War. By making a public commitment to keep Soviet missiles out of Cuba, Kennedy dramatically increased the domestic political and foreign policy costs of allowing the missiles to remain after they were discovered. A threat originally intended to deflect pressures on the administration to invade Cuba would have made that invasion very difficult to avoid if Soviet leaders had not agreed to withdraw their missiles.

Israel chose not to practise immediate deterrence in 1973. Its leaders were convinced that Egypt would only attack when it could neutralise Israel's air force. Confidence in deterrence blinded Israel's leaders to the growing desperation of Sadat and his imperative to find a limited military strategy that would achieve his political objective. Israel's leaders worried instead that limited defensive measures on their part might provoke Egypt to launch a miscalculated attack.

Even if Israel had practised immediate deterrence, the evidence suggests that it would have made no difference. It is unlikely that public warnings and mobilisation of the Israel Defence Forces would have deterred Egypt; Sadat had expected Israel to mobilise its reserves and reinforce the Bar-Lev Line in response to Egyptian military preparations. He was surprised and pleased that Israel did not take defensive measures and that Egyptian forces did not sustain the high casualties that he had anticipated and was prepared to accept (Stein, 1985).

When the cease-fire negotiated jointly by Moscow and Washington failed to stop the fighting, Brezhnev threatened to consider unilateral intervention. The United States resorted to immediate deterrence to prevent a Soviet deployment. This was not the first time since the war began that Kissinger had attempted to deter Soviet military intervention. As early as 12 October, he told the Soviet ambassador to the US, Anatoliy Dobrynin, that any attempt by the Soviet Union to intervene with force would 'wreck the entire fabric of US–Soviet relations' (Kissinger, 1982: 508). Later that day, he warned the Soviet ambassador that any Soviet intervention, regardless of pretext, would be met by US force (p. 510). On the evening of 24 October, when Brezhnev asked for joint intervention and threatened that he might act alone if necessary, the United States went to a DEFCON III alert.

Immediate deterrence was irrelevant since Brezhnev had no intention of sending Soviet forces to Egypt. Soviet leaders had difficulty understanding why President Nixon alerted US forces. Brezhnev and some of his colleagues were angered, dismayed and humiliated.

Deterrence had diverse and contradictory consequences for superpower behaviour. General and immediate deterrence were principal causes of the missile crisis, but general deterrence also facilitated its resolution. In 1973, general deterrence contributed to the outbreak of war between Egypt and Israel and provided an umbrella for competition between the United States and the Soviet Union in the Middle East. Immediate deterrence failed to prevent the superpower crisis that followed, but general deterrence constrained the Soviet leadership and helped to resolve the crisis. These differences can best be understood by distinguishing between the strategy and reality of nuclear deterrence.

The strategy of deterrence attempts to manipulate the risk of war for political ends. For much of the Cold War, Soviet and US policymakers doubted that their opposites were deterred by the prospect of nuclear war. They expended valuable resources trying to perfect the mix of strategic forces, nuclear doctrine and targeting policy that would succeed in restraining their adversary. They also used military build-ups, force deployments and threats of war to try to coerce one another into making political concessions. In Berlin and Cuba, these attempts were unsuccessful but succeeded in greatly aggravating tensions.

The reality of deterrence derived from the inescapable fact that a superpower nuclear conflict would have been an unprecedented catastrophe for both sides. Superpower leaders understood this; by the late 1960s, if not earlier, they had come to believe that their countries could not survive a nuclear war. Fear of war, independent of the disparity in the strategic capabilities of the two sides, helped to keep both US and Soviet leaders from going over the brink and provided an important incentive for the mutual concessions that resolved the Cuban missile crisis. The moderation induced by the reality of deterrence helped to curtail the recklessness associated with the strategy of deterrence in the late 1950s and early 1960s.

The contradictory consequences of deterrence are not fully captured by any of the competing interpretations. Proponents of deterrence have emphasised the positive contribution of the reality of deterrence but ignored the baneful consequences of the strategy. The critics of deterrence have identified some of the political and psychological mechanisms that made the strategy of deterrence provocative and dangerous. But many ignored the ways in which the reality of deterrence was an important source of restraint.

When and why does deterrence work?

Proponents of deterrence have advanced two constraining reasons for its putative success. The conventional wisdom holds that deterrence restrained the Soviet Union by convincing its leaders that any military action against the United States or its allies would meet certain and effective opposition. Those who credit deterrence with preserving the peace assume that in its absence the Soviet Union would have been tempted to use force against its Western adversaries or their allies in the Middle East.

Throughout the Cold War, the US leaders regarded their adversary as fundamentally aggressive and intent on expanding its influence by subversion, intimidation or the use of force. Soviet leaders were frequently described as cold rational calculators who were constantly probing for opportunities. They carefully weighed the costs and benefits and abstained from aggressive action only if its costs were expected to outweigh the gains. At the outset of the Cuban missile crisis, Soviet expert Charles Bohlen told the Ex Comm, Kennedy's advisory group, that Lenin had compared Soviet foreign policy to a bayonet lunge: 'If you strike steel, pull back; if you strike mush, keep going' (Sorenson, 1965: 677). In this context, peace at times looked precarious to US leaders and their remarkable success in avoiding war needed an extraordinary explanation. The strategy of nuclear deterrence provided the explanation.

The strategy of deterrence seemed ideal for coping with a fundamentally aggressive and opportunity-driven adversary. It sought to prevent Soviet aggression by denying its leaders opportunities to exploit. The United States consequently developed impressive military capabilities – general deterrence – and publicly committed itself to the defence of specific interests – immediate deterrence – when it appeared that these interests might be challenged. The conventional wisdom, eloquently expressed in many of the scholarly writings on deterrence, assumed that Soviet aggression would wax and wane as a function of Soviet perceptions of US military capability and resolve. Soviet leaders would be most restrained when they regarded the military balance as unfavourable and US resolve as unquestionable (NSC 68, 1950: 264; Pipes, 1977; Aspaturian, 1980; Podhoretz, 1980; Luttwak, 1980).

The evidence from the crises in 1962 and 1973 do not support this assessment of deterrence. In 1962, the strategy of deterrence provoked a war-threatening crisis and, in 1973, nuclear deterrence provided the umbrella under which each sought to make or protect gains at the expense of the other until they found themselves in a tense confrontation.

The alternative interpretation holds that fear of nuclear war made both superpowers more cautious than they otherwise would have been in their competition for global influence, and thereby kept the peace. While far more convincing than the argument which credits the strategy of nuclear deterrence with preserving the peace, this explanation also is not fully persuasive. The reality of nuclear deterrence had a restraining effect on both Kennedy and Khrushchev in 1962 and on Brezhnev in 1973. When superpower leaders believed that they were approaching the brink of war, fear of war pulled them back.[3]

It is difficult to judge how much of the fear of war can be attributed to nuclear weapons, but the pattern of war avoidance was well set before the 1960s when the strategic nuclear arms race greatly accelerated (MccGwire, 1994: 215–17). At the time of the Korean War, the United States had only a limited nuclear arsenal, but Stalin may have exaggerated US ability to launch extensive nuclear strikes against the Soviet Union.[4] Secretary of Defense Robert McNamara subsequently testified that President Kennedy worried primarily that the missile crisis would lead to a conventional war with the Soviet Union (Welch, 1989). Other members of the Ex Comm disagree; they say it was the threat of nuclear war that was in the back of their minds, and probably, the president's (Welch, 1989). McNamara also admits that he had little expectation that a conventional conflict could be contained. 'I didn't know how we would stop the chain of military escalation once it began' (Hawk's Cay Conference, Lebow Record).

Soviet leaders during the missile crisis also worried about war, but neither the written record nor the testimony of Soviet officials offers any evidence of the kind of war Khrushchev thought most likely. There is no evidence that Khrushchev or Kennedy speculated about war scenarios; they were desperately trying to resolve the crisis. They had no political or psychological incentive to investigate the consequences of failure – quite the reverse. Their fear of war remained strong but diffuse.

In 1973, the United States did not see superpower war as a likely possibility, but Soviet leaders worried actively about war. They feared the consequences of a conventional Soviet–Israeli engagement somewhere between the Canal and Cairo, or an accidental encounter at sea. However, there is no evidence that Soviet speculation progressed to more detailed consideration of how either could escalate to nuclear war. Again, the fear of war was strong but diffuse. Soviet leaders did not fear only nuclear war, but any kind of Soviet–US war. Their fear translated into self-deterrence; Brezhnev ruled out the commitment of Soviet forces on Egypt's behalf before the United States practised immediate deterrence.

The absence of superpower war is puzzling only if at least one of the superpowers was expansionist and aggressive. On the basis of the evidence now available, the image that each superpower held of the other as opportunity-driven aggressors can be discredited as crude stereotypes. Khrushchev and Brezhnev felt threatened by what they considered the predatory policies of their adversary, as did US leaders by Soviet policies. For much of the Cold War, Soviet leaders were primarily concerned with preserving what they had, although, like their US counterparts, they were not averse to making gains that appeared to entail little risk or cost. Serious confrontations between the superpowers arose only when one of them believed that its vital interests were threatened by the other.

With the benefit of hindsight it is apparent that although both superpowers hoped to remake the world in their image, neither Moscow nor Washington was ever so dissatisfied with the status quo that it was tempted to go to war with the other, or even threaten war, to force a change. It was not only the absence of *opportunity* that kept the peace, but also the absence of a strong *motive* for war. Without a compelling motive, leaders were unwilling to assume the burden and responsibility for war, even if they thought its outcome would be favourable. In the late 1950s and early 1960s, when the United States might have destroyed the Soviet Union in a first strike with relatively little damage to itself, US leaders never considered a preventive war. The Soviet Union never possessed such a strategic advantage, but there is no reason to suspect that Khrushchev or Brezhnev had any greater interest than Eisenhower and Kennedy in going to war. The reality of deterrence helped to restrain leaders on both sides, but their relative satisfaction with the status quo was an important cause of the long peace.

Nuclear threats and nuclear weapons

The role of nuclear threats and nuclear weapons in Soviet–US relations during the Cold War runs counter to much of the conventional wisdom. Throughout the Cold War, superpower leaders expected their adversary to exploit any strategic advantage for political or military gain. Consequently, they devoted scarce resources to military spending to keep from being disadvantaged. For four decades Soviet and US leaders worried about the political and military consequences of strategic inferiority. These fears, coupled with the 'worst case' analysis each side used to estimate the other's strategic capabilities, fuelled an increasingly expensive arms race. In the late 1940s, the Soviet Union made an intensive effort to develop its own nuclear arsenal in the aftermath of Hiroshima and Nagasaki. In the early 1950s, both sides developed thermonuclear weapons. Following the success of *Sputnik* in 1957, the United States accelerated its commitment to develop and deploy ICBMs. President Kennedy's decision to expand the scope of the US strategic buildup in the spring of 1961 triggered a reciprocal Soviet decision. The Reagan buildup of the 1980s was a response to Brezhnev's intensive spending of the previous decade and a widespread if misplaced concern that it had bought the Soviet Union a strategic advantage.

This pervasive fear of strategic inferiority was greatly exaggerated. We offer a set of general observations about the impact of nuclear threats and nuclear weapons that summarise our arguments based on the new evidence. These observations must remain tentative until additional evidence becomes available about other critical confrontations during the Cold War and about the role of nuclear weapons in Sino-US and Sino-Soviet relations.

Leaders who try to exploit real or imagined nuclear advantages for political gain are not likely to succeed. Khrushchev and Kennedy tried and failed to intimidate one another with claims of strategic superiority in the late 1950s and early 1960s. Khrushchev's threats and boasts strengthened Western resolve not to yield in Berlin and provoked Kennedy to order a major strategic buildup. Kennedy's threats against Cuba, his administration's assertions of strategic superiority and the deployment of Jupiter missiles in Turkey – all intended to dissuade Khrushchev from challenging the West in Berlin – led directly to the Soviet decision to send missiles to Cuba. Both leaders were willing to assume the risks of a serious confrontation to avoid creating the impression of weakness or irresolution.

Credible nuclear threats are very difficult to make. The destructiveness of nuclear weapons makes nuclear threats more frightening but less credible. It is especially difficult to make nuclear threats credible when they are directed against nuclear adversaries who have the capability to retaliate in kind. Many Soviets worried about nuclear war during the missile crisis but Khrushchev judged correctly that Kennedy would not initiate a nuclear war in response to the deployment of Soviet missiles. Khrushchev's principal concern was that the president would be pushed into attacking Cuba, and that armed clashes between the invading US and the Soviet forces on the island committed to Cuba's defence would escalate into a wider and perhaps uncontrollable war.

In 1973, the US alert had even less influence on the Soviet leadership. It was inconceivable to Brezhnev and his colleagues that the United States would attack the Soviet Union with nuclear weapons. They did not believe that the interests at stake for either the United States or the Soviet Union justified war. The US nuclear threat was therefore incomprehensible and incredible.

Nuclear threats are fraught with risk. In both 1962 and 1973, US leaders were uninformed about the consequences and implications of strategic alerts. In 1973, they did not understand the technical meaning or the operational consequences of the DEFCON III alert and chose the alert in full confidence that it entailed no risks. During the missile crisis, when conventional and nuclear forces were moved to an even higher level of alert, it was very difficult to control alerted forces. Military routines and insubordination posed a serious threat to the resolution of the crisis.

Evidence from these two cases suggests that there are stark trade-offs between the political leverage that military preparations are expected to confer and the risks of inadvertent escalation they entail. US leaders had a poor understanding of these trade-offs: they significantly overvalued the political value of nuclear alerts and were relatively insensitive to their risks (Lebow, 1987).

Strategic buildups are more likely to provoke than to restrain adversaries because of their impact on the domestic balance of political power in the target state. Stalin, Khrushchev and Brezhnev all believed that strategic advantage would restrain adversaries. Khrushchev believed that the West behaved cautiously in the 1950s because of a growing respect for the economic as well as the military power of the socialist camp. He was convinced that the visible demonstration of Soviet power, through nuclear threats and the deployment of missiles in Cuba, would strengthen the hands of the 'sober realists' in Washington who favoured accommodation with the Soviet Union. Khrushchev's actions had the opposite impact: they strengthened anti-Soviet militants by intensifying American fears of Soviet intentions and capabilities. Kennedy's warnings to Khrushchev not to deploy missiles in Cuba and his subsequent blockade were in large part a response to the growing domestic political pressures to act decisively against the Soviet Union and its Cuban ally.

Brezhnev's strategic buildup was a continuation of Khrushchev's programme. US officials considered that the Soviet buildup continued after parity had been achieved. Soviet strategic spending appeared to confirm the predictions of militants in Washington that Moscow's goal was strategic superiority, even a first strike capability. Brezhnev, on the other hand, expected Soviet nuclear capabilities to prevent the United States from engaging in 'nuclear blackmail'. Instead, it gave Republicans the ammunition to defeat President Carter and the SALT II agreement. The Soviet arms buildup and invasion of Afghanistan contributed to Ronald Reagan's landslide victory in 1980 and provided the justification for his administration's massive arms spending. US attempts to put pressure on the Soviet Union through arms buildups were equally counter-productive.

Nuclear deterrence is robust when leaders on both sides fear war and are aware of each other's fears. War-fighting, MAD and finite deterrence all mistakenly equate stability with specific arms configurations. More important than the distribution of nuclear capabilities, or leaders' estimates of relative nuclear advantage, is their judgement of an adversary's intentions. The Cuban missile crisis was a critical turning point in Soviet–US relations because it convinced Kennedy and Khrushchev, and some of their most important advisors as well, that their adversary was as committed as they were to avoiding nuclear war. This mutually acknowledged fear of war made the other side's nuclear capabilities less threatening and paved the way for the first arms control agreements.

By no means did all US and Soviet leaders share this interpretation. Large segments of the national security elites of both superpowers continued to regard their adversary as implacably hostile and willing to use nuclear weapons. Even when Brezhnev and Nixon acknowledged the other's fear of war, they used the umbrella of nuclear deterrence to compete vigorously for unilateral gain. Western militants did not begin to change their estimate of Soviet intentions until Gorbachev made clear his commitment to ending the arms race and the Cold War.

Deterrence in hindsight

The Cold War began as a result of Soviet–US competition in Central Europe in the aftermath of Germany's defeat. Once recognised spheres of influence were established, confrontations between the superpowers in the heart of Europe diminished. Only Berlin continued to be a flashpoint until the superpowers reached a tacit understanding about the two Germanies in the mid-1960s.

The conventional and nuclear arms buildup that followed in the wake of the crises of the early Cold War was a reaction to the mutual insecurities they generated. By the 1970s, the growing arsenal and increasingly accurate weapons of mass destruction that each superpower aimed at the other had become the primary source of mutual insecurity and tension. Moscow and Washington no longer argued about the status quo in Europe but about the new weapons systems each deployed to threaten the other. Each thought that deterrence was far less robust than it was. Their search for deterrence reversed cause and effect and prolonged the Cold War.

The history of the Cold War provides compelling evidence of the pernicious effects of the open-ended quest for nuclear deterrence. Michael MccGwire captured the pernicious effects of deterrence dogma on Western attitudes, ethics and policies, which he summarised under seven major indictments; he argued consistently that the Western theory of nuclear deterrence had a particular dogmatic quality which was not shared by the more practical approach of the Soviets

(MccGwire, 1985/86). Be that as it may, nuclear weapons also moderated superpower behaviour, once leaders in Moscow and Washington recognised and acknowledged to the other that a nuclear war between them would almost certainly lead to their mutual destruction.

Since the late 1960s, when the Soviet Union developed an effective retaliatory capability, both superpowers had to live with nuclear vulnerability. There were always advocates of preemption, ballistic missile defence or other illusory visions of security in a nuclear world. But nuclear vulnerability could not be eliminated. Mutual Assured Destruction (MAD) was a reality from which there was no escape short of the most far-reaching arms control. Even after the dissolution of the Soviet Union and the proposed deep cuts in nuclear weapons, Russia and the United States will still possess enough nuclear weapons to destroy each other many times over.[5]

Nuclear vulnerability distinguished the Soviet–US conflict from conventional conflicts of the past or present. In conventional conflicts, leaders could believe that war might benefit their country. Leaders have often gone to war with this expectation although, more often than not, they have been proved wrong. The consequences of war turned out very differently than leaders in Iraq in 1980, Argentina in 1982 and Israel in 1982 expected.

Fear of the consequences of nuclear war not only made it exceedingly improbable that either superpower would deliberately seek a military confrontation with the other; it made their leaders extremely reluctant to take any action that they considered would seriously raise the risk of war. Over the years they developed a much better appreciation of each other's interests. In the last years of the Soviet–US conflict, leaders on both sides acknowledged and refrained from any challenge of the other's vital interests.

The ultimate irony of nuclear deterrence may be the way in which the strategy of deterrence undercut much of the political stability the reality of deterrence should have created. The arms build-ups, threatening military deployments, and the confrontational rhetoric that characterised the strategy of deterrence effectively obscured deep-seated, mutual fears of war. Fear of nuclear war made leaders inwardly cautious, but their public posturing convinced their adversaries that they were aggressive, risk-prone and even irrational.

This reckless kind of behaviour was consistent with the strategy of deterrence. Leaders on both sides recognised that only a madman would use nuclear weapons against a nuclear adversary. To reinforce deterrence, they therefore tried, and to a disturbing degree, succeeded in convincing the other that they might be irrational enough or sufficiently out of control to implement their threats. Each consequently became less secure, more threatened and less confident of the robust reality of deterrence. The strategy of deterrence was self-defeating; it provoked the kind of behaviour it was designed to prevent.

The history of the Cold War suggests that nuclear deterrence should be viewed as a very dangerous medicine. Arsenic, formerly used to treat syphilis and schistosomiasis, or chemotherapy, routinely used to treat cancer, can kill or cure a patient. The outcome depends on the virulence of the disease, how early the disease is detected, the amount of drugs administered, and the resistance of the patient to both the disease and the cure. So it is with nuclear deterrence. Mutual deterrence can prompt mutual caution. Too much deterrence, or deterrence applied inappropriately to a frightened and vulnerable adversary, can fuel an arms race that makes both sides less rather than more secure and provoke the aggression that it is designed to prevent.

The superpowers 'overdosed' on deterrence. It poisoned their relationship, but their leaders remained blind to its consequences. Instead, they interpreted the tension and crises that followed as evidence of the need for even more deterrence. In retrospect, both sides would probably have been more secure without any nuclear weapons. But once nuclear weapons were developed and used against Japan it became impossible to put the nuclear genie back in the bottle with a secure stopper at its mouth. Despite its rhetoric to the contrary, the United States was unprepared to give up its advantage, and the Soviet Union was committed to developing its own nuclear arsenal. Still, the superpowers would have been wise to have resisted the temptation to develop thermonuclear weapons, intercontinental ballistic missiles and multiple independently targeted re-entry vehicles (MIRVs). MIRVs were particularly destabilising because they conferred an advantage to offence, and made both sides feel more insecure and more committed to programmes that seemed to confirm the other's worst case assumptions about their motives.

The superpowers were unique in their resources, level of technical sophistication and numbers of nuclear weapons that they developed and deployed. We have to be careful in drawing wider lessons. Bearing this caveat in mind, there do seem to be some important political parallels. Nowhere do nuclear weapons appear to have conferred real security benefits. In the Middle East, the Indian subcontinent, and in Argentina and Brazil until changes of government in both those countries put an end to their nuclear weapons programme, the attempt or actual development of nuclear weapons was the catalyst for adversaries to develop their own weapons of mass destruction. As with the superpowers, this made both sides more insecure because it made them feel vulnerable and was taken as evidence of the other's hostile intentions. The superpower experience should serve as a cautionary tale for the leaders of these countries and of those countries contemplating the possible development of nuclear arsenals.

NOTES

1   Interview with Leonid Zamyatin, Moscow, 16 December 1991 (see also Khrushchev, 1990: 156–7; Troyanovsky, 1992).
2   See Lebow, 1981, pp. 82–97, for a discussion of the four traditional prerequisites of deterrence. For an alternative set of hypotheses about the conditions essential to deterrent success, see Lebow and Stein, 1990: 59–69.
3   There is also evidence that the fear of war influenced Soviet behaviour in Korea. Joseph Stalin had encouraged Kim Il Sung to attack South Korea in June 1950 in the expectation that the United States would not intervene. When Washington did intervene, Stalin, afraid that the North Korean attack would provoke a Soviet–US war, quickly signalled interest in a cease-fire (Schecter with Luchkov, 1990: 144–7).
4   Oleg Grinevsky contends that Stalin feared that even a few atomic bombs dropped on Moscow would have been enough to destroy the communist experiment (interview with Oleg Grinevsky, Stockholm, 24 Oct. 1992).
5   By 2003, if the cuts proposed in the START II treaty are implemented, Russia will cut its missiles to 504 and its warheads to 3,000 and the United States will reduce its missiles to 500 and its warheads to 3,500

REFERENCES

Aspaturian, Vernon (1980) 'Soviet Global Power and the Correlation of Forces', *Problems of Communism*, no. 20 (May–June).
Betts, Richard K. (1987). *Nuclear Blackmail and Nuclear Balance* (Washington, DC: Brookings Institution).
Bundy, McGeorge (1988) *Danger and Survival: Choices About The Bombs in the First Fifty Years* (New York: Random House).
Dziak, John J. (1981) *Soviet Perceptions of Military Power: The Interaction of Theory and Practice* (New York: Crane, Russak).
George, Alexander L. and Smoke, Richard (1974) *Deterrence in American Foreign Policy: Theory and Practice* (New York: Columbia University Press).
Holloway, David and Sharp, Jane M. O. (eds.) (1984) *The Warsaw Pact: Alliance in Transition?* (London: Macmillan).
Jones, Christopher D. (1981) *Soviet Influence in Eastern Europe: Political Autonomy and the Warsaw Pact* (New York: Praeger).
Khrushchev, Sergei (1990) *Khrushchev on Khrushchev: An Inside Account of the Man and His Era*, trans. William Taubman (Boston: Little, Brown)
Kissinger, Henry (1982) *Years of Upheaval* (Boston: Little, Brown).
Lebow, Richard Ned (1981) *Between Peace and War: The Nature of International Crisis* (Baltimore: Johns Hopkins University Press).

(1983) 'The Cuban Missile Crisis: Reading the Lessons Correctly', *Political Science Quarterly*, no. 98 (Fall).

(1987) *Nuclear Crisis Management: A Dangerous Illusion* (Ithaca: Cornell University Press).

Lebow, Richard Ned and Gross Stein, Janice (1990) *When Does Deterrence Succeed and How Do We Know?* (Ottawa: Canadian Institute for International Peace and Security).

(1994) *We All Lost The Cold War* (Princeton: Princeton University Press).

Luttwak, Edward N. (1980) 'After Afghanistan', *Commentary*, no. 69 (April).

MccGwire, Michael (1985/6) 'Deterrence: The Problem – Not The Solution', *International Affairs*, vol. 62 (1). Also in *SAIS Review*, no. 5, Summer–Fall 1985, pp. 105–24.

Morgan, Patrick M. (1977) *Deterrence: A Conceptual Analysis* (Beverley Hills: Sage Library of Social Science).

NSC 68 (1950) 'United States Objectives and Programs for National Security', *Foreign Relations of the United States, 1950*, vol. I (Washington, DC: Government Printing Office, 1977), 14 April.

Pipes, Richard (1977) 'Why the Soviet Union Thinks It Could Fight and Win a Nuclear War', *Commentary*, no. 64 (July).

Podhoretz, Norman (1980) 'The Present Danger', *Commentary*, no. 69 (April).

Remmington, Robin Allison (1967) *The Changing Soviet Perception of the Warsaw Pact* (Cambridge: MIT Center for International Studies).

Schecter, Jerrold L. with Luchkov, Vyacheslav L. (trans.) (1990) *Khrushchev Remembers: The Glasnost Tapes* (Boston: Little Brown).

Schlesinger, Arthur (1965) *A Thousand Days: John F. Kennedy in the White House* (London: Deutsch).

Sorenson, Theodore C. (1965) *Kennedy* (New York: Harper and Row).

Stein, Janice Gross (1985) 'Calculation, Miscalculation and Conventional Deterrence. I: The View from Cairo', in Robert Jervis, Richard Ned Lebow and Janice Gross Stein, *Psychology and Deterrence* (Baltimore, MD: Johns Hopkins University Press), pp. 34–59.

Troyanovsky, Oleg (1992) 'The Caribbean Crisis: A View from the Kremlin', *International Affairs* (Moscow), no. 4–5 (April/May).

Welch, David A. (ed.) (1989) *Proceedings of the Hawk's Cay Conference on the Cuban Missile Crisis. CSIA Working Papers, No. 89–1* (Cambridge, MA: Center for Sciences and International Affairs) mimeograph.

4   A Cold War life, and beyond

Ken Booth
with Michael Herman, Donald C. F. Daniel,
John McDonnell, Michael Clarke, Cori E. Dauber

This chapter is radically different but intimately related to the others. It explores some of the major themes of the book by focusing on one individual's work. There are six main justifications for this. (1) It was argued earlier that Cold War structures were created, sustained and dismantled by human agents. A fuller understanding of the period requires the examination of individual lives, and not simply the decisions of governments. (2) The chapter offers students of strategy/security studies some insights into the sociology of their subject. Some of the most interesting thinkers (and some of the most influential) are not necessarily the best known, and students of international security during the Cold War overwhelmingly mistook opinion (fashionable/ ethnocentric/self-interested) for objectivity. (3) The chapter hopes to empower students to think for themselves, rather than taking the easy option of thinking today what their elders and betters thought yesterday. There may not be much space for individuals to transcend their early conditioning and to exercise their ideas and imagination, but there is always some. The chapter shows that if an individual feels strongly about something, and has the knowledge and methodology to back it up, then he or she can make a difference. (4) The individual who is the subject of this chapter, Michael MccGwire, is one of the most interesting contributors to the debate about the Cold War and beyond. He was in the 1970s and 1980s an important figure in the US public policy debate about the Cold War, though not in his own country. Furthermore, as Russia again becomes a bogeyman in some Western eyes, his analyses of (Soviet) Russia as a world power with a particular geostrategic perspective, history, legitimate set of interests and unique politico-cultural tradition are of contemporary relevance – as is his contribution to the debate about the future of nuclear weapons. (5) There is a growing recognition of the interplay between theory and experience. The philosopher Mary Midgley has argued that it is 'quite extraordinary' how epistemology has neglected the very important aspect of knowledge offered by 'knowing people' (1994, pp. 63–5). There are different ways of seeing the world, and this can best be understood by looking at concrete cases. To reach this angle we need *know* the individual, in the ordinary but very significant personal sense, as well as the general facts. To understand the Cold War and beyond we therefore need to understand how the Cold War made subjects and how subjects made the Cold War. Finally (6) this book would not have been written without Michael MccGwire. He has enriched the lives of each of the contributors. We hope this book is not only a tribute to him but that this brief portrait says enough about him to encourage others to grit their teeth, work hard and believe in the importance of what they are doing. These qualities, allied to historical imagination and a sense of human solidarity are crucially important if the future of international security is to be better than its past.

The plan of this collaborative chapter is simple. Specific aspects of MccGwire's work will be analysed by five experts. I will provide context and continuity with a linking personal account.

[K.B.] Before his intensely Cold War life, as practitioner and theorist, Michael MccGwire lived an intensely varied life as a child of the British Raj and young naval officer. He was born in Madras in 1924, his maternal grandfather had been in the Indian Civil Service and his father worked in a merchant company. His mother was a daughter of empire. At the age of eight Michael was at school in Lausanne, Switzerland, learning French and the piano. Soon afterwards the great depression resulted in enforced early retirement for his father, and in 1935 this rather Victorian family – descended from the Chiefs of Fermanagh in Ireland – settled in Swanage, a cosy coastal town in Dorset, where they learned to live in genteel poverty. When the time came to decide what to do with Michael – a boy with an excess of energy and ideas, who made friends easily, had an impetuous streak, and was not scholarly – entry to the Royal Naval College at Dartmouth, at thirteen, was logical. It made economic sense in comparison with Britain's traditional fee-paying public schools and his father (convinced since 1933 of the dangers of Hitler and German rearmament) may have thought that if his son had to fight for his country, it be better done at sea than in the trenches.

At Dartmouth, MccGwire proved to be a 'natural' leader. He was good at games, energetic, full of initiative, a respecter of tradition and sensible rules, and prone to bouts of original thought and hooliganism. He won school prizes, typically the works of Kipling and Corbett's naval history (the latter sold unread twenty-five years later); and he ended up as a chief cadet captain (equivalent to Head Boy) which brought with it the coveted King's Dirk (equivalent to the Sandhurst Sword of Honour). But for him, like other young men in Europe at the time, life's choices were narrowing dramatically. He had already decided that the navy would not satisfy his (still unformulated) aspirations, and that he would leave once the war was over. But first there was duty. In May 1942, when they had all turned 17, MccGwire's Dartmouth term went to war, as midshipmen on battleships and cruisers. Already one half of the previous May's intake that had gone to sea were dead. In the next three years, though the tide of war had turned, 12 per cent of those who began with him were lost.

For young naval officers these were years of involvement in great events, danger, fear, activity and boredom, and acute lack of sleep. MccGwire's ships participated in a Malta Convoy, the North African and Sicilian landings, Anzio, Salerno and operations in the Adriatic, the invasion of Normandy and motor torpedo operations against coastal convoys on the French, Belgian and Dutch coasts. When victory came in Europe, MccGwire was in a destroyer on its way to the Pacific, where the navy's task – once victory had been secured there – was to try to tidy up a volatile region. This involved a range of jobs, including defending a grounded coaster against pirates, driving a Hong Kong ferry during a strike, spraying Foochow with DDT, handing Sumatra back to the Dutch, being the advance man for his admiral's official visit to the French in Saigon, showing the flag in Borneo and rescuing landing craft caught by a typhoon. The responsibilities of these tumultuous years – created by the clear-cut issues of fighting a world war and tidying up the remains of empire – had seemed quite natural to a young British naval officer born in India. What proved a radical shock came with his ship's re-deployment to the Mediterranean in 1947 for the Palestine Patrol, whose task was to block Jewish immigration into Palestine, where the British, faced by pressures on all sides, were trying to hold the ring as the Mandatory Power. The Palestine Patrol was a brutal experience for everybody involved. What was particularly shocking to some of the naval officers carrying it out was what they saw as the betrayal of Britain by the United States, ostensibly its closest ally, and especially Washington's overt and covert support for illegal Jewish immigration, including the exploitation for political ends of vulnerable and desperate refugees crammed into dangerously overcrowded ships. This was MccGwire's first education in some of the nastier complexities of international politics, as opposed to its brutal simplicities in war.

At the end of 1947 a more pleasant education beckoned, when he went to Cambridge to learn Russian. He was a volunteer, but the attraction was the prospect of university life, not the subject. His appetite had been whetted by contact with RNVR graduates in the wartime navy, and then seeing demobilised officers going home to take degrees. At Cambridge his fellow officers on the Russian course were split between lovers of the language and literature, and fierce anti-communists (the later defector, George Blake, was one such). MccGwire scraped through the course, mostly learning his Russian living with an émigré family in Paris, where he discovered how British politics looked to the French. At Cambridge he also discovered European federalism from those ex-servicemen who had pledged 'never again' as they had fought their way across Europe a few years earlier. These experiences led him to become a strong supporter of European integration, and a critic of the regressive policies of successive British governments and of the patronising attitudes of many British people towards continental Europe.

On his return to the navy, now with a Russian qualification, MccGwire spent a year as navigator of a ship in the Fishery Protection Squadron. For much of 1949 he worked around arctic Norway and the Murman coast. He developed a deep respect for the people of this barren region, and was also fascinated by its landscape and strategic location. He proposed to the Admiralty that he be seconded to learn Norwegian, but the idea was rejected. Instead of returning to a mainstream job, he volunteered for loan service with the Australian Navy, then short of experienced officers. While running ships and training new entrants, he discovered in Australia another perspective on the world, and also met Helen, whose own contribution to this story – here unspoken because of space – perfectly exemplifies Cynthia Enloe's thesis about the role of women in the running of the international political system (1989, esp. ch. 5).

When MccGwire returned to England in 1952, a chance encounter with a naval friend from the Cambridge course led him to turn down a fast-track opportunity in the Training Squadron at Rosyth, and instead decide to work at GCHQ, the government's signal intelligence organisation at Cheltenham (that had taken over from the famous wartime operation at Bletchley Park). This was MccGwire's first real encounter with 'the Soviet threat'. At the time he shared the general view that international communism, manipulated from Moscow and backed by the might of the Red Army in Europe, represented a world-wide threat to British interests and the future of the United Nations. The common-sense opinion, which he shared, was that the 'next war' would be against the Soviet Union. Part of MccGwire's time at GCHQ was spent on the submarine construction desk where he deduced (correctly) that the Soviets had embarked on a programme to build 72 medium-type submarines a year; this was assumed (incorrectly) to imply they were planning a future battle of the Atlantic. In this desk job he learned the importance of verbal precision and analytical integrity. Before leaving it, he organised the production of the navy's first Russian naval dictionary.

Following GCHQ MccGwire returned to sea, as first lieutenant of a fleet destroyer. The latter's task involved showing the flag and training for war in home waters and the Mediterranean. During this period MccGwire himself spent a week in 1956 as liaison officer aboard a Soviet destroyer accompanying the Soviet leader Nikita Khrushchev on his much-publicised visit to Britain. After this, rather than step up the established promotional ladder with another operational job, MccGwire took his last opportunity to be assistant naval attaché in Moscow. He arrived there with his growing family in mid-1956, and for the next two years participated in the Cold War equivalent of the front line – providing intelligence from within the Soviet Union under continuous close surveillance. With other Western attachés, his visits ranged from Murmansk in the north of the Soviet Union to Odessa, Tbilisi and Baku in the south, and from Astrakhan down the Volga to numerous visits to Leningrad on the Baltic. From these experiences, and close proximity with Foreign Office colleagues and the wider diplomatic community, there grew in his mind an ever more complex picture of both the Soviet Union and international politics in general. One dimension of this was his growing dissatisfaction with the negative character of the Western posture of containment. This was evident, for example, in what he saw as the moralistic anti-Soviet attitude of US society. There were two other alienating experiences, this time specifically in relation to British policy. The first was the Suez operation in November 1956, which he saw from Moscow as a humiliating display of Britain's political and military ineptitude, and which also diverted attention from the Soviet invasion of Hungary. This damage to British interests was then compounded by the defence review which shifted resources from conventional forces to the so-called independent nuclear deterrent – of which MccGwire was an early critic. When he left Moscow in August 1958, MccGwire still believed that the Soviet Union represented the kind of threat posed by Germany in the 1930s, but he had acquired a new 'feel' for Russia and East–West relations. He now believed that containment as practised was a deeply flawed and over-militarised posture, and he was convinced that British policy was backward-looking and insular. The next four years helped the doubts crystallise.

Now a commander, MccGwire went to the staff course at the Royal Naval College Greenwich, where one of his exercises involved simulating the role of a 'Kremlin Planner'. This helped him conclude that in no circumstances would it be in Soviet interests to initiate premeditated war. The corollary, that Soviet military doctrine was basically reactive, was corroborated by information from a fellow student, a former Soviet bloc naval officer, who provided evidence that the Soviet Navy's primary concern in 1945–7 had been to defend its fleet areas against the threat of Western seaborne invasion. This reactive character on the Soviet Navy's part then explained that the reason behind the annual buildup of 72 medium-type submarines identified at GCHQ had not been to fight another battle of the Atlantic, but to defend Soviet shores. After Greenwich, MccGwire spent six months at the US joint services staff college in Norfolk, Virginia, where the need to write a thesis provided him with the opportunity to sort out his ideas on how the West should approach the 'problem' of the Soviet Union. He was then appointed as a war planner on the staff of the Supreme Allied Commander, Atlantic. He played the 'Red' side in a NATO-wide exercise, learning how worst-case assumptions lead to grossly inflated threat assessments. During his two years in the Plans and Operations Division at SACLANT, he worked on the problem of how to start resupplying Europe 180 days after a nuclear 'exchange', an experience which made him acutely conscious of the surreal nature of such activities, and also of the problematic nature of what was taken to be hard evidence about Soviet war planning. He was now convinced that the latter did not reflect an urge to aggression but rather represented prudent planning for a contingency the Soviets wanted absolutely to avoid, but could not afford to lose if it happened. It was during this period, as he began reassessing the strategic environment, his work and his life, that MccGwire started writing. The first outlet was the *Naval Review,* an inspired Royal Navy institution dating from 1911. Its articles are in-house and unclassified, but in the spirit of encouraging professional debate in a hierarchical institution, are encouraged to be anonymous. MccGwire's first article opposed the British nuclear deterrent.

It was during his time at SACLANT that MccGwire finally decided what he wanted to do with his life. He had enjoyed working on an international staff, and had found that he could make things happen in an international context that were not possible in a national one. He had also become increasingly convinced, in many areas of international politics, that British policy was part of the problem and not the solution. He concluded that it was necessary to move from national service to international service. Twenty years of world war and Cold War since going to sea in 1942 had convinced him of the need to change the world, and if he did not yet know exactly how, working in the United Nations seemed the logical place to start. Consequently, he planned to leave the Navy after his next appointment, which was as head of the Soviet section of naval intelligence. Before he took this up, however, the opportunity arose to be the executive officer (commander) of the tender (depot ship) of the Second Submarine Squadron. This proved an especially positive experience, enabling him to get to know the sub-marine community at first hand, enjoy dealing once more with the nuts and bolts of naval life, and at the same time continue writing. He published articles on the problems caused to the British Navy by having primary responsibility for the nuclear deterrent (Polaris), his disappoint-ment at the navy's failure to stand up fully to civil servants, his objections to nuclear weapons, his proposals to change the structure of the navy and his views about operational issues. Such opinions must have been an irritation to senior officers, but this had been one of the reasons why the pressure valve of the *Naval Review* had been created a half-century earlier.

MccGwire's period as head of Soviet naval intelligence – which he had become convinced needed major restructuring – coincided with the growth of the Soviet Navy in the mid-1960s. This growth was manifest in more sophisticated technology and in semi-permanent and then permanent operations outside their traditional fleet areas. In particular, Soviet warships began to tail the ships of the US Sixth Fleet in the Mediterranean on a continuous basis. An assessment of MccGwire's contribution to British naval intelligence at this period, and the role of intelligence in general during the Cold War is the subject of the next essay by a former colleague.

NAVAL INTELLIGENCE

Michael Herman

Michael MccGwire made his first identifiable contribution to inter-national security as a commander in the Royal Navy, when he ran the Soviet naval section of the British Defence Intelligence Staff (DIS) between 1965 and 1967. Intelligence was the lens through which Western governments saw the Soviet Union. MccGwire in these two years had a personal impact on the way the lens was focused and the picture of the Soviet Navy presented to the Western policymaking brain. The effect is part of Cold War history, but it also suggests general lessons about intelligence and policy.

In taking over the DIS job MccGwire was unusual in coming to Whitehall with previous intelligence experience. As a regular naval officer he had had a fighting war at sea in the Second World War, but in the post-war period had volunteered to learn Russian and in the early 1950s worked at the British Signal Intelligence organisation (GCHQ) at Cheltenham, which was where I first met him. Along with some standard naval postings he subsequently did a two-year tour as assistant naval attaché in Moscow in the pre-satellite era, when defence attachés provided almost the only Western eyes on new Soviet weaponry. Few naval officers then sought intelligence jobs of these kinds since they did nothing for promotion prospects, so there was a regular pattern of senior naval officers in the DIS learning their jobs as they went along with no previous experience to guide them. MccGwire, on the other hand, joined the organisation knowing the subject and what needed to be done in it.

His section was the authority for information and operational assessment about the Soviet Navy. Feeding in to it were the massive data flows available from the various kinds of covert collection, but the section was the thinking body which transmuted this information into usable intelligence for the various levels of government's decision-making machinery and the navy's own command system. Before MccGwire's arrival the work had been carried out as a fairly routine operation, and those who worked there still remember the way he transformed the atmosphere. Partly this was through personal leadership. He brought an inspirational style of management – of which we had had a foretaste in Cheltenham, where he transformed GCHQ's Rugby Football Club from the weakest team in the district to a competent body of enthusiasts – to his mixed service-civilian Whitehall staff. His personal qualities also gave him a wide range of NATO intelligence contacts, particularly in North America; his impact on the international conference machinery for appraising Soviet naval power was a foretaste of the charisma which was a feature of his later academic life.

But the style served a method and a cause. For some years naval intelligence had coasted along on settled assumptions. The nature of the Soviet threat was felt to be well established, and intelligence's functions were seen mainly as keeping track of Soviet numbers, equipment and tactics and supplying the navy with the other information it would need for fighting a war. MccGwire approached the job with a different conviction, that the available data properly handled could answer more searching questions on what the Soviet Navy was actually *for*. The result was a two-year crusade of which one of his staff wrote at its conclusion that, 'It is my sincere belief that he has succeeded in contributing something tangible to the security of the country and to the stability of the world in a way that is not given to many of us to do' (private communication, July 1967). At the end of it, despite the award of an OBE and the prospect of promotion, he stuck to his intention of retiring to take a degree and pursue a different career.

MccGwire's method, attempting to get behind numbers to intentions, depended on a sensitivity to evidence and the kinds of inference that could be drawn from it; he recalls that it was working earlier at GCHQ that he had learned this professional rigour. A prerequisite was a widespread reorganisation of the section's data-handling and retrieval system; as a result it struck me nearly twenty years later that the naval data base in the DIS was still better than those on the other Soviet services. But this was just the infrastructure. The essence of the new approach was seeing new questions that needed answering, and finding new ways of testing hypotheses against evidence. By the mid-1960s US satellites were providing detailed photographs of Soviet naval vessels and equipment, and NATO-wide tracking systems gave a reasonably good account of their movements. Intelligence had become quite good at answering 'what? where? when?' questions, but assumed the answers to 'why?' questions to be self-evident. Threats to Atlantic communications and aims of politico-military 'power projection' were assumed to be the self-evident objectives of Soviet naval power. To draw on an old debate about historical writing, naval intelligence (like much other Western military assessment) was like old-fashioned 'scissors-and-paste' history, fitting incoming evidence uncritically into an established conceptual framework (Collingwood, 1939: 77–8).

MccGwire's contribution was to formulate 'why?' questions to detailed evidence and use the answers to rebuild the conceptual framework. A key element in his own thinking had been Yugoslav information at the British Naval Staff College in 1959 that Soviet staff exercises at the Frunze academy in 1945–8 had focused on defending the homeland against Western Normandy-type invasion. Intelligence analysts had always pursued the details of Soviet naval hardware and construction programmes, but without much curiosity about the reasons for the differences from the Western equivalents; it was enough that 'the Russians do things differently'. The MccGwire approach worked from the details to the underlying Soviet naval requirements and thence to Soviet assumptions, interests and intentions; and in this way sought evidence of policy and doctrinal changes over the course of time.

A small example can be given from his later book, in which the armament of Soviet vessels built in the 1950s was cited as evidence that they were designed to defend the four Soviet fleet areas against Western maritime assault, not to attack Western trade routes. Thus:

The large-type Zulu class [submarine] carried air defense weapons that would have been needed if the submarine had had to surface in the mid-Atlantic. The mass-produced medium-type Whiskey class carried no air defense weapons but mounted a 100-millimeter gun. This combination would have been useless against ocean commerce but would be very effective when operating within range of shore-based support against amphibious assault forces, particularly at night. Similarly the cruiser/destroyer surface action groups that were then building had a role to play in the fleet areas, but the cruisers had little chance of surviving as ocean raiders, the role ascribed to them by the West. (MccGwire, 1987: 361n)

Of course gun armament was only a small part of the evidence for naval objectives in the 1950s; conclusions depended on taking all the evidence in context and studying the overall naval programmes. But the Whiskey example illustrates the links that could be traced between detailed hardware and underlying concepts.

Working in this way, MccGwire in 1965–7 succeeded in getting the official British intelligence estimates rewritten, with a new picture of Soviet maritime objectives. This was that Soviet naval expansion was a move forward in strategic defence, supporting the traditional mission of defending the homeland against attacks from the sea. The presence of their ships in the Eastern Mediterranean and South Norwegian Sea reflected the requirement to pose a peacetime counter to the capability of US carriers and Polaris submarines for launching nuclear strikes against the Soviet industrial heartland.

This had some permanent effects on naval intelligence; it seemed to me twenty years later that the naval part of the DIS was still the best of the services at getting inside Soviet thinking. But the British naval policymakers concerned with the size of their navies never accepted MccGwire's conclusions completely, and by 1970 it also sat uncomfortably with a US Navy that faced cuts in the wake of Vietnam. Both the British and US naval lobbies had strong interests in fostering the image of a Soviet fleet bent on world-wide power projection and challenging Western naval supremacy. Three years after he left the DIS the British naval hierarchy issued what amounted to an anathema against the 'MccGwire thesis'.

Nevertheless, his reappraisal had at least opened up threat interpretations for some permanent debate. During the Middle East wars of 1967 and 1973 there was probably less Anglo-American anxiety about the Soviet naval presence in the Mediterranean – 'marking' the US Sixth Fleet – than if it had been accepted without question as evidence of a Soviet attempt to take over Egypt. And his work in the 1960s was the foundation for his own contribution in the 1970s – as an academic, not a naval officer – in understanding the subsequent Soviet naval role of defending the SLBM 'bastions' in northern waters. This in turn led to his later work on Soviet military power as a whole. On this I remember that his early drafts in the 1980s hit me with the clarity of revelation; the data on the USSR that we in British intelligence were producing seemed for the first time to fit into a credible doctrinal framework, instead of showing just an 'inexorable' Soviet pursuit of military superiority. For all this, MccGwire's work in 1965–7 was seminal.

Of course it is still too early to know how far the Soviet archives will confirm MccGwire's interpretations in detail. But their value did not depend on being uniformly right. British intelligence on the USSR was not on the whole staffed by ideologues; nevertheless it was wedded to a 'set', two-dimensional view of the target that subconsciously underwrote the Cold War and bipolar world. MccGwire set a precedent for digging deeper.

This has some implications for Western intelligence even in the late 1990s. Britain has never invested enough brain-power in the DIS's 'all-source' analysis, as compared with the covert collection agencies. The mystique of collection derived from the breaking of Enigma in the Second World War has encouraged the services to assume that the work of the DIS can be done effectively by any competent staff-trained officer, without previous intelligence experience. Civilian specialists have been employed mainly as supporting analysts, without pay and status comparable with those offered to the intelligence collectors elsewhere. There is a general failure to recognise the crucial role of detailed analysis and assessment in the final intelligence product.

This state of affairs is compounded by the inherent problem of intelligence's relationship with its customers. It has to be on their wavelength if it is to have credibility with them. But the military customers have a characteristic mindset and are a natural interest group with good reasons to press for 'worst case' estimates. Armed forces' peacetime prospects and equipment are proportionate to the size of the perceived threats; and if war happens the servicemen bear the direct consequences of previous underestimations. Service officers on short tours in intelligence have little incentive to challenge assessments that benefit their parent services, and are vulnerable to pressures for conformity.

There is no simple answer to what is a US as much as a British problem, but the MccGwire example suggests the case for intelligence quality and independence. The British DIS and its US opposite numbers need national attention; they are major elements in national perception and are not just integral parts of the armed forces. Intelligence should be closer to the fast track of appointments for promising service officers, but the key is developing defence intelligence's own institutional professionalism.

MccGwire showed what can be achieved if the organisation manages to put itself in the enemy's place. Writing of the British wartime Joint Intelligence Staff (JIS), Donald McLachlan recorded that it

set out consistently and stubbornly to see the various problems put before it exclusively from the enemy's point of view . . . The value of this way of looking at the facts and prospects of war was considerable; not so much for its positive grasp of the enemy point of view – though this was the main business of intelligence – as for its critical influence on the concourse of facts, ideas, political and personal influences pressing on the conduct of the war in London and Washington. 'But this is how the enemy may, or must, see it; these are his resources, his positions, the distances he has to cover, the principles of strategy he has so far followed. He *is* probably capable of this but he is certainly not capable of that'; this kind of staunch reminder, from a small body of men who gradually achieved a collective intellectual integrity which no amount of ministerial cajolery could shake, was salutary. (McLachlan, 1968)

The MccGwire impetus was to bring these principles to military matters in peacetime.

This is history. But 'threat assessments' are still the military's weapon in its fights with Treasuries; and the dangers of stereotyping will still apply even with new threats like Russian irredentism or Muslim fundamentalism. Intelligence's professionalism is based on empathy with its targets. Those in charge of defence intelligence should be selected to encourage it to do more than just provide information.

Intelligence may not be able to find the truth; even less may it be able to persuade others that it has found it. But keeping the players honest, not permitting disreputable arguments to thrive, pointing out where positions are internally contradictory or rest on tortured readings of the evidence would not be a minor feat. While it would not save the country from all folly, it would provide more assistance than we get from most instruments of policy. (Jervis, 1991: 179–80)

MccGwire demonstrated that intelligence in this mode can contribute to a safer world – but it is very dependent for this on individuals of vision and stature.

[K.B.] By the second half of the 1960s Michael MccGwire had an almost unrivalled knowledge of the Soviet Navy. Nevertheless, he applied to retire in July 1967, at the end of his appointment heading Soviet naval intelligence. Not surprisingly, he was asked to withdraw the application – there were hints of further promotion – but he stuck to his aim, and wrote an inspiring letter to his staff explaining why. In the previous year a series of fortunate introductions had led to the director of the United Nations Development Plan (UNDP) offering him the prospect of serving as a resident representative responsible for UNDP activities in some part of the developing world. Although national quotas prevented him from being hired in the short term, he was led to believe that there would be further openings in the next few years. While marking time, he decided to indulge his hankering for formal education. It proved decisive. A series of accidents and incremental decisions condemned him to become an academic.

On retirement at 42, and with five young children, MccGwire cashed his very limited naval pension to become a student. He secured a place at the University of Wales, Aberystwyth (UWA) to study International Politics (which he thought he knew about) and Economics (which he thought he needed to know about) as the bases for a career in international service. UWA had a tradition of being sympathetic to mature students with irregular academic qualifications – or in this case none at all – while rural depopulation in mid-Wales meant plenty of empty farm-houses with low rents and lots of space for large families.

Present at my first seminar as a university teacher – an introductory course in International Politics – was a man who was well over twice the age of the majority of the other students. They were mostly straight from school and mid-sixties cool. Michael MccGwire was better dressed than the rest, and looked uneasy, two qualities I never glimpsed again. Almost at once he began criticising the dominant theory of the subject, the political realism identified with theorists such as Hans J. Morgenthau. MccGwire had no illusions about how little he knew, but he believed he could recognise a bad argument when he saw one, in any field, and thought academic International Relations full of them. He began to revel in the discovery of new fields of knowledge and theories that he had not known existed. Inevitably, though, and reluctantly, he became drawn into what was now becoming a public debate about the intentions and capabilities of Soviet naval expansion.

During his first year as a student, MccGwire was asked by one of his professors to comment on a book on the Soviet Navy. He agreed, and quickly concluded that it was an attempt by the US naval lobby to inflate the Soviet threat – for obvious purposes. He also realised for the first time how much serious information there actually was available in the open literature, and this led him to agree to a commission from the then Institute for Strategic Studies (ISS) in London to write a book of his own on the Soviet Navy. A 120,000 word manuscript was produced over the next two years, a feat which naturally interfered with his activities as a student. For its own reasons the ISS decided not to proceed to publication. Even so, it proved a decisive piece of writing, for it resulted in the development of the original methodology that underlay his later work, and it enabled him to provide – based entirely on open source material – all the detailed analyses of Soviet ship-building programmes, deployment patterns and naval characteristics that quickly led him to become such a controversial and important figure. Some of the manuscript was subsequently published in article form from 1968 onwards, some got picked up in Washington and was read into the US *Congressional Record*, and some appeared in chapters in books in the burgeoning field of Soviet naval studies. The 'MccGwire thesis', that Soviet naval development was best understood as a counter to the weapons and doctrines of superior Western naval power, began to reach the interested public.

The promised opening in UNDP had not materialised by the time MccGwire graduated in 1970. Fortunately, a lecturing position came up at UWA. He was asked to teach British defence policy, a concept which his practical experience had suggested was an oxymoron, but whose study led him to appreciate how little he had actually known about the period through which he had lived. Soon after beginning this job, he was approached by Dalhousie University in Canada to become the first Professor of Maritime and Strategic Studies in its Centre for Foreign Policy Studies. He accepted this interesting challenge, but on the under-standing that it was still his intention to join UNDP. In the event he stayed at Dalhousie for eight busy and enjoyable years, because national quotas meant that openings into international service did not materialise for a UK citizen, now in his fifties. At Dalhousie, not for the first time in his career, MccGwire rewrote his job description. He moved away from teaching strategic studies (for which he had been hired) to running innovative courses on the United Nations and the Law of the Sea, extending their scope to encompass the environmental, social and economic aspects, as well as the political and military. He was also involved in the plans for an Institute for Marine Policy Studies, aimed at the needs of Third World coastal states. As he became an increasingly prominent writer and speaker, especially in North America, the aca-demic grip tightened, though he protested about some of its ways, from the individualistic posturing of many academics to the practical irrele-vance of much theorising. The grip tightened in part because of his increasing involvement – despite himself – in the great Soviet naval debate which by the early 1970s had become a major issue in strategic studies.

Visiting Washington in 1972, MccGwire realised that the opposing sides in the Soviet naval debate there never talked to each other. He therefore offered Dalhousie as the venue for a workshop, to which he would bring relevant specialists together from all sides. On neutral territory and under his chairmanship, he hoped that something interesting would emerge; it did. His workshop on Soviet naval developments proved a great success, and stimulated further meetings, in which his collaboration with the US Center for Naval Analyses played a significant role. The workshops – conceived, organised and orchestrated by MccGwire – led to the growth of an 'epistemic community' that remained important in Soviet studies for the next two decades. They also led to the publication of three edited books, the size of doorsteps, which remain the key works on the Soviet Navy during the Cold War. In these ways MccGwire made a decisive contribution to Western thinking about the Soviet Navy, as is evident from the section below, written by a naval specialist at the US Naval War College.

SOVIET NAVAL STUDIES

Donald C. F. Daniel

One of the ultimate accomplishments for an academic is to be recognised by his peers as a seminal thinker in his field, furthering its substantive content and identifying fruitful approaches, sources of data or methodologies. That Michael MccGwire achieved such recognition is well evidenced in the extent to which he is cited in books and journals and has been featured in conferences. An academic of practical bent, his ultimate aim was to affect Western defence policymakers, especially those of the United States, by describing the content of and, more importantly, explaining the objectives underlying Soviet military declarations and behaviour. He feared that ill-conceived Western decisions, based on erroneous assumptions about Soviet actions and motives, could exacerbate East–West tensions and possibly even precipitate nuclear conflict if unchecked.

MccGwire's academic career did not begin by focusing on Soviet military policy in the main. Rather, his initial concentration, which provided the foundation for his reputation, was on the Soviet Navy. This section concerns itself with that part of his career in order to account for the recognition he received and the influence he exercised.

One factor is that MccGwire arrived on the academic scene at a fortuitous moment, a period of upsurge in Western interest in the navy of the USSR. In the late 1960s and early 1970s the Soviet Navy was building an ocean-going fleet and making its presence felt through forward deployments (to the Mediterranean beginning in the early

1960s and the Indian Ocean and the Caribbean in the late 1960s and early 1970s), large exercises (such as *Sever '68* and *Okean '70*), and crisis response (such as in the 1970 Jordanian crisis, the 1971 Indo-Pakistani War, and the 1967 and 1973 Arab–Israeli conflicts). In 1971–2 the Soviet Navy's commander-in-chief, Admiral Sergei Gorshkov, personally fuelled concern about Moscow's intentions for its navy by his unprecedented publication of a series of eleven articles entitled 'Navies in War and Peace'. All of these developments were given considerable publicity by Western naval leaders and observers who genuinely feared an increased naval threat to Western maritime superiority. Even *Time* magazine devoted one of its 1968 covers to a drawing of Admiral Gorshkov superimposed over the scene of a partially-submerged submarine and the caption, 'Russia's Navy: A New Challenge at Sea'.[1]

This upsurge in Western interest provided fertile ground for MccGwire to make an impact, and five reasons explain why he in particular became so prominent. One was his background, which went far to establishing his credibility on Soviet naval issues when he began his academic career in the late 1960s. MccGwire had been an officer in the Royal Navy, from which he retired as a commander in 1967, and it is particularly significant that he served as assistant naval attaché in Moscow from 1956 to 1958 and as the head of the Soviet naval section of British defence intelligence between 1965 and 1967. In the latter capacity he became well known to his counterparts in the United States and Canada when he headed the UK team in the yearly 'CANUKUS' (Canada, United Kingdom, United States) meetings which focused on naval intelligence matters.

A second reason is that, from the onset of his speaking out publicly, his arguments provoked interest by virtue of their relative novelty and, to many, their logic and explanatory value. While his fundamental argument about how to approach Soviet affairs may seem self-evident today, this was not the case twenty-five years ago when Cold War perspectives caused many to regard MccGwire as iconoclastic. One needed, MccGwire stressed, to focus on more than *what* the Soviet Navy was doing; one also needed to ask *why*: what motives or objectives impelled the Soviet Union to develop and deploy its navy as it did? Both the question and MccGwire's answer called on people to put aside ethnocentric lenses and to recognise that much of what Moscow did militarily was not so much part of a well-laid-out programme to achieve global hegemony as it was a reaction to what the West was doing.

Many observers in the United States and Western Europe accepted as axiomatic that, as a superpower in nuclear and land warfare, the USSR was slowly and surely moving towards the Western great power model of a blue-water navy intended to be strategically offensive in nature and charged with acquiring influence in peacetime and commanding distant seas in wartime. MccGwire challenged this view; he stressed that one must not, in the Colomb and Mahan tradition, view command of the sea as an end in itself, but rather as a means to a larger end. Maritime strategy, he argued, is not about control of the sea but 'about the *use* of the sea' (using it for one's own purposes and preventing its use to one's disadvantage) and within that context, he went on, Moscow's fundamental purpose was defence of the homeland against the maritime axes of attack (MccGwire, 1976: 15, 19–24, emphasis in original). He saw Soviet naval construction and deployments as responses to the threat posed by the US Navy – specifically its ability to operate at great distances and launch airplanes or missiles with nuclear charges to strike the Soviet homeland.

MccGwire credits a Yugoslav naval officer with sensitising him on the need to view Soviet military developments from the perspective of Soviet objectives, of what Moscow believed it needed to do and not what ethnocentric Western observers concluded it should do. The officer had been at the Frunze Academy in the first years after the Great Patriotic War and had learned there that the Soviet Navy was being designed to counter seaborne invasion. This surprised MccGwire because he knew that the NATO navies had no intention of conducting such an invasion, but he found that hypothesis did indeed explain much of what Stalin's fleet had done in the first decade or so after the war.

This experience was instrumental in shaping MccGwire's objectives-oriented approach to Soviet naval affairs. He refined the approach over time and gave considerable thought to the variables which should be attended to and how information should be combined. As he came to apply it, the approach entailed bringing together what the Soviet Navy built, how it operated, and what its spokesmen said, and placing these variables in the larger context of Soviet planning and doctrine about war and the possibility of war. In particular, when sifting through information – such as changes in construction patterns, for example – he sought to establish turning points in Soviet policymaking, and their rationales. The end result was a comprehensive and richly textured analysis.

A third reason is that MccGwire did more than arrive on a changing scene with differing viewpoints about how to think about the Soviet Navy both methodologically and substantively. Ultimately more significant was the central role he played in shaping Soviet naval analysis as a distinctive subfield of military or strategic studies in general and Soviet security studies in particular. The precedent had been set earlier by the publication of Robert Herrick's ground-breaking *Soviet Naval Strategy* (1968), but it was MccGwire who really followed through. Working as he did for organisations which did classified analyses for the US government, Herrick was constrained in ways MccGwire was not. The latter had considerably more freedom as a professor at Dalhousie University in Halifax, Nova Scotia, and later as a senior fellow in the Foreign Policy Studies Program of the Brookings Institution in Washington.

Convinced of the need 'to raise the level of informed analysis and debate' about the Soviet Navy, MccGwire initiated and chaired while at Halifax in 1972, 1973 and 1974 three workshops on Soviet naval developments (MccGwire, 1973: vii). These were milestones in Soviet naval studies and had lasting impact in two ways. One is that the participants, who numbered about eighty overall, came to see themselves as part of a larger intellectual entity, as members of what was in effect a cohesive field of study. As MccGwire wrote after the first conference, held in October 1972, 'At the closing session it was decided that the seminar had served a useful purpose and should reconvene in October 1973. Meanwhile, to provide some continuity . . . the participants constituted themselves into an informal Soviet naval studies group. It was felt such a group could serve as a focus for studies . . .' (1973: ix). The second way the workshops had lasting impact is that each resulted in a substantial volume of papers which uniquely and comprehensively brought together the major authors (including MccGwire himself) and issues in the field (MccGwire, 1973; MccGwire, Booth, and McDonnell, 1975; MccGwire and McDonnell, 1977). Policymakers or scholars interested in the Soviet Navy could not avoid reference to these volumes. They were crucial for helping shape the terms of the debate for several years.

The Dalhousie workshops were exemplars of another reason accounting for MccGwire's influence. He actively associated himself with colleagues who themselves had some influence on other academics as well as on decision-makers. Instrumental in helping him establish such contacts in the United States in the early 1970s was his association with the Center for Naval Analyses (CNA), a think-tank which supports the US Navy, and particularly with analysts there such as Robert Weinland, James McConnell, Robert Herrick, Bradford Dismukes and Barry Blechman. In addition, he forged links with the National War College (where he was asked in 1977 to chair a large conference bringing together Washington officials and policy analysts concerned with Soviet naval affairs), the Naval War College (where he played central roles in highly important war games and lectured regularly to the chief of Naval Operations Strategic Studies Group), and Congressional staffers (for whom he acted as a consultant on naval matters generally). Finally, MccGwire's move to the Brookings Institution allowed him to be a permanent and active contributor to Washington defence debates.

While in Washington MccGwire was part of a group of analysts from think-tanks and the intelligence community who met regularly to analyse Soviet writings. He also organised the Washington Area Forum on Soviet Affairs, which held monthly meetings at Brookings for high level officials and others, to discuss and assess the significance of developments in the Soviet Union and the implications for US policy. Earlier, MccGwire had run a more intensive series on the US Navy, the focus of a very different debate. His summaries of those sessions incisively laid out the major elements of current issues, and this writer well remembers those meetings and the comments which officials made to him about how useful they were.

A last reason is MccGwire's personality. He does not hold back, enjoys give-and-take and has the courage of his convictions. Not only the content of his arguments but also the vigour and relish with which he presents them make him a sought-after speaker. In addition, his willingness to tell people what they do *not* want to hear buttresses his credibility, earns him respect and contributes to his being viewed as an intellectual force to be reckoned with. Especially in his early academic years, he was very much in the minority as he, in effect, called upon his audiences to question their own assumptions, revise their perspectives on Soviet attitudes and behaviour, and ultimately reconsider their own policy preferences *vis-à-vis* the USSR.

In sum, MccGwire's impact on Soviet naval studies was partly fortuitous. He arrived on the scene at a time when people were very interested in what he too was interested in, the Soviet Navy, but his impact would have been nil and he would have remained essentially unrecognised by his peers had he not reacted as he did to the opportunity afforded by that rising interest. MccGwire did what few academics are fortunate enough to do: be centrally instrumental in helping shape a field of studies. With the passing of the Cold War and of the USSR, the Soviet Navy's successor has lowered its profile and the field of study concerning it has lost its lustre. MccGwire himself moved on in the 1980s to focus the bulk of his attention on the broader Soviet military. Nevertheless, these facts do not lessen his achievement nor the relevance of his work in those years when many in the West were justifiably concerned about the naval intentions and capabilities of the Soviet Union.

During his first decade out of the navy, MccGwire's hope of changing the world by working for the United Nations gradually weakened. He would have made a great administrator, but the UN's loss was the MccGwire family's gain. He settled into the life of a reluctant academic, and to a far greater extent than he wished, he was constantly pulled back into military matters. He accepted that war and the threat of war are not going away in a hurry, and so studying them is important; he was just disappointed that he himself had to keep doing the studying. But his experience had instilled duty. While at Dalhousie in the 1970s he raised the profile of Canadian strategic studies to a degree it had never had before, nor has had since.

MccGwire's work on the Soviet Navy in the 1970s – both general surveys and finegrained hardware analyses – required him to have a detailed understanding of US naval operational behaviour and philosophy. The broad perspective and accumulating knowledge which came from studying both navies, combined with his own naval experience, led him to think about navies in general in original ways. He was therefore asked in the 1970s to work on studies on a wide range of topics, including strategic ASW, naval arms control, cruise missiles at sea, seaborne intervention, power projection and various geostrategic surveys of regions and waterways. His expertise inevitably drew him to Washington, and to North American service and war colleges. In 1979 he was recruited by the Brookings Institution in Washington, a long-established think-tank with a reputation for thorough research and conclusions some US administrations found uncomfortable. He was appointed to work on the future of the US Navy, then a live political issue. He had doubts about the project – he had not left the British Navy in order to study the US one – and he also enjoyed the independence and opportunities afforded by his Dalhousie post. But family factors predominated, and he moved south. In so doing he was given an opportunity he would not have missed, to be a policy analyst in Washington during the second Cold War.

Characteristically, MccGwire's research project at Brookings – 'Six Hundred Ships – the Navy and National Security' – led him to assess US naval requirements from first principles, devise new methodological tools, work back through construction programmes, build up expertise in defence budgeting, and produce interesting and ingenious conclusions. Because the Reagan administration insisted that the Soviet Union had more capability than it 'needed' for defensive purposes (which implied that it must be planning to use the ostensible surplus for offensive reasons) MccGwire was asked by the Congressional Research Service to see whether his method of assessing Soviet naval requirements (tasks/capabilities) could be applied to the other branches of the Soviet armed forces. The key question was: how much *did* the Soviets need? A successful pilot study led to a decision to produce a monograph on the subject; this also meant setting aside the 600-ship project (which in any case events were overtaking, with Congress having authorised two new carriers). But what had been intended as a fairly short and straightforward exercise took on a different complexion when MccGwire discovered that the evidence about the structures and characteristics of the other Soviet services did not support prevailing Western assumptions about Soviet doctrine and strategy. He followed the evidence, and by piecing together the all-service jig-saw he was able to identify key decisions in Soviet military policy and strategy; in particular he identified a reformulation in late 1966 of Soviet doctrine about the likely nature of a world war (which in turn led to a new list of military priorities and a far-reaching and protracted shift in strategy), and he was able to spot at an early stage that there had been another far-reaching reformulation of military doctrine in January 1987, this time about the probability of world war. The significance of the 1987 downgrading of the threat of world war removed the longstanding requirement for Soviet forces to be stationed in Eastern Europe, and allowed the political and economic arguments for withdrawal to prevail (MccGwire, 1988). This exhaustive examination of Soviet military and foreign policy resulted in the publication of two outstanding contributions to the analysis of Soviet military behaviour. Their significance is discussed next by a Soviet/Russian policy analyst.

SOVIETOLOGY

John McDonnell[2]

Michael MccGwire made significant contributions to Sovietology both in methodology and in substance. He developed a fresh approach to the study of Soviet national security policy based on what he termed 'objectives analysis'. He used this methodology to identify major shifts in Soviet military doctrine and to demonstrate the impact on Soviet behaviour of changing assumptions about the nature of a possible world war. The methodology of objectives analysis was implicit in his earliest work on the Soviet Navy, but he refined and expanded it as his interest in Moscow's foreign and defence policies broadened and deepened. The outcome can be seen in the two substantial volumes written during his decade at the Brookings Institution (MccGwire, 1987, 1991).

MccGwire was interested from the start not merely in discovering the 'what' of Soviet policy, but also the 'why'. It was not enough, in other words, to determine what weapon systems in what numbers the Soviets had built over a given period, nor to describe how these had been deployed and employed. The fundamental point was to identify the motivations that had shaped the decisions to build and field these systems, with an eye to forecasting future Soviet behaviour. The predictive orientation of objectives analysis is one of its strongest features; this provides a basis for judging the value of the approach and the accuracy of its findings even for those not fully steeped in its methodology.

Explaining the 'why' of Soviet policy, if it was to go beyond the circular reasoning of offering an interpretation and then selectively citing evidence in support of it, meant developing a set of testable hypotheses. These are set forth in MccGwire's approach as Soviet military planning assumptions, a hierarchy of strategic objectives deriving therefrom, which in turn yield operational missions and force requirements expressed concretely in procurement programmes, deployment patterns and so on. MccGwire's use of objectives analysis started out as an inductive process, when his initial work on the Soviet Navy yielded repeated discontinuities in ship-building programmes that cried out for explanation. The awareness of repeated changes in Soviet naval and military policies indeed lies at the heart of objectives analysis, because identifying and dating changes in policy makes it possible to investigate both the reasons for policy shifts and their consequences.

Objectives analysis is characterised by three key features. First, the focus is on Moscow's perspective, on the viewpoint of a notional Soviet war-planner, which means thinking in terms of Soviet requirements, rather than Western vulnerabilities. Second, analysis is directed at the political-strategic level, i.e., at the Soviets' most likely course of action, rather than at the military technical level, which is concerned with worst case assumptions about what the Soviets might do to exploit Western tactical vulnerabilities. And third, the evidence is examined in its full and proper context, with initial hypotheses about Soviet plans and intentions tested against the concrete facts of weapon procurement, force structuring, deployment patterns and so on. MccGwire emphasised particularly the danger that lay in impressionistic and superficial use of Soviet public statements and writings that are deliberately vague, ambiguous and intended principally to communicate with domestic audiences rather than the Western analysts (1987: 353–66).

Soviet statements and writings and military themes were, of course, a primary source of information for Western analysts, especially those working in an unclassified environment. Far from dismissing these sources as merely propaganda at best, if not deception at worst, MccGwire increasingly exploited such material in dating and explaining major shifts in Soviet defence policy. He demonstrated the strengths and weaknesses of textual analysis through careful comparisons of successive editions of major works published in the 1960s, such as Marshal Sokolovski's *Military Strategy*, in detailed examinations of Admiral Gorshkov's writings from the 1970s, and in exploring the dramatic revolution wrought by Gorbachev's 'new thinking' about international relations in the 1980s. Throughout, he emphasised the importance of taking account of the full context of such writings and the hazards to intellectual rigour of selective quotation.

MccGwire's development of objectives analysis as a basic methodology for the study of Soviet national security policy led directly to his major contribution to Sovietology: the identification of fundamental shifts in Soviet military doctrine. Indeed, analysis of Soviet military doctrine became the central focus of MccGwire's work in the 1980s, since he believed that changing Soviet assumptions about the nature of future warfare dictated the alterations in policy that followed. More than most Western security analysts, MccGwire stressed the importance of comprehending Soviet military doctrine as a whole and of trying to understand the basic tenets that provided the framework of Soviet policy formulation. And when he was identifying Soviet requirements, because he was not encumbered by Marxist–Leninist theology or by other parochial concerns, MccGwire could lay out this doctrinal framework and its detailed implications in a more straightforward manner than a Soviet General Staff planner was likely to.

MccGwire identified nearly a dozen significant shifts in Soviet military doctrine in the four decades following the Second World War. No attempt can be made here to summarise his full periodisation of doctrine and its contents (see, especially, MccGwire, 1987: 13–67; 1991: 14–45). But the two most fundamental changes in Soviet military doctrine should be noted, since they dwarfed all other shifts in Soviet thinking in their consequences. First was the 1966–7 assessment that a possible world war need not inevitably involve nuclear exchanges, and second was the 1987 decision to make prevention of world war the highest Soviet security objective.

Starting in the late 1940s, Soviet military doctrine was predicated on the possibility of a third world war, and it set as its basic strategic objective the avoidance of losing such a war. This central assumption – the possibility of world war – and its corollary chief objective – to avoid losing – remained unchanged over the next four decades, though a series of shifts took place regarding the likelihood and nature of such a war. In the late 1950s, for example, it was accepted that nuclear weapons would play the primary role in such a war, with nuclear exchanges between the USSR and the United States determining its outcome. In late 1966, however, the key assumption that world war would inevitably and almost immediately involve nuclear strikes against one another's home-lands was reassessed.

Soviet achievement of strategic parity threw increasing doubt on the willingness of the United States to put itself at risk of nuclear war in Western Europe's defence. NATO's adoption of the policy of flexible response suggested that war in Europe might remain conventional in nature or might involve only limited use of nuclear weapons. MccGwire identified a wholesale reordering of Soviet doctrinal priorities that stemmed from Moscow's acceptance of the possibility that world war could remain conventional and that massive intercontinental nuclear exchanges could be avoided. In planning for the contingency of world war, avoiding the nuclear devastation of the Soviet Union now became a top priority. This meant a drastic reduction in the incentive to launch pre-emptive nuclear strikes, particularly against the United States, to avoid retaliation in kind. It meant that Moscow could and should plan for a rapid conventional campaign in Europe to defeat NATO and deprive the United States of a foothold on the continent. And it meant preparing for a prolonged world-wide conventional war in the event Washington refused to accept the resulting new status quo.

None of these doctrinal changes indicated an increased Soviet will-ingness to unleash aggression in order to expand the socialist camp or enhance Moscow's power. But they did entail a major expansion of Soviet conventional offensive capabilities, especially in Europe, and this served only to strengthen Western fears about Soviet aims. In addition, the changes also drew the Soviets deeper into competition with the West in the Third World, as Moscow sought to build the infrastructure needed for the second, prolonged phase of possible world war. And while these doctrinal shifts facilitated a reversal of Soviet policy to one favouring strategic arms control, the need to continue preparing for the possibility of world war going nuclear, as well as to match Western technological advances, meant no sharp end to the East–West arms race.

The end result of the 1966–7 decisions was that what began as a seemingly modest reassessment of the nature of a possible world war led to Soviet measures on a wide scale that raised tensions, encouraged Western counter-measures, and made such a war more likely. This was a classical case of unintended consequences in security policy. The advent of the Reagan administration in Washington, prepared to assume the worst of both Soviet intentions and capabilities, and committed to raising the stakes aggressively, exacerbated already deteriorating relations, leading the Soviets under Andropov to revert to views of the prospects for war akin to those of the late Stalinist period. But as MccGwire noted, Reagan was a lucky president, and never more so than in the emergence of Gorbachev as what would prove to be the final Soviet leader.

MccGwire argues that Gorbachev and his supporters recognised the need to democratise Soviet politics, to redirect resource allocations from the military to the civilian sector of the economy, and therefore to redefine security policy to avoid an ever-expanding arms race and to defuse tensions with the West. Gorbachev recognised (in MccGwire's reconstruction) that Soviet preparation for the contingency of world war served only to make such a war more likely. In January 1987, Gorbachev made what MccGwire calls an 'audacious' decision that Soviet military doctrine would henceforth be predicated on the assumption of 'no world war', rather than on the self-imposed requirement to prepare for the possibility of such a war. World war would be averted by political means, with military preparations for this contingency now having a secondary priority.

The 1987 decision overturned the most fundamental tenet of Soviet military doctrine and had implications more far-reaching than the 1966–7 shift described above. The collapse of the USSR in the wake of the abortive August 1991 coup cut short the full playing out of these implications, but two developments that occurred by the end of 1990 illustrate its enormous significance. First, by eliminating the requirement for conventional superiority in Europe, this doctrinal shift led directly to the unilateral reductions in Soviet military manpower that Gorbachev announced in December 1988, as well as to the rapid achievement of a conventional arms control agreement entailing highly asymmetrical Soviet reductions. And second, by undercutting the need to maintain a cordon of military allies in Eastern Europe, either as a springboard for offensive operations against NATO or as a defensive buffer in case of NATO attack, it facilitated Soviet acquiescence to the removal of six communist regimes and to the dissolution of the Warsaw Pact.

Three characteristics stand out in MccGwire's thinking and in his approach to the study of the Soviet Union. First, his patience for the tedium of data collection, for accumulating the evidence that is necessary for achieving the ambitious goal of constructing a theory of Soviet national security policy. Second, his rigour and discipline in drawing out the implications of the evidence and then extrapolating hypotheses that can be tested to confirm one's initial judgements –

plus a readiness to accept their negation. And third, his creativity and imagination, both in constructing the overarching framework of analysis and in presenting it to the reader through vivid analogies. In his most succinct description of his methodology, MccGwire draws on cartography, geology, astronomy, physics and chemistry on the way to concluding that palaeontology may provide the closest parallel to objectives analysis (1991: Appendix A, especially p. 447). While always keeping military analysis at the centre of his attention, MccGwire insists on the importance of context, recognises gaps in his own knowledge, and never hesitates to ask questions of his colleagues. Where helpful he will also adopt – with suitable acknowledgement – the ideas of others. His writings draw from history, economics, international relations, political science, sociology and philosophy. While demonstrating the centrality of military doctrine in understanding the post-war evolution of the Soviet Union, his work reaches far beyond the narrow scope of mainstream strategic studies.

[K.B.] In addition to publishing extensively during his time as a policy analyst at Brookings, MccGwire became what is now called a 'public intellectual'. In the Washington of the Reagan years his reputation and expertise were valued much more than in the stuffy atmosphere of Whitehall. Among other things, he testified to Congress, his expert knowledge was employed in global war games run by the US Naval War College, and he was drawn into the debate about Reaganite nuclear policy reflected in the controversial pastoral letter by the Catholic bishops of America (which contained major reservations about the morality of nuclear deterrence). Brookings was an ideal base for such activities, with its access to the policy community, its tough seminars, its reputation for integrity, its rigorous analysis, and the way it managed to combine the best of academic, business and service values. He counted himself lucky to have been there when John Steinbruner was running the Foreign Policy Program and Bruce MacLaury was president. He grew in this atmosphere, and Brookings – like other organisations in which he had worked – benefited from his capacity as an energiser, skill as a facilitator, and experience in handling people and getting things done. Attending to the human relations side of whatever he is involved with has always been crucial, and has meant that MccGwire has published less than he might – a privilege not allowed to conventional academics these days. Meanwhile, his reputation spread beyond Washington. Fundamentalists in the Reagan administration rejected his conclusions about Soviet behaviour set out in *Military Objectives* (1987), but the War Colleges were open to his ideas as were independent thinkers in Europe (especially in the Nordic countries) and in East Asia.

The urgency of the nuclear debate in the West in the 1980s stemmed from a widespread concern that the confrontational words and deeds of the Reagan administration would exacerbate relations with the Soviet Union to such a degree that an uncontrollable nuclear crisis might result. MccGwire was repeatedly drawn back to nuclear issues; as a result, his knowledge grew about the genesis of the theory of nuclear deterrence, the gaps between theory and practice, the problems of arms control and the way in which theory was manipulated to justify new weapons programmes. At the same time, his studies of Soviet military policy led him to believe that the Soviets did not subscribe to nuclear deterrence theory as propounded by the Western – mainly US – strategic community. Fortunately, the advent of Gorbachev and his 'new political thinking' about international relations began to help to defuse the tensions of the second Cold War, though the US administration sought to consolidate its strategic superiority through the START negotiations, despite the mounting evidence of a fundamental shift in Soviet policy. This drive only abated after the disintegration of the Soviet superpower in 1991. By then, in any case, US defence concerns were shifted to the new dangers of nuclear proliferation, 'loose nukes' and – in the aftermath of the Gulf War – growing anxiety that nuclear weapons in the wrong regional hands could threaten the global conventional capability of the United States. These concerns led some in the US defence establishment to favour the marginalisation of nuclear weapons – and in some cases their complete elimination 'if only we knew how' – though these views were not shared by everybody. In defence circles in Whitehall, for example, such talk fuelled worries that ideas about 'nuclear marginalisation' might take hold in Britain, and this led a prominent former official to publish a preemptive article explaining why the three Western nuclear powers needed to retain their nuclear capability (Quinlan, 1993). MccGwire, back in Britain after retiring from Brookings in 1990, was provoked to respond. So began a debate which – allied to the growing legal and environmental pressures against nuclear weapons – has still not run its course.

Although MccGwire's contribution to thinking about international security remains most commonly identified with sea-power and Sovietology, he has made a consistent and significant contribution to the central debate about nuclear weapons. One piece of work, 'Deterrence: the Problem not the Solution' (MccGwire, 1985/6) is widely recognised as being seminal, to use the much overused term, because of the novel way it shifted the argument from the alleged benefits of nuclear deterrence to its political and other costs. Between 1960 and the early 1990s he accepted nuclear weapons as a material fact that could not be wished away; what he focused on was what he saw as the pernicious doctrine of nuclear deterrence, which justified arms racing and not only undermined moves towards the relaxation of tension with the Soviet Union but actually made war more rather than less likely. Since 1993 his focus has been on the new possibilities opened up for thinking about the elimination of nuclear weapons, a concern driven by his belief in the dangers inherent in the continued existence of these weapons. In the current debate his focus on the comparative risks of a policy of nuclear elimination as against the continuation indefinitely of policies in which nuclear weapons structure 'defence' postures is proving persuasive. His long contribution to professional thinking and the public policy debate is assessed in the next section by a British defence specialist.

NUCLEAR DETERRENCE

Michael Clarke

Throughout his professional life Michael MccGwire has been out of step with the conventional wisdom of the Western strategic community. First, he seemed to be left behind by the march of a subject – nuclear deterrence – which in the 1950s and 1960s many believed could be worked out with mathematical precision. To some, he seemed to have little grasp and less interest in the so-called calculus of deterrence, and the ways that nuclear deterrence could be defined through theories of escalation, extended deterrence, limited war, graduated response and even the minutiae of arms control. Then, in the 1980s and early 1990s he seemed to be way out in front of the subject, urging that the time had come for a fundamental paradigm shift in strategic thinking, arguing that the logic of deterrence theory and so much that flowed from it was in fact deeply illogical, and that alternatives which would seem naive even to novices in strategic studies were in fact both worldly and within our grasp if only we were prepared to make the necessary imaginative leap. And now, in the post-Cold War world, as the strategic studies community rethinks its role, MccGwire emerges as a remarkably consistent thinker on strategic studies in general, and nuclear deterrence in particular. It was his critics and their conception of the subject which vacillated, piled angels on to pinheads and gave incoherent practice the attire of theoretical elegance. For several decades, Michael MccGwire has been the boy in the crowd shouting that the nuclear emperor has no clothes, and now most of the international relations community mutters audibly that the emperor, if not naked, is at least scantily clad.

His contribution to thinking about nuclear strategy rests on two pillars. First, he has long argued that strategic analysis had to be based on a thorough grasp of the national politics of the actors who were engaged in thinking about nuclear weapons. Strategy in the abstract would always be a poor guide to policy in the real world. The second pillar, which developed somewhat later in his work, was a powerful critique of Western strategic thinking in general. Even in terms of its own influential abstractions, he later argued, such thinking was infused with a deep political disutility.

The first pillar of his contribution to the nuclear debate grew out of his background in intelligence and his intimate knowledge of the Soviet Union and the way in which its military establishment thought and operated. He always had the vision to turn the map upside down and look outwards from the Soviet Union rather than inwards from the West: he insisted that those who lived there were *people* with their own backgrounds, traditions, neuroses and concerns. He would not allow Westerners, in particular Americans, automatically to adopt the moral high ground, as they invariably did during the Cold War. He argued that Soviet policy-makers had perfectly logical reasons for most of the general policies they adopted and that none of these policies constituted a master plan for global military domination. He believed that the ignorance and abstractions of Western deterrence theory posed a bigger threat of war than the Soviet military. MccGwire was always scathing about the fact that theories of strategic deterrence were articulated in the Cold War of the 1950s and 1960s by people who had very little knowledge of the Soviet Union or the Russian language. It was not even 'Kremlinologists' who worked out the theory on which US defence policy and hence much of what passed for international security rested in the post-war period: it was mathematicians, economists and other axiomatic disciplines who for the most part had become fascinated with the logical dimensions of deterrence theory and in turn provided abstract justification for a US defence establishment determined to codify its military superiority over all potential adversaries. Perhaps for these reasons, MccGwire was inclined to bring a counter-intuitive approach to the subject of nuclear strategy: he disliked what he found and developed his own ideas over a number of years without having a clear sense of what conclusions he would reach, other than that they must stay close to political and military realities. This aspect of his thinking on deterrence found its most mature expression in his two major books on Soviet military thinking, written while at Brookings

(MccGwire, 1987, 1991). These are discussed elsewhere in this chapter; for present purposes their significance is partly that ideas which were once regarded as no more than an apologia for Soviet aggression are now widely accepted, and that his analysis leads to the conclusion that we should probably count ourselves lucky to have come through the Cold War without a serious breakdown in the edifice of nuclear deterrence.

He argues that the West was always in a position to escape from – or at least greatly ameliorate – the effects of nuclear confrontation. If we had accepted that the prime Soviet objective was to avoid war (rather than risk one in the cause of communist expansion) then it would have been clear that there was very little *latent* 'aggression' which could be, or needed to be, deterred by nuclear means. But instead Western strategic thinkers gave us an elaborate justification for an expensive and ultimately dangerous nuclear arms race. If they had been a little more interested in the Soviet military and a little less interested in the application of abstract modelling to politico-strategic relationships, the history of the Cold War might have been rather different.

The second pillar of MccGwire's contribution to nuclear deterrence thinking builds on this. His distrust of deterrent theorising goes back to the beginning of the independent British nuclear deterrent. The early 1960s saw him arguing vigorously – while still a naval officer – in the columns of a number of specialist journals against this concept. 'My nerve is NOT breaking', he thundered in 1962, 'but my *patience* is severely strained by the blind emotional reaction induced in some protagonists of the deterrent whenever anyone dares to discuss the subject in terms other than of bigger and better bombs'.

In those days, his arguments primarily concerned the proliferation of nuclear weapons and the controversial notion that Britain could make a positive contribution to nuclear non-proliferation by refusing to go down – and then acting to discourage others from going down – what he described as a nuclear cul-de-sac from which there was no escape. For he saw nuclear deterrence as a fundamentally apolitical construct, particularly in the British case; it was insufficiently related to the political objectives British governments sought to achieve and was grotesquely disproportionate to any objectives to which it *was* linked. The most tangible objectives of an independent British deterrent – political influence with the United States, seats at the world's 'top tables' and so on – were simply trivial in relation to the long-term risks. He saw the dangers of nuclear proliferation early, and recognised that non-proliferation had to begin somewhere, and where better than in the country in whose armed services he was a rising figure? By the mid-1980s he had developed in some detail the argument that the 'problem' of international security in the Cold War was not the Soviet Union but *war itself*. This belief had always been a prime concern of Soviet defence planners. Deterrence, said MccGwire, was not a solution to the problem of war, still less a solution to the problem of the Soviet Union, but rather it was itself a significant part of the problem of international security. For Moscow, it created a war neurosis which affected its military planners who genuinely feared a global war, either by design or accident, and who were determined not to lose it. For the West, it created a comforting illusion that we were being efficiently defended; when in fact it was based on a false premise and tended to justify continuing weapons development in the West, quite unrelated to any real temptation to aggression that Soviet leaders may ever have felt. As more and diverse weaponry was recruited to the aid of 'deterrent credibility' so the concept became increasingly devoid of real meaning. Two particular articles of MccGwire's expressed these thoughts: 'The Dilemmas and Delusions of Deterrence' (1984) and 'Deterrence: The Problem, not the Solution' (1985). There were also a number of contributions at about the same time in the debate over the strategic defence initiative (SDI). These served as a focus for him not only to comment on the SDI itself, but also to criticise the fundamental assumptions of the programme, including the intellectual paucity of the deterrent logic which backed it up. The SDI began – at least in the view of President Reagan – as a way of breaking out of nuclear deterrence, but almost from the moment of his SDI speech in March 1983, it became yet another exotic technology justified precisely because it was going to safeguard and stabilise deterrence.

For MccGwire the pursuit of long-term stable nuclear deterrence is a chimera. It cannot be stable with two, let alone multiple, players. A world of several active nuclear players – the world towards which we are gradually but steadily drifting – is one in which a nuclear attack some-where at some time is virtually assured. And the catastrophe of a failed nuclear threat outweighs any rational political purpose. Before 1989, his arguments were based on the belief that nuclear deterrence represented the wrong way for the West to deal with the USSR; now his arguments are that nuclear deterrence represents an even greater folly if it is intended as some over-arching mechanism of a more abstract world order.

For the British defence establishment, the British independent deter-rent is regarded as serving a number of explicit deterrent purposes: it deters war between the major powers who already possess nuclear weapons; it helps deter the use or acquisition of chemical and bacter-iological weapons on the part of others; it helps deter threats by non-Western nuclear states in the future; and it helps deter the temptation to which 'rogue states' might succumb, of dashing for nuclear possession in a world that was steadily disarming (Quinlan, 1993). There are many other political arguments put forward to justify British nuclear weapons, such as the belief that they confer political influence, but MccGwire attacks the logic at its strongest, rather than its weakest, points. MccGwire refutes each of the pro-nuclear arguments in detail, on the basis either that nuclear means do not have to be used to achieve such objectives, or else that the conditions which would prevail in a non-nuclear world would render the objectives meaningless. A nuclear free world would be a new political arena which would significantly change the political objectives the major powers would seek to pursue (MccGwire, 1994).

More importantly, certain basic points are being missed in the present debate. MccGwire argues that comparisons between a nuclear and a non-nuclear world have to be drawn from an equal baseline. The comparison should be between the likely circumstances of a non-nuclear world in twenty to thirty years time, as against the likely conditions in the world in twenty to thirty years time if nuclear proliferation continues. Too often, he says, the comparison is made between the brief honeymoon we have so far enjoyed since the end of the Cold War and the relative uncertainties of a nuclear free world in, say 2020. But the real comparison should be between a nuclear free world in 2020 and a world of *continuing proliferation* by then. For it is much more likely that the low-salience nuclear world we now have will by then have reverted to the high salience nuclear world which has been the norm over the last half century. The question is not so much whether a nuclear free world is 'feasible and desirable' but rather whether it is 'feasible and preferable' to the likely alternatives if longer-term trends in proliferation are sustained.

To escape from the dilemmas of nuclear deterrence, in other words, it is necessary to accept first that we *can* escape. MccGwire insists that we can take advantage of the brief honeymoon presented by the end of the Cold War and utilise the fact that a nuclear weapons free world is (probably for the last time) feasible. Once its feasibility is accepted then the calculus of risks and possibilities to address the insecurities that will arise in twenty to thirty years time changes drastically. Many 'breakout' problems would be largely irrelevant once it is accepted that a genuinely nuclear weapons free world can be constructed and policed. But what makes us think that the major powers would be prepared to police such a system? Simply because – as more insiders are recognising – if they knew how to rid the world of nuclear weapons, it would be entirely in their national self-interests to do so. A world of proliferating nuclear weapons, and a century in which Asian powers will be more dominant than Western ones, will be a century in which the present status quo powers would be a great deal more secure in a nuclear-weapons-free environment.

These mid-1990s arguments represent the most developed expression of MccGwire's views, and bring the wheel virtually full circle. Nobody in the defence establishment who supports nuclear weapons, he says, has come up with a list of vital security objectives which cannot be achieved by non-nuclear means, or which would not become simply irrelevant in a non-nuclear world (MccGwire, 1995a, 1995b). And the nuclear genie is not so far out of the bottle that it cannot still be recaptured. The world has realistic expectations of banning chemical weapons in a comprehensive Chemical Weapons Convention; why not for nuclear weapons, which rely on far more specific and controllable technologies than chemical weapons production? MccGwire is leading the way in putting the onus of explanation on the supporters of nuclear deterrence. It is not up to the advocates of a non-nuclear world to try to explain why the world *should not* have nuclear weapons, he says, it is for the deterrence theorists to prove to us why we now *should*. The responsibility is now on pro-nuclear opinion to make a sensible case for the continuance of such a bizarre approach to peace and security: the nuclear emperor is beginning to feel exposed.

[K.B.] As a policy analyst in the Washington hot-house in the 1980s MccGwire's reputation had grown. In a policy debate characterised by specialists in constant public session he was seen as an original figure in a key issue area. Controversy was a constant companion: the public disagreement with Western naval establishments over the 'MccGwire thesis', disagreement with some naval analysts over the interpretation of aspects of Soviet naval policy, criticism by some reviewers for his interpretation of Soviet military policy in his major books, and confrontation with the Reaganites over his root-and-branch critique of nuclear deterrence. In the late 1980s he had devoted his public energy to trying to convince the US political establishment that fundamental change was underway in the Soviet Union and of the importance of meeting the Soviets half way, rather than pocketing Soviet concessions and demanding more as their 'legitimate' right (MccGwire, 1989). But alongside the controversy was the fact that his work was noticed. It was frequently cited, while his name appeared regularly in the Prefaces and Acknowledgements of books whose authors expressed their indebtedness to his help. In 1990 the US secretary of defense and the chairman of the Joint Chiefs of Staff were invited during a Congressional Hearing to explain why they did not accept his views.

In 1990, beyond UK retirement age, MccGwire left Washington. He was sad to leave the Brookings Institution, happy to leave the subject area (or so he thought), and satisfied that the Cold War had ended – an outcome he put down to audacious changes on the Soviet side rather than enlightened thinking on the part of the West. But the subject area, and his old habit of getting involved, did not go away. On his return to Britain he joined the Faculty of Social and Political Sciences at Cambridge University as a part-time member of the Global Security Programme (GSP). The interdisciplinary richness of Cambridge, which he actively helped foster, opened his mind to new ideas and ways of thinking about the global future.

The GSP was intended to eschew immediate policy issues and to look some twenty to thirty years ahead. To that end MccGwire revived his long-standing proposition that the 500 year period which had seen Europeans achieve global domination was coming to an end. He argued that while the 'Euro-Westerners' were still strong they should expand, follow and enforce the rule of law in the international system. They would then have hope of looking themselves to its protection when, as world population and other trends made certain, they became relatively weak in the decades ahead. He believed that international conventions banning weapons of mass destruction would be an important first step along that road (MccGwire, 1994). These arguments are part of the reason why he has been so opposed to lawless behaviour by Western states and their allies: if *we* do not live by the rules when *we* are the most powerful, how can we expect *others* to behave towards *us* with restraint when we no longer have that primacy? More immediately, in terms of his Cambridge post, he was concerned to define and delimit the concept of global security, which he regarded as an evocative label with warm overtones but little intellectual substance. He delimited the subject area by reference to the three main categories of problem that had long shared public attention at the international level: military confrontation and conflict; social and economic development; and environmental degradation. What fundamentally defined 'global security' for him were threats in some way connected to the survival of the human race (recognising that the definition of 'survival' is itself in contention). However ill-defined, he thought the label 'global security' useful in part as a way of giving priority to certain issues. In this respect he believed that the crucial question was not *what* needed to be done but *how* to bring about the changes needed in attitudes, values, social relations and political structures if the necessary responses were to be implemented.

MccGwire left Cambridge in 1993, for the second time, intending in retirement to pursue intellectual interests unrelated to international security. But, as ever, world affairs intruded. In particular, there has been continuing Western triumphalism about the Cold War and especially its end; this provoked him to turn back to his work about Soviet attitudes and behaviour, and to continue arguing that the Soviet Union did not have an urge to military aggression – a belief that fuelled Cold War arms racing and fuels military postures against Russia today. He also became embroiled in the debate about the new possibility of a nuclear weapon free world, mentioned earlier, a possibility given momentum by serious talk in US arms control circles about nuclear marginalisation, the negotiations on a Comprehensive Test Ban Treaty, the Review Conference of the Nuclear Non-Proliferation Treaty and the Canberra Commission set up by the Australian government to recommend how (not whether) to eliminate nuclear weapons. MccGwire continues to oppose Britain's pro-nuclear defence establishment, and contributed three papers to the Canberra Commission. It is his belief that if this opportunity is not taken to drive down and ultimately eliminate nuclear weapons, pressures for vertical and horizontal nuclear proliferation will at some point decisively increase, as happened during the Cold War. His critiques on behalf of the anti-nuclear case, consistent over three decades, are the more compelling because of his experience and reputation as a strategist's strategist.

In this period of renewed debate about international security, MccGwire's detailed knowledge of Soviet military behaviour has been essential, since so much of the argument, implicitly or explicitly, relates to what has been remembered and forgotten about the Cold War. To repeat Tina Rosenberg's words in the Introduction: 'The memory of the past is a prize worth struggling for.' His earlier work is also central to his latest writing, which argues against the extension of NATO eastwards. His Washington experience tells him that the impetus for this policy, which he believes will prove counter-productive, comes from US domestic politics, and is not the result of some dispassionate analysis of what is needed for long-term security in Europe. His own analysis leads him to conclude that the West is in danger of repeating the misperceptions and mistakes of the 1943–7 period. The dangers include demonising Russia, allowing minority opinions in Washington to determine policy, disregarding Russia's legitimate interests, failing to show sensitivity to Russian fears and being unwilling to believe other than that, since the Soviet Union lost the Cold War, we must have been (and be) right.

Because the wheel in some senses is turning full circle on these issues, MccGwire's intellectual investment in Soviet affairs has not been consigned to only historical interest. But it is not only his distinctive conclusions that are relevant; he also developed distinctive *ways* of arguing. Jack Snyder, for example, in a study group report on methodology in Soviet studies, noted how MccGwire's work was unique in combining a holistic approach with deductive logic and positivist testing procedures (1988: 191–2). MccGwire himself considers that his methodology derived directly from his attempt to understand the particular character of the Soviet procurement system; this allowed him to work back from weapons programmes to doctrinal and other decisions, which were crucial to his explanation of Soviet policy over time. However, he thinks that his 'objectives analysis' can be applicable to many kinds of historical research (including revisionary analyses of the 1945–90 period, using Soviet archival material) and can also be used in contemporary policy analysis when another government's or institution's behaviour is crucial to formulating one's own policy. MccGwire's approach attracted not only the attention of specialists in Sovietology and security but also a specialist in argument. As the section below shows, she sees continuing relevance in MccGwire's methodology, even in a post-Soviet world, because of the insights it offers about the study of the attitudes and behaviour of apparently impenetrable and enigmatic states.

TALKIN' THE TALK

Cori E. Dauber

In the wake of the euphoria over the collapse of the Soviet Union and the end of the Cold War, one might assume that a *post-hoc* evaluation of the debate over Soviet military doctrine, and Michael MccGwire's role in that debate, would be purely academic. Despite the excitement over the ability to use previously unavailable Soviet sources to determine who in the Western debate was 'right', can we learn from these evaluations? Is there any point in taking the time to determine who was right, if anyone, or is nothing at stake beyond bragging rights? In short, does any of the work done on the Soviet Union have anything to say about where analysts go from here?

I would like to begin by positioning myself from a disciplinary perspective. My disciplinary 'home' would generally be called either rhetorical criticism or 'argument studies'. Rhetorical critics are interested, broadly stated, in the way people use symbols, especially linguistic symbols, in the production and creation of persuasive strategies. My own work has centred on the study of texts produced in the Western debate over deterrence. Thus I examined that debate during the Cold War, not with an eye to determining who was 'right' or not, since that is frankly beyond my expertise, but with an eye to determining how the structure of the argument that was taking place might lead us to consider some arguments but not others, to view the nature of international relations in a certain way, to interpret events from the perspective of a very particular frame of reference or interpretive lens (Dauber, 1993). So, as an example, now that we have access to vastly improved historical understandings of the Cuban missile crisis, a variety of authors have produced works based on new historical information. Better data means we come closer to knowing what 'really' happened (the quotation marks here refer to the belief in my own field that historical understandings are always shaped by the interpretive lens of the person making the judgement, and not to imply any disagreement or critique of any particular arguments), and therefore permits the development of lessons that are far more helpful and realistic then those currently available. While I have not yet done the work, I would take an entirely different approach towards the data on the missile crisis. Rather than saying the old lessons can now be displaced by better lessons, my interest as a rhetorical critic would be in assessing the old lessons themselves, not in order to assess their accuracy or helpfulness, but in order to understand the way they subsequently shaped our understanding of the Cold War. The Cuban missile crisis became a textualised event, generated a vast literature, and a set of understandings about the nature of crises in general and Soviet and American relations in particular that came to be seen as 'common sense' or 'common knowledge'. From a historian's perspective we might now say that those lessons were wrong, but right or wrong they had an influence on the way people approached the issues. The question, to my mind, then becomes what influence they had.

My interest in the deterrence debate has led me to focus on the way various competing schools of deterrence theory functioned as arguments, and in particular the way they worked from textualised evidence to normative conclusions about defence policy. My argument has been that, for most authors in the debate, the deterrence theories provided an overarching framework from within which explanations for evidence were generated. Rather than the evidence being confirming or disconfirming of the theory, the theory works to explain evidence in a fashion that retains the theory's consistency. Thus the invasion of Afghanistan by the Soviet Union in 1980 is not taken as final proof of anything. Those who believed in an expansionist and aggressive Soviet Union generated an interpretation of the invasion consistent with that picture: it was the beginning of the Soviet drive towards the Persian Gulf. Those who believed in a pragmatic and defensive Soviet Union also generated an interpretation consistent with their theory: the invasion was intended to maintain a friendly buffer state on the Soviet border. Because the theory drives the interpretation of the evidence, and not the other way around, there is no basis for choice between these two obviously exclusive assessments of Soviet behaviour.

What initially caught my attention about MccGwire's work on Soviet military policy was that, given his rigorous focus on a self-reflexive methodology for the assessment of evidence, he was able to set up tests for his interpretations. In other words, because he examines evidence in an interactive fashion, where each specific interpretation yields hypotheses about what should be found in other forms of evidence, if his interpretation of the initial piece of evidence was correct, his interpretations are, even before complete access to Soviet records, *falsifiable* (Dauber, 1989).

It is this sensitivity to method that makes MccGwire's work pertinent to this post-Cold War period and, I would argue, it is precisely the importance of MccGwire's work to the future that distinguishes him from other participants in the Western debate. There are many authors whose work is now open to confirmation or disconfirmation, as MccGwire's is. The difference is that when most work is checked against the documents of a no longer opaque adversary, what we will have confirmed or disconfirmed is their instinct, their sensitivity to Soviet actions, their precision in articulating their beliefs. If, on the other hand, MccGwire's work is confirmed, then it is a broad based method, an approach to assessing evidence, that is confirmed. It is a method that can be adapted to other opaque enemies and other fragmentary pieces of evidence in the arena of international affairs. (It is certainly not my intent here to argue that we can ever fully escape the interpretive nature of such assessments, but the fact that all judgements are interpretive does not mean that we are unable to make comparative evaluations or assessments of competing interpretations.)

From the perspective of specialists in argument and rhetoric the Western debate over Soviet military doctrine is an example of competing argument structures. In other words almost every participant in that debate could be categorised based on the underlying assumptions they made, both about the Soviet Union itself and about the nature of nuclear war. One set of authors (call them believers in counterforce) based their argument on the premise that the Soviet Union was intrinsically, unalterably aggressive (whether that was believed to develop from communist ideology or Russian civilisation is for our purposes irrelevant) and that the United States, in order to deter the Soviets, had to appear ready to fight and win a nuclear war. A second set of authors (call them believers in Mutual Assured Destruction or MAD) based their argument on the premise that the Soviets were fundamentally defensive, and that deterring them required an ability to ride out a first strike, and a willingness to avoid threatening the Soviet ability to do the same (Gray, 1984; Jervis, 1984).

While much has been written about these two schools of thought and the differences between them on a wide array of issues, from force structure to arms control, from missile defence to weapons accuracy, what is important to the argument scholar is the fact that while *substantively* distinct these two approaches are *structurally* identical. That is to say, each starts with assumptions about the nature of the Soviets, and proceeds to interpret the available evidence in light of those assumptions. The elaborate theoretical structures of the schools of nuclear deterrence serve to generate explanations for available forms of evidence and individual pieces of evidence alike. Evidence is thus denied its power to confirm or contradict, since the theoretical structures are always capable of explaining any evidence as ultimately consistent with the initial assumptions, which provide the interpretive lens, or framework, within which evidence is explained and understood, as the Afghanistan example above should make clear. Similarly, Soviet decisions to eliminate certain classes of weapons could be taken to disconfirm images of them as always on the offensive. But the assumptions of offensive orientation, however, easily generate interpretations of such moves as inauthentic, designed to lull the West into a false sense of security.

And therein lies the difference between MccGwire's work, particularly *Military Objectives in Soviet Foreign Policy* (MccGwire, 1987), and *Perestroika and Soviet National Security* (MccGwire, 1991), and the bulk of the Cold War debate over both nuclear and conventional doctrines. Elaborate structures which permit the spinning out of explanations precede the analyst's encounter with individual elements of evidence. MccGwire inverts this analytical process. His work moves from the evidence to the search for an explanation. Thus although the evidence is still interpreted (necessarily so, since no fact speaks for itself), the interpretation *precedes* the development of an overall analytical framework. This allows for a cross check, where the analyst can generate a series of hypotheses saying, in effect, if my assessment of this piece of evidence is accurate, then I should be able to find the following kinds of evidence. Rather than calling for explanations that permit a consistency to be imposed *upon* the evidence, MccGwire's approach makes it possible for interpretations of different individual pieces of evidence to confirm or disconfirm one another. This is also, I believe, why MccGwire is unique in combining in his articulation of Soviet doctrine, elements common to both the counterforce and MAD-based analyst. Because his approach goes beyond the analytical frameworks available to most authors, his assessment concedes arguments other authors must contest. So while a MAD author must reject *any* articular indicative of an offensive orientation, and a counterforce author must reject *any* indication of a defensive orientation, since such evidence would undermine the essentialist nature of the foundations of their argument, MccGwire alone can finesse both kinds of evidence. He makes arguments that a MAD author would be quite comfortable with, but he also makes arguments a counterforce author would be comfortable with, combining elements of both to provide a far more elegant assessment than is otherwise available.

Furthermore, it is MccGwire's approach which permits an authentic voice to emerge from the evidence. In other words, when MAD or counterforce authors encounter an individual piece of evidence, the first determination that must be made is whether or not the evidence is 'authentic'. All evidence is presumed to fit into one of two neat categories: it is either 'authentic', a legitimate window into Soviet intentions, or 'propagandistic', a calculated and contrived item, designed to manipulate Western perceptions. The problem has been that in many cases the dividing line used by the individual analyst has been whether or not the item in question is consistent with their foundational assumptions. In either case, though, any indication that the evidence was *intended* for Western consumption dooms it to the dust heap of irrelevance. Automatically it is assumed that anything meant from the Soviet side to be communicative is disregarded.

Both sets of authors see the US military force structure, primarily, during the Cold War, the nuclear force structure, as fundamentally communicative. It was designed to send a message to the Soviets about what we would do based on what we could do. Yet the same was not believed to be true about the Soviets. We built to communicate; they built to prepare. Thus any sign that they were building weapons for the same reason we were, to send a message to the other side, was rejected out of hand. That is a fairly large blind spot on the part of Western analysts. If in fact the Soviets did perceive weapons systems as we did, as a means of non-verbal communication, then the Western debate was at the most basic level incapable of determining that. Because of his ability to check individual pieces of evidence against other pieces of evidence, MccGwire did not need to be nearly as rigid in his categorisation of evidence. By using different evidence and indeed different forms of evidence to develop an overarching framework in which it is the totality of evidence which builds towards the conclusion, it was MccGwire, virtually alone in this debate, who was able to look at the Soviets as potentially attempting to influence our perceptions of them. It seems to me that virtually every other participant in the debate over deterrence theory begs the question: what if the Soviets were in fact doing the same thing we were? If that is the case then it seems to me the entire project falls apart. For that would mean that they were building weapons in order to construct for us a portrait of themselves that would deter, basing their determination of what would deter us on a portrait of the US, based on an interpretation of our deployments, which were built based on our assessment of what would deter them, based on our determination of who they were, based on an interpretation of the weapons they had in fact built based on their interpretation of what we had built. If there is any validity to this, and MccGwire's work suggests there is, then we were less in the realm of geopolitics than we were trapped together in a House of Mirrors, where nothing was as it seemed. If both sides were building weapons systems to deter with no evidence that can be trusted other than the other sides' weapons deployments (since words can lie but it is assumed that deployments cannot) then the entire deterrence project *vis-à-vis* the Soviets is cast into serious doubt.

It is only MccGwire's work that sees this as a possibility, and begins to move beyond the conundrum to a method that can be taken as an exemplar for dealing with opaque adversaries. The notion that the post-Cold War world would be a world without conflict has already been disproved. The potential for conflict means we must be prepared to interpret the behaviour of more nations and more cultures. Because MccGwire's methodology offered a system for approaching sets of evidence, and not a theory which began with assumptions about the Soviets, it has the potential for teaching us how to approach questions regarding the military objectives of other opaque states such as Iraq or North Korea. If so, it then has lasting meaning even in a post-Cold War era.

[K.B.] The justifications for this chapter were made in the introductory paragraph. The claim we are making is that its subject is an individual whose life and work has been radically interesting, shows an expanding consciousness, deserves recognition, throws light on the central concerns of the book and is of continuing relevance. In this story there are lessons and some encouragement for those students of statecraft and security who want to be other than the 'dreary comforters' of the powerful. In conclusion I want to emphasise four inter-related themes.

Beyond one's culture

One of the key features of MccGwire's work has been his ability to overcome cultural and national blinkers. It was more from him than anyone that I learned about the problems caused by ethnocentrism in the theory and practice of strategy. From him I discovered that the drama of international politics is not primarily a morality play, but a tragedy.

A constant theme has been MccGwire's objection to the moralistic claims of Western superiority in world politics, and in particular those of the United States. During the Cold War this moralising was usually directed against Soviet behaviour, but when he looked at Western actions in the Third World, or in what he called the superpowers' 'national security zones' he found there was not much that was different in their urge to dominate. He regarded Western enthusiasm for nuclear deterrence as exhibiting the much criticised Leninist principle of the ends justifying the means. Furthermore, he believed that the danger of nuclear war – which he felt was palpable in the first half of the 1980s – stemmed from the dictates of Western deterrence dogma and not from some imagined Marxist mission. Moralising can lead to misleading analyses and counter-productive policies. This was the case in the Cold War, when the West dealt with the Soviet Union as the magistrate threatens the law-breaker – rather than as a competitive entrepreneur. Illustrations of skewed analysis are plentiful. On the rise of the Soviet Navy, some of his critics were so blinkered by their own ideology, national viewpoint or institutional interests that they could not or would not recognise the force of a better argument – namely that Soviet naval growth could only be properly understood in the context of its historical and technological inferiority in relation to Western navies. With this in mind he persuasively argued, for those who would listen, that too much Western thinking was driven only by a concern with Western vulnerabilities and Soviet strengths. Since Soviet naval planners looked at the confrontation from exactly the same but opposite point of view, the resulting alarmism was mutually reinforcing.

More recently, at the end of the Cold War, MccGwire has been sceptical of liberal triumphalism. He argues, for example, that Western democracies continue to cause major problems in international affairs as a result of their brutal behaviour in the Third World and their selfish domestic politics. He challenges the widespread assumption that, just because liberal democracies have built tolerable societies at home, their foreign policy behaviour must therefore be tolerable. He points out that while the Soviets killed a great number of their *own* people, particularly in the interwar years, the West in general and the United States in particular have killed a great number of the people of *other* nations, either directly in war (Vietnam, Cambodia and so on) or indirectly by sustaining brutal civil wars (Angola, Afghanistan and so on), some of which continue well beyond the end of the Cold War.

Beyond conventional wisdom

Whether or not one agrees with the conclusions he reaches, one of the main features of MccGwire's work has been his willingness to follow an idea. This is evident, in detail, in his re-creation of decision periods in Soviet military policy, and in his hardware analysis. In comparison with those strategic commentators who throw together newspaper cuttings in search of another publication, MccGwire writes immensely detailed background papers in the search for validity. Consequently, to his friends, he is a symbol of thoroughness and active resistance to official lies, academic bullshit and resting on one's laurels. The earlier sections show what can be achieved if an analyst has a good method, area expertise, knowledge, integrity and the capacity for hard work; and a willingness to think for one's self and challenge conventional wisdom.

MccGwire has followed an idea through, regardless of the work entailed or where it led. This has been true in terms of policy analysis and his personal life. His career shows intellectual independence, avoidance of fast tracks and easy options, freedom from passing ideological fashions or national demands, a refusal to be taken in by the propaganda of London, Washington or Moscow, and a determination to see a job through until the end. Because of this integrity, controversy has never been absent. His critics have included the top brass in the British and US navies, other Soviet and naval analysts, the pro-nuclear academic strategic studies community, and the British defence establishment. In the public debate, critics have said that he was 'soft on communism', that his position was unacceptably based on 'moral equivalence' between East and West, that his analysis of the Soviet Union has been too rational, that he has been a 'happy positivist', and that he was 'starry-eyed' about Gorbachev. I will leave the reader to judge. For my part I hope this chapter will draw new attention to his work. Some is of historic value, dealing with the Soviet Navy and the alarms and problems of the Cold War. But there is more than that, including ideas about methodology, analytical rules-of-thumb, and insights to be drawn from US–Soviet relations that may be relevant to the way the West relates to Russia today. In terms of rules-of-thumb in threat analysis for example, his work usefully emphasises the need to think of the adversary's *vulnerabilities* and not just *strengths*; the importance of 'national security zones' for powerful countries; the desirability of avoiding the 'Colonel's fallacy' (that is, do not mistake an adversary's contingency planning for its strategic ambitions), the importance of balancing requirements and capabilities, identifying lead times and decision periods, relating tasks to the surplus or deficit of requirements, and clarifying the distinction (as in 'deterrence theory') between the recognition of a reality ('a fact of life') and a theory.

Beyond one's self

MccGwire has been the human face of the organisations in which he has worked. He has done his own job – and more – but has also helped others to do theirs. The latter is neither done enough, nor praised enough, in academic life. Regrettably, what gains credit these days is (published) output, not (human) input. By temperament and training, throughout his career, MccGwire has been a great organiser, facilitator, creator of opportunities for people, bringer together of like-minded individuals, critic, energiser, mover and shaker, and a believer in getting people together to see if the sparks would fly. He is a generous person, who gives people ideas and *bon mots*; for him the spread of the idea is more important than its ownership. In these ways he has been much more influential than any public record would suggest. Such a person is not always easy to work with, nor live with, and in the latter regard the great silence in this account (hinted at earlier) is Helen, who dealt with the disruptions and professional risks, who tended the large family, and who has always provided an anchorage.

MccGwire's rich life has been, and continues to be, a journey of intellectual and personal hope. The actual life has been the text, as well as the work. Imagination, integrity and hope successively reinvented it. To reinvent the future of international security it will be necessary to reinvent its academic exponents from the coopted individuals who served selfish national interests and profit-seeking defence industries in the Cold War, and their equivalents today. This is not impossible; this chapter has shown, literally in one life, the growth of a consciousness from national to global security.

Beyond the moment

For MccGwire the future has always had priority. This requires imagination as an analyst and confidence as an individual; but it also requires pragmatism as a policy advocate, since change in the short run is only possible within political bounds. From an early age MccGwire wanted to change the world, and still does. He has undoubtedly changed other people's worlds, and this is a necessary start to reinventing the future, for as Gandhi said: 'We must be the change we wish to see in the world.'

By tracing the work and thinking of Michael MccGwire – as a naval officer at the end of empire, within the British defence establishment at the height of the Cold War, as an academic during the years of détente, as a policy analyst in Washington during the New Cold War and the Gorbachev years, and in retirement as a thinker about global security – I hope that this chapter has given some ideas to those concerned about the future, and their own part in it. This story asks us to hold up a mirror to our own lives and work. It asks us whether we make use of whatever space we have to resist the dangerous or regressive common-sense of the day, whether we show a human face in the organisations in which we work, whether we energise the hopeful, and whether we grow through experience. It is only by more of us responding positively to such questions that societies will reinvent the future in ways that promise greater human security.

NOTES

1 A copy of the cover is found after the title page of Polmar (1974). The specific date the cover appeared is not given.
2 The ideas expressed in this section are those of the author and do not necessarily represent the views of any agency of the US Government.

REFERENCES

Collingwood, R. G. (1939) *An Autobiography* (London: Oxford University Press).
Dauber, Cori (1989) 'Validity Standards and the Strategic Debate', *Defense Analysis*, vol. 5(2), 115–28.
(1993) *Cold War Analytical Structures and the Post-Post War World* (Westport, CT: Praeger Press).
Enloe, Cynthia (1989) *Bananas, Beaches and Bases: Making Feminist Sense of International Politics* (London: Pandora).
Gray, Colin (1984) 'Warfighting for Deterrence', *Journal of Strategic Studies*, vol. 7(11), 5–27.

Herman, M. E. (1996) *Intelligence Power in Peace and War* (Cambridge: Cambridge University Press).

Herrick, Robert Waring (1968) *Soviet Naval Strategy: Fifty Years of Theory and Practice* (Annapolis, MD: United States Naval Institute).

Jervis, Robert (1984) *The Illogic of American Nuclear Strategy* (Ithaca, NY: Cornell University Press.

—— (1991) 'Strategic Intelligence and Effective Policy', in A. S. Farson, D. Stafford, and W. K. Wark (eds.), *Security and Intelligence in a Changing World* (London: Cass).

MccGwire, Michael (1976) 'Maritime Strategy and the Super-powers', in *Power at Sea: Part II: Super-Powers and Navies*, Papers from the IISS 17th Annual Conference, Adelphi Paper no. 123 (London: International Institute for Strategic Studies), pp. 15–24.

—— (1984) 'Dilemmas and Delusions of Deterrence', *World Policy Journal*, vol. 1(4), 745–68.

—— (1985–6) 'Deterrence: The Problem not the Solution', *International Affairs*, vol. 62(1).

—— (1987) *Military Objectives in Soviet Foreign Policy* (Washington, DC: The Brookings Institution).

—— (1988) 'A Mutual Security Regime for Europe', *International Affairs*, vol. 64(3), 361–79.

—— (1989) 'The New Challenge of Europe', in Armand Cleese and Thomas Schelling (eds.), *The Western Community and the Gorbachev Challenge* (Baden-Baden: Nomos Verlagsgessellschaft), pp. 283–303.

—— (1991) *Perestroika and Soviet National Security* (Washington, DC: The Brookings Institution).

—— (1994) 'Is There a Future for Nuclear Weapons?', *International Affairs*, vol. 70(2), 211–28.

—— (1995a) 'The Possibility of a Non-Nuclear World', *Brassey's Defence Yearbook 1995* (London: Brassey's).

—— (1995b) 'Eliminate or Marginalize?: Nuclear Weapons in US Foreign Policy, *The Brookings Review.*

MccGwire, Michael (ed.) (1973) *Soviet Naval Developments: Capability and Context* (New York: Praeger).

MccGwire, Michael, Ken Booth and John McDonnell (1975) *Soviet Naval Policy: Objectives and Constraints* (New York: Praeger).

MccGwire, Michael and John McDonnell (1977) *Soviet Naval Influence: Domestic and Foreign Dimensions* (New York: Praeger).

McLachlan, D. (1968) *Room 39* (London: Weidenfeld and Nicolson).

Midgley, Mary (1994) *The Ethical Primate. Humans, Freedom and Mortality* (London: Routledge).

Polmar, Norman (1974) *Gorshkov: A Modern Naval Strategist*, A Report Prepared for the Office of the Director, Defense Research and Engineering, Department of Defense (Falls Church, VA: Lulejian and Associates).

Quinlan, M. (1993) 'The Future of Nuclear Weapons: Policy for Western Possessors', *International Affairs*, vol. 69(3), 485–96.

Snyder, Jack (1988) 'Science and Sovietology', *World Politics*, vol. 40(2), 169–93.

Part 2

Post-Cold War: powers and policies

5   Can the United States lead the world?

John Steinbruner

Clearly the United States does lead the world in some major ways. It operates the largest single national economy and does so on relatively open terms that serve to engage other national economies as well. It provides a primary impulse for technical development in a variety of areas, some of which are transforming the basic circumstances of all human activity. It possesses a uniquely capable military establishment, the only one with full global reach and the only one able to perform the most advanced military missions. It maintains a highly diverse society that to some degree incorporates most of the world's cultural traditions and stimulates many of the world's popular aspirations. For these reasons the United States commands attention, inspires emulation, and incites reaction – all features of what is generally meant by the idea of leading.

But just as clearly the issue of world leadership goes beyond the obvious fact that the United States is inherently consequential. Leadership worthy of the name involves appropriate, explicitly formulated and successfully implemented intention. To lead the world under current circumstances, the United States would have to initiate a deliberate redesign of the international political order and would have to undertake the major innovations in policy and in institutionalised arrangements necessary to bring it about. The qualities necessary for such an exercise are not automatically conferred by size, prominence or even historical achievement. It is not yet evident whether the United States will be able to rise to the occasion.

Doubts on that point are justified by the difficulty the United States is having in emerging from the conceptual and institutional grip of the Cold War.[1] The end of that particular confrontation has been universally acknowledged and political rhetoric has been suitably adjusted, but the military posture developed to prosecute the Cold War has not been fundamentally altered. Nor has the supplemental legacy of economic division been entirely overcome. United States defence policy no longer designates a specific enemy but none the less continues preparations for large-scale war anywhere in the world on very short notice, as if there were a continuing strategic confrontation. The central elements of foreign policy remain subordinated to that familiar conception. The nature of the new strategic context has not yet been absorbed.

The difficulty is understandable in human terms. With the ending of the Cold War, the United States emerged, apparently triumphant, from what was for forty years the primary organising commitment of the national government. It spent in the course of that time the equivalent of over $11 trillion in today's currency creating and maintaining a military establishment that is now unquestionably the most capable in the world. The prevailing political consensus that was forged in the course of that effort is proud of the accomplishment and highly committed to preserving its most satisfying feature – the fact that extensive preparations for a full-scale war did not result in having to fight one. Predominant political opinion in the United States is inclined to view the new world situation from the traditional perspective of deterrence and containment and to react to it with variations of the same methods.

Were that to be the entire story, it would undoubtedly be a decisive impediment to the exercise of world leadership. But the pressure of events makes the indefinite continuation of established attitudes unlikely. It is reasonable to imagine that a radical shift in basic strategic circumstances will eventually call forth a commensurately dramatic redirection of policy. That possibility makes the question of US world leadership an interesting one.

The new strategic context

There are at least two fundamental developments at work whose combined implications are powerful enough to alter the basic conditions of international politics and to override entrenched political sentiment in the United States. They are respectively the ongoing revolution in information technology and an impending surge in the world population.

The revolution in information technology is already a familiar event in terms of its immediate manifestations even if its full implications are still obscure. Over the past two decades the inherent costs of performing the basic functions of storing, processing and long-range transmission of information have undergone precipitous declines. Though agreed measures of these cost declines have not been fully established, they clearly amount to several orders of magnitude – factors of a thousand to a million or more.[2] That appears to be the largest efficiency gain of any commodity in economic history, and the unfolding consequences are correspondingly strong. Highly facilitated information flows are stimulating a globalisation of economic activity and in fact the spontaneous formation of an integrated international economy. This process is also diffusing technology and is changing the basic circumstances of making military investments.

At the same time we are encountering an unprecedented surge of world population – the rapid rise associated with an exponential growth sequence before it reaches some natural or induced limit. The world population is projected to double by the middle of the next century, adding roughly a billion people per decade over the next five decades.[3] Ninety-five per cent of the increase will come in what are currently the poorest communities. Both the scale and the composition of this surge will have consequences powerful enough to affect, potentially even to dominate international politics.

Since the revolution in information technology and the population surge are well outside the bounds of any historical experience, it is prudent to assume that many important implications are yet to be discovered and that some major surprises are likely to be encountered. Nonetheless some central features of this new strategic environment are already apparent.

Economic performance will clearly be an objective of overriding priority. Unless the globalising economy successfully extends its reach to those people in the lower economic strata, where the population surge is occurring, then the coherence of many if not all political systems is likely to be in question and some would almost certainly be torn apart. The expansion of economic participation required to assure a favourable trend in standards of living implies that the global economic product will have to increase by a factor of five or more, including a probable tripling of energy and agricultural production. That in turn implies that massive investment programmes will have to be undertaken, bringing about large structural and technical shifts within virtually all national economies. It also implies an increasing sensitivity to the balances of material flows and to their environmental effects, a development likely to be of decisive importance in the more burdened regions and potentially so on a global scale as well.

The national governments subjected to these implications can expect to experience a diffusion of their own power; that is, the ability to determine the outcome of matters they care about. Information technology is enabling, probably in fact compelling, the decentralisation of many decision processes, thereby eroding the degree of control they can expect to exercise within their societies. It is simultaneously driving the global extension of basic economic activities thereby dispersing effective control into the international economy as a whole. In responding to new problems under new circumstances, national governments will almost certainly have to evolve far more effective and more consequential patterns of collaboration. This is the context in which leadership will have to be exercised.

The leading problems

It is not realistic to expect the United States or any other political entity to cope all at once with the full agenda posed by the ongoing transformation of the international order. The scope of effects is too large and the uncertainty too great to impose that expectation. The adjustment of policy and the working out of new political relationships will necessarily occur in dealing with a sequence of specific issues that serve to provide practical focus. That means that the processes of adjustment, like changes in weather, will be impossible to predict in determining detail very much in advance of when they occur. But, again like weather, we can anticipate what the main patterns will have to be.

Economic integration will be a sustained preoccupation as the information revolution works its inexorable effects. The powerfully entrenched instincts of national governments to preserve control over access to their economies and to manoeuvre for comparative advantage will have to give way to the design of common methods of managing a globally extended economy. In the leading sectors of that economy national identity is being eroded under the impulse of technical change and market logic. A series of compelling regulatory problems are being posed having to do with the control of dangerous products and materials, and these simply cannot be handled on a national or regional basis. In the trailing sectors of the international economy, the issues of distribution pose a common threat of monumental proportions. Again, economic participation will have to be extended to the population surge occurring at the base of the global economy if basic civil order is to be preserved, and it is difficult to imagine a global economy operating successfully without basic civil order. The obvious if poorly specified connection between economic performance and social order makes the absorption of labour a general international problem of major importance and requires labour intensive strategies of development that do not yet exist.

Overcoming the long isolation of the centrally planned economies in the former Soviet Union and in China is a particularly demanding part of this general economic agenda. This isolation was largely self-imposed, but it was also systematically reinforced during the Cold War by the industrial economies who were assertively led in that enterprise by the United States. An elaborate set of trade restrictions were constructed that have been mitigated but not entirely dismantled. The new situation requires not only the removal of these formal restrictions but their replacement with policies of assertive engagement to pull these economies out of their ingrained isolation.

Systematic cooperation among the major military establishments is also a necessary preoccupation, since that is the logical and indeed the only feasible way of reacting to the truly radical shifts that are occurring in the basic problems of security. Large-scale ground offensives designed to seize and hold territory – historically the primary focus of strategic calculation and of military investment – are no longer the dominant concern for the simple reason that in most important instances classic aggression of this sort is infeasibly expensive. With modern technology large offensive operations can be detected and disrupted in their initial stages, and even an initial success could not be sustained. Basically, in the new era political jurisdiction cannot be maintained by coercive means since that method is ruinously inefficient in economic terms.

Moreover, the traditional problem of massive aggression intended to acquire territory is being superseded as a security concern by capacity for long-range destruction. That presents itself in two forms – the ability to attack precisely defined targets and the ability to cause mass casualties in human populations. The potential to develop both of these capabilities is being proliferated by the inexorable diffusion of technology. Information technology is itself inherently internationalised, and its use is internationalising access to most other technologies as well. Many of the technologies that are relevant to advanced weapons applications are being developed in commercial markets for commercial application and general access to them cannot be denied as a practical matter. That means that advanced delivery system technology and most of the materials required to make weapons of mass destruction will be accessible to small states and substate organisations. That will not confer the ability to seize territory but it will propagate the potential for producing severe social and economic damage. Weapons of mass destruction and weapons of precision delivery share the characteristics that they are strategically meaningful in small numbers regardless of what the overall balance of military capability might be.

Finally, it is apparent that the primary political source of threat is no longer the impulse for imperial or irredentist expansion but rather the danger of internal disintegration. The globalising economy is producing rapid structural shifts in patterns of production and is stripping away the protective devices used by national governments to buffer their populations from the effects of these shifts. This process has imposed endemic austerity on some regions serious enough to undermine not only the authority of a particular political regime but also the entire legal structure on which it is based. In extreme instances of this process basic civil order can break down, and in those instances armed intimidation becomes the residual form of social organisation. Disintegration of this sort has recently occurred in a sufficient number of places to suggest that a general pattern may be emerging. Against the background of the impending population surge that constitutes a sharp warning.

The major tasks

The basic problems of economic integration and military stabilisation present at least two immediate tasks that the United States or any other aspiring world leader would have to undertake with a fair degree of urgency. These are respectively the creation of an international security arrangement for Russia and the development of an effective international operation for restoring legal order in instances where it has radically broken down. There is in addition a third task that is also urgent but somewhat less immediately pressing; namely, the redesign of arrangements for controlling proliferation.[4]

Russia

Russia is unavoidably the central problem of military stabilisation. Russia has inherited the core of the Soviet military establishment, including provisionally and hopefully all of its nuclear weapons. It faces the problem of relocating and redesigning its military deployments to defend its new territorial configuration. It must undertake that effort while undergoing a massive transformation of its economy, its political system, and indeed of its entire society. The Russian military establishment cannot be expected to handle the security burdens this situation creates without receiving much more substantial reassurance from the international community than has yet been contemplated.

At the moment the Russian military planning system aspires to preserve a military establishment of more than 1.5 million people. This is the minimum deemed necessary to preserve core nuclear deterrence, to protect against an imaginable conventional ground attack in the Far East and tactical air assaults from the West, and also to cope with flaring episodes of civil violence along their southern border. Though these images of potential threat may appear unlikely to the rest of the world, in the traditional logic of military planning they are at least as plausible as the ones the United States is currently using to set standards for its military deployments. So are the force structure conclusions derived from them.

Those conclusions, however, are wildly unrealistic in economic terms. Russia would have to spend nearly $100 billion per year to sustain a 1.5 million person establishment even if it could produce comparable equipment at half the cost the United States experiences. As prices in the Russian economy adjust to world standards, the full financial requirements of the planned military establishment would exceed $200 billion. The officially enacted defence budget of 40 trillion rubles, nominally comparable to $20 billion at the time it was approved, is not considered to be a full accounting of all that the Russian economy actually spends on defence. But whatever the true amount is, it almost certainly falls well below the minimum sustaining requirement. Defence spending increases to meet the full requirement are highly unlikely. Such an allocation would not only threaten the process of economic regeneration but also require a degree of coercive political recentralisation that probably has become infeasible but at any rate would be self-defeating. The inevitable world reaction would require yet more unrealistic levels of military preparedness.

That situation poses the most serious international security problem at the moment. If indefinitely continued, sustained underfinancing of the Russian military establishment will assuredly cause its internal deterioration, and there are a series of very grave consequences that could readily result – the loss of control over large weapons inventories and a destructive interaction with the process of political reform foremost among them. The disintegration of Yugoslavia has provided a chilling hint of what could happen. If that large set of risks is to be avoided, however, the Russian establishment will probably have to be cut to less than half of the current planning aspiration in order to preserve its internal coherence. That in turn requires some very systematic arrangements to provide reassurance. A coherently planned reduction will not be undertaken if those who are doing it believe the consequence is indefinite exposure to unmanageable external threat.

Systematic reassurance of this sort that Russia requires is not an adversarial process and in that sense it is fundamentally different from the traditional practice of arms control which was designed to constrain a continuing confrontation. The applicable measures are similar, however. Their basic purpose is to relieve military pressure and to convey confidence in legitimate security requirements. That is accomplished by holding force deployments below the levels necessary to stage overwhelming offensive operations and by introducing transparency rules and standards for force operations that preclude any surprise attack. As long as these deployment standards and operating rules were maintained, the participating military organisations would be able to determine with fair certainty that they do not face any immediate prospect of a major engagement and that they would have a reasonable period of warning before such a circumstance could arise. The primary financial burden that the major military establishments acquired during the Cold War was due to their commitment to prepare for large conventional force operations on short notice.

In the Russian case there are four specific measures of reassurance that would be important. First, a substantially smaller Russian military establishment with some 500,000 to 700,000 people would have to acknowledge that it could not immediately block a ground incursion into Siberia by unconstrained Chinese military forces. With adequate financing a smaller Russian force might well have more actual capability than the current one does, but it could not aspire to complete self-sufficiency. Hence China would have to be an integral participant in establishing measures of systematic reassurance. Second, at whatever overall level of deployment, the Russian air defence system is not likely to be able to handle the sophisticated air incursions that Western countries are technically capable of mounting – a matter of particular historical sensitivity. Measures of reassurance would involve full integration into the military air traffic control arrangements for Western Europe. That would give them access to the most advanced technology and would prevent air incursions from being prepared without their knowledge. Third, for reasons of operational safety, the nuclear weapons component of a smaller Russian establishment should be relieved of the burden of maintaining a rapid reaction deterrent capability, that is, the capacity to initiate full-scale retaliation in response to tactical warning. Fully adequate and inherently safer deterrent postures can be designed that are operationally and financially less draining, but they must be jointly implemented and do necessarily involve cooperative surveillance and warning arrangements. Fourth, at whatever size, the Russian military establishment cannot be left with the full burden of dealing with civil violence in former Soviet republics, just as no single national military establishment or even regional organisation can be expected to handle this type of problem. This issue in particular requires substantial elaboration of international security collaboration.

Defence of legal order

Over its first five years, at least, the massive reordering that began within the former Soviet bloc in 1989 has been much more peaceful than most people would have imagined for societal changes of such sweeping proportions. Moreover, the ending of the global ideological competition that defined the Cold War has terminated many of the regional conflicts associated with it. The common perception of the new era, however, is hardly that of benign transformation. The phenomenon of the collapsed state has emerged as the source of a particularly troublesome form of violence.

Whether the phenomenon itself is new or merely the context in which it is occurring, radical disintegration of political authority within a nominally sovereign state has recently progressed in several instances to the point that fundamental legal order could not be maintained. When that occurs, normal commerce and consensual politics cease as well. Criminal gangs and irregular militia spontaneously emerge as the residual form of social organisation, and they sustain themselves by plundering those outside their scope of allegiance. Since their span of control is limited, the victims are bound to be neighbours, identified by whatever ethnic or cultural distinction is well enough defined to be practical. With no means of protection the victims are vulnerable to virtually all forms of depravation, and the progressive decay of all human standards sets in. Bosnia, Rwanda and Somalia have been especially prominent but not unique instances of this process.

During the course of the Cold War the opposing alliance systems acted to contain incipient instances of political disintegration within their respective jurisdictions in defence of what they considered to be critical strategic interest. In doing so, both sides acquired hard lessons regarding the difficulties of intervention. The strategic rationale has departed with the Cold War, but the hard lessons are well remembered. Neither the United States nor any other major power is inclined to undertake an assertive intervention to preserve civil order – not in the early stages of deterioration when it is most feasible; certainly not in the later stages of full disintegration when it becomes most urgent. This attitude is in fact so well established in the United States that on the basis of current domestic opinion one might proclaim a doctrine of disengagement.

Such a doctrine could not be sustained, however, by the international community as a whole. The instances of radical political disintegration are potentially numerous enough and sufficiently acute to compel eventually a systematic defence of legal order. Otherwise the flow of refugees from victimised populations, the stimulus provided for illegal organisations, and the destructive precedent being set will propel the virus of disintegration well beyond the immediate cases. If left unattended, the process is capable of threatening legal order generally.

The requirements of an assertive defence are substantial. A new rationale for intervention would have to be established that both qualifies the traditional rights of sovereignty and limits the qualification. Presumably that would be based on the preservation of human rights so fundamental that the systematic and extensive denial of those rights would constitute a forfeiture of sovereignty by the state involved and an obligation for the international community to establish basic protection. The principle itself is obviously difficult; the measurements and judgements required to apply it even more so. Such a doctrine would have to be developed, legitimised and enforced by a comprehensive coalition, fairly representing the international community as a whole. It could not be undertaken by any single country or regional grouping. Moreover, the enforcement operations would have to be of very sophisticated design jointly undertaken by the sponsoring coalition – not the sort of thing that can be improvised quickly from standard military operations in response to sensational atrocities.

The doctrine, the coalition and the enforcement operations for circumstances of radical political disintegration cannot be subsumed under the traditional practice of deterring and defeating a wilful aggressor. All three require significant innovation and lengthy preparation. A policy development of that scope simply could not be accomplished without a leading initiative from the United States which possesses in the wake of the Cold War the predominant military establishment. The official US annual defence budget is five times larger than that of any other single country's and is comparably larger than the combined budgets of all the non-allied countries bordering the regions of conflict. The combined official defence budgets of Russia, China, Iran, Iraq, Syria, Libya, India and North Korea, for example, are about 20 per cent of the United States budget. Even accepting that Russia and China in particular spend substantially more on defence than is accounted for in their official defence budget, United States defence expenditures more than double the combined total of these countries.[5] As a consequence of this disparity, the United States has the only establishment in position to project military power on a global basis and the only one able to undertake some of the most advanced military operations. It sets the international standard and its capacities would be indispensable for any collaborative operation of significant scale. The magnitude of its capability imposes unavoidable involvement and corresponding responsibility for leadership.

Management of materials and technologies

The global extension of the international economy and its necessary expansion in scale will assuredly pose problems of management and regulation that have never before been encountered. The remarkable progression of science, clearly vital to meeting the necessary standards of economic performance, is also creating products and materials that inherently require much more systematic monitoring and management than has been the historic practice. More than 1,200 metric tons of plutonium has been created, for example, in the course of making nuclear weapons and operating nuclear power reactors, and it continues to accrue at the rate of 70 metric tons per year. In addition to its explosive properties, it is one of the most toxic substances known. Unless disposed of by some method yet to be established, it will remain extremely dangerous for hundreds of thousands of years. The security, accounting and storage procedures established so far are not remotely adequate to handle safely the global extension of this substance, and there are many others that pose different but highly burdensome problems.

The traditional method of controlling dangerous substances is to license use and access. Bureaucratic approval, in other words, is to be imposed and those without it are to be denied access. That method, however, is essentially hopeless in a globalising economy that is inexorably diffusing basic access to materials and technology. There is no central bureaucracy with the competence to impose this form of control, and it is quite apparent that none will be created. Even if that were feasible in principle, which it probably is not, virtually everyone can appreciate that such a cure is likely to be intolerable however serious the disease.

Fortunately, the radical advance of information technology, involving the full spectrum of capability from sensing to storage to processing to long-range communication, is enabling a different method of regulation based on systematic rules for disclosure and monitoring.[6] In principle, sensitive materials and products of all sorts can be labelled and tracked throughout their entire life cycle if there is systematic agreement to do so. Thus the maker of a weapon, for example, or any product with environmentally sensitive materials would have to label and register it at the point of production and would similarly have to record any sales transaction or other disposition. There would be criminal sanctions for evasion or misrepresentation but otherwise legitimate trade could proceed without prior approval. If that is done routinely and automatically, strong incentives for self-regulation can be created and the organised, bureaucratic form of it can be concentrated on instances of violation with a far better chance of detecting them and reacting to them than the current system of regulation allows. Moreover the data that would be generated by such a system would provide at least part of what is required to understand the various human and environmental interactions that the globalising economy is producing.

Despite inherent need and basic technical feasibility, a systematic disclosure and monitoring arrangement of this sort is very far from international consciousness at the moment, and there are critical problems of policy that would have to be solved to produce a practical arrangement. Largely these have to do with rules for access and use of the resulting information. The instincts of national governments for controlling information for their own purposes and for conducting adversarial intelligence operations are deeply ingrained, and they will be predictably very slow to accept the imperatives for a comprehensive collaborative process. Probably a fair amount of unhappy experience will have to be absorbed before the basic idea is taken seriously enough to develop it. Nonetheless this development is a predictably looming task of world leadership.

The record so far

A generous judge might conclude that in the initial stages of the new era the United States has displayed some appropriate instincts while still remaining well short of understanding or accepting its ultimate requirements. That assessment is hardly reason for satisfaction; but, for those independently inclined to do so, it does give some basis for making an optimistic projection. As usual, it is easier to be pessimistic on the basis of the record so far.

The optimistic case can best be made by reference to the promotion of open trade arrangements. In pursuing NAFTA and the GATT agreement and even in bilateral trade talks with Japan, the United States has generally defended the international extension of economic activity and has more or less restrained its own domestic political pressures for protection. Similarly it has led its more reluctant G7 and NATO partners into tentative forms of engagement with Russia. The policies developed so far do not have the scope or impulse or even yet the full character of those that are ultimately required for the new circumstances, but at least they are steps in a promising direction.

On the matter of regulating proliferation and environmental consequence the optimistic case is much weaker. Some appropriate rhetoric can be cited but very little that counts as serious commitment.

On the defence of legal order it is difficult to be even that positive on balance. The actions taken in Bosnia, Somalia and Rwanda were clearly designed to limit involvement rather than to master those situations and the lessons so far extracted have reinforced the initial reluctance. Like the rest of the world the United States is still seeking to avoid responsibility.

But at the moment it is simply too early to answer the question. World leadership is certainly necessary, and necessity is supposedly the mother of invention. If one speaks of the culture of the United States as distinct from the government, it is certainly quite inventive. Someone must be the father in this situation, and the United States as a whole is better positioned than any other society. For whatever it is worth, as a member of that society, I believe that it will eventually rise to the occasion and that the real question is how much grief will have to be absorbed before it chooses to do so.

NOTES

1 Parts of the text that follows have been adapted from Steinbruner (1995).
2 For a rough indication of the trend see Moravec (1988), pp. 61–2.
3 This corresponds to the medium projections issued by the United Nations, McNicoll (1992) and by the World Bank, Bos and Bulatao (1992). The projections count on the continuation of a declining trend in fertility rate currently being observed in much of the world. Particularly rapid fertility rate declines might plausibly hold the population surge to the low UN projection – an 8 billion peak in 2025 with a gradual reduction thereafter back to the current 5 billion level, Seckler and Cox (1994). There is also uncertainty on the high side, however.
4 This agenda is outlined in Carter *et al.* (1992) and in Nolan (ed.) (1994).
5 The official budget figures are those reported by the International Institute for Strategic Studies, 1994 except that the official Russian figure is used instead of their purchasing power parity estimate. The latter estimate raises the Russian figure to nearly $80 billion, and it is generally believed that China's defence expenditure, nominally reported as $6 billion per year, actually falls in the range of $30 to $40 billion per year. Using these larger estimates the combined total for the set of countries listed is still less than half of the United States' annual expenditure.
6 The design of a regulatory arrangement based on systematic disclosure rules is discussed by W. Reinicke, 'Cooperative Security and the Political Economy of Nonproliferation' in Nolan (1994).

REFERENCES

Bos, Eduard and Rodolfo A. Bulatao (1990) 'Projecting Fertility for All Countries', Working Paper of the Population and Human Resources Department of the World Bank (Washington).

Carter, Ashton, William Perry and John Steinbruner (1992) *A New Concept of Cooperative Security* (Washington, DC: The Brookings Institution).

International Institute for Strategic Studies (1994) *The Military Balance 1994–1995* (London: Brassey's).

McNicoll, Geoffrey (1992) 'The United Nations' Long-Range Population Projections', *Population and Development Review*.

Moravec, Hans (1988) *Mind Children* (Cambridge, MA: Harvard University Press).

Nolan, Janne (ed.) (1994) *Global Engagement: Cooperation and Security in the 21st Century* (Washington, DC: The Brookings Institution).

Reinicke, Wolfgang (1994) 'Cooperative Security and the Political Economy of Nonproliferation', in Janne Nolan (ed.), *Global Engagement: Cooperation and Security in the 21st Century* (Washington, DC: The Brookings Institution).

Seckler, David and Gerald Cox (1994) 'Fertility Rates and Population Projections: Why the United Nations Low Population Projection is Best', Center for Economic Policy Studies Discussion Papers (Arlington, VA: Winrock International Institute for Agricultural Development).

Steinbruner, John (1994) 'United States Security Relationship with Russia', in hearing before the United States House of Representatives, Armed Services Committee, 103rd Congress, 2nd session (Washington, DC: Government Printing Office), 17 Mar.

(1995) 'The Strategic Implications of Emerging International Security Conditions', presented to the Conference on American–Israeli Relations and the New World Order (The Hebrew University of Jerusalem).

6   Can Russia escape its past?

Oles M. Smolansky

Geography and history

In contrast with the maritime powers of the West, Russia before Peter the Great was essentially a land-locked state. Access to the Baltic Sea was blocked by Sweden and to the Black Sea by the Ottoman empire. Hence, the Muscovite urge to expand had to be directed eastward. After the defeat of the Mongols in the fifteenth century, Russia's *Drang nach Osten* resulted in the annexation of the vast Siberian landmass, taking Russian settlers to the shores of the Pacific Ocean. In the process, Russia established a contiguous land empire which, in its communist incarnation, outlasted its Western counterparts.

The advent of Peter the Great (1696–1725) marked the dawn of a new era in Russian history. Not content with Moscow's preoccupation with Asia, Peter was determined to Westernise his country by transforming Russian society and by removing the physical obstacles – Sweden and the Ottoman empire – which had barred Russia's access to the maritime routes to the West. In defeating Sweden, Peter opened the Baltic Sea to Russian commerce. The job of establishing Russia as a Black Sea power was completed by Catherine the Great (1763–96).

Expansion to the east and the south continued during the nineteenth century with the result that, by the time the communists gained power in 1917, the Russian empire covered a vast area, stretching from Eastern Europe and the Transcaucasus to Central Asia and the Far East. In the process, Russia had conquered territory from the Ottoman and Persian empires, had overrun the independent khanates of Central Asia, and had annexed a large portion of Chinese territory. As a result, Russia/USSR became a multinational empire inhabited by over 100 ethnic groups which belong to some 10 distinct language groups, many Christian denominations, the Sunni and Shia branches of Islam, as well as some Eastern religions.

Geography has conditioned the behaviour of the Russian rulers in other ways as well. During the nineteenth century, St Petersburg had worked hard, but without success, to gain control of the Turkish Straits.* Initially, the communist regime renounced such imperial ambitions but, in 1944–5, Stalin requested Western permission to establish Soviet bases in the Straits area. He was unceremoniously turned down. Similarly, since the late nineteenth century, Russia had coveted the ice-free ports situated in southern Manchuria. In 1945, Stalin demanded access to them as part of the reward for the Soviet entry into the war against Japan. On that occasion, Washington acquiesced. However, after Mao Zedong's victory in 1949, Stalin returned the ports to China. It is instructive that in both instances geography had prevailed over communist ideology. Some twenty-five years after the Bolshevik leaders had denounced the 'imperialist avarice' of the tsars, Stalin concluded that control of the Straits and of the Manchurian ports – let alone of the Baltics and the rest of Eastern Europe – was, after all, vital to the security of the USSR. At that juncture, Stalin's thinking, now influenced by geopolitics rather than ideology, paralleled that of his imperial predecessors.

It is equally important to note, however, that geographic requirements are not immutable and that their importance is subject to change. For example, Stalin did return the Manchurian ports to China and, after 1945, did not raise the issue of the Straits. In these instances, his behaviour can be explained in terms of political as well as technological considerations. Specifically, it made no sense to maintain Soviet forces on the territory of communist China against Mao's expressed wishes. Similarly, no Soviet government could rationally contemplate seizing territory from a country protected by the Western alliance. Subsequently, technological advances, including the advent of nuclear weapons and delivery systems, significantly decreased the military-strategic importance of the Turkish Straits.

Returning to history, in the process of building an empire, the Russians acquired vast stretches of territory, inhabited by both Slavic (Belorussians, Ukrainians) and non-Slavic populations. In an attempt to control them, the Russians followed neither the British nor the French colonial models but developed their own approach. Before 1917, the policy of Russification was conducted mainly in the Slavic areas. In the other regions, particularly in those inhabited by the Muslims, the local population enjoyed considerable religious, cultural and linguistic freedom. However, everywhere it was clearly understood that advancement was possible only through service to the empire. The advent of communism

---

* In this context, 'control' is defined as ability to determine as to who will and who will not be able to use a strategic location for his own purposes. Such ability can be acquired either by means of occupation or by suitable international arrangements.

brought with it Stalin's dictum that national minorities were free to develop their respective cultures provided the latter were 'Bolshevik in content'. For this reason, 'bourgeois nationalism' (interpreted as a drive to establish independent states) was ruthlessly persecuted throughout the entire existence of the USSR.

Some of these same issues have been inherited by the Russian Federation (RF) since the collapse of the Soviet Union. For instance, the problem of how to deal with nationalism of the non-Russian minorities within the Federation and in the newly independent states along Russia's rim is a highly relevant issue which is bound to affect the future of Russia and of the other former Soviet republics. Specifically, like its imperial and communist predecessors, the RF embraces dozens of non-Slavic and non-Orthodox nationalities, some of which – notably Chechnya – are trying to wrest autonomy, if not outright independence, from Moscow. And beyond its borders, the Kremlin must determine how to treat the former Soviet republics, or what is called the 'near abroad'. The Baltic states (Lithuania, Latvia, Estonia) have regained political independence; however, they are destined to live in Russia's shadow and will, for a long time, remain bound to it economically. Of the rest, Belarus has shown particular interest in reestablishing political and economic union with Russia. Others, like Ukraine, Kazakhstan, Turkmenistan and Azerbaijan have jealously guarded their independence, while Armenia and Tajikistan, engaged in major conflicts, have depended on Russia for survival and have, therefore, opted for close military, political and economic cooperation with Moscow. Georgia, because of the Abkhazian conflict, agreed to the reintroduction of Russian troops to its territory, while the other republics have displayed varying degrees of interest in the Russian connection.

Political culture

The November 1917 revolution swept away the empire and brought to power Russia's Communist Party, headed by Lenin. Generally speaking, however, no matter how effective the demolition of the old order might be, no revolution has ever succeeded in totally eradicating the cultural vestiges of the past. Rather, with the passage of time, old values interact with the revolutionary culture and either subvert it or, at least, leave a distinct imprint on it.

In retrospect, it would appear that the 1917 revolution never completely destroyed 'old Russia'. One striking parallel between the tsarist and Soviet political culture was the survival of the authoritarian form of government. Barghoorn defined authoritarianism as a political system in which the power of the state was concentrated in the hands of the chief executive and the policies decreed from above were implemented by 'a centralised hierarchy of bureaucrats'. The system of checks and balances, characteristic of the democratic form of government, either did not exist or was ineffective (Barghoorn and Remington, 1986: 2). On all of these counts, the Soviet political system closely resembled that of Imperial Russia.

The history of the Russian Orthodox Church provides another example of the continuity of the country's political traditions. An important and relatively independent institution in Muscovite Russia, the church was placed under government control by Peter the Great. Outlawed by the communists, it was resurrected by Stalin in 1942 to help awaken the will of the embittered Soviet populace to resist the Nazi attack. In a close parallel to its fate under the empire, the church became an obedient servant of the Soviet state. In the 1990s, the religious establishment has taken tentative steps to assert itself against governmental authority. Nevertheless, the church remains subordinated to the government which finances many of its religious activities.

In 1881, in a reaction to the spreading revolutionary zeal among Russia's youth, Alexander III promulgated rule by emergency decree. It required police permission to establish newspapers and to have access to library books. It also conferred upon the authorities the right to conduct surveillance over politically suspect individuals. Adopted and perfected under the Soviet regime, these measures have, for the time being, disappeared from the current Russian political scene.

To carry out political repression, Imperial Russia created a secret police apparatus, Okhrana, which grew considerably in the late nineteenth and early twentieth centuries in response to the intensifying revolutionary activity of the disaffected segments of the population. However, these tsarist efforts fade into insignificance in comparison with the extent and the quality of repression introduced by the communists. While the revolutionary Cheka conducted extermination of the Russian upper classes, Stalin's GPU/NKVD organised mass terror of truly staggering proportions. In the post-Stalin period, the CPSU refrained from using mass terror. Nevertheless, the KGB remained a feared and efficient organisation which hunted down suspected political dissidents. Since political dissent is sanctioned in the RF, the involvement of the secret police in politics has been greatly reduced.

Another aspect of the Russian political culture which flourished during the Soviet period was 'the existence ... of bureaucracies answerable to powerful chief executives'. Lenin's early egalitarianism proved unworkable and, by the late 1920s, the communist bureaucrats enjoyed special privileges that were denied to ordinary citizens: higher salaries, better housing, special stores and others (Barghoorn and Remington, 1986: 13–14). The *nomenklatura*, the Soviet equivalent of Peter the Great's 'Table of Ranks', has survived the collapse of the USSR. This is not surprising because, to govern Russia, its current leaders, who themselves are former CPSU and government functionaries, need the services of qualified middle and lower level bureaucrats, members of the armed forces, secret police and diplomatic establishments, and managers of various enterprises. To win and keep their allegiance, the leaders – who themselves have long been beneficiaries of the traditional reward system – encourage the retention of the old benefit structure.

Parallel to the perks runs the practice of corruption among public officials. Endemic in tsarist Russia, it decreased in the early Soviet period, increased sharply after Stalin's death, and has become rampant in the 1990s. Indeed, it has now reached astronomic proportions, as evidenced, in part, by the deposits of tens of billions of dollars by various officials in Western bank accounts.

Finally, nationalism emerged as a powerful motivating factor in Russia's foreign and domestic affairs in the nineteenth century. Supplanted by 'communist internationalism', Russian nationalism re-emerged triumphantly during the Second World War, when Stalin, who, despite his humble Georgian origin, was a Great Russian chauvinist at heart, resurrected it, along with the Orthodox Church, as a means of combating Nazi Germany. Russian nationalism subsided after Stalin's death but has made a strong comeback since the collapse of the USSR.

In sum, its 'Russian' origins played an important part in the Soviet political culture. Russia's geography and history combined to foster the growth of an authoritarian form of government which, in the twentieth century, fused with the Marxist notion of the 'dictatorship of the proletariat', to produce one of the most brutal regimes in the history of mankind. With the dissolution of the USSR, the influence of these traditional factors on Russia's political culture is very much in evidence today.

Politics

Since the political system of the Russian Federation is still in its infancy, it is difficult to predict how and in which direction it is going to evolve. Optimists believe that a full-blown democratic system in Russia is but a question of time. Pessimists argue the opposite, pointing out that, given the country's political traditions, a return to an authoritarian system is a more likely outcome of the present tribulations.

Neither course is historically preordained or inevitable. What history does suggest is that the Western models of democracy have no significant roots in Russia's political culture. The existence of an independent judiciary is virtually without precedent; the legislature, after the ascendancy of the Muscovite state, has been either non-existent or under tight executive control; and the executive power – often unlimited – has essentially resided in the person of the tsar/emperor or the general secretary of the CPSU. Constitutions, if any, merely sanctified the existing order. Nevertheless, in the post-Soviet period, a new constitution has been framed and adopted, providing for a strong presidency but also for an independent legislature and a judiciary. The former has been elected and has begun to assert itself against the executive branch, while the Constitutional Court, due to legislative indecision, is yet to be set up. Independent political parties of various persuasions exist and have competed against each other in democratically contested elections. In short, the seeds for the development of a new political system appear to have been planted.

Whether the democratic institutions in Russia will have the opportunity to develop depends on many factors. Among them are: the willingness of the head of the executive branch to nourish the democratic system by enabling the other branches of government to develop free of executive *diktat*; the ability of the government to improve Russia's economic performance, thus foreclosing the possibility of mass upheavals caused by economic hardships; relative political stability, including non-interference by the military in the country's politics; and the supportive attitude of the industrial West. Since the success of the democratic experiment hinges on so many variables – some of them intangible – the pessimists, as noted, have argued that a reversion to authoritarianism is only a question of time. They list the success of Vladimir Zhirinovskii's misnamed Liberal-Democratic party and of the communists in the December 1993 elections in support of their contention.

The assumption that a return to authoritarianism is inevitable is open to question. It is true that the Russian electorate is deeply disenchanted with Yeltsin and his policies. On the crucially important economic scene, little progress had been made by the liberal reformers, who initially enjoyed Yeltsin's full support. Their place has now been taken by the old Soviet managers and technocrats, headed by Premier Chernomyrdin, who advocate a more measured pace of market reform. But neither group has done well, as attested to by the steadily declining production rates, growing unemployment and inflation. These problems have been magnified by the financial plight of the intelligentsia and of individuals on fixed incomes, by the spread of corruption, and by the rise of organised crime. In the sphere of foreign relations, too, many Russians have been disturbed by what they perceive as Yeltsin's lack of assertiveness. Many resent the fact that their country has been reduced to the status of a second-rate, albeit nuclear, power whose interests are routinely disregarded by the West.

Nevertheless, in this writer's opinion, Zhirinovskii's popularity rests on a fragile foundation. That is to say, in demonstrating their displeasure with Yeltsin and in casting their votes for the extremists of the right and the left, the voters delivered a powerful message which has been received not only in the Kremlin but also in the West. However, to assume on the basis of this evidence that someone like Zhirinovskii has a chance of being elected president is to miss the mark. The Russian electorate is sufficiently discriminating to understand that it is one thing to use this posturing buffoon to make a point with Yeltsin but an entirely different matter to elect him president of Russia. Moreover, it should be borne in mind that Zhirinovskii's success may yet prove to be his political undoing. The Liberal-Democratic party, an important faction in the new Russian parliament, has not been able to translate its victory into any tangible gains for the disaffected electorate. In this sense, many Russian voters now view the Liberal-Democrats as an integral part of an ineffective establishment.

The communists, at the other extreme, are a different matter. Still, most Russians understand that a return to Soviet style, one party rule is not feasible. Hence, most communist parties in the former USSR and in Eastern Europe have adopted a 'democratic approach' to politics and are content to function in a multiparty setting. 'Reform communists' have returned to power in freely held elections in Poland, Hungary and Lithuania and, other things being equal, could do so in Russia as well. The surge in popularity of Communist Party leader Gennady Zyuganov in the mid-1990s reflected the strength of nostalgia for aspects of the Soviet past in some sectors of opinion. But even if the new communists were ever to come to power, they would promote policies that would have been unthinkable during the Soviet period.

For the rest of the 1990s there will be a jockeying for position to replace the ailing Yeltsin. Will the successor be some as yet relatively unknown figure standing in the wings? Will it be the populist General Lebed, of Afghanistan and Chechnya fame? Or might it still be Alexandr Rutskoi and his 'irreconcilables', strong on nationalism and the reunification of the ex-Soviet space, but with no workable programme for the economy? It will be a political struggle of great intensity and importance, and with implications far beyond Russia. For the moment the main point is that work to establish a democratic form of government in Russia has begun, and if the state of the economy permits, these efforts should in time produce a society governed by laws.

Economy and the social order

The monumental changes that have occurred in the former USSR and Eastern Europe since 1989 caught Western experts by surprise. In retrospect, most now agree that the collapse of the Soviet Union was precipitated by the campaign to restructure the Soviet economy. Initiated by Andropov in 1982, perestroika gathered full steam under Gorbachev in the latter half of the 1980s. Several reasons are usually cited to explain the decision to launch the economic reform movement. One was the wasteful economic system which, for over seventy years, paid no attention to world market prices and which, during the 1970s and 1980s, squandered over $150 billion, earned from the foreign sales of fuel on imports of food, feed and consumer goods. Another was the failure to join the 'high tech' revolution which had occurred in the West in the 1970s. Yet another complicating factor was the existence in the USSR of an unwritten social contract. Introduced with Stalin's industrialisation programme in the late 1920s, it provided for full employment and price stability. In exchange, the Soviet public had to put up with shortages of consumer goods and housing, free but often inferior medical care, and a highly repressive police state.

Perestroika did not resolve any of these major problems. Hence, the question of Russia's future economic well-being depends on the Kremlin's willingness and ability to restructure the entire society inherited from the Soviet Union. Put differently, to achieve economic prosperity, Russia will have to re-make its societal structure (or social order), meaning the political, economic and juridical-institutional arrangements of the old USSR. In the context of the *political* dimension of the social order, Russia, as noted, has taken the initial step by dismantling the monopoly power structure of the former Communist Party. In the process, the direct influence of the CPSU on the society was formally eliminated, but its indirect impact is still very much in evidence. This phenomenon is explained by the fact that, even after the dissolution of the USSR, many former communists, as noted, continue to occupy prominent positions in the high echelons of the military and secret police establishments, as well as in the administrative and managerial bureaucracy. The influence which they continue to wield is bound to hamper the efforts to restructure Russian society.

Turning to the *economic* dimension of Russia's social order, it will be recalled that, in 1929, the USSR introduced what is known as quantitative-output planning. All prices, wages, rents and foreign exchange were subject to different forms of rationing devices, designed to enable the state to cope with the existing shortages. Industrial firms were given yearly output plans, cast in terms of weight or rubles, while the collective farms had mandatory delivery plans and fixed prices for their production.

The shift from quantitative-output planning to a market economy will not be easy. The right-wing elements as well as the 'Eurasians', who resent Russia's close cooperation with the West, have little use for Western economic ideas. Moreover, the managers of the former Soviet enterprises are quite comfortable with the system in which nearly a quarter of the entire output finds its way into the 'underground economy'. Finally, the newly established mafias, too, prefer the old, corrupt system because it is easier to penetrate and manipulate.

The third dimension of Russia's social order refers to the country's *institutional* arrangements. Unlike the Soviet societal structure, where privately owned means of production were taboo, the new order will presumably be built on the privatisation of land and of the industrial and trade sectors. Russia will also have to create new privately owned commercial banks, which will finance the activities of genuine entrepreneurs, as well as stock and commodity exchanges. These measures, if implemented, will help expand the private sector of the economy.

In addition to the privatisation process, Russia will have to pass and enforce pertinent legislation. As the country gradually moves towards a market economy, the prevailing uncertainty with respect to the legal foundations of private entrepreneurship has wrought havoc. As a result, genuine privatisation has often been replaced by *prikhvatization*[*] which is nothing but legalised theft. And it is for this reason that 'shock therapy' (big or small) has failed to move Russia into a market-type economy.

Neither has the RF been able to bring order to its monetary reform. The present situation is marked by coexistence of open and repressed inflation. The former is the order of the day and the ratio of government debt to the Gross Domestic Product is enormous. The authorities fear that failure to support large government-owned enterprises will lead to massive unemployment and civil disorders. Yet, while the uncertainty continues and the freshly printed ruble notes keep these enterprises afloat, industrial production is on the decline, as Russia continues to utilise its antiquated 'assembly-line' technology. To complicate matters

---

[*] From the Russian verb *prikhvatit'*, meaning 'to grab'.

further, as the volume of output has declined, unit costs have risen sharply.

It may well be that Russia's industrial sector will have to go bankrupt in order to enter the 'high tech' age. However, to emerge in these circumstances, the Schumpeterian innovator will have to be given certainty of the law with respect to property rights, easy access to credit in genuine commercial banks, and a guarantee of freedom from punitive taxation by either the government or the mafia. As of this writing, the introduction of many of these reforms is not yet in sight.

Nevertheless, one cannot be entirely pessimistic about Russia's longer-term economic prospects. It possesses enormous wealth in the form of natural resources and of a well-educated labour force, capable of transplanting advanced 'high tech' manufacturing methods to Russia. And, as Gerschenkron once wrote, technological backwardness can be overcome by means of a 'quantum leap'. However, the problem, historically as well as now, is that Russia's industrialisation programmes have been carried out not by private entrepreneurs but by the government. The circumstances described above make it virtually certain that the authorities – rather than private individuals – will dictate the extent and the tempo of the reforms. Their record does not inspire undue optimism.

Foreign policy

According to the pronouncements emanating from Moscow, the new Russia has welcomed the dissolution of the USSR and has expressed support for the independence and territorial integrity of the former Soviet republics. At the same time, the Kremlin has made clear its determination to remain involved in the affairs of the 'near abroad'. Among the stated reasons for its position are: concern for the safety and well-being of the Russian population in the ex-Soviet republics; apprehensions about Russia's national security; and economic interests.

Approximately 25 million Russians are thought to reside outside the RF: 12 million live in Ukraine, and in Latvia and Estonia they form large minorities (30–40 per cent of the population). While the Russians residing in the Slavic republics (Ukraine, Belarus) suffer no ethnic discrimination, the opposite is true of Estonia, Latvia, as well as some Muslim republics. As a result, concern about their fate has been elevated by the Yeltsin administration to one of its political priorities in the 'Near Abroad'. However, various republics interpret Moscow's attitude on this issue as interference in their internal affairs and regard the issue itself as a Kremlin lever to influence their respective policies.

According to official sources, the main threats to Russia's national security from the 'Near Abroad' emanate from two distinct sources. They are: military problems, including the presence of nuclear weapons on the territory of Belarus, Ukraine and Kazakhstan, and the threat of Islamic fundamentalism. With respect to the first set of problems, it is important to note that the tactical nuclear weapons – that is to say, the only category which could have been used in a war against Russia – were handed over to Moscow in 1992. What remains on the territory of the other republics are strategic ICBMs which, during the Cold War, had been aimed at the North American targets. Of the nuclear republics, only Ukraine possesses the technical expertise to reprogramme the ICBMs, a process that would take several years to complete. In short, despite expressions of Moscow's continued concern about the nuclear weapons deployed in the territory of the former USSR, they do not constitute a current or near-term threat to the national security of Russia.

The same is true of Islamic fundamentalism. The Kremlin's apprehension is reportedly caused by regional as well as internal considerations. In 1992, a civil war between the forces of the old-line communist government and of the political opposition broke out in Tajikistan. Fearing defeat, the Marxist leaders turned to Moscow for help. Sensing an opportunity to counter the growing Turkish and Iranian influence in Central Asia, the Kremlin obliged. As a result, Russian troops are now engaged in combating the rebels who operate from Afghanistan and enjoy the moral and material support of Kabul and Tehran. To justify its military intervention in the Tajik civil war, Moscow presents it as a crusade against Islamic fundamentalism.

More genuine is the Kremlin's concern about the future of Islam in the territory of the Russian Federation itself. The country's Muslim population, while not too numerous, is concentrated in some strategically and economically important areas (e.g., northern Caucasus, Tatarstan). In some of them, the influence of Islam, which reinforces the nationalist tendencies of the Muslim minorities, is on the rise. The combination of nationalism and religion is bound to impede Moscow's efforts to integrate and control the Muslim minorities. The problem is a very real one, but it has nothing to do with Islamic fundamentalism.

Since the Soviet economy had been highly centralised, the dissolution of the USSR has wrought havoc with the economies of the former Soviet republics. Many of them continue to depend on Russia for their supply of fuel (oil, gas), while the RF relies on its neighbours for deliveries of raw materials, food and some types of equipment. Hence, Moscow has consistently called upon the newly independent states to reintegrate the ex-Soviet space politically, militarily, and, above all, economically. The Commonwealth of Independent States (CIS) is the current version of functional unity advocated by the Kremlin. Most republics have followed the Russian lead, while others, led by Ukraine, refused to accept full membership. Generally speaking, the CIS does not appear to be a viable entity and will one day be replaced by something else. One thing is certain, however. Russia will not abandon its quest to reintegrate the ex-Soviet space because, on this issue, rare harmony prevails across the entire Russian political spectrum.

In this pursuit, Moscow holds important trump cards. As noted, Russia remains one of the world's largest oil and gas producers which has traditionally satisfied the requirements of its fuel-hungry neighbours. The ability to control this spigot has given the Kremlin considerable leverage to be used as it sees fit. Moreover, as the centre of a far-flung empire, Moscow traditionally controlled the political and administrative apparatus of the entire state. It was also the country's educational centre, where the most gifted republican cadres came to study and to gain experience. The ties established in this manner are still in evidence today. The same applies to the republican armed forces, bureaucratic and managerial establishments. Last but not least, the Russian army has been able to interject itself into local and regional conflicts which erupted in the ex-Soviet space after the collapse of the USSR (Tajikistan, Moldova, Georgia).

In contrast, in the 'Far Abroad', i.e., the world beyond the former Soviet borders, Russia's role has decreased dramatically since the early 1990s. This process is likely to continue in the years to come. Many Russians, as noted, genuinely resent the sharp decline of the international prestige and power of their state. Some argue that the end of the Cold War and the normalisation of relations with the Western powers have been bought at an exorbitant price: the unification of Germany, the dissolution of the Warsaw Pact and, eventually, of the USSR itself; and the withdrawal from Eastern Europe. Most understand, however, that although Russia is still feared because of its vast nuclear arsenal, its economic collapse has made it impossible for Moscow to regain its former leading role on the world scene.

In the clash between the 'Westerners', who advocate close cooperation with the West, and the 'Eurasians', who oppose it, the Yeltsin administration has sided with the former. In June 1994, Russia joined NATO's 'Partnership for Peace' programme and entered into an economic partnership with the European Union. Yeltsin's decision to stay the pro-Western course was made in spite of the rising nationalism and anti-Westernism in Russia. These sentiments are fed by desperation, born out of conviction that the orderly Soviet state system was destroyed for no worthwhile purpose. Instead, many Russians now see their society and economy as being controlled and manipulated by unscrupulous and corrupt politicians, bureaucrats and managers, many of whom work closely with the mafia. To combat these ills, many Russians have turned to nationalism and its values, explaining, in part, both Zhirinovskii's early popularity and Yeltsin's own attempts to jump on the nationalist bandwagon by pursuing a more assertive foreign policy.

Be that as it may, it is unlikely that the Russian empire will ever be restored. Instead, Russia is likely to emerge as a great power which will exercise considerable and, in some instances, decisive influence in the ex-Soviet space. It will be able to do so by virtue of its relative military and economic power; of its ability to promise, and deliver, improvement in the economic lot of many republics; and of the plain reluctance of some nationalities to separate themselves entirely from the Russians, under whose control they had lived for a very long time.

Conclusion

By now, it should be evident that Russia's future hinges on the state of its economy: its condition will affect the country's political development and its relations with the outside world. As demonstrated in December 1993, strong dissatisfaction with Yeltsin's failure to deal with the deterioration in the standard of living caused a significant part of Russia's electorate to cast their votes for the extremes of the political spectrum. Popular discontent has also fed the flames of Russian nationalism, leading the Yeltsin administration to conduct a more assertive foreign policy.

As argued earlier, the present state of the Russian economy does not inspire optimism: industrial production is declining at a catastrophic 25 per cent a year; unemployment is on the rise; the rate of inflation is still high; and billions of dollars continue 'to flee' the country to the safety of the Western banks. This means that future reforms will have to take place in conditions of economic retrogression. Moreover, aversion to 'big shock' therapy, continued procrastination, and the insistence on 'we know what to do and how to do it less painfully', will only raise the costs of reform in the future. In short, Russian leaders have chosen to disregard the lessons learned in post-1945 West Germany, where the fascist-type economy was converted into a highly successful capitalist welfare economy, and, more recently, in Eastern Europe, where Poland and the Czech Republic underwent 'shock therapy' and abandoned their quantitative-output economies.

Nevertheless, to compare present-day Russia with Weimar Germany, defeated in the First World War, ostracised politically, and devastated economically, seems far-fetched. Post-Soviet Russia did lose its super-power status but has not been humiliated militarily or politically – it remains a powerful and respected member of the international community. Economically, Russia is not only not paying any reparations but is also a beneficiary of Western assistance. At present, its leaders lack the will to introduce major economic reforms but, given the choice between reform and possible collapse, they will, eventually, have to respond to this challenge in a positive manner.

In sum, the question posed in the title of this chapter – can Russia escape its past? – may be answered in the following fashion. If one means the Soviet past (a one-party communist dictatorship, a state command economy and an enlarged empire), the answer is an unqualified 'yes'. Russia is on the way to shedding it and a return to the old USSR is, in this writer's opinion, virtually impossible. If, on the other hand, one means historical Russia (nationalist, authoritarian, economically struggling and keen for respect), then the answer must be couched in more ambiguous terms. Political, economic, institutional and legal reforms are at an early stage and have encountered varying degrees of opposition from powerful vested interests. One hopes that enlightened self-interest will eventually steer Russia toward genuine political democracy and a viable market economy, but the going is bound to be rough and Russian history offers little encouragement.

REFERENCES

The list below contains the references for this chapter together with suggestions for further reading on its main themes.

Aslund, Anders (1989) *Gorbachev's Struggle for Economic Reform* (Ithaca, NY: Cornell University Press).

Barghoorn, Frederick C. and Thomas F. Remington (1986) *Politics in the USSR*, 3rd edn (Boston: Little, Brown).

Brzezinski, Zbigniew (1989) *The Grand Failure* (New York: Scribners's).

Dallin, Alexander (1992) 'Causes of the Collapse of the USSR', *Post-Soviet Affairs*, vol. 8(4), 279–302.

Dunlop, John B. (1993) *The Rise of Russia and the Fall of the Soviet Empire* (Princeton, NJ: Princeton University Press).

Florinsky, Michael T. (1960) *Russia: A History and Interpretation*, 2 vols. (New York: Macmillan).

Friedrich, Carl J. and Zbigniew Brzezinski (1956) *Totalitarian Dictatorship and Autocracy* (Cambridge, MA: Harvard University Press).

Hewett, Ed A. (1988) *Reforming the Soviet Economy* (Washington, DC: The Brookings Institution).

Hosking, Geoffrey (1990) *The Awakening of the Soviet Union* (Cambridge, MA: Harvard University Press).

(1992) *The Road to Post-Communism: Independent Political Movements in the Former Soviet Union* (New York: Pinter).

Kaiser, Robert G. (1991) *Why Gorbachev Happened: His Triumphs and His Failure* (New York: Simon and Schuster).

Lewin, Moshe (1989) *The Gorbachev Phenomenon: A Historical Interpretation* (Berkeley: University of California Press).

Malia, Martin E. (1994) *The Soviet Tragedy: A History of Socialism in Russia, 1917–1991* (New York: Free Press).

Remnick, David (1993) *Lenin's Tomb: The Last Days of the Soviet Empire* (New York: Random House).

Suny, Ronald Grigor (1994) *Nationalism, Revolution, and the Collapse of the Soviet Union* (Palo Alto, CA: Stanford University Press).

White, Stephen (1979) *Political Culture and Soviet Politics* (New York: St. Martin's Press).

Yakovlev, Alexander (1993) *The Fate of Marxism in Russia* (New Haven, CT: Yale University Press).

7 Imperialism, dependency and autocolonialism in the Eurasian space

Karen Dawisha

The contemporary debate about the future of politics in the Eurasian space comes back again and again to 'the Russian question': will the Soviet Union, having collapsed, reassert itself, this time as a new Russian empire?[1] Some analysts in the West and elsewhere moved quickly from euphoria over these long-suppressed nations gaining independence to concern over whether they would be able to resist or survive in the face of any renewed Russian imperial drive. Books and articles started to fill the shelves analysing Russia's potential strength, assessing the foreign policy impact of its domestic political divisions, speaking of the Russian impulse to empire, and chronicling the near-total obsession which elites in neighbouring countries have with managing the relationship with Moscow (Reddaway, 1993a, 1993b; Hill and Jewett, 1994; Pipes, 1994).

Many of the authors point to the difficulties faced by elites in all the new states, including Russia, in developing a conception of national interest which would orient their foreign policies beyond the Eurasian heartland (Dawisha and Parrott, 1994: ch. 6). But the frailties both of the new states themselves and of the institutions for formulating foreign policy within them limit their ability to extend the focus of their external politics outside the Eurasian orbit. The fact that the inter-relationships amongst these fifteen states are likely, for the foreseeable future, to occupy the first rank of their concerns means that the international system will also interact with them through the prism of these relationships. Consequently, the ability of the world community to effect change in these relationships will depend on having a clearer understanding of their essential nature. This underlines the importance of analysing them dispassionately and with a yardstick which could be applied more generally and is unchanging over time.

The task can be approached by posing a number of questions about the whole range of possible relationships between Russia as the 'metropolitan power' and the other new states:

164

The metropolitan power:
- Do all great powers have rights and responsibilities?
- How does one distinguish between a great power's 'legitimate interests' in the area surrounding its borders, and 'imperialism?'
- What are the prerequisites for the emergence of an imperial power?
- Can a country with low state capacity and no avowed official ideology of imperialism nevertheless be an empire? In other words, can a 'naked emperor' exist?
- What are the rights and responsibilities of Russia in the territory of the former Soviet empire?
- What would Russian imperialism look like today?

The states on the periphery:
- How dependent are the former republics on Moscow?
- Can these new states break out of a cycle of dependence on Moscow that in some cases is so great as to constitute virtual autocolonisation (defined as the process whereby elites or populations in a target country seek and accept a diminuation in their state's sovereignty in hopes of receiving enhanced material, security, or other benefits from a metropolitan state)?
- Is dependence on Moscow in the objective interest of at least some of these new states some of the time?

The international system:
- Will the major actors in the international system allow Russia to emerge as a *de facto* imperial power?
- Alternatively, can it prevent Russian imperialism from emerging?
- What measures can be used to increase the former republics' independence from Russia?
- Is dependence on Moscow sometimes in the interest of the West and other external powers?

Imperial prerequisites

An empire as a polity and imperialism as a system of ideas which guides policy intersect conceptually, in that the first is an outgrowth, a result, of the latter. This apparently trivial and obvious point gets to the heart of the first requirement of empires, namely that they be established on purpose, with the objective of the elites in the metropole gaining unfair advantage through coercion or its threat over countries or territories in the periphery and for the purpose of promoting definite state interests. Thus the definition provided by Schumpeter in his earliest works of imperialism as 'the objectless disposition on the part of a state to unlimited forcible expansion' (Schumpeter, 1927: 7) or the old argument that the British empire expanded 'in a fit of absent-mindedness' simply misses the point that states do not expand *for no reason*. Such an expansion may, in the fullness of time, prove to have been irrational or unwise, but the original impulse to expand has to have been a conscious one on the part of the elites designed to serve what elites perceive to be state interests. Moreover, a policy of imperialism pursued by the centre is, of course, unlikely to be advertised as such, but it is important nevertheless to include in one's conceptualisation of imperialism the effort by one country to wrest formal sovereignty from another. It is, therefore, more than the exercise of influence over the policies of another country.

As such, while it is highly unlikely now that any state would openly declare in advance that it was going to create an empire, nevertheless, it would be more than possible to determine whether a state has the interest, the capacity and the will necessary to pursue such a course. While there are great differences on other issues pertaining to imperialism, authors are agreed that the drive to empire has to serve some set of overarching interests: whether economic (as with the British drive in India), messianic (as with the missionary expansionism of Iberian catholicism), or ideological (as with Bolshevism in the USSR). While the motivations may differ, nevertheless they must be present in order for the foreign policy of a state to be characterised as imperialistic. In this sense, Winston Churchill's statement that 'the empires of the future are the empires of the mind' informs the discussion by pointing to the central aspect of intent.

Discerning intent is particularly important in the case of those states which have a heritage of imperial behaviour or which are geographically large and economically powerful. Failure to consider the motivation of elites in the metropole, therefore, would lead one to blur the conceptual distinction between, for example, French policies in Algeria before and after independence. Factoring in the change in Algeria's formal status and the changed motivation of French elites allows one to distinguish between an imperial–colonial relationship, on the one hand, and a great power–developing state relation, on the other. Both are relations of inequality, but quite different both in their essence and in the level of independent action open to Algeria. Thus, the economic deprivations of the Algerian population under colonial rule were directly attributable to French policies, and the result was the rise of the Algerian FLN which successfully fought a war of liberation. On the other hand, the economic deprivations of the population after independence were due less to French policies than to Algeria's generally unfavourable position in the world economic system. Certainly France can be accused of pursuing a policy of neo-colonialism whereby it sought to limit the economic and thereby the political independence of Algeria. But, in addition, the economic hardships encountered by the population were blamed by them on the corruption and stasis of the local elite, with the result that over time Islamic movements opposed to indigenous politicians arose to challenge authority. These politicians, seeking to stay in power but lacking the domestic legitimacy to do so, looked to the international system to support an internal coup which imposed martial law, while making the regime once more dependent not on France alone this time but on those major Western powers which supported the coup. In so doing, the military leaders diminished the independence of their own state.

Failing to see the differences in the two scenarios leads one to fail to draw the distinction between the process of imperial disintegration and nation formation on the one hand and national disintegration and what might be called autocolonisation on the other. The impulse for imperialism comes from the metropole; the impulse for autocolonisation comes from the periphery. In the former, the motivation to expand comes without taking into account, or against, the wishes of people in the periphery. Autocolonisation takes place at the behest and with the support of either the elites or the population in the periphery. One can name many instances during the Cold War when otherwise illegitimate elites in the Third World adopted a pro-Western or pro-Soviet stance in order to receive security assistance which would keep them in power. They used the assistance to ruthlessly suppress domestic opposition and generally did not institute democratic reforms or guarantee human rights. Meanwhile, Swiss bank accounts swelled as local elites plundered their national wealth while their people's standard of living dipped even below colonial standards. On the other hand, populations, too, can set a process of autocolonisation in motion. Protestants among the population of Northern Ireland, for example, prefer union with Britain even with direct rule, to an independence which would leave them open to what they believe would be inevitable pressure for union with the south. The support by the Kurds inside northern Iraq for the establishment of UN-mandated no-fly zones is one example, the support by Bosnian Muslims for establishing UN-governed areas is another. Both have in common the population's willingness to accept a diminution or elimination of their own rights as citizens of a country in return for personal protection.

It is certainly possible that there might be parallels now or in the future in the relations between Russia and the rest of the new states.

Russian imperialism and autocolonisation among the new states

To take the case of Russia first, its continuing pre-eminence in Eurasia as the dominant geographic colossus and economic power gives it enormous natural advantage. Comprising over three-quarters of the territory of the former Soviet empire and over one-half of its total population (a figure which rises to almost two-thirds if citizens of Russia and ethnic Russians abroad are combined), Russia can be expected to continue to exert an overbearing presence in the calculations of its neighbours.

To conclude from this alone, however, that Russia will 'naturally' exercise imperial ambitions over the other new states is to overdetermine for geography. Russia's geographic capability did not prevent invasions by much smaller countries in centuries past, nor has it allowed Russia such an overarching advantage as to satiate previous rulers in Moscow and deter them from expansion. Just as Japan invaded the much larger China at the outbreak of the Second World War, and China has managed to have equitable relations with the much smaller South Korea in recent decades, relative smallness or largeness is not in and of itself a guide to motivation.

Where geography becomes a factor is in enhancing capability. When given the political will to create an empire, the size and extent of natural resources are important inputs into any state machine bent on imperial expansion. It is a common fallacy that states build empires to become rich: states, and/or their leaders, may seek additional enrichment, but in fact, significant state resources are required to undertake and sustain colonial expansion. States bent on expansion may be motivated by the lure of wealth, but in order to launch a successful and sustained policy of expansion, they themselves must possess significant capacity: full coffers, large armies and navies, and extensive excess production capabilities large enough to support, and profit from, wars of conquest and occupation.

The level of capacity needed is of course relative and not absolute: the resources required are in inverse relationship to the resistance offered not only by the population in the area invaded, but also by other great powers and by the international system. All the European imperial powers of the late nineteenth century, including Russia, were already powerful when they entered the so-called 'golden age of empires'. When the empire costs more than it yields, institutional interests and ideas like prestige and *mission civilisatrice* come to the forefront. Clearly, however, once the population in the metropole begins to shoulder the burdens of expansion, a core domestic constituency for empire is lost.

In Russia, were imperialism to reassert itself, it would require both motive and capability. There is no lack of right-wing leaders and parties in Russia who are motivated to promote the re-establishment of Greater Russia within the borders of the former Soviet empire. And indeed, this is crucial because historically, it has been individuals and political groups who have acted as the agents for the germination of the imperial idea. Whether considering Cecil Rhodes (whose own vision of capitalist imperialism in South Africa came to be adopted by the British) or the pan-Turanists in Ottoman Turkey (who sought unsuccessfully in the dying days of the Ottoman empire to revive it on the basis of the unity of all Turkish-speaking peoples), or the Russian explorer Skobelev (whose 'discoveries' of Turkestan helped motivate the Russian imperial expansion), these individuals and groups have mobilised society and elites to expend the resources necessary for expansion. They have worked with the intellectual elites to develop the essential myths which have undergirded and sustained expansion and they have fostered an intellectual climate in which any challenge of these myths is seen as subversive of the broadest goals of society. Certainly in Russia, most nineteenth-century writers and intellectuals gave powerful support to the idea that Russia's identity is an imperial identity.

These groups and individuals are ultimately important, however, only to the extent that either they become influential or their ideas become 'the ruling ideas'. Thus, before any leader can recapture the states on Russia's border, he must first capture power in Russia. Several attempts by these forces to capture power by force have failed, and such a result by the electoral procedure now in place is also not very likely. Observers worry, however, that as economic and internal conditions deteriorate in Russia, and in particular as the public grows weary of the increase in lawlessness, public support for the institutions of democracy may decline, particularly if a leader emerges who can appeal to the growing sense that Russia has been humiliated, and deserves redress. The electoral success of Vladimir Zhirinovskii must be seen in this light, in so far as while his 20 per cent of the votes was not enough to be elected, it was a signal to the anti-democratic forces that this kind of pro-imperial rhetoric has solid resonance amongst the population and is there as a reserve when needed. One can in this scenario see echoes of the earlier views expressed by Hannah Arendt (1951) that imperialism may gain such popularity that the mob which supports it can rise up to destroy other institutions, including both nascent capitalism and democracy.

This raises the question whether Russian imperialism could be born out of the struggle of political forces within the country itself: that is, whether, in their quest for gaining power, groups would mobilise imperial sentiment for narrow political gain. This would presuppose that these forces could win an election, and that having won they would feel pressured to act accordingly. This view of motivation argues that empires are built almost willy-nilly, without what Michael MccGwire would call a strict planning cycle, and largely as a result of the combination of domestic pressures and lack of constraints by the international community. Certainly there are historians, A. J. P. Taylor (1954) among them, who view the entire experience of the construction of empires in the nineteenth century as largely a result of political competition and narrow diplomatic oneupmanship. Along these lines Bismarck is said to have remarked to a subordinate in 1884 that 'all this colonial business is a sham but we need it for the elections'.

In Russia, pro-imperial views increasingly began to filter into the highest echelons of the political, military and economic elites during 1994, and from there began to shape a more assertive foreign policy. Public opinion polls in Russia have consistently shown the public's rejection of foreign entanglements, and popular sentiments against committing conscripts to the war in Chechnya ran high. At the same time, anti-Western feelings were on the increase, and there was remarkably little opposition to many of the actions which have caused concern that Russian foreign policy is seeking a reassertion of empire: actions like the declaration of Moscow's mayor that Sevastopol in the Crimea was the eleventh district of Moscow, or the re-establishment of military bases in Georgia, or the demand that the elimination of Belarus' central bank be a precondition for accepting Belarus' request for economic union with Russia. Moreover, elite articulation of views openly dis-avowing any Russian 'rights' in the near abroad began to recede, suggesting that an elite consensus, supported by a minority within public opinion, may emerge favouring a resurgence of Russian imperi-alism, and differing only on the means to be used, and the objectives to be pursued in each country. Several analysts in the West (Prizel, 0000) have documented the emergence of this consensus which it is important to monitor, not least because the impact of the rhetoric of the Russian right on Russia's relations with neighbouring countries like Ukraine is very significant in its own right.

Evidence suggests however that that there is insufficient state capacity to implement a sustained policy of imperial expansion particularly if military force were required. Indeed it would appear that much of the state's capacity in the foreseeable future will be focused on preventing the boundaries of Russia from shrinking even further, particularly given the location of so many restless national minorities at the periphery, especially in Chechnya but also elsewhere in the North Caucasus and in Siberia.

In sum, therefore, the Russian state currently possesses neither the capability nor the unified will to reassert its imperial persona. But Russia has many conflicts on its borders, and many opportunities for gaining advantage. Also, history has shown that the political culture of a country can rather swiftly be changed from the politics of humiliation to the politics of *revanche* (France after 1870, Germany in the 1930s, Egypt after 1967). It cannot be excluded that the political culture in Russia may see an equally swift transformation.

When analysts consider the prospect for a reassertion of Russian imperial activities beyond the mere expression of sentiment, they primarily deal with scenarios in which the new states of the 'near abroad', struggling to establish and maintain their independence, resist such efforts by all means available, including force of arms. And to be sure, many of Moscow's actions in the period since independence have met with resistance. Indeed it could be said that a central feature in the national identity of many of the new states is the imperative of resistance to any renewed Russian drive. This is particularly true in Latvia and Estonia, in western Ukraine, in western Moldova, in Azerbaijan, and unfortunately for Russia, also within Russia in the north Caucasus. It is less a part of the central governing *raison d'état* in Central Asia, Armenia, Georgia, eastern and southern Ukraine, eastern Moldova, Belarus and Lithuania. Whereas, in the first group, there is a solid consensus amongst the elites and the population that independence for their countries means independence from Russia, the situation in the latter group is not so clear cut. The existence of historic ties, of common Slavic roots, of a common economic infrastructure still centred in Russia, of Russophone elites, and of large numbers of Russian nationals settled in and intermarried with the local population living within these countries are just some of the factors which favour a continued Russian influence.

But how do conditions which favour Russian influence translate into circumstances which produce autocolonisation? There would appear to be two primary motivations for autocolonisation: security and economic. In the first, the country, the elites, the population or all three, are so absorbed in a military conflict whether civil or interstate that they see a Russian presence as a means of either tipping the conflict in their favour or suppressing it altogether.

In Georgia, both the Abkhaz separatists and the Georgian state authorities called on Russian military support to tip the balance in their favour and then to maintain the peace once the threat of separatism had subsided. In the process, the government acceded to Russian demands for basing rights in the country, bases which would be used both to promote Russia's interests and to support President Shevardnadze's own embattled base of power if needed.

In Armenia, the government has repeatedly tried to enlist Russian military support in its conflict with Azerbaijan over Nagorno-Karabagh, receiving critical supplies of oil for its own 1994 offensive into western Azerbaijan. Both Armenia and Russia seek the weakening of Azerbaijan: Armenia so as to promote its own claims to Nagorno-Karabagh and Russia so as to gain access to Azerbaijan's oil and weaken Baku's potential for reasserting its historic role as the beacon for the spreading of pan-Turkic and Islamic appeals north and east from the Middle East. In the process, Azerbaijan elites who have taken power have sought to protect the country from Armenia by acceding to virtually all Russian demands, including ceding ever-larger percentages of stock in Azerbaijan's oil industry to Russian firms, and closing down the offices of the Azerbaijani Popular Front. The Azerbaijanis had decided that the only way to buy security from Armenian attacks was to start down the road of auto-colonisation in their relationship with Russia.

In Ukraine and Belarus, both President Kuchma and President Lukashenko ran on platforms in their 1994 campaigns which promised a much closer relationship with Moscow. With the defeat of their predecessors, President Kravchuk and President Shushkevich, it was heralded in many newspapers in these two countries that 'two out of the three traitors of Minsk had been defeated'. It had been a meeting between Kravchuk, Shushkevich and Yeltsin in Minsk in 1991 which had led to the break-up of the USSR. Obviously there are strong forces in both countries, and especially in western Ukraine, which favour independence from Russia and will fight to maintain it, but Russia's strong economic performance *relative* to the dismal situation in Ukraine and Belarus, and for that matter in all of Central Asia as well, has predisposed these countries to rely on Russia economically.

The move away from trade dependency on Russia which was expected after independence did not happen anywhere except in Estonia. The elites in all the other countries appeared unable or unwilling to act on their economic independence from Russia. Needless to say, autocolonisation may be transitory: given the speed and circumstances of the collapse of the USSR, the presence of so many elites and populations so unprepared for independence is historically unique. It may be that with the passage of time these elites or the next generation may come to value independence more. At the same time, Russia is unlikely to recede as a geopolitical presence in the area, and the temptation to empire will have to be contained by more than the questionable will of elites in these bordering states.

Imperialism and the international community

While empires have existed in both the modern and ancient worlds, the 'Age of Empires' really lasted for the briefest period from the mid-1800s to the First World War. During this time, virtually all the European powers expanded their power, culture and economic influence by means of the formal acquisition of territories world-wide. The very essence of the international system was itself imperialist. The wars between empires (as with the Crimean War, and the endless wars in the Balkans) which broke out in this period were not about the unacceptability of empire *per se* but about the fate of contested territory between empires. Consequently, alliances among empires could be established, agreements not to attack one's flank when at war with another empire could be signed, and all in all, discussions about the rights of nations and peoples to self-determination could be sacrificed to the interests of maintaining a balance of power within Europe.

But now that a century has passed, and the USSR – in some ways an empire – has collapsed, the talk of empire, specifically the possibility of the re-emergence of a Russian empire, has resurfaced. The USSR succeeded in the early 1920s, in a weak and divided international community, in establishing itself and incorporating by force many of the territories of the former Russian empire. Would the international community allow such a phenomenon to be repeated today?

Several important factors mitigate against such a repetition. First there is the greater awareness among the elites in the neighbouring countries of the nature and potential of Russian power. All display an acute knowledge of Russia's potential and a caution about its future orientation which signal the fact that states on Russia's borders are stronger and more aware now than they have ever been in the past and, therefore, they provide a significant deterrent in and of themselves to expansion: for example, reabsorbing Kazakhstan today, with its cities, educated elite, developed infrastructure and communications links to the outside world would be a far more difficult task than it was in the 1920s when the indigenous peoples were nomadic, illiterate, geographically isolated and had no history of independent statehood.

Second, the international system has come to more fully accommodate as governing norms the principles of state sovereignty, national self-determination and the inadmissibility of the use of force to change boundaries or legitimate governments (Katzenstein, 1993). To the extent that force has been sanctioned by the international community through the United Nations, it has been to uphold these norms (as in Kuwait, Haiti or Bosnia). It is practically inconceivable that the international community would support a wholesale Russian policy either of using force to absorb states that are recognised as sovereign and independent or of systematically undermining by the use or threat of force democratically elected governments within those states. Not only would such a policy bring international censure, but many of the international institutions to which Russia has turned in an effort to restructure its economy would undoubtedly conclude that the upturn in military spending which such a policy shift would necessitate would so weaken Russian economic recovery as to negate the very basis on which the original loans and investments were made. In this way, the international community could both isolate and punish Russia economically for any policy of expansionism. The extent to which that punishment would be effective either in deterring the adoption of the policy in the first place, or, failing that, in ensuring that Russia would be economically unable to pursue such a policy would depend on the extent to which not only the policy has domestic support within Russia which could be sustained even with hardships, but also that the Russian economy first becomes integrated within the international economic system. Russia has moved significantly to introduce capitalism and integrate itself into the international political and economic system, to the point that some economists think the economy could not be returned to an autarchic and state-planned model without catastrophic disruption (Aslund, 1994b). It is becoming increasingly difficult, therefore, to identify elites who would benefit economically from such a renewal of imperial policies which isolated Russia from the global community.

The international system has ceased to be ruled exclusively by *laissez-faire* and *realpolitik* principles alone. It has become more norm-governed. However, inequalities within the system are still acute, dependence is more often the watchword than interdependence and great powers still hold tremendous sway. These facts are as apparent in Eurasia as anywhere else, and this is the subject of the last section.

Russia's national security zone

While there is scant evidence of a renewed and concerted Russian drive for empire, nevertheless Russia has moved from pursuing an inchoate policy towards the countries on its border to one which has clearly marked the area out as an area of vital interest, akin to Michael

MccGwire's (1991) important conception of a 'national security zone'. While Russia may not be moving to re-establish empire, it has affirmed that the area surrounding its state borders is critical to its well-being and security. All states have national security zones – only the strongest have the capability to promote their interests within them. The conceptual distinction between an empire and a national security zone is more than a difference of degree: the former has no basis in current international norms and laws, the latter allows one to focus on the natural interplay of relations between great powers and smaller states, an interplay in which great powers are infinitely more constrained than imperial powers and small states have significantly more leeway than colonies. In policy terms, while it is inconceivable that the international community would support a reassertion of Russian imperialism, it is by no means certain that all Russian activities in its national security zone would be condemned.

As the largest and strongest country of the former USSR, and the one which benefited the most from the institutional inheritance of the Soviet state, Russia is in a position of enormous comparative advantage. Russian leaders have often exercised this advantage to the detriment of the other new states. Thus, Russia has used its position as the least dependent economy in the former Soviet space to exert economic pressure, particularly through the supply or withholding of energy. Russian leaders have maintained their interest in all the new states joining the Commonwealth of Independent States which Russia dominates. And the Russian military, via a network of formal basing agreements, contingents 'temporarily' stationed abroad, loan-service personnel, and peace-keeping missions sanctioned by regional treaties, is the only force in the Eurasian space capable of a sustained independent action beyond its borders.

Because of the fragility and comparative weakness of most of the new states, Russia is able to exert enormous leverage with relatively little effort. The way in which Russia has been able to shift between the Armenians and the Azerbaijanis, by supplying energy to one side and then another, or by withdrawing relatively small numbers of forces here and then deploying them there, shows its ability alternatively to punish and to reward without itself suffering significant or proportionate loss.[2]

Russia's military presence in Tajikistan, its legal claims to Crimea, and the protection accorded in Russia's military doctrine to ethnic Russians living abroad are issues which spring from different situations and political motivations. But they nevertheless reflect an overall consensus in Russia that at a minimum the former Soviet area constitutes a natural Russophone zone over which Moscow has 'always' been able to exercise influence. Even President Yeltsin and Foreign Minister Kozyrev, long associated with a view of foreign policy which emphasises international and Western links, have long come to embrace the notion that 'the sphere of Russia's economic, political, and humanitarian interests extends to the entire post-Soviet space' (*Segodnya*, 30 September 1994).

The central point is that the other new states, however hostile to Russia, yet being weaker and more fragile, nevertheless need it. The fact that Russia has been willing to provide substantial and continued energy and trade subsidisation (to the tune, according to IMF estimates, of $17 billion in 1993 alone) shows the extent to which Russia is both aware of these needs and concerned not to destabilise these countries. Certainly, not all the new states regard Russia as inherently untrustworthy as a partner. Belarus, with an economy which is even more inflation-ridden than Russia's, has tried to forge an economic union with Moscow, only to be kept at arms length on certain monetary issues. And virtually no state has not continued to rely heavily on Moscow for continued trade, for expertise, or as the centre of Eurasia's communications network. Certainly in the modern era it has never before occurred that the imperial centre has collapsed with some of the 'colonies' so unprepared psychologically for independence (Olcott, 1992). This reliance comes about not necessarily because of any nefarious design by the current Russian government, but because these countries (with the partial exception of Estonia) have yet to be incorporated into any regional or global network which bypasses Moscow. As Disraeli once said, 'colonies do not cease to be colonies just because they are independent'.

In this context, therefore, it is necessary to distinguish between the fact of Russia's self-perception as the dominant power in the region and the other countries' objective dependence. The legacy of the Soviet empire has left them dependent, but overcoming the consequences of that dependence is primarily the responsibility of these new states themselves. Much the same phenomenon as witnessed following the emergence of post-colonial Africa and the Middle East can be expected in Eurasia. Many leaders in these states, faced with almost intractable problems, have already chosen to blame Moscow as an excuse for their inability to implement a credible development strategy.

Looking at the patterns which have emerged in the decades since decolonisation began in the developing world, one can find many reasons to conclude that the process in Eurasia will be equally difficult but substantively different. The proximity of the former colonial power, in particular, and the harsh economic straits that Russia finds itself in, predispose one to conclude that the interrelationship between Russia and its neighbours is likely to be more intense than between most former colonial powers and their newly independent states. Russia will not have the 'luxury' of having a debate about casting off 'the white man's burden' as the British did when discussing the benefits of withdrawal from India, because 25 million Russians found themselves in these new states after the breakup of the USSR and because Russia's weak economy makes these states a more natural partner than India was for Britain. And as for the other new states in Eurasia, they cannot easily form regional security systems to bolster their independence from their former colonial masters, as the newly independent African and Middle Eastern states did in the Organization of African Unity and the Arab League, because whereas Britain, France and Portugal withdrew over the horizon when these empires collapsed, Russia continues to reside in their midst.

By far the most realistic course, therefore, to avoid autocolonisation would be to promote interdependence. Such a course would be difficult for the reasons elaborated above: the legacy of *diktat* and distrust, the domestic political climate in many of the new states which fuels mutual antagonism on all sides, and an international climate which alternately promotes Russia as a great power in its national security zone and punishes it for exercising the prerogatives of such a power. Absence of consensus and clear thinking about the distinction between illegitimate imperial behaviour and a range of legitimate actions which Russia could take to promote its interests within its national security zone all contribute to the problem. Moreover, states which are not truly independent cannot participate in an interdependent world: and until the states bordering Russia make further strides, their full participation will remain only a distant objective.

NOTES

1 The author would like to thank Michael MccGwire for his comments on this chapter and for his initial comments on imperialism, and its need for closer definition and scrutiny, which he made at the Russian Littoral Project conference on Eurasian Security Issues and Western Concerns, at Barnett Hill Conference Centre, England, in July 1994.
2 A partial catalogue of Russian activities abroad and a full justification of all such activities was presented in a report by the director of the Russian Foreign Intelligence Service, Yevgeniy Primakov, and published in full in *Rossiyskaya gazeta*, 22 September 1994.

REFERENCES

Arendt, Hannah (1951) *The Origins of Totalitarianism* (New York: Harcourt, Brace, Jonanovich), rev. edn 1973.

Aslund, Anders (1994a) *Economic Transformation in Russia* (New York: St. Martin's Press).

(1994b) 'Russia's Success Story', *Foreign Affairs*, vol. 73(5) (Sept./Oct.), 58–71.

Bonner, Elena (1993) 'Yeltsin and Russia: Two Views', *The New York Review of Books*, vol. 40(8) (22 Apr.), 16–19.

Crow, Suzanne (1994) 'Why Has Russian Foreign Policy Changed?' *RFE/RL Research Reports*, vol. 3(18) (6 May).

Cunliffe, Marcus (1974) *The Age of Expansion: 1848–1917* (Springfield, MA: G. & C. Merriam Co.).

Dawisha, Karen and Bruce Parrott (1994) *Russia and the New States of Eurasia: The Politics of Upheaval* (Cambridge: Cambridge University Press).

Hill, Fiona and Pamela Jewett (1994) ' "Back in the USSR": Russia's Intervention in the Internal Affairs of the Former Soviet Republics and the Implications for United States Policy Toward Russia', Ethnic Conflict Project, Strengthening Democratic Institutions Project (John F. Kennedy School of Government, Harvard University), Jan., 1–90.

Katzenstein, Peter J. (1993) 'Coping with Terrorism: Norms and Internal Security in Germany and Japan', in Judith Goldstein and Robert Keohane (eds.), *Ideas and Foreign Policy: Beliefs, Institutions, and Political Change* (Ithaca, NY: Cornell University Press).

Lough, John (1993) 'The Place of the "Near Abroad" in Russian Foreign Policy', *RFE/RL Research Reports*, vol. 2(11) (12 Mar.).

MccGwire, Michael (1991) *Perestroika and Soviet National Security* (Washington, DC: Brookings Institution).

Olcott, Martha B. (1992) 'Central Asia's Catapult to Independence', *Foreign Affairs*, vol. 71(3) (Summer), 108–31.

Pipes, Richard (1994) 'Imperial Russian Foreign Policy', *Times Literary Supplement*, no. 4755 (20 May), 3–5.

Prizel, Ilya (1998) *National Identity and Foreign Policy: Nationalism and Leadership in Poland, Russia and Ukraine* (Cambridge: Cambridge University Press).

Reddaway, Peter (1993a) 'The Role of Popular Discontent', *The National Interest*, vol. 31 (Spring), 57–63.

(1993b) 'Russia on the Brink', *The New York Review of Books*, vol. 40(3) (28 Jan.), 30–6.

(1993c) 'Yeltsin and Russia: Two Views', *The New York Review of Books*, vol. 40(8) (22 Apr.), 16–19.

Schumpeter, Joseph A. (1927) *Imperialism and Social Classes* (New York: Kelley), rev. edn 1951.

Taylor, A. J. P. (1954) *The Struggle for Mastery in Europe, 1848–1918* (Oxford: Clarendon Press).

Tolstaya, Tatyana (1992) 'Intellectuals and Social Change in Central and Eastern Europe', *Partisan Review*, vol. 59(4), 568–73.

(1994) 'The Struggle for Russia', *The New York Review of Books*, vol. 41(12) (23 June), 3–7.

8   Western Europe: challenges of the post-Cold War era

Catherine McArdle Kelleher

What does the future hold for Western Europe? The fall of the Berlin Wall bred contending theories of Western Europe's fate in the absence of the Cold War framework of superpower protection. On one side were the neo-realists, projecting a bleak future which would see the re-emergence of traditional power politics and old rivalries. On the other side, integrationists were predicting an explosion of cooperation and an extension of Western European security and prosperity eastward. The only point of agreement was that there would be serious hurdles to overcome in the post-Cold War world.

This chapter will begin by examining the neo-realist argument, with an eye towards explaining why it is overall too pessimistic in its predictions. It will then examine the challenges facing Western Europe, and the European Union (EU) in particular, and explain what must be done if the future for Western Europe is to be brighter than the neo-realists would have it.

The neo-realist vision of Europe

The end of the Cold War was followed almost immediately by a strong sense of nostalgia, a longing for a period in which everyone had grown comfortable in their given international roles – where inter-European squabbles were sublimated to the struggle between the superpowers, the result being an unprecedented period of stability in Western Europe. This romanticism was most prevalent in neo-realist thought, and was exemplified by the writings of scholars such as John Mearsheimer (1990) and Owen Harries (1993). The neo-realist argument posited that the end of the Cold War was bound to usher in a new period of dangerous instability. With the Soviet menace receding, the United States was sure to disengage from Europe in order to tend to its own house. This, in turn, would put the European powers back at each others' throats as they became increasingly insecure without a hegemon to keep them 'in line'.

The key to the neo-realist post-Cold War world was power relations among nation states. Cooperative economic institutions like the European Community (EC), while convenient for unity against a communist menace (be it from within or without), would not be able to supersede the 'traditional' rivalries of the continental powers – notably France and Germany. The EC, by this argument, was a child of the Cold War. Designed to provide a united economic front against the Soviets, and surviving only through US sponsorship (or at least toleration), it was doomed to disintegrate as the United States lost interest and traditional power rivalries overrode the economic cooperation that had evolved in the shadow of the hegemonic contest over the continent.

Yet now, more than a half decade into the post-Cold War world, the EU is still standing and indeed seems to be moving forward after a successful outcome for the Maastricht Treaty. With some notable exceptions, such as the Croatian and Slovenian recognition issue (Steinberg, 1994; Woodward, 1995), the Western European powers seem at least as united as before the fall of the Berlin Wall, with continued Franco-German cooperation serving as the engine for closer cooperation. The neo-realist argument has not held up under the weight of history, at least in regards to the European Community and the outlook for European cooperation. Why is this so?

The neo-realist argument laboured under three important false assumptions. First, it assumed the EC was a product of the Cold War, an attempt to provide an economic counterpart to NATO in order to stave off the communists. This was simply not the case. Rather, the EC had its genesis in a confluence of two factors. On the one hand, the drive for Western European integration through the EC was an attempt to find a final cure for the endemic Franco-German rivalry and to eliminate the spectre of German domination of Europe, factors which had launched two world wars and innumerable earlier conflicts.

One need look no further than the Schumann Plan, which proposed developing the European Coal and Steel Community (ECSC) and served as the jumping off point for further European integration, to find evidence of this motivation. The ECSC was in the minds of Schumann and Monnet long before the Soviet menace became prominent. Indeed, the seeds of European cooperation on a functionalist model were germinating in the mind of Jean Monnet as early as the 1920s (Cook, 1981; Monnet, 1989). The Schumann plan was designed to take coal and steel production – two vital components of the military industry – out of national (read German) hands. It was a direct reaction to German reconstruction and totally consistent with other French policies, such as internationalisation of the Ruhr, for constraining German war-making capacity. While somewhat coterminous with the beginning of the Cold War, superpower concerns had little to do with the EC's genesis.

Similarly, the Dunkirk Treaty (predecessor of the Brussels Treaty, which led in turn to the WEU) was a direct reaction to World War II. A defensive alliance of France, Britain and the Benelux countries against *German* aggression, this too had little to do with the Cold War. Indeed, when the Brussels Treaty was revamped in 1954 into the WEU, it was primarily intended to serve as a *counter-weight* to NATO (at least by the French), to allow for European integration outside of superpower domination (Garnham, 1988; Cromwell, 1992; Kelleher, 1995). While the Soviet menace (and US support) no doubt strengthened these institutions, the initial moves towards European integration had roots much deeper than the deterioration of East–West relations in the late 1940s.

The birth and growth of the EC can be seen more accurately as an attempt to avoid the economic nationalism of the 1920s and 1930s which fed the interwar catastrophes and, ultimately, contributed to a second world war. The interwar years proved that economic Darwinism was not feasible, that a system of 'cooperative engagement' involving the European powers and the United States would be necessary to avoid repeating the mistakes of the interwar years. The Marshall Plan, which made aid for economic reconstruction in Europe contingent on cooperation among recipient states, exemplified this new approach to international economic cooperation.

The foreign policy results of the plan have been well debated, yet scholars often forget that the plan was more an outgrowth of Congressional consternation at the slow pace of reconstruction than a grand scheme to woo Eastern Europe from the Soviets and create an economic Bloc in Europe (De Porte, 1979). The Congress approved the Marshall Plan (with severe reservations) only after United Nations Relief and Rehabilitation Agency (UNRRA) assistance had proved prohibitively costly and inefficient. The plan was approved because it implicitly mandated cooperation among the European powers and the sharing of sensitive national economic data as a precondition to receiving aid. The plan was thus able to virtually eliminate economic nationalism on the continent, creating an atmosphere of openness and trust among previously competitive European states, and forcing the French and Germans (and others) to work closely together for their mutual rehabilitation. Thus it was a combination of more long-term historic factors that led to the growth of the EC and European cooperation, not the immediate dangers of the Cold War.

The second misapprehension of the neo-realists was that the United

States would indeed abandon the European continent when the Cold War ended. While there has been some domestic pressure for a reduced presence in Europe, the United States has not completely disengaged from the continent. In part, this is because of the instability in Russia that followed the fall of the Soviet Union. The failed August 1991 putsch in Moscow, as well as the Yeltsin–Duma standoff which followed in autumn 1993, sobered the United States to the realities of the security situation in post-Cold War Europe (Gorbachev, 1991; Arbatov, 1994; Garthoff, 1994). But even apart from that, the United States has perhaps finally learned, after the lesson of two world wars, that its continued physical presence on the continent is a primary guarantor of Western European security. While the US leadership is probably more confident than ever before of the possibilities of European cooperation, there is enough *realpolitik* left in US policy-makers to hedge against any possible revisionism. Thus the United States is likely to remain actively engaged in security and cooperation in Western Europe for the foreseeable future – through continued leadership in NATO, a continuing military presence, and continued support for Western European integration through the EU. The US leadership wants this, key European leaders (especially the British, Germans and French) want it, and, at least until instability in Russia subsides, the situation demands it (Kelleher, 1995).

The final misapprehension of the neo-realists was that the Europeans would revert immediately to traditional 'balance of power' politics. If two world wars, separated by economic nationalism and German (and Soviet) revisionism, has taught the Europeans nothing else, it has taught them – at least the West Europeans – that the old system of international politics was not sustainable. Indeed, fifty years of cooperation since the late 1940s has no doubt taught the European powers that a coordinated Europe has much more pull in the international arena than a disunited and internally competitive Europe. If anything, national self-interest tells the Europeans that there is more to gain in a globally interdependent international system dominated by economic relations from co-operation than from conflict amongst themselves – especially if they are to maintain a co-equal position with the United States and Japan in the global economy. The continued opposition in Germany – both popular and among the leadership – to nuclearisation and renationalisation of defence attests to the fundamental shift in attitude of the Europeans, and, perhaps most importantly, the Germans, away from traditional power politics on the continent (Kelleher, 1993: notes 19, 21, 27).

However, for all the shortcomings of the neo-realist position, it is not without merit; for it does raise legitimate concerns about the future of

Western Europe. Even though the Cold War was not the genesis for European cooperation, its end does pose serious challenges to continued cooperation. In particular, the EC, now European Union (EU), as the embodiment of post-war European cooperation, must adapt to a continually changing and increasingly uncertain European landscape if it is to survive and move forward. Specifically, this will require a fundamental re-examination of three major issue areas: first, it must address its internal relations (popularly referred to as 'deepening'); second, it must address the evolution of its external relations – including both 'widening' to the countries of the European Free Trade Area (EFTA) and Eastern Europe, and a redefinition of the transatlantic relationship; finally, it must re-examine the 'German Question', establishing a role for a newly unified (and economically dominant) Germany within a united – or at least cooperative – Europe.

Internal relations: deepening

The first concern, deepening of existing European Union structures, is of particular importance to 'Europeanist' states such as France and Germany and to the EU leadership in Brussels as well. These groups feel that current EU institutions must be strengthened if they are to weather the post-Cold War transition and emerge stronger, more united and on a level footing with other major powers – especially the United States and Japan. Deepening is a complex issue, but can be broadly defined by three processes: examining new forms of federalism, the continuation of integration measures along lines which have already shown some success, and institutional restructuring.

The first concern, examining new forms of federalism, is perhaps more theoretical than immediately practical. Most of the concerned parties (with the exception of only the most idealistic) have recognised that the EU will not be capable of developing along federalist lines in the US tradition (the discussion below is based on Sbragia, 1992). While the United States has always in the past served as 'the' model for federalism, it has become increasingly clear that such a model will not be sustainable in Western Europe. Thus the European and EU leadership must explore other options for closer integration which can serve as a blueprint to guide integrative steps.

One option which has emerged is a sort of 'federation of sovereignty', wherein member states establish a system of joint decisionmaking in lieu of ceding power to the EU. This approach is already being tried, as plans for the European Central Bank (ECB) allow for pooled sovereignty rather than a system akin to the US Federal Reserve. National

Central Banks will have ultimate authority, but will make European decisions jointly. This option, seemingly more confederative than federative, approximates the intergovernmental model which has driven the EU to date. As Sbragia notes: 'Integration has ... proceeded through the willingness of national governments to submit to one another – not to the Commission' (1992: 270). This option for federation is on the more conservative side, as it allows for only minimal (if any) evolution of decisionmaking above the national level, and is in some ways reminiscent of the 'Gentlemen's Courts' of the eighteenth and nineteenth centuries.

Another option, one which has gained currency among Europeanist states, is federation along German lines. According to this system, the state units are wholly responsible for policy implementation and administration, and have influence over policymaking as well. States have representation as one 'house' of the German parliament (the Bundesrat), and have co-equal powers with the federal government in some defined policy areas, e.g., education and cultural affairs. This federal system provides a proven, workable alternative to the US model, one which gives the constituent states more latitude within a system tighter than confederation. Indeed, many of the principles of subsidiarity are consistent with a German federative approach.

The German model, though, has some obvious drawbacks. One of the most glaring (at least for the present) is that it is a *German* model. Politically, the possibility of adopting a German form of government will be a sticky subject, as many European states – especially the smaller ones – could well see adoption of this model as an indication of German domination of the EU. Fears of a resurgence of German hegemonic instincts, even if contained within the EU framework, are still real, if not always directly expressed. The German economic system is already the *de facto* hegemon in Europe. Adding a made-in-Germany political structure could prove too much for European cooperation.

Examining the federation question, then, will prove no easy task. The choice between a minimalist, intergovernmental approach and a federative (though German-influenced) approach will no doubt involve much debate and may produce some third, hybrid system which incorporates elements of both. *Some* blueprint, however, will be vital if the EU is to emerge from the transition period stronger and more mature. The Inter-Governmental Conference (IGC) in 1996 was the perfect opportunity to construct such a blueprint.

The second concern with deepening, continuation of ongoing integration, is important on a much more substantive level. Using the now well-worn 'bicycle' analogy of the structural-functionalists, the EU must continue to move ahead with its programmes if it is not to fall over. This means focusing on strengthening programmes with which the EU has had proven success (especially in the economic realm) while forging stronger integrative ties in other areas, such as Common Foreign and Security Policy.

Specifically, this means ensuring that the outstanding legislation necessary for the completion of the 1992 initiative is enacted, and focusing more energy on progress towards Economic and Monetary Union (George, 1991). Even with the EMU crisis of the mid-1990s, EMU has shown promise. A *de facto* Deutschmark zone exists in central and northern Europe, and even some of the countries which have had currency crashes (notably France and Spain) have made a genuine commitment to keeping their currencies within the original, less forgiving exchange rate bands which preceded the crisis. Also, most EU states have made a commitment to give their central banks more autonomy in keeping with Maastricht criteria for setting up the ECB.

These events, coupled with continuing economic recovery in the UK, and the beginnings of recovery in Germany and elsewhere in Western Europe (not to mention the now well-established use of the Ecu as a unit of account), bode well for the future of EMU. While EMU will probably not develop exactly as envisioned in the Delors report of 1989 (Committee for the Study of Economic and Monetary Union, 1989), it *is* developing. Most recently, this has meant a proposal for a 'variable speed' Europe, wherein 'core' countries which are ready for close cooperation now (notably France, Germany and the Benelux states) can move forward while more peripheral states move towards closer cooperation at a pace they can sustain. This is good news for European integration (though perhaps not so good for Eurosceptics), as it means closer economic cooperation well into the future. This continued development of EU cooperation is essential if the EU 'bicycle' is to continue to move forward.

Finally, and perhaps most importantly, deepening must include institutional restructuring. With a federative blueprint to guide them, European leaders must restructure existing EU institutions to both streamline and strengthen decisionmaking and enforcement. This may include addressing the 'democratic deficit' by increasing the powers of the European Parliament in order to avoid the development of a 'cartel of governments'. It may also include expanding the scope of weighted-majority voting in the Commission. It will almost definitely mean expanding the mandate and authority of the European Court of Justice (ECJ). If the EU is to manage the transition period, it must have institutions in place which will be strong enough to manage substantial change in Europe and flexible enough to adapt to the addition of new member states.

External relations: widening

The challenge of widening is one of the most crucial issues facing the EU and its member states in their external relations. Widening is not only an immediate concern – at least two, and perhaps as many as six, new members from EFTA will enter the EU shortly – but also a longer-term problem. The EU must deal with the applications of Eastern European states in the future – indeed, perhaps sooner than they think – as well as those of Turkey, Malta, Cyprus and eventually perhaps even Ukraine.

The near-term concern is the easiest to swallow, but is by no means a simple matter. The shocks to EU member states and to EU institutions as well of expansion to the EFTA countries – Austria, Sweden, Finland and Norway – will be cushioned by the fact that most EFTA states will eventually be net contributors; they are all 'northern tier' countries with high standards of living and developed industrial sectors. Additionally, many of the EFTA applicants already adhere or come close to EU standards and policies as a matter of convenience, making their transition to equal partnership much easier.

The difficulties, though, are more bureaucratic and political. One is the effect of expansion on EU institutions, mentioned previously. This difficulty has led to a political battle between 'Europeanist' members (France, Germany) and 'Atlanticist' members (Britain, Spain, Ireland). The Europeanists have tried to delay widening, putting priority on deepening first – ostensibly so that the new members could be more easily ingested, but also to forestall any widening which would make creating consensus more difficult and would threaten accelerated progress towards tighter federation. The Atlanticists have promoted widening to the EFTA countries, for a variety of national and policy reasons. Britain, for example, would like to constrain the domain of the Brussels bureaucracy and slow deepening, primarily to minimise the deepening of current cooperative economic structures to more integrated common (but still ultimately national) policies. Spain, on the other hand, would welcome new members who would donate to, but probably not threaten, monies it receives through the regional development funds. Ireland, representative of many smaller Western European states, is hedging against Franco-German domination of the EU by welcoming the addition of new members, which would by definition dilute the combined voting power of France and Germany.

While these problems may seem manageable, they pale in comparison to the problems endemic to widening into Eastern Europe and beyond. While the EFTA applicants have fully developed market economies, none of the probable Eastern European applicants have. Most or all potential Eastern European applicants are still facing a difficult transition from centrally planned to market-based economies, and are thus likely to be net recipients of EU funds for some time, further straining the resources of the EU (and especially the regional development fund). Compounding the economic problems is the fact that the political situation in many of those countries is not yet stable. Underdeveloped economies and unstable internal politics are a poor recipe for countries aspiring to full membership in such a 'club' as the EU.

Even if these problems are overcome, there remains the issue of commitment on the part of Eastern European applicants. Eastern European countries may seek membership more for identity purposes than because of a commitment to full compliance with EU norms. While keen on accruing the economic benefits and international stature resulting from membership, these countries are not likely to be enthusiastic about the concept of transferring sovereignty to another outside body, given their recent and painful emergence from the Soviet Union's control. Thus granting membership to at least some of the applicants from Eastern Europe may put undue stress on EU integration.

In addition to these practical matters, there are political problems within the EU over EU accession. The 'Southern tier' countries are opposed to admitting any new members who might take away some of 'their' development money. France has opposed quick entry for the central European states because of the effects on deepening. And many of the member states fear the development of a North-Central European voting 'bloc' in the EU, led by Germany, if all of these states were to be added to the reorientation that will accompany the addition of the EFTA states.

Yet for all these problems, expansion is inevitable if the EU is to survive in the post-Cold War world. The question is no longer whether, but when, to expand. The EFTA countries will enter sooner rather than later (with at least Austria and Sweden entering soon), and probably more smoothly than is expected. The question of when to admit the Eastern European states is more troublesome. Poland, Hungary and the Czech Republic will undoubtedly be in the first in, as they are the farthest along the road to being market democracies. The fact that their economies are not fully developed, or their political systems not yet mature, may become less of a factor in the future, if the Greek and Spanish accessions are any indication. Also, the fears of a voting 'bloc' are probably overstated, as the new democracies would no doubt make a point of exerting independence from Germany. In any event, any voting arrangement within the EU would be preferable to the development of a new 'Mitteleuropa' outside of EU control.

The point is that the EU must expand. It is probably the most direct way to promote democracy in the East, the only way to promote economic development there in any systematic fashion, and an important way to extend a zone of security over the region through inclusion into Western 'clubs' as well as political and economic development. These things are crucial not only to the new democracies, but to the EU as well. Western Europe can ill afford to have a perpetually unstable and possibly violent region in its backyard, and would rather avoid an experience parallel to the continuing challenges faced by the United States in Latin America.

So both Western Europe and the new democracies of the East have a vested interest in moving forward, including (to the extent that it is possible) the new democracies eventually into a broader and stronger EU. For the near future, though, full membership seems unlikely. The expansion plan currently in vogue envisions a Europe of concentric circles, with the EU at the core, the EFTA states in the second tier and the Eastern European states in the outer circle. What this plan does not entail, and indeed what is for now off the agenda of the EU, is expansion to include those nettlesome others – Turkey, Cyprus and Ukraine. For various reasons, none of these countries is likely to see an invitation to EU membership for some time to come. Turkey is considered too peripheral, too politically unstable and too abusive in human rights fora to warrant membership; Cyprus has been a political mess for over thirty years, with no resolution in sight; and Ukraine is again too peripheral, and would unnecessarily antagonise Russia. Yet for the rest of Central and Eastern Europe, and definitely for the EFTA countries, some form of membership is only a matter of time.

Transatlantic relations

The other most vital external concern of Western Europe (and EU member states in particular) is the maintenance of transatlantic relations after the end of the Cold War. The rhetoric of the immediate post-Cold War era on both sides of the Atlantic was that the United States would remain committed, would remain a 'European power', and that Western Europe would welcome with open arms a continued US involvement in continental affairs. The Transatlantic Declaration of November 1990,

Bush's 'Partners in Leadership' speech, and numerous other events signalled that relations would remain strong.

Some began to doubt early on, however, that transatlantic relations would be able to remain the same. As the threat of the Cold War receded, the United States and Europe would have to base relations more on economics than security. Almost immediately, however, problems arose in the Euro-Atlantic relationship. The most glaring was the row over the Uruguay Round of the GATT. Conflicts over CAP reform, audio-visual issues and a host of other, less sensitive, sectors put into serious doubt the ability of the United States and Europe to maintain relations 'as usual' when economic competition replaced security co-operation as the primary locus of relations. The eleventh-hour compromise over the GATT did little to ease these doubts.

Three major post-Cold War crises, however, reinforced in no uncertain terms the necessity of continued US–European partnership and of US leadership of a united West. The first, the Gulf War, saw the United States take the early lead in coordinating (indeed, dominating) the Western response to Iraqi aggression. While the allied response to the War was strictly an *ad hoc* affair, it was clear that the United States was *the* leader, with the major nations of Europe playing a supporting (though not insignificant) role (Kelleher, 1994, 1995).

The second crisis, the war in Yugoslavia, saw the EU attempt to take the lead. The repeated failure of the EC/EU to bring a resolution to the conflict, and the eventual involvement of the UN and United States (both in negotiations and through NATO) made clear to the Europeans that they could not as yet lead as a cohesive unit, and that US involvement and leadership was still necessary, at least for the near-term future.

The third crisis, the ongoing turmoil in the former Soviet Union (and especially in Russia) served to convince actors on both sides of the Atlantic that a US presence would be necessary for some time. The failed coup of August 1991, and later the Yeltsin–Duma conflict which came to a head in October of 1993, opened the eyes of all concerned to the fact that, while the Cold War might be over, the instability which followed would require a continued commitment to solidarity and cooperation.

It is clear to both the governments of Western Europe and the United States, then, that cooperation will continue well into the future. Economic conflicts will undoubtedly arise between them, and there may indeed be less emphasis on showing a united front. Yet when the really serious issues are at stake, it is likely that transatlantic relations will hold fast.

All this leaves one question unanswered: where does the future of a Common Foreign and Security Policy (CFSP) for the EU lie? Given the poor showing of the EU in the Yugoslav crisis,[1] and given the attitude on both sides of the Atlantic (with the possible exception of France) that the United States and NATO will dominate European security for the near future, the options for CFSP and/or development of an autonomous European defence pillar under WEU auspices are limited. What seems to be emerging is a role for a semi-autonomous Europe in 'out of area' conflicts, especially peacekeeping missions. The proposed Combined/Joint Task Force (CJTF) initiative attempts, among other things, to earmark NATO assets for use by EU or other organisations for peacekeeping and other missions. If this proposal proves successful, it will allow Europe to develop a semi-autonomous force under the 'wing' of NATO, a role for which some Europeanist states (notably France) are grooming the Eurocorps. It will also allow Europe to develop CFSP in more evolutionary fashion, rather than thrusting it prematurely onto the world stage. In any case, the United States will remain a primary European power for some time to come.

Germany's role in the new Europe

Central to all these pressing issues is the reemergence of the 'German Question' – how to deal with a reunified, rejuvenated Germany in the centre of a changing Europe. Germany is clearly the economic, and some would argue political, leader in Europe. It has the largest and strongest economy in the region, a unique position on the continent geographically, and, with the addition of the eastern *Länder*, close to 25 per cent of Western Europe's population. However, it also has a disappointing track record as a unified state in terms of relations with its neighbours, at least up until 1945. For these reasons, finding an answer to the German Question will be a central task for Europe.

In regards to deepening, the German Question has influenced events by serving as a motivational factor. With the end of the Cold War and superpower hegemony, France (and other states) pushed vigorously to enmesh Germany more tightly within European institutions to prevent Germany attempting to 'go it alone'. As stated previously, European integration and tying Germany to European institutions has been a consistent French policy, and has become only more urgent with the end of the Cold War.

Germany, to its credit, has been in the forefront of the move towards closer integration. Whether because of fear of its own power, guilt over an inglorious past, a need to reassure edgy neighbours, or a genuine belief in the merits of integration, Germany has pushed every bit as hard as France for institutional deepening (it does not hurt that the agenda and shape of integration are heavily influenced by German concerns). With roots predating the Cold War, such integrative efforts are likely to continue and to strengthen European cooperation.

The German Question has similarly been central to the widening issue. The reasons have been stated previously, but bear repeating. Widening to the EFTA countries is desirable to many European states as a counter to Franco-German hegemony in EU decisionmaking structures. It is similarly desirable to Germany because it will take some of the economic pressure off Germany, the largest net contributor to the EU, and will add more Nordic states to the mix – Sweden, Austria, Finland and Norway. All are in the Deutschmark zone, and all are largely supportive of German concerns in economics and politics, in diplomacy and in trade policy.

Widening to the east also has been strongly influenced by the German question. Fears of German economic domination of the region (Germany is the largest European trading partner of every Visegrad state), and of an emerging 'Mitteleuropa' have put pressure on the EU to admit these Eastern states, or at least offer some sort of associate status, in order to retain some influence in the region and again discourage Germany 'going it alone' (a prospect unsettling to many in Germany as well).

On the security front, the German question has caused perhaps the most difficulty. This is not surprising, as German military adventurism was a major contributing cause of the deadliest European conflicts in this century. Providing for greater German involvement in European defence without raising the ghosts of Germany's military past is proving to be a delicate task.

On the one hand, many Western European states have come to believe, especially after the experiences of the Gulf War and Yugoslavia, that Germany must shoulder more of the burden of European security policymaking, and especially European involvement in peacekeeping. It is no longer acceptable for Germany to be simply the paymaster while other European nations offer up blood for peacekeeping operations. This has led to calls for direct German military participation, something Germany is loath to consent to, both because of historic problems of the Nazi past throughout Europe and the domestic political costs of any change in the present situation.

Yet, at the same time, there is significant aversion on the part of Western European states to expand German military involvement, because of history and the threat of renationalisation of defence. This has led to a stronger push for immersing Germany in a *European* defence identity, through EU and the Eurocorps (Kelleher, 1995). While the development of these two organisations has somewhat strained trans-atlantic relations, the United States nevertheless is generally supportive of tying Germany more strongly into multilateral Western European arrangements in the security field. Indeed, in *realpolitik* terms, it is as much the possibility (however remote) of a renationalised German military as it is fear of instability in the East which will keep the United States committed to Europe for the foreseeable future (Leech, 1991: p. 42). With Germany at the core of all the major issues confronting Europe in the post-Cold War world, then, a re-examination of the German Question is crucial to Western Europe's future.

Conclusion

It seems, then, that while the neo-realists were perhaps too pessimistic about the future of European cooperation, many of their concerns have some basis. Western Europe, and particularly the EU and its member states, face several crucial tests in the transition period from the Cold War to an uncertain future. Indeed, how long the transition period lasts will in large part be determined by how Western Europe responds to the challenges which lie ahead. If the EU can manage deepening and widening (whether in tandem or in order), if strong bonds are main-tained across the Atlantic, and if a reunited Germany finds a role with which all the major actors are comfortable, the post-Cold War world could well be marked by unprecedented cooperation. If Western Europe is not up to the challenges, though, the dark predictions of the neo-realists may well prove true. Such an outcome is too negative to be ignored. The challenges of the next five years may well shape inter-European and transatlantic relations for the next hundred. Western Europe must learn from the past, and build on it for the future.

NOTE

1 It is important to note that the EU was but one of the many of the organisations and states to fail in Yugoslavia. However, since the EU itself set Yugoslavia as a test case for its ability to act in unison in foreign policy issues, the failure of CFSP in Yugoslavia was particularly damaging.

REFERENCES

Arbatov, Georgi (1994) 'A New Cold War?', *Foreign Policy*, no. 95 (Summer), 90–104.

Committee for the Study of Economic and Monetary Union (1989) 'Report on Economic and Monetary Union in the European Community' (Luxembourg: Office of Official Publications).

Cook, Don (1981) *Ten Men and History* (New York: Doubleday).

Cromwell, William (1992) *The United States and the European Pillar* (New York: St. Martin's Press).

De Porte, Anton (1979) *Europe Between the Superpowers: the Enduring Balance* (New Haven: Yale University Press).

Garnham, David (1988) *The Politics of European Defence Cooperation* (Cambridge: Balliger).

Garthoff, Raymond L. (1994) *The Great Transition: American–Soviet Relations and the End of the Cold War* (Washington, DC: Brookings Institution).

George, Stephen (1991) *Politics and Policy in the European Community* (Oxford: Oxford University Press).

Gorbachev, Mikhail (1991) *The August Coup: The Truth and the Lessons* (New York: HarperCollins).

Harries, Owen (1993) 'The Collapse of "The West"', *Foreign Affairs*, vol. 72 (Sept./Oct. 1993), 41–53.

Kelleher, Catherine McArdle (1993) *A New Security Order: The United States and the European Community in the 1990's* (European Community Studies Association), ns. 19, 21, 27.

(1994) 'Cooperative Security in Europe', in Janne E. Nolan (ed.) (1994) *Global Engagement: Cooperation and Security in the 21st Century* (Washington, DC: Brookings Institution), pp. 292–351.

(1995) *The Future of European Security: An Interim Assessment* (Washington, DC: Brookings Institution).

Leech, John (1991) *Halt! Who Goes Where?: The Future of NATO in the New Europe* (London: Brassey's).

Mearsheimer, John (1990) 'Back to the Future: Instability in Europe After the Cold War', *International Security*, vol. 15 (Summer), 5–56.

Monnet, Jean (1989), *Memoires* (Paris: Fayard).

Sbragia, Alberta (1992) *Euro-Politics: Institutions and Policymaking in the "New" European Community* (Washington, DC: Brookings Institution).

Steinberg, James B. (1994) 'The Response of International Institutions to the Yugoslavia Conflict: Implications and Lessons', in F. Stephen Larrabee (ed.) *The Volatile Powder Keg: Balkan Security After the Cold War* (Washington, DC: American University Press), pp. 233–74.

Woodward, Susan (1995), *Balkan Tragedy: Chaos and Dissolution After the Cold War* (Washington, DC: Brookings Institution).

Robert O'Neill

Europe and intervention after the Cold War

In a volume on international security it can no longer be taken for granted that Europe has any right to be treated as an actor of dominating importance. The end of the Cold War has de-emphasised the role of NATO in world affairs. Global security is no longer primarily affected by the relationship between NATO and the Warsaw Pact. Rather the foci of attention now are the Security Council, its permanent members individually, a number of regional bodies, of which NATO and the European Union are but two, and the many crisis-ridden parts of the world which cry out for assistance.

Europe none the less has a considerable amount to offer as a supporter of security elsewhere. It is not, nor is it ever likely to be again, the principal provider of forces and resources for foreign military intervention as it was for so long between the fifteenth and twentieth centuries. The battering its component states gave to each other in the two world wars severely attenuated its long-held and formidable capacity to reach out and rearrange affairs in the Middle East, Africa, Asia, the Pacific and Latin America. Since 1945 it has been the United States which has borne the principal burden of leadership and commitment in international security affairs, chiefly by example. In the case of the Gulf War we saw another mighty intervener – although with resources not military contingents – in Japan.

None the less, since 1945, the states of Western Europe have not been absent as intervening powers in the name of international law. France and Britain have been involved in many, if not most, of the major conflicts of the post Second World War period. Italy, the Netherlands, Belgium, Spain and Portugal have also fought in several. And Germany is now poised to re-enter the field, cleared legally, if not fully in a political sense, of the burdens of past misadventures. The 1994 decision of its Constitutional Court that peacekeeping operations under the aegis of the United Nations do not conflict with the special requirements of the constitution regarding the use of force has removed the final obstacle to active security partnership outside the old NATO sense of self-defence.

Western Europe still has substantial military forces and considerable expertise in their use, particularly in areas which used to be part of the colonial empires. It has the means to project those forces over great distances. Its states have considerable experience in nation-building in other parts of the world. And despite their difficulties, are not the economies of the states of Western Europe much stronger than a generation or two earlier? Europe not only has capabilities to play a security role in the world but it also has economic and security interests in doing so, and, arguably, the moral obligation to help those struggling towards its own levels of peace and cooperation. The clamour of international public opinion to criticise European ineffectiveness in the Bosnian crisis shows very clearly that the world expects Europe to play a major part outside its own borders.

Further, we know that it is unrealistic to expect that the United States will continue to shoulder the burden of intervention and other forms of security assistance to the extent that it has in the period since 1945. But we also recognise a new potential contributor to international security in Japan – increasingly powerful, and slowly coming to terms with its troubled past so that it can play a more active role in securing peace around the world. Mindful of the G7 mechanism which links this peculiarly rich, democratic and militarily secure group of states, which have so many interests in common, it would seem obtuse not to keep in mind the prospect that Europe's long-term security role in the world will be played in partnership with the United States and Japan rather than in any separate sense.

Europe's prime security responsibilities after the Cold War

But where and how is European influence likely to be needed most in the short and mid-term futures? On the borders of the European Union lies a broad sweep of troubled countries: the arc embracing Central and Eastern Europe, the eastern Mediterranean and the Maghreb. If parts of that sweep of troubled states erupt in conflict or if government breaks down there, Western Europe will be directly affected, and in some cases may be the only members of the G-7 to suffer. Japan and the United States may be willing to provide some assistance but their European partners will be expected to take the lead. The further one goes from the eastern border of the EU into Russia the greater will be the obligation on the US and Japan to assist, but in the heartland from Germany to Russia, Western Europe clearly has to take the lead.

The extent of Europe's security interests does not stop at the boundaries of its neighbouring regions. The flagrancy of Saddam Hussein's disregard for international law demands a response from the whole international community, Europe included. Weapons of mass destruction remain a global problem, of increasing proportions. Crime, drugs and terrorism can intrude from abroad, wherever airlines fly or cargo vessels ply. The human agonies of central Africa, the Horn of Africa and Cambodia simply cannot be ignored by any state which claims to have a commitment to uphold justice and democracy, and whose people know of the tragedies afflicting other sectors of humankind. And Europe will have to bear its share of the teamwork involved in strengthening the fabric of peace and international order through the United Nations and whatever subsidiary or regional organisations are established to these ends. Fortunately similarities between the causes of insecurity in Eastern Europe and in developing countries further afield underline the possibility for shaping a common approach to dealing with them.

The legacies of the past century of conflict

Before considering policies for the future it is well to look at the constraints of our current context – constraints set by the learning process through which Europe has been in the twentieth century. This experience has influenced the policies and attitudes of all of us, from political leaders, their civil and military advisers, leaders of public opinion and others who think professionally about security matters through to public opinion – those whose votes determine ultimately what our taxes go to and how large our armed forces are. There is an almost unanimous view that major inter-state wars in Europe advance the interests of nobody and should be consigned to history. They are not impossible, but their probability is extremely low, and we can keep it so by intelligent pre-emptive action, by state-building in a context of lessons derived from our past unhappy experience.

The First World War demonstrated that the maintenance of stability in Europe is a multilateral problem. There is no invisible hand to keep its nations from colliding with each other. If all interpretation of state behaviour is done on a unilateral basis by other states, suspicions and mistrust will accumulate. The need for multinational bodies to iron out differences and uphold the peace is virtually universally accepted, and has been acted upon. The League of Nations was not a brilliant success but nor was it a total failure. Building on the lessons of the 1920s and 1930s the founders of the United Nations have been able to develop something better, something which, for all its inadequacies, is becoming more effective and influential. Europe itself has the Organisation (formerly Conference) on Security and Co-operation in Europe (OSCE), backed by the EU, NATO and the WEU. But the foundation of peace, continent wide, has to be through an organisation which links it all together.

The destructiveness of modern weapons has inspired numerous attempts at disarmament and out of their failure has grown the more productive approach of arms control – which admittedly does not yet have much impact on the conventional arms trade, but it has inhibited the proliferation of nuclear, biological and chemical weapons. There is a realisation, widely but not universally shared, that their development and transfer is more of a threat to international security than a support. States have a common interest in limiting the nature and numbers of weapons that they have, and most understand that arms races are interactive events. It is more widely accepted that one country's security is often bought at the cost of subjecting another to a new threat. Continent-wide security requires an arms control framework which includes all member states of Europe, and which is supported by confidence-building measures.

One of the legacies of the era of world wars which is not so helpful is the Munich syndrome: the idea that only the weak and deluded can fail to confront an aggressor, rapidly and with overpowering force. Quite apart from the simplistic misunderstanding of Chamberlain's policy which this critique implies, let us not forget the view of his most robust of challengers, Winston Churchill, that 'Jaw, jaw is better than war, war!' At a time when regional strongmen or dictators are well enough equipped to inflict immense damage on their neighbours, even though it may be to their own ultimate cost, Churchill's advice seems to have even more merit than in the era when he first enunciated it. It served the world well during the Cold War and it would be foolish for European leaders to forget it in the years ahead. Peace is upheld by conferring, consulting and cooperating together – again on a continent-wide basis, not in sealed packages.

Perhaps the most important lesson of the past century of conflict is that ultimately public opinion is the dominant force in both national and international politics. The communist system was very strong, but when it persistently failed to deliver the political freedoms and the economic and social benefits that its masters and subjects knew to be available in the West, it lost vital credibility with those who had to uphold it. Eastern

European governments know that to keep their seats they have to offer much higher standards of living than at present and far wider choice in terms of employment and social development, recreation and enjoyment. Western governments have to respect the reluctance of their voters to pay heavy taxes to support large military establishments or to underwrite foreign commitments of doubtful relevance to their own living standards. This does not mean that no such commitments can be undertaken, but governments have to be circumspect. Public opinion in this field is not an iron prohibition but a general constraint on policy. Governments and constitutions, if they are to survive, have to offer their citizens interesting and rewarding lives, not just place demands and duties on them. Economy of effort is a vital component of security policies which have to run the gauntlet of public opinion – strengthening the case for taking preemptive action rather than waiting until major conflict has erupted on our borders.

Finally, we have to take into account human nature. The instinct to resort to violence when frustrated or threatened has been deeply seated in our stock for hundreds of thousands of years. We needed those drives to survive, both in competition with other species and against the threat of other human beings. It will not be massaged out of our systems in the next few years just because the ideological conflict that Francis Fukuyama confuses with the course of history has ended. Violence is being, and will be, used whenever men and women feel that they have no other recourse, through their governments, their religions, their employers or their social institutions to avoid disaster for themselves and their families. The leaders of religious, ethnic and immigrant communities, and of political parties or factions thereof, will continue to draw on this source of influence and exploit it both for indirect leverage in bargaining and for direct effect in conflict when all else seems likely to fail. Thus it is more at this level than that of nations that we must aim our policies in post-Cold War Europe.

Europe's new security challenges

Turning from the lessons of past experience to the future, it is clear that we have to confront a series of security challenges which are quite different in nature to those of the past century. The principal threat to the security of Europe is no longer major international war initiated by other European powers but an avalanche of chaos falling on the West from the Centre, East and South, possibly reinforced by some of the remaining elements of military power left from the Cold War, including nuclear warheads. A less dire, but more probable danger is an overflowing into the West of the consequences of domestic strife in a single state in the region of stress and change.

The causes of such dangers lie primarily in the weak, defective political structures of most of the states on Europe's southern and eastern flank. They give little back to their citizens in return for what they supply with their own labour and the privations that they have to tolerate. Some are still ruled by oppressive governments, which discriminate against minorities on ethnic, ideological, religious or gender grounds. In many of them corruption and maladministration are rife. Several are disintegrating or, like Yugoslavia, have already disintegrated. Most have economies which do not produce what their citizens really want to buy in the face of open competition from external suppliers. They are crucially short of capital for development. They are trying to enter the international economic system more fully at a time when the developed states are bracing themselves under the chill wind of competition, lower market protection and down-sizing. Their social infrastructure is weak, with poor provision for care of the sick and the aged, and pension schemes which are meaningless. Their educational institutions are starved for resources, not only libraries and laboratories, but also faculty members to replace those brain-drained away to more developed countries. Some have military forces which do not respect the primacy of civil authority and are a law unto themselves. Their trade unions are weak. Standards of local government are poor and the police are severely inadequate to preserve order and give people a high sense of confidence that they and their property will be safe.

These weaknesses have already led to the collapse of state authority in Yugoslavia and they threaten stability in many of the former component states of the Soviet Union. Algeria and Egypt are under stress. Romania and Bulgaria are making very slow progress towards robust health. A serious worsening of this situation is the prime security challenge facing Europe in the generation ahead. There is a military component to it, but in general this challenge is far wider in nature than those of preceding eras, particularly that of the Cold War.

A need for greater emphasis on conflict prevention

There is a clear and pressing need for action, both to contain conflict and to prevent it. It is greatly to be regretted that more was not done to pre-empt and contain communal strife in the former Yugoslavia before it broke up. In the event the crisis was worsened by Germany's hasty recognition of Croatia's claim to be a separate state. Had there been even a modicum of contingency planning purely among the states of

Western Europe, the breaking-up of Yugoslavia would surely have been handled more effectively, with less open resort to arms and more emphasis on negotiation. At least they could have tested whether a negotiated settlement would have been possible without the sudden rush into war.

Pre-emptive action has been applied through Western, regional and United Nations agencies in other trouble-prone parts of the world, such as South-East Asia, to considerable effect. There the excellent final result was due largely to indigenous determination and effort, not least through the formation of ASEAN and the cooperation which it has led to. But the whole process was assisted in its early stages in the 1950s and 1960s by support from Britain and the United States. The recent establishment of the ASEAN Regional Forum has put ASEAN at the peak of a secure and prospering network which extends throughout East Asia and the Western Pacific.

In the context of the 1990s, where states clearly will not accept unwelcome advice, considerable care has to be taken in deciding on which sectors external assistance should focus. The intrusion of ideas seen to be subversive of their power bases will not be tolerated by governments not fully committed to the tenets of democracy. Here some difficult decisions will be necessary because contradictions between the human rights aspirations of Western taxpayers and the nature of governments being assisted are bound to arise. But there is nothing new in this, as anyone associated with assistance programmes for developing countries knows well. It is certainly not a valid reason for turning one's back on troubled states in the hope that the wider problems that they pose for international order and security will evaporate without further action.

The provision of assistance in the building of democratic states with thriving economies, and endowed with internal and external security, calls for expertise on a wide series of fronts, civil and military. Clearly security still has an important military dimension, but the way in which the term has been used in public debate in the period of the New World Disorder, i.e., the years since 1990, suggests that all too few have incorporated this broader, integrated view into their own thinking. Perhaps this tendency is to be explained by our failure to develop effective means of conflict-prevention assistance, leaving everything, even humanitarian relief missions, to be done by armed forces once the situation has gone beyond the point of open bloodshed.

Western assistance teams will have to be tailored to particular situations, but most will require specialists in democratic practice, law, local government, public health, communal relations, religious affairs, urban development, economics and business development, policing and military affairs. The nearer the situation to actual violence the greater the military component must be. It will never be absent, even if the need is only for advice on how the democratic essentials of civil–military relations are to be implemented in societies which have either never followed them or have neglected them for a very long time. Although the most obvious areas in which such assistance teams might be deployed are Central and Eastern Europe and the southern shore of the Mediterranean, composite groups of this nature would also be relevant for regions further away, particularly in Central and Southern Africa. In other words, the development of this form of preventive security assistance would both serve Europe's direct needs and help to meet its obligations on a global basis.

How should Europe develop its conflict-prevention capabilities?

Essentially Europe faces a problem of organisation in this regard. Already within the social fabrics of virtually all the members of the European Union are persons with the necessary skills. They are to be found in government service, national and local, business, academia, voluntary organisations of many kinds, the armed forces, regular and reserve, and the ranks of the retired and unemployed. But none of their parent states has attempted to put these persons together into integrated functional teams for service in troubled areas abroad. Rather, experts have been sent abroad in an *ad hoc* and non-integrated manner to take part in wider missions sponsored by bodies such as the UN and private aid agencies. A few have come together under the aegis of the EU, NATO, the OSCE and the WEU, especially for observer tasks, but these have been sent well after the time at which assistance could have been truly preventive of violence.

Furthermore, even though the component personnel for such teams exist in the main, this cannot be said for those who would have to give them leadership and direction, and to plan well ahead for their deployment. When teams are sent abroad today they tend to address a narrow band of the security spectrum rather than the full range needed in statebuilding, in the context of an immediate security crisis. Thus special training will have to be provided for those charged with leadership, and it will have to be done in such a way that it does not unduly blinker those receiving it. The development of such training will require a major intellectual effort by participating governments and the academic and research community supporting their efforts. It would be the first serious effort to meet the challenge of developing a new operational concept of security since the end of the Cold War.

What organisations can Europe use for action?

The OSCE

The most obvious body to oversee the strengthening of security is the OSCE as it embraces both halves of Europe, bringing in everyone involved, from the United States and Canada in the west to Russia in the east. In theory at least it has also the breadth of vision to cover most of the security problems of the area of prime concern to Western Europe. The OSCE has been encouraged to develop and do more by the European Union, under the aegis of its security group within the framework of the Common Foreign and Security Policy, and the OSCE now has a secretary general. Unfortunately it has little capacity to take decisions and implement them. Its constitution requires unanimity, which will often prove elusive in contentious security matters. It has very few analytical or planning staff and its capacity for controlling complex, sensitive and dangerous operations is virtually non-existent. Sadly the OSCE is unlikely ever to become the right vehicle for active security cooperation, as distinct from dialogue, because its members do not wish to see it become a powerful regional actor in its own right. In that sense its composition is too powerful for its own good. None the less, OSCE's role as a forum for discussion of security issues is indispensable, and its Programme for Immediate Action is an important step in the right direction. This programme requires member states to adopt common rules of politico-military behaviour, to implement fully the treaties governing conventional force levels in Europe and the non-proliferation of weapons of mass destruction, to develop further the existing Vienna agreement on confidence-building measures and to participate in the global exchange of information on military matters. Its Forum for Security Co-operation is also useful, especially for subregional arms control matters.

NATO

A much more promising agent of cooperation is NATO, and its post Cold War additions, the North Atlantic Co-operation Council (NACC), the Partnership for Peace linkage (PFP), and the Rapid Reaction Corps (RRC). NATO itself remains the security guarantor of last resort in Europe. It is the bedrock on which all else is founded. It is the ultimate bulwark against nuclear blackmail from Russia or any other nuclear weapons state. It has a planning capability unmatched by any other security body. It can take decisions quickly and effectively and it has a well-developed command and control system for field operations. In short, without it Europe would be in a very worrisome state. Hence its European members have a very strong interest in ensuring that the alliance retains the strong support and interest of the United States in European security affairs – no easy challenge in the 1990s and beyond.

But NATO's expertise lies essentially in the military field. It has for most of its life been focused on deterring the threat of massive attack by the Warsaw Pact, rather than on preventing or containing socio-political or communal threats within its area of operation. The Atlantic Treaty has provision for cooperation in the non-military aspects of security but it has never really branched out into this field. Essentially this expansion of the treaty's coverage was a sop to Lester Pearson, to ease his internal political problems in having the Canadian parliament ratify the treaty, rather than a statement of serious intent.

The establishment of the North Atlantic Co-operation Council (NACC) has created a useful forum for discussion of military matters between NATO members and former Warsaw Pact states. It is an important token of NATO's good offices, and its intentions to eliminate serious causes of misunderstanding on military matters, but it is a consultative body and its focus is essentially military in nature.

The series of agreements with Central and Eastern European states known as the Partnership for Peace have widened and intensified the areas of practical political and military cooperation, including the development of potential for joint peacekeeping operations. The PFP cell at Mons affords a foothold for small missions from the participating states outside NATO's ranks. But the arrangement only underlines the basic reluctance of NATO members to bring the eastern states into more active partnership and offer them some security guarantee. And, of course, the cooperation fostered under PFP does not extend beyond the military and political realms.

NATO has been criticised for playing only a marginal role in the Bosnian conflict. To the extent that the outcomes of that conflict have been determined by the ground forces of the local combatants, this verdict is correct. NATO none the less has mounted air operations which have imposed some limits on the scope of the actions which could be undertaken by the combatants, particularly by the Bosnian Serbs, and this containing influence has probably also had a beneficial effect on Slobodan Milosevic and his government in Belgrade. While NATO has not played a dominant role in a conflict which it had the military power to halt, it has shown itself to be a factor which has to be weighed by potential aggressors, even within the borders of existing states.

Sadly, NATO's deterrent power in such situations is very limited. If a strongman wishes to act with his own ground forces against those of a non-NATO neighbour in South-eastern Europe, the lesson of the past two years of conflict in Yugoslavia is that NATO probably will not wish to intervene. Admittedly the abolition of the strict definition of the area in which NATO forces could operate, and the willingness of the Germans to take part in peacekeeping operations, have done much to strengthen NATO's credibility as a guardian of the peace. But they have not done much for NATO's capacity to prevent conflict through addressing its social and economic roots.

The European Union

Under the Maastricht Treaty, not only do we have the European Union but also a Common Foreign and Security Policy. The European Union is potentially the most important provider of security outside the strictly military field. Its competence extends to cover all the political, economic and social issues which are at the heart of security problems on the Union's periphery, and it has the capacity to take and implement policy decisions. It also has the ability to widen its membership and integrate the most trouble-prone parts of Europe into its own structure. But we know from the recent sad history of European integration, particularly the debates on the ratification of the Maastricht Treaty, that there is at present very little consensus on further integration, let alone on building an effective security linkage within the EU.

The more Atlanticist governments, particularly the British, are opposed to taking any action which will set up a competing organisation with NATO. Although the French government remains interested in limiting the scope of United States authority in European affairs, it does not wish to drive the United States out altogether. Europe is also suffering from a general nationalist backlash against federalist designs, monetary union, Brussels and the directives which emanate from it, and the apparently overreaching ambitions of former EC President Jacques Delors and his multitudinous minions. In this situation the EU does not seem to be a feasible means for developing what is necessary to strengthen security on the whole continent.

In order to obtain Danish ratification, substantial exemptions were granted from participation in the fields of defence, citizenship and judicial affairs, setting a precedent which could lead to the unravelling of a delicate structure that has been long in the building. Obviously the other members of the Union were gambling that the forces of integration would assert themselves once the ratification debates were through, bringing Denmark back into line with the other eleven, but events could still go in either direction. In the meantime, the current for integration in the other major powers seems to have died.

In the economic field the prospect for a major, albeit indirect, EU contribution to security is more optimistic. The Union is reaching out to Central and Eastern Europe through trade and cooperation agreements, supported by the European Bank for Reconstruction and Development, and the PHARE programme of economic assistance. The Hurd–Andreatta proposals for regular liaison between the EU and eastern associate countries were accepted, bringing their governments into consultation on CFSP matters, and thereby underpinning economic cooperation with political dialogue. But more formal linkage will clearly take many years to achieve, even in the case of the most eligible, the Visegard Four, and by the Baltic states. And Russia, Belarus and Ukraine, not to mention the states of the Balkans and the Caucasus, seem likely to remain beyond the pale of membership. Obviously the plan for economic cooperation and assistance will have to extend far wider than the circle of those who might be expected to join the EU over the next fifteen years.

But this kind of economic support is not enough by itself to underpin a really secure region on Europe's borders. Furthermore, much of the rationale for this economic assistance is limited to the economic sphere itself. The *leitmotiv* seems to be: 'If you can make money by investing in the region then do so by all means: if not, don't.' This line of reasoning simply ignores the security dividends of economic assistance, not to mention the longer-term economic costs to EU members of having to rectify chaos and even fight a war. We need a new type of calculus which takes the total sum of costs and benefits into account, not merely the direct economic consequences. And this has to be a matter for governments and the EU itself, not for the private sector.

The Western European Union

The remaining means of influence open to the states of Western Europe is their own Western European Union. This organisation, resurrected by the French as a counterpoint to NATO in the mid-1980s, is now enjoying a vigorous new lease of life, at least as a debating and planning mechanism, if not as a potent force in European security affairs. After a period when NATO and the WEU tended to be seen by members as rivals, both have settled into a cooperative relationship. It is a somewhat one-sided partnership because NATO has most of the assets which the WEU would need to undertake sustained deployment, particularly command and control facilities, transport and logistic support. And NATO has now cast off the inhibition of being unable to operate outside of the NATO area.

As the embodiment of the Western European powers' determination to have some defence capability which is independent of that provided by the United States, the WEU is valuable, but constant care will have to be taken to see that its very existence does not weaken NATO's cohesion. At present that is not a danger, and given even the French willingness to retain NATO, the separate purpose and roles of the WEU are somewhat unclear at present. Its major limitation is very similar to that of NATO: it is essentially another military means of ensuring security. Like NATO, it lacks competence in the economic and social aspects which are such dominant causes of conflict in and around Europe today.

What else is needed?

Thus there is at present no body, alliance or other grouping in Europe which addresses comprehensively the security problems of the post-Cold War era. We have seen a heavy price paid on our very doorstep for this absence in Croatia and Bosnia. This will not be the end of such bloodshed and suffering. The states of Western Europe are *the* proximate group of powers with resources to contain and remedy these problems. The United States is unlikely to play more than a supporting role. If Europe cannot look after its own bordering regions, why should the United States take the lead, many Americans will ask of any president who proposes a major intervention.

Europe now needs to create a body which can help maintain and strengthen security in these regions. To meet the Cold War it created NATO. To meet the new problems it needs something different. It must be an organisation which has diverse competences and skills, but all aimed at the long-term building of secure, prosperous states which ultimately can either take their place as members of the European Union, or enter into long, close and peaceful association with it. Such a body does not have to be large, or have many permanently dedicated components. In essence it should be a linkage, reporting both to the North Atlantic and the European Councils, with planning arms covering each of the key determinants of security: economic development, political development, social policy, international relations, military planning and development, and arms control. It could profit by taking a leaf out of NATO's book in terms of its planning, mobilisation and command and control capabilities – not on anything like the same scale, but giving the organisation the means to analyse developments, foresee crises and other contingencies, and then plan action to deter, preempt or contain them. A natural name for this body would be *The Alliance for Development in Europe*. The term 'alliance' signifies partnership in facing a common enemy – chaos – and 'for Development in Europe' specifies the task to be undertaken to defeat the enemy. But, given the current political climate, naming such a body so clearly may prevent it from being born at all. Rather than run this risk it may be better, in the short term at least, to leave it with a low profile as just a functional linkage of officials and military officers working quietly together.

This body would need to work on several time scales – the long term for economic and social development, the mid term for military force development and political reforms, and the short term for peacekeeping, conflict resolution or peace enforcement. It would not be enough simply to coordinate the short-term aspects of this work (as happens at present) because the other areas also require special attention from a security perspective. If economic development is fostered entirely according to economic criteria millions will starve or be dispossessed. If social change is fostered without an eye to security, competing groups can collide on the road to affluence and harmony. If political reform is undertaken without paying heed to security requirements it can lead to weakness and lack of cohesion. Excessive focusing on military forces can also undermine security.

The challenge to thinkers, in government, the armed services, the research institutes and the media now is to develop a new science of security which fits the new era, in much the same way that military strategy of the pre-nuclear era had to adapt to the Cold War. The products of their thought then need to be applied to a new structure which can shape practical policy and help implement it. This is an area in which Europe can take the lead and show the way to other regions, enhancing its own standing *vis-à-vis* the United States, Japan and the countries on its periphery for which it can do the most. Indeed the United States and Japan should be drawn into consultative partnership with this linkage, both to keep them informed and to have the benefit of whatever direct support they might be willing to offer for policies which also advance their own security interests.

Without such broad planning and executive capability, Europe and its bordering regions are likely to drift on, blindly hoping for the best in 1930s style, until a major crisis arises to compel action. This will inevitably be both extremely costly to resolve and corrosive of trust and confidence among Europe's partners. It is time to wake up to the demands of a new era in international and European affairs before the ship goes onto the rocks.

REFERENCES

The list below consists of suggestions for further reading on the chapter's main themes:

Forster, Anthony (1994) 'Variable Geometry: WEU and the European Security Identity' (unpublished paper delivered at St Antony's College European Studies Centre, Oxford), 10 May.
Jopp, Mathias (1994) *The Strategic Implications of European Integration*, Adelphi Paper 290 (London: International Institute for Strategic Studies).
Kelleher, Catherine McArdle (1994) 'Cooperative Security in Europe', in Janne Nolan (ed.), *Global Engagement* (Washington, DC: Brookings Institution), pp. 293–351.
Munuera, Gabriel (1994) *Preventing Armed Conflict in Europe*, Chaillot Papers 15/116 (Paris: Institute for Security Studies, Western European Union).
NATO Press Service (1994) *Partnership for Peace: Declaration of the Heads of State and Government* (Brussels: Press Communiqué M-1(94)3), 11 Jan.
NATO Press Service (1994) *Meeting of the North Atlantic Cooperation Council in Istanbul, Turkey: Report to ministers by the NACC Ad Hoc Group on Cooperation in Peacekeeping* (Brussels: Press Release M-NACC-1(94)47), 10 June.
NATO Press Service (1994) *Statement issued at the Meeting of the North Atlantic Cooperation Council in Istanbul, Turkey* (Brussels: Press Release M-NACC-1(94)48), 10 June.
NATO Press Service (1994) *Ministerial Meeting of the North Atlantic Council in Istanbul – 9 June 1994* (Brussels: Press Communiqué M-NAC-1(94)46), 9 June.
NATO Press Service (1994) *Summary of Conclusions of Discussions between The North Atlantic Council and Foreign Minister of Russia Andrei Kozyrev* (Brussels: Unnumbered Press Release), 22 June.
O'Neill, Robert (1992) 'Securing Peace in Europe in the 1990s', in Beatrice Heuser and Robert O'Neill (eds.), *Securing Peace in Europe 1945–62, Thoughts for the Post-Cold War Era* (London: Macmillan), pp. 313–30.
Political Committee of the Assembly of the EU (1994) *WEU in the Process of European Union*, Document 1417 (Assembly of the Western European Union), 10 May.

I am grateful for research assistance in preparing this paper to Holly Wyatt-Walter of St Anthony's College, Oxford, and Juliet Sampson of the International Institute for Strategic Studies, London.

10   A new Japan? A new history?

Geoffrey Hawthorn

The material future of East Asia is clear. Japan's GNP is second only to that of the United States. Even though their economic growth, like Japan's, is now slowing, Singapore, South Korea and Taiwan have also reached a high level. Others in the region, including China, are growing quickly, and those that are not are set to. Politically, however, in itself and in its implications for the rest of the world, the East Asian future is opaque. Some observers, especially in the United States, foresee a new military power, even a threat. Some, especially in Japan, see something more peaceably 'civilian'. Some expect a less dramatic change. But no-one doubts that East Asia will be a force, and that the kind of force it will be will be determined largely by Japan.

The arguments

Self-described 'realists' see no reason to believe that a future that contains a rich Japan will be different. 'For a country to choose not to become a great power', Kenneth Waltz argues, 'is a structural anomaly. For that reason, the choice is a difficult one to sustain. Sooner or later, the international status of countries has risen in step with their material resources. Countries with great-power economies have become great powers, whether or not reluctantly.' Waltz believes that Japan will overcome its deep resistance to nuclear weapons, and realising that such weapons make alliances less necessary, hold a new balance of power in the world against the United States and a nuclear Germany (1993: 50, 55, 64, 66; also Huntington, 1993; Layne, 1993). Those inclined to expect hegemony predict a Pax Nipponica. William Dietrich has suggested that by 2015, Japan's per capita GNP will be four times that of the United States. Japan will dominate every leading industry and control the world's financial flows. The other East Asian economies will be in a second tier, the United States and Western Europe in a third. And against the claim that 'hegemons' always generate a concerted resistance (Waltz, 1993: 76), Dietrich expects the other two great powers to accept Japan's by then decisive contribution to world order (1991: 263–6; also Williams, 1994: 4).

The more idealistic agree that Japan will deploy its growing power, but argue that it will do so in a more distinctively 'civilian' way (Maull, 1991; Taira, 1993; Tsuru, 1993: 212–35). The new 'world banker', suggests Funabashi Yoichi, a journalist working in the United States, will (or should) 'design and contribute to the building of an international order based on something more than economic growth' (1994: 12–13): on giving assistance to poorer countries (Japan became the world's largest bilateral aid donor in 1989, and channels a higher proportion of its aid than any other donor through the multilateral institutions), on international peacekeeping (the Diet has agreed that Japan's Self Defence Forces can take part in United Nations exercises for this purpose), on the extension of human rights (Japan aligned itself with the West at the UN conference in Vienna in 1993) and on encouraging environmental protection.

Others are more circumspect. Economically, Japan may be a rising star, an important financial market and the world's largest creditor, and on occasion able to determine what, economically, other states can do (Helleiner, 1990; Huntington, 1993; Strange, 1994). But in so far as any individual state can now do so, the United States, in itself and through its domination of the international financial institutions, continues to shape the world economy, and like Western Europe, is far from beaten. Moreover, the circumspect add, Japan shows few signs of wishing to extend its economic power to other realms. On the contrary. It is and may remain a 'reactive' state, unwilling – and because of its lack of vision and the 'immobilism' of its domestic politics, perhaps also unable – to take any initiative of its own (Calder, 1988b; Pyle, 1992). At most, it will continue actively to avoid collective security agreements, of which it has no experience, and seek to maintain the low-cost, low-risk strategy of military protection by the United States that it adopted under Prime Minister Yoshida Shigeru in 1952. It will be willing to increase its financial contributions to US forces on its territory (it raised this to 50 per cent in 1995), and make whatever other concessions it has to in order to avoid becoming a great military power (Inoguchi, 1993; Langdon and Akaha, 1993; Pharr, 1993; Johnson and Keehn, 1995).

These differences of opinion are not surprising. The reach of Japan's economy, relations between all the states in North- and South-east Asia, Japan's reaction to defeat in 1945 and the standing of its Mutual Security Treaty with the United States, its internal politics and those of the other East Asian countries, together with wider conceptions in the 1990s of the nature of national interest and international security, are complex matters, are changing, and connect, if they do, in ways that the protagonists themselves are still trying to understand.

Japan's economy

Even though Yoshida, who, with American support, crystallised it, would never admit the description, Japan's post-war economic policy has been what in the West would be called 'mercantilist'. 'Post-war Japan defined itself as a cultural state holding the principles of liberalism, democracy and peace', a former vice-minister of the Ministry of International Trade and Industry (MITI) conceded in 1988, 'but these were only superficial principles [*tatemae*]. The fundamental objective [*honne*] was pouring all of our strength into economic growth' (quoted by Pyle, 1993: 122).

Tsuru Shigeto has nicely described the 'administrative guidance' for this growth (1993; Johnson, 1982 is the classic Western study). At the start, there was *mugi-fumi*, 'treading on wheat nurseries', strengthening young plants by massaging their roots. Thus stimulated, firms were promised *yamagoya*, 'mountain shelters'; if they over-reached themselves and had difficulty, there would be relief. No-one forced anyone to do anything, and where there were laws, as there eventually were on prices, these were almost always 'undrawn swords' whose mere existence made the guidance 'cut better'. MITI would sometimes take the initiative, sometimes not. But where necessary it would provide the best information it could on overseas markets, bring the potential participants together, work in concert with the 'window guidance' of the Bank of Japan, arrange tax breaks, provide licences to import technology and protect firms from foreign competition. In forty years, the country's GNP increased 152 times.

But this period of directed growth is now past. In the later 1980s, the successful corporations were able to generate sufficient profits to repay their debts, further increase their spending on research and development, invest abroad, diversify their production and speculate in securities and land. They were stimulated into doing so, ironically, by the Plaza Accord in 1985, the first of a series of international measures pressed by the United States and intended to redress the imbalance of trade between Japan and the other industrial economies. The revaluation of the yen under the Accord did at first deliver the blow to Japan's competitiveness that the United States intended. But the corporations responded by cutting costs and increasing investment to the extent to which, within two years, this had as a proportion of GNP exceeded the record set just before the end of the Bretton Woods agreement and the first oil-price rise at the beginning of the 1970s. In 1987, through six of the Group of Seven (Italy did not participate), the United States retaliated in the Louvre Accord on trade. This reduced its overall trade deficit, but made little impact on that with Japan. In 1989, responding to Tokyo's apparent willingness in the Maekawa Reports in 1986 and 1987 to consider 'structural change', Washington tried again with a Structural Impediments Initiative. This was intended to raise domestic demand in Japan and reduce the high rate of savings and investment in the new 'super industrialism', the *heisei*, of later 1980s. But Prime Minister Nakasone Yasuhiro declared that the central targets were ones that Japan could only 'do its best to meet in the medium to long term'. In February 1990, Washington indicated to Nakasone's successor Kaifu Toshiki that unless Tokyo acted more decisively, it would reconsider the Mutual Security Treaty. Kaifu conceded (Pyle, 1992: 93, 106; Takenaka, 1994; Williams, 1994: 64).

Since 1991, however, Japan has had reasons of its own to reform. Economic growth has slowed, perhaps irreversibly. Many firms have found themselves overextended, and, with the help of a strong yen, have been drawing money back from abroad to service the debts they incurred at home in the bubble of the later 1980s and to maintain their domestic balance sheets. They have also returned some of the manufacturing they had devolved to countries to the south. For fear of increasing its trade surplus, however, Tokyo cannot significantly weaken the yen by lowering interest rates. For fear of unemployment, which has been rising slightly as firms cut costs further, and seeing no other reason to disturb an arrangement that has worked so well, it resists more radical industrial deregulation. Its governments have so far moved only to a modest reduction of income tax and in order to maintain the yen against the ecu, to a promise, which they may not be able to keep, of a degree of financial deregulation by 2001.

Japan in Asia

To maintain their market shares, Japanese corporations have been increasing their investments in the United States and Western Europe. They have also extended their investment in their own region. In 1987, Japan agreed a New Asian Industrial Development Plan for what were then the six ASEAN countries. In 1990, a Ministry of Finance Committee on Asia–Pacific Economic Research expanded on this by recalling Japan's old model of a staggered 'flying geese' formation of the region's economies. 'It is necessary', it said, 'that what Japan used to do should be done by the Asian Newly Industrialising Economies', South Korea,

Hong Kong, Taiwan and Singapore, that 'what the Asian NIEs used to do should be done by ASEAN countries' (it diplomatically excepted China), and that 'Japan should enter into a far higher division' (quoted by Pyle, 1992: 135). In a different image, some outside the country as well as within it have dared to speak of Japan's future function as Asia's 'brain'. Substantial increases in aid, investment and trade between industries and firms in East Asia (and the expansion also of trade within them), together with Japan's domination of the Asian Development Bank, are now benefiting economies in the third tier as much as Japan itself. Malaysia, Thailand and China are the most recent instances, Vietnam is the next and Cambodia will follow (Arase, 1993; Sakurai, 1994).

The ASEAN countries have welcomed Japan's interest in the security of their region, so long as the responsibility for the security of Japan itself is shared with the United States and Japan does what it can (as in the attempt to restore an indigenous regime in Cambodia) to work through the UN. Indeed, in response to the Industrial Development Plan, and realising that under the influence of its then foreign minister, Nguyen Co Thach – eventually fired in 1991 for having failed in his attempt to secure the support of the European Community, the United States and ASEAN against China – Vietnam was moving away from its dependence on the Soviet Union, a move which might eventually enable the whole region to detach itself further from the established great powers and China, ASEAN went so far as to agree that Japan could represent it at G7 and other summits to which it was not itself invited. Even Indonesia, perhaps in this respect the most reluctant, agrees that ASEAN's ties with Japan should be strengthened. And all the members of the association, which since 1995 has included Vietnam, are keen that Japan should be active in bringing in the hitherto excluded states, including Burma (for which, since the coup in 1962, and with only a slight interruption after the army's suspension of democracy in 1988, Japan alone has provided international assistance) (Chittiwatanapong, 1993). In return, ASEAN has accepted Japan's apologies for its wartime occupation of South-east Asia and not opposed its support for those politicians who are sympathetic to its interests there now (Wong, 1991).

Tokyo is understandably less direct in its political relations with Beijing. The Chinese are bitter still about the Japanese occupation of the east and north of the country between 1937 and 1945. Beijing has been extending its 'blue-water' navy in order, it is thought, to advance its claims to the Paracel and Spratly Islands and Senkaku and to restrain Taiwan. For this and other reasons, not least its support for a time for the Khmer Rouge, it has been thought by some in Thailand, Cambodia and Vietnam still to be a waiting 'tiger in the woods'. But the Peace and Friendship Treaty that Beijing signed with Tokyo in 1978 (and which includes a general 'anti-hegemony' clause, directed at the time at Moscow) remains in force. And with a GNP that is still little more than one-eighth the size of Japan's (although better in real terms per capita and in its consequences for welfare than the dollar equivalent with the yuan would suggest (United Nations Development Programme, 1994)), China's need for Japanese credits, investment, aid and trade will, for some time at least, neutralise whatever threat it is inclined to make.

Japan in turn cares more than any other country in the region (except North Korea) about its good relations with China, and resumed these as soon as it decently could after the incident in Tiananmen Square in 1989; indeed, its move to put the resumption of aid to Beijing on the agenda of the Houston summit in July 1990 marked its first decisive initiative at any such meeting. But in deference to Western opinion, Japan has also done nothing (at least publicly) to exempt China from its first explicit Official Development Assistance Charter in 1992, in which it warns potential recipients that it will in future pay more attention to their military expenditures, their development and production of 'weapons of mass destruction', their trade in arms and their willingness to promote democracy and attend to human rights.

For the same reason, Japan has also politely agreed to the political conditions that have been put upon aid to Central and Eastern Europe in the charter of the European Bank for Reconstruction and Development (Yasutomo, 1993), and has itself been directly interested in Russia's economic reconstruction. (MITI produced a Russian translation of how Japan achieved its economic growth. There is none in English.) This interest, however, has been dampened by the uncertainty in Tokyo about whom it can reliably deal with in its eagerness to invest in the exploitation of eastern Russia's natural resources. And there is still the irritating issue of the continuing Russian refusal (so dependent has the Yeltsin government been on nationalist sentiment) to countenance the return of the northern Kurile Islands and formally conclude the state of war that the Soviet Union declared on Japan in August 1945.

Japan's more immediate difficulty in the region is with the two Koreas (Arase, 1993: 115–16). In its decision to move to export-led industrialisation after 1961, the new South Korean military administration was at first eager to fly in the slipstream of Japan's credit and technical transfers. But the lifting of restrictions on trade unions after the resumption of civilian rule in 1987 has tripled the costs of skilled labour in the country and exposed industry's neglect of research and development. The result is that this industry can no longer compete with the lower-cost economies in South-east Asia, to which it is now, like Japan, exporting production; it has had to price goods produced in South Korea itself that are in many cases inferior to those from Japan at levels close to Japan's own. South Korean firms are now therefore attempting to move up the product cycle.

Political relations also are tense. Although Seoul has been pleased at last to receive an official apology for Japan's occupation of the peninsula between 1905 and 1945, it continues to resent the treatment of the descendants of those Koreans who were taken to Japan in this period, is annoyed at Tokyo's reluctance to return some works of art, and has an unresolved dispute about sovereignty over the island of Tokto (Takeshima). It is also angry at Tokyo's decision not only to apologise but also, in its anxiety about the effects of instability on the peninsula, actually to compensate Pyongyang for its colonial past and indicate its willingness to extend further help. South Korea is caught between not wishing to see the North sustained by others and not wanting itself to bear the likely costs, which the West German experience with the East made clear to it, of further rapprochement and a possible reunification. Until such rapprochement takes place, Japan in turn is anxious about the fact that North Korea's armed forces are considerable (with missiles that can reach Japanese cities) and that South Korea's, over which Washington has given Seoul more discretion, exceed its own in both equipment and men, and are not constrained from being deployed aggressively abroad. Behind the *realpolitik*, moreover, there is the unspoken knowledge on both sides, evidently awkward in the light of the relations between the two countries in the twentieth century, that the imperial house and civilised society itself in the Japanese islands may derive, in the distant past, from Korea.

Japan's national security

Within little more than a year of Washington's threat in February 1990 to discontinue it, the original rationale of the Mutual Security Treaty between the United States and Japan, to counter the supposed Soviet threats in East Asia, had gone. In his new constitution for Japan, General MacArthur had at first wanted the country to renounce both the sovereign right of war and arming for its own defence. His principal drafter thought the general's second wish unreasonable and persuaded him to abandon it. In Washington itself, there was almost at once regret about the first. John Foster Dulles, despatched in June 1950 to conclude the Allied Occupation, tried to persuade Tokyo to agree to a more active collective security agreement – a North Atlantic Treaty Organisation for the Pacific – with Australia, New Zealand, the Philippines, perhaps Indonesia and the United States itself. But Yoshida did not want to be closer than he had to be to other states in Asia and the Pacific or, unlike Konrad Adenauer in the Federal German Republic, to the West. Subsequent Japanese administrations have used the relevant constitutional article to resist nuclear rearmament, prohibit the manufacture and sales of arms, and (which MacArthur's constitution had not intended) to refuse until 1992 to collaborate in the use of force by the UN. In 1960, in the greatest public turmoil that Japan has seen since the war, the Mutual Security Treaty was revised, pointedly removing Washington's demeaning commitment to intervene in disturbances within Japan itself and extending Tokyo's own to what the constitutional article required it to think of as its self-defence. By the 1980s, the strains within what was not, in Japan, to be called the 'alliance' (a foreign minister actually resigned for describing it as such) increased. Moscow was increasing its air and sea forces in the Far East, and Washington was pressing Tokyo to share more of the costs. But despite Nakasone's conciliatory tone, the adjustments were few and relatively slight.

The treaty remains in place, and neither party shows any sign of wanting to revoke it. (In September 1994, the former Socialist Party, then governing in a coalition with the Liberal Democrats, agreed to end its long-standing opposition to it.) It allows the United States to retain a presence in East Asia and Japan to restrain the United States, it enables Japan militarily to restrain itself (Pharr, 1993), and it increases the confidence of those who remember Japan's past aggression and fear China. In return, Tokyo has agreed to consider its trade surplus (meanwhile making concessions to Europe to seek support against the United States) and to extend aid to states in the South and Central and Eastern Europe that are important to Washington.

Japan's domestic politics

'Japanese decisions', Henry Kissinger thought, 'have been the most farsighted and intelligent of any major nation in the postwar era' (1979: 324, quoted by Pyle, 1992: 23). Their rationale, for Japan itself and the other East Asian states, remains. Japan's economic interests, global and regional, together with its wish not to make enemies and harm those interests by becoming a more orthodox power and forming potentially divisive alliances – political, military or economic – are more than sufficient reasons for it to want to continue as it has been doing. And the other East Asian powers, impressed by its economic example, eager for its credit, investment, technology, aid and trade, relieved by its wish to keep a US presence in the region, and uneasy still with each other, are pleased for it to do so. There have nevertheless been questions about whether these decisions will continue to be made in the same way, and how far the international situation will allow them to be.

Tamamoto Masura may be right to say that the alien imposition of a liberal democratic constitution has for the past forty-five years freed the Japanese from having to think about how, politically, their success has been possible (Tamamoto, 1994; 194). But what many Americans have seen as one of the country's great liabilities, 'its inability to articulate universalisable norms, values and principles' (Langdon and Akaha, 1993: 274), others, regarding this as a strategic pragmatism, see as a supreme advantage (Schmiegelow and Schmiegelow, 1990). It is certainly a mistake to say, with an influential Tokyo intellectual, that the success has turned on 'non-Western organisational principles' (Murakami Yasusuke translated and quoted by Pyle, 1992: 139). The 'principles' have at best been tacit. Japan is a *kokumin*, in the Chinese characters literally a 'nation-country-people'. It is also a *kokka*, a political community or association (with a hint also of family) which, as the *Kojien* dictionary explains, 'has exclusive sovereignty and power to rule' and does so in the exercise of *kokyo-seisaku* or 'public policy', where 'public', in contrast to its connotation in the West of discursive and incipiently critical independence, implies benevolent but unrestrained state power (Williams, 1994: 110–11). There is nevertheless no denying the effectiveness with which, domestically and internationally, this *kokka* has been able to turn modernity – until now, in Takeuchi Yoshimi's phrase, 'the self-recognition of Europe' – to its advantage. Williams has even suggested that post-war Japan may eventually be seen as 'one of the great political experiments of history' (1994: 190–1; Takeuchi quoted at 191).

To hostile eyes, however, this experiment is now failing (Wood, 1994: 31–66). Politics in Japan have been dominated by the Liberal Democratic Party. This has been beholden to the interests of producers, factionalised and open to charges of financial scandal. Its character has owed much to the electoral system. All but one or two Japanese constituencies have elected between two and five candidates, but voters have been allowed to express a preference for only one. Candidates from the same party have thus been forced to compete with each other, and since they have been able to be elected with as little as 10 or 15 per cent of the vote, have appealed to particular interests. Once in the Diet, moreover, they have tended not only to be bound to those interests but often also to spend up to three days a week in their constituency to sustain their support. The LDP has accordingly been divided against itself in dense networks of personal ties which make risky initiatives next to impossible. And its elected members have not had the incentive or the time to concentrate on issues of international importance.

The consequence is that the prime minister, his office and the LDP Cabinets have been weak (weaker, perhaps, than in any other parliamentary state) and have by default given power to the civil service. This is staffed by the country's most able graduates, and maintains what has been called the 'high art' or public administration that is characteristic of all the older Asian societies. But the speed and often also the coherence of its decisions have been hampered by overlapping but fiercely guarded spheres of responsibility, the effects of which (apart from the hitherto small size and low standing of the Ministry of Foreign Affairs) are especially noticeable in the formation of international policy: in decisions on aid, for instance, for which four departments have responsibility, and in those on defence, where officials seconded from other ministries have had most say. When initiatives have occurred, therefore, they have often been taken not by the executive or any wider collective authority within the administration but by ministries which have often tried to further enhance their power by making alliances with foreign governments and multilateral institutions (Calder, 1988a, 1993).

Yet after growing public dismay at illegal payments to the political class, electoral reverses for the LDP in the 1980s and 1990s, new parties, a series of fragile coalitions and much discussion, there has been electoral reform. In the election in October 1996, two-thirds of the Diet was for the first time elected in new single-member constituencies and the remainder by proportional representation. This, it was hoped, would produce a more concerted opposition. In the event, the turnout in that election was lower than ever, and the opposition actually fragmented. The LDP formed a new cabinet alone, and did so in its usual manner, by rewarding the most powerful factions. The coalitions of interest, it is true, are shifting. The influence of the large corporations remains, but those of agriculture and small business are declining in favour of a more influential (if politically less hostile) labour force and a variety of other urban concerns. But the intended strengthening of the executive seems distant. And even if electoral reform does eventually produce a politics that is more responsive, as Western liberals have hoped, to a greater variety of internal interests (Pempel, 1993: 123–90), there is less external reason than at any time since 1950 to expect the consensus on foreign policy to change.

Japan's international interests

The direction of this policy, moreover, is now more consistent than it has been with beliefs beyond East Asia about what national interests are and what matters for international security. It is mistaken to suppose that the end of the Cold War has marked the end of the defensive and incipiently aggressive competition between nation states. No East Asian state, certainly, is rash enough to suppose that it has. Indeed, it is possible to read the evidence in such a way as to infer that, like China after its break with the Soviet Union, Japan intends to become a traditional 'great power' with a second-strike nuclear capacity (Layne, 1993: 37–9; also Calder, 1996). This evidence, however, consists largely of speculations about Japan's increasing resort to nuclear energy, which is more plausibly explained by its uneasy past dependence on Middle Eastern oil, and of statements made in irritated reaction to hostility now in the United States. It has to be set against the inherent reasonableness, for its own self-interest, of what Japan has actually done in the past forty-five years, the inherent reasonableness of its continuing to do it (unlike Germany, it sees no need to bind itself politically in order to succeed economically), the extent to which this will suit the other East Asian states, including China, and America's unwillingness still, contested though that is within the United States itself (Johnson and Keehn, 1995; Nye, 1995), to let any other power or association of powers in which it is not itself dominant take precedence.

Recent governments in Japan, however, and those elsewhere in East Asia are clear that if they are not to generate even stronger hostility to their economic success and their relative indifference to liberal principles, they must be seen more willingly to be contributing to what the West construes as international security. Japan, which has until recently been the only state in the region in a position to do so, had hoped that making a purely financial contribution would suffice. That is why, in reaction to pressure from the United States, it agreed to increase its support for US forces in Japan, to extend its aid to states beyond its own sphere of interest in the Caribbean and Africa, and to pay (most conspicuously in contributing $13 billion to the coordinated assault on Iraq in 1991) for nominally international adventures. But it now sees that it has to do more. The embarrassing disarray in Tokyo about how and how far to support the attack on Iraq (a dispute that was more disturbing in Japan itself than the collapse of the Berlin Wall in 1989 or the end of the Soviet Union two years later) led in 1992 to a reversal of the decision not to contribute men and material to the UN's peace-keeping operations. (The Diet insisted, however, that it could do so only after a cease-fire and that members of the Self Defence Forces must remain under Japanese command and not engage in aggressive action.) In the same year, Japan published its new charter for Overseas Development Assistance. In 1993, it was conspicuous in siding with the West against other Asian states, most especially China, Malaysia and Singapore, in the defence of civil and political rights at the UN conference on the issue in Vienna. It has also gained respect for its part in UN operations in Cambodia, Bosnia and Mozambique and for Rwandans in Zaire. In return for its financial contributions and these new political moves, it is asking more insistently for a permanent seat on the UN Security Council and for increased voting rights in the International Monetary Fund and the World Bank.

A turning point?

For the foreseeable future, therefore, the traditional realists are almost certainly mistaken about East Asia. The less traditional, who see new 'civilian' powers there, confuse the means with the end. Japan itself may be more uncertain now about its relations with the United States. The United States is certainly not yet clear about its own post-Cold War policy for East Asia (Johnson, 1995). But Japanese governments show no sign of wishing to discontinue their strategy of persuading the United States to take joint responsibility for the country's security and of working in concert with all the other governments they can. This will enable them to continue to give priority to Japan's national economic interests, to indicate what they believe is a sufficient responsiveness to the new international concerns, to quieten their critics at home and abroad, to satisfy the strong domestic aversion still to revising the 'Peace Constitution' (Katzenstein and Okawara, 1993; Tamamoto, 1994), to soften the fears they can still arouse in the other East Asian states and the fears these states can still arouse in each other, and to retain Japan's integrity and pride. To the other East Asian states also, it is the economic future that now matters most. To assure that future and avoid conflict between themselves, they too will concentrate on economic cooperation ('the business of diplomacy is business', the Thai prime minister said in 1989) and not wish otherwise to disturb the direction in which the West, in itself and through the international institutions, wants to take the world into the next century (Pharr, 1993; Oksenberg, 1994).

This is what prudence would dictate. Cooperation, however, does not entail cultural convergence. The United States can no longer assume that in East Asia it will be watching over countries that accept its rhetoric of liberty and democracy as a model for themselves. Polls in Japan do still suggest that perhaps no more than half the Japanese people regard Japan as a 'first-class country', but three-quarters of them also believe that it now surpasses the United States in economy, education, science and technology. Pride will displace deference to its post-war protector. The same is true of South Korea and Thailand. China has never lost its sense of itself. In Singapore, Indonesia and Malaysia, a once quiet indifference now has an edge of defiance (Chan, 1993; Mahatir and Ishihara, 1995). And there is little reason to expect anything different in Vietnam and Cambodia. These societies can only in the grossest sense be thought (like 'the West' itself) to be part of a single 'civilisation'. But they are all encouraged by their capacity to manage modernity, and see no reason politically to abandon the assumption that it is the ruling party that is best able to enhance the benefits of social cooperation. They are neither liberal nor enthusiastically democratic, and see no good reason to become so.

It is accordingly wrong to suppose that they are now at 'a particularly critical turning point' in their history (Fukuyama, 1992: 242–4), forced to choose between their own past and the future of someone else's. And unless one believes with Samuel Huntington that 'the sustained international primacy of the United States is central ... to the future of freedom, democracy, open economies, and international order in the world', and that East Asia cannot therefore be allowed an equal say in international affairs, it would be wrong also to suppose, as Huntington does, that the 'civilisations' of East and West must clash (1993: 83; contrast Iriye, 1994). Quite the opposite. It is precisely because the East Asian societies, most especially Japan, are too proud to want to convert others that there is hope for a future that includes them: a future which could in this respect lie 'beyond the end of history' as we have known it since 1945.

REFERENCES

I thank Barry Keehn, Camilla Lund and John Thompson for their helpful comments on earlier drafts of this chapter.

Arase, David (1993) 'Japan in East Asia', in Tsuneo Akaha and Frank Langdon (eds.), *Japan in the Posthegemonic World* (Boulder, CO: Lynne Rienner), pp. 113–36.

Calder, Kent E. (1988a) *Crisis and Compensation: Political Stability and Public Policy in Japan* (Princeton: Princeton University Press).

(1988b) 'Japanese Foreign Economic Policy Formation: Explaining the Reactive State', *World Politics*, vol. 40: 517–41.

(1993) 'Japan's Changing Political Economy', in Danny Unger and Paul

Blackburn (eds.), *Japan's Emerging Global Role* (Boulder, CO: Lynne Rienner), pp. 121–31.

(1996) *Asia's Deadly Triangle: How Arms, Energy and Growth Threaten to Destabilise Asia-Pacific* (London: Nicholas Brealey).

Chan, Heng Chee (1993) *Democracy and Capitalism: Asian and American Perspectives* (Singapore: Institute of Southeast Asian Studies).

Chittiwatanapong, Prasert (1993) 'Japan's Roles in the Posthegemonic World: Perspectives from Southeast Asia', in Tsuneo Akaha and Frank Langdon (eds.), *Japan in the Posthegemonic World* (Boulder, CO: Lynne Rienner), pp. 201–31.

Dietrich, William (1991) *In the Shadow of the Rising Sun* (University Park, PA: Pennsylvania State University Press).

Fukuyama, Francis (1992) *The End of History and the Last Man* (London: Hamish Hamilton).

Funabashi, Yoichi (1994) 'Introduction: Japan's International Agenda for the 1990s', in Yoichi Funabashi (ed.), *Japan's International Agenda* (New York: New York University Press), pp. 1–27.

Helleiner, Eric (1990) 'Money and Influence: Japanese Power in the International Monetary and Financial System', in Kathleen Newland (ed.), *The International Relations of Japan* (London: Macmillan), pp. 23–44.

Huntington, Samuel P. (1993) 'The Clash of Civilizations?' *Foreign Affairs*, 72(3), 22–49.

Inoguchi, Takashi (1993) 'Japan's Foreign Policy in a Time of Uncertainty', in Inoguchi (ed.), *Japan's Foreign Policy in an Era of Global Change* (London: Pinter), pp. 117–38.

Iriye, Akira (1994) 'The United States and Japan in Asia: A Historical Perspective', in Gerald L. Curtis (ed.), *The United States, Japan and Asia: Challenges for US Policy* (New York: Norton for The American Assembly), pp. 29–52.

Johnson, Chalmers S. (1982) *MITI and the Japanese Miracle: The Growth of Industrial Policy, 1925–1975* (Stanford: Stanford University Press).

(1995) 'History Restarted: Japanese–American Relations at the End of the Century', in *Japan: Who Governs? The Rise of the Developmental State* (New York: Norton), pp. 296–323.

Johnson, Chalmers and E. B. Keehn (1995) 'The Pentagon's Ossified Strategy', *Foreign Affairs*, 74: 103–14.

Katzenstein, Peter J. and Nobuo Okawara (1993) 'Japan's National Security: Structures, Norms and Policies', *International Security*, 17(4), 84–118.

Kissinger, Henry (1979) *White House Years* (Boston: Little, Brown).

Langdon, Frank and Tsuneo Akaha (1993) 'The Posthegemonic World and Japan', in Frank Langdon and Tsuneo Akaha (eds.), *Japan in the Posthegemonic World* (Boulder, CO: Lynne Rienner), pp. 265–82.

Layne, Christopher (1993) 'The Unipolar Illusion: Why New Great Powers Will Arise', *International Security*, 17(4), 5–51.

Mahatir, Mohamad and Shintaro Ishihara (1995) *The Voice of Asia: Two Leaders Discuss the Coming Century* (Tokyo: Kodansha International).

Maull, Hans W. (1991) 'Germany and Japan: The New Civilian Powers', *Foreign Affairs*, 69(5), 91–106.

Nye, Joseph S. (1995) 'The Case for Deep Engagement', *Foreign Affairs*, 74(4), 90–102.

Oksenberg, Michael (1994) 'China and the Japanese–American Alliance', in Gerald L. Curtis (ed.), *The United States, Japan and Asia: Challenges for US Policy* (New York: Norton for The American Assembly), pp. 96–121.

Pempel, T. J. (1993) 'From Exporter to Investor: Japanese Foreign Economic Policy', in Gerald L. Curtis (ed.), *Japan's Foreign Policy after the Cold War: Coping with Change* (Armonk, NY: Sharpe), pp. 105–36.

Pharr, Susan J. (1993) 'Japan's Defensive Foreign Policy and the Politics of Burden Sharing', in Gerald L. Curtis (ed.), *Japan's Foreign Policy after the Cold War: Coping with Change* (Armonk, NY: Sharpe), pp. 235–62.

Pyle, Kenneth B. (1992) *The Japanese Question: Power and Purpose in a New Era* (Washington, DC: American Enterprise Institute Press).

Sakurai, Makoto (1994) 'Japan's Role in Economic Cooperation and Direct Foreign Investment', in Yoichi Funabashi (ed.), *Japan's International Agenda* (New York: New York University Press), pp. 143–63.

Schmiegelow, Henrik and Michele Schmiegelow (1990) 'How Japan Affects the International System', *International Organisation*, 44: 553–88.

Strange, Susan (1994) *States and Markets: An Introduction to International Political Economy*, 2nd edn (London: Pinter).

Taira, Koji (1993) 'Japan as Number Two: New Thoughts on the Hegemonic Theory of World Governance', in Tsuneo Akaha and Frank Langdon (eds.), *Japan in the Posthegemonic World* (Boulder, CO: Lynne Rienner), pp. 251–63.

Takenaka, Heizo (1994) 'Japan's International Agenda: Structural Adjustments', in Yoichi Funabashi (ed.), *Japan's International Agenda* (New York: New York University Press), pp. 164–86.

Tamamoto, Masuru (1994) 'The Ideology of Nothingness: A Meditation on Japanese National Identity', *World Policy Journal* (Spring), 89–99.

    (1995) 'Reflections on Japan's Postwar State', *Dædalus: Journal of the American Academy of Arts and Sciences*, 124 (Spring), 1–22.

Tsuru, Shigeto (1993) *Japan's Capitalism: Creative Defeat and Beyond* (Cambridge: Cambridge University Press).

Waltz, Kenneth N. (1993) 'The Emerging Structure of International Politics', *International Security*, 18(2), 44–79.

Williams, David (1994) *Japan: Beyond the End of History* (London: Routledge).

Wong, Anny (1991) 'Japan's National Security and Cultivation of ASEAN Elites', *Contemporary South Asia*, 12: 306–30.

Wood, Christopher (1994) *The End of Japan Inc.: And How the New Japan Will Look* (New York: Simon and Schuster).

Yasutomo, Denis T. (1993) 'The Politicisation of Japan's "Post-Cold War" Multilateral Diplomacy', in Gerald L. Curtis (ed.), *Japan's Foreign Policy after the Cold War: Coping with Change* (Armonk, NY: Sharpe), pp. 323–46.

11   New China: new Cold War?

Michael Cox

Introduction

Historians of the twentieth century tend to think of history – and more often than not write about it – in terms of important 'turning-points'. They do so partly because it makes for a more interesting read. They are also impelled to because the modern era in particular is littered with dramatic moments. Upheavals like the Russian revolution, the Wall Street crash or Hitler's coming to power are not merely dramatic, but, more fundamentally, transitional events which quite literally turn the world upside down and alter our ways of thinking about it. By this simple measure, the Chinese revolution of 1949 clearly has to be viewed as one of the great historical turning-points of the epoch.

First, though the revolution gave birth to an era of chaos, it also brought to a conclusion one of the most unstable and bloody periods in China's history – one which had witnessed the collapse of an ancient imperial dynasty in 1911 and the subsequent disintegration of the country, followed in turn by revolution in the 1920s, intervention by Japan in the 1930s and, finally, China's insertion into a wider global war in 1941. Nor was this all. After having defeated his main rivals in the pro-Western Guomindang after a lengthy civil war, Mao not only ended the country's humiliating subordination to foreign powers but united China's vast territories under one single, sovereign authority. The revolution also brought about one of the major transformations of our time by wrecking the social base of the old landlord elite. This upheaval was extraordinarily brutal – somewhere close to a million people died as a result – but probably of material benefit to at least 60 per cent of the Chinese peasantry (Spence, 1990: 517). Finally, the revolution in China had massive international repercussions. Apart from the turmoil it created within Asia itself, Mao's stunning victory had a chilling impact upon the evolution of an already well-established superpower conflict. Indeed, it is difficult to imagine the Cold War without China. The Chinese revolution after all was a critical factor in the US decision to rearm. It also created a panic in the United States which led directly to the scourge of McCarthyism. And it changed the course of the Korean War. In fact, we now know (for sure) that Stalin would not have endorsed the North Korean attack upon South Korea without Chinese support; and if China had not then intervened in the autumn of 1950, there is every chance the United States and UN forces would have liberated the whole of the Korean peninsula. As it turned out, China not only managed to save North Korea, but went on to fight a long and bloody war against US–UN forces which prolonged the military conflict and deepened the already great political divide between itself and the United States - one which it took until the 1970s to overcome (Barnett and Reischauer, 1970).

The historical significance of the Chinese revolution of 1949 is thus clear. But with the passage of time, and in particular with the collapse of communism, we are perhaps liable to forget now how ideologically attractive China once seemed to be – especially after it abandoned the Soviet economic model in 1958 and adopted what looked like a more egalitarian and less bureaucratic version of socialism. For a time what came to be known as the 'Chinese road' attracted a large international following (Wheelwright and McFarlane, 1973). This included, amongst others, Third World militants sceptical of Soviet revolutionary credentials, a number of radical theorists in the West who were drawn to Mao's utopian economic ideas, academic Sinophiles and a loose coalition of well-meaning people in the West who were keen to see historically wronged and materially underdeveloped China succeed in a world still dominated by the two superpowers. What might be termed 'fellow travelling' (or giving Mao and China the benefit of the political doubt) became rather fashionable for a time. This form of painless solidarity – made all the more palatable because of US intervention in Vietnam – was often accompanied by a good deal of wishful thinking. But so long as the United States vilified the regime and excluded it from membership of the international community, many felt morally bound to support China from afar. No doubt if the United States had adopted a less aggressive stance towards the regime, things might have turned out differently. But there was little risk of that. The Cold War made normal relations with China impossible. The United States remained bound by treaty to support the claims of Taiwan against the communists. And during the 1960s at least, many senior US policymakers (such as Dean Rusk) tended to regard Beijing rather than Moscow as being the more serious political threat to global order. China's more explicit support for the armed struggle in the Third World, its shrill denunciations of imperialism, and its apparent indifference towards the consequences of nuclear war together convinced the Washington establishment that having 'lost' China to communism in 1949, there was no way in which this malignant revolutionary presence could ever be drawn back into the international fold (Barnett, 1960).

The process by which China was partially drawn back into the fold constitutes another of those critical 'turning-points' of the twentieth century. Though obviously the result of other changes in the wider international system – including a strong US desire to exploit the ever-widening division between the USSR and China – three individuals were critical to the process: President Nixon, whose global vision made the opening to China possible in the first place; Mao himself, who recognised the strategic necessity of tilting towards the United States in order to balance the power of the Soviet Union; and Deng Xiaoping who, having rejected the political and economic excesses of Maoism, embarked on a new economic course after Mao's death in 1976. Deng's initial aim was to restore order and normality after the upheavals of the Cultural Revolution. But Deng had a larger goal which was to get the party to substitute development for class warfare and abandon what he saw as the false path of economic isolation. Though resisted by some and suffering a temporary set-back following the Tiananmen Square massacre in 1989, Deng pursued his policies with dogged determination. The results, as I shall demonstrate, were impressive: so impressive in fact that many now assume that it is but a matter of time before China translates its new-found economic power into political influence on the world stage. China it would seem has a very bright international future. Indeed, according to many analysts, China – the new 'Orient Express' of the East – is *the* future and will dominate the international system of the twenty-first century in much the same way as Britain before the First World War and the United States after 1945 (Kristof and Wudunn, 1994).

Before looking critically at some of the claims now being made about China's future prospects, it is necessary to examine the character of the reform programme and its economic impact upon China. The argument I will advance is that while the reforms have undoubtedly helped transform China, they have in the process generated a series of contradictions which have made the country highly unstable. Because of this, there is little chance of China's leaders gradually relaxing their grip on power or permitting freer expression for its people. Moreover, having observed the collapse of the various communist regimes in Eastern Europe in 1989, followed two years later by the disintegration of an apparently invincible Soviet Union, they are convinced that liberalisation is bound to lead to chaos and anarchy. Democracy and human rights, they feel, are 'Western' luxuries which the country simply cannot afford. But if China is not bound for liberal democracy, as this essay will argue, this raises a critical question about the country's relationship with the outside world. For if exponents of the 'democratic peace' thesis are right in arguing that authoritarian powers are more inclined to be aggressive than those which are not, then there is every reason to assume that China will pose a serious threat to its neighbours in the future. The argument cannot be lightly dismissed, but in my view many of the worse case predictions now being advanced about China's international behaviour are based upon an exaggerated conception of the nation's real capabilities. It is thus imperative to provide a balanced assessment of Chinese power. Otherwise, there is a danger that having escaped from the twisted logic of one Cold War with the Soviet Union, the United States, in particular, could easily get sucked into planning for another one with China. In the conclusion however, I shall try to demonstrate that while such an outcome is not beyond the bounds of historic possibility, there are powerful, countervailing factors pushing in the other direction. In other words, we are not heading towards a new Cold War in the Pacific region.

Modernising China

China's status as an emerging economic superpower reflects both its size and growth since the late 1970s. Unfortunately, in the rush to eulogise Deng, contemporary Western analysts tend to overlook the important role played by China's previous leaders – including Mao himself. This is not to ignore the irrationalities of Maoism. The Great Leap Forward, for example, which tried to increase production on all economic fronts at an unprecedentedly high rate after 1948, was an economic disaster. Nor should we forget that when Deng finally took over in 1976, social order was poor, industrial absenteeism endemic and corruption prevalent. But one should not underestimate Chinese economic achievements before he set out to modernise the country (Evans, 1995: 224). As an official US report on the Chinese economy conceded in 1978, in spite of many political set-backs, one simply could not ignore 'the record of positive rates of growth in both agriculture and industry in China's economic development' since the revolution of 1949. In this sense, Mao and his fellow leaders had already 'created a significant economic base for the new leadership to build on in their attempts to modernize China's economy'. Moreover, as the report pointed out, whilst the Cultural Revolution between 1966 and 1969 impeded industrial development, its economic impact overall was not huge. As subsequent figures released by the government in Beijing made clear, though the upheavals of the late 1960s generated a good deal of economic dislocation, they were not an economic disaster. Indeed, in agriculture, there was a quite rapid growth in output throughout the late 1960s and early 1970s (Joint Economic Committee, 1978: x).

When Deng began his reforms therefore he was able to build upon a solid pre-existing economic base. The fundamental problem with this base of course was that it was never likely to develop to the advanced level where it could secure China a place at the international top table. Furthermore, though it was able to provide the vast majority of its people with some degree of economic security – no mean feat in the context of Chinese history – it did not really allow them to prosper. Moreover, though the Chinese economy had been able to develop in an 'extensive' sense, like all other socialist systems in the twentieth century it did not have the capability of developing intensively by raising the productivity of labour or successfully incorporating and efficiently utilising high technology. Secure in its own economic laager and shielded from comparison with the wider world, it was doomed to remain a low productivity economy in a dynamic and rapidly evolving global capitalist system (Guocong, 1986: 59–77).

Deng did not have a plan so much as a series of specific goals. These he lumped together under the broad heading of the 'four modernisations', a term originally formulated by the father of reform and long-time foreign minister, Zhou En-Lai, in 1975. In the event Deng's modernisation strategy probably went much further than anything originally conceived of by Zhou – or even by Deng himself. Philosophically justified on the sound empiricist grounds that one had to 'seek truth from facts', his larger objective was to liberate the economy from the shackles of central planning while all the time insisting that the purpose was not to undermine socialism but rather to build a new form of socialism 'with Chinese characteristics' (Eckstein, 1997).

Deng's reforms after 1978 aimed to change China's economic relations in at least three ways. The first was by transforming the way in which the Chinese peasant worked. What this necessitated (and in the end led to) was the effective decollectivisation of Chinese agriculture. In formal terms this did not involve a transfer of ownership from the state to the individual. Nevertheless, it did allow peasant families to control their land and dispose of their agricultural surplus in ways they thought fit. It also permitted the better-off peasants to accumulate land and hire and fire labour. Indeed, the main beneficiaries of the reforms have clearly been the village *nouveaux riches*, notably peasants from the wealthier villages, households with more or better-skilled labour power and those able to contract for the best land or other assets.

Deng's second goal was to try and change the nature of industrial management. He hoped to do this by allowing individual firms more autonomy while forcing managers to think more seriously about the quality and price of goods produced by their enterprise. Though gradual and piecemeal in character – for example, there was never any attempt made to privatise state enterprises – the main objective of these reforms was to help shift the emphasis away from production for production's sake to production more geared for the market. Implemented in three stages between 1978 and 1993, the reforms in industry were normally given a localised trial before being implemented on a nation-wide basis. In this way, Deng believed Chinese industry could be transformed while avoiding unnecessary upheaval (Harding, 1987).

Finally, in pursuit of the dream of economic modernisation, the leadership opened China's economic door to the world market. This involved, amongst other things, the creation of 'special economic zones' in the coastal provinces close to Hong Kong, Shanghai and Canton; the legalisation of direct foreign investment (the greater part of which was to come from Taiwan and the Chinese diaspora); and the establishment of a serious export sector. The implications of these various alterations in China's economic relationship to the capitalist world should not be underestimated. For the better part of thirty years, the regime had regarded any form of economic association with the outside world as being either unnecessary or ideologically threatening. Now, in the post-Mao era (though not without some lingering fears about the dangers of going global) Deng and his supporters impelled the country towards a closer though not complete integration into the world market (Lardy, 1994).

The most obvious result of these connected reforms has been a marked improvement in the material circumstances of many Chinese people. According to one calculation, Chinese annual per capita income stood at somewhere between $425 and $2,000 in 1995. Another (more optimistic) estimate placed it at a much higher level between $1,500 and $3,000. This hardly made China a rich country. But the figures did point to a measurable increase in living standards made possible by an impressive and sustained rate of growth. Again, different statistics tell rather different stories about Chinese growth under the reforms, but if the official Chinese position is to be believed, the annual real growth rate between 1980 and 1992 was just under 10 per cent per annum. Figures from the World Bank paint more or less the same picture. Indeed, the World Bank not only accepts that there was extraordinary growth after 1980, but predicts that China's economy will continue to grow at 8-10 per cent per annum until the turn of the century. A longer-term projection by Australian economists is even more upbeat and anticipates that if the current rate of growth continues, China's economy will be even larger than that of the United States by 2020, provided the present direction and momentum of economic reforms are maintained (Funabashi, Oksenberg and Weiss, 1994).

The rapid growth of the Chinese economy has been accompanied (some would insist, been made possible) by an important change in its underlying structure. Before 1978 there was little or no economic activity outside the plan. Since the reforms began, however, things have changed considerably, and there has been a vast expansion of the private sector. This has been particularly marked in the special economic zones and the larger coastal cities. Here there has been the most rapid growth of private economic activity, facilitated on the one hand by the influx of foreign investment, and on the other by the increase in the number of companies (both Chinese and foreign owned) producing for the export market. But even outside the special zones there have been significant changes, and by the middle of the 1990s literally thousands of small semi-privately-run concerns were operating outside of central control. Again, it is difficult to make a precise calculation about their overall contribution to the economy. But it is estimated that over a third of China's total industrial output now comes from this sector, a good deal of which has been created by township and village enterprises to serve local or community needs (*Financial Times* Survey, 1993).

Finally, any assessment of the reforms has to take account of China's changing position within the international market-place. Recall that when Deng began in 1978, China was an irrelevant factor in the world economy, its share of world trade then being no more 0.5 per cent of the world's total. This made it thirtieth in the league table of exporters (in 1977 China's total trade turnover was no more than $15bn). By 1992, however, China was exporting over $121bn of commodities and importing $115.7bn. This made it the tenth largest trader in the world, excluding Hong Kong. Moreover, although the state sector continued to account for much of this trade, by 1990 over 20 per cent of exports were coming from foreign enterprises, and another 20 per cent from the decentralised, semi-private township and village enterprises. This did not necessarily make China a completely open, 'free trade' economy. None the less, it was another clear indication of the important trans-formation which had occurred since it was announced by one of the theoreticians of reform in 1980 that 'by paying special attention' to its 'comparative advantage in manpower and national resources' the country would be able to increase its 'total exports', and by so doing not only accelerate the process of economic reform at home, but help China become an altogether more serious player in the broader international system (Cable and Ferdinand, 1994: 243–62).

Modernisation and its contradictions

The reforms have clearly made China a wealthier country with a now significant trading sector and a real economic presence in the Asia-Pacific region, one which is bound to be enhanced with the addition of Hong Kong to its list of economic assets in 1997. But as has oft been observed, the most dangerous period in the history of any authoritarian regime is when it attempts to carry through meaningful reform. This particular historical 'law' is certainly one which the Chinese leadership seems to have taken seriously since 1978, and for this reason no doubt have maintained the tightest political control. In terms of their own interests, they have probably been wise to do so. After all, in the space of just under fifteen years they have implemented what amounts to social revolution in the countryside. They have favoured certain regions over others while trying to shake up a huge, inefficient industrial state sector. They have, in addition, asked serious and disturbing questions about the economic policies of the previous regime, cast an historical cloud over the founder of modern China and done a great deal to undermine traditional socialist values. Finally, they have opened up the country to contact with – and thus the danger of contamination by – the outside world. Forced to implement a series of far-reaching economic reforms that might ultimately undermine the very authoritarianism that guarantees social order and continued economic growth, it is perhaps understandable that the Chinese leadership has shown little enthusiasm for tampering with the political system.

Though justified in classical Marxist–Leninist terms, the main reason for the leadership's tenacious refusal to countenance any change in the political superstructure has less to do with ideology or a devotion to the ideals of Marx (an argument difficult to sustain in an era of growing elite privilege and corruption) than practical politics. Many Chinese may have benefited from the process of modernisation but millions have not. The costs of what has sometimes been referred to as 'market Stalinism' are not hard to discern. For instance, as a result of the reforms in the countryside, many peasants have, in narrow economic terms, become surplus to requirement. Indeed, according to one estimate, by the early 1990s there were about 100 million rural labourers in China who were either without work or underemployed. Many more of course remain desperately poor or have been disadvantaged by the reforms. This not only poses an economic problem, but a possible threat to political order as well. In fact, some analysts believe that whereas China's leaders could count on the support or acquiescence of China's peasantry in 1989 at the time of Tiananmen Square, they could not do so a few years later. Certainly, there is evidence to indicate that rural agitation is on the rise. In 1993, for example, it was recorded that the police and paramilitary forces had to deal with more than 600 cases of armed unrest in the countryside. In one particular case, it was reported that spontaneous protests by farmers in Sichuan led to smashing and looting, followed by the beating up of local cadres. There have also been several reports of attacks on local officials by irate farmers and of battles breaking out between villages over property rights and access to water. There are even rumours that long-defunct secret societies have re-emerged in the villages, a development that is of some concern to the leadership in Beijing because they hold the possibility of more organised protest (Benewick and Wingrove, 1995: 117).

But there is no need to travel to the Chinese countryside to see the downside of the reforms. One can observe it more dramatically in the shape of the 50 million or so poor and near-destitute migrants who at any one time are on the move, desperately looking for work in the towns or in the boom cities of the south and east. This vast horde of migrant peasants have now become an almost permanent feature of China's urban landscape, and can normally be found dozing on their bundles at city railway stations waiting for a train or a job. Some inevitably drift into alcoholism, crime and prostitution and seem to be viewed by many urban dwellers with almost the same combination of fear and disdain that the English once reserved for immigrant Irish labourers. The regime takes a somewhat more instrumental view. The new itinerants, in its view, are an essential source of cheap labour without which the great building boom in the emerging cities would be impossible. On the other hand, they represent an obvious threat to law and order. The regime has some reason to be concerned. Crime after all is on the increase, especially in the coastal cities and the special economic zones; and it is particularly high amongst the floating population drawn to the cities by the prospect of employment.

The emergence of what Marx would have justifiably characterised as a 'reserve army of labour' is however only one manifestation of new and potentially explosive contradictions in the new China. Equally significant has been the widening of pre-existing economic gaps between the various provinces. Historically, if one of Mao's conscious aims was to unite the nation by building his own primitive version of peasant socialism, then one of the unintended results of Deng's market reforms has been to weaken China's economic unity by allowing some regions to flourish and others to languish. Certainly, as a result of the reforms, there has been a marked increase in the powers and resources of the more prosperous provinces – all of which have become markedly more self-confident and willing to shape their own economic agendas irrespective of what the central government might wish or decree. The dynamic of uneven economic development has also created a situation in which the more advanced regions (notably Guangdong, Fujian, Zheijiang, Shanghai, Shangdong and Jiangsu) have demanded a real degree of economic autonomy from Beijing. Equally, as the more advanced coastal regions have become more prosperous by becoming more completely integrated into the world market, they have not only drifted away from the centre but from the poorer regions in the interior as well. In turn, the minority peoples of the interior – especially those living near the northern and western frontiers – are finding that they now have almost nothing in common with those from the more prosperous areas in the south and east. Significantly, these various peoples (7 per cent of China's population but occupying 60 per cent of the land) are becoming politically assertive in an era of modernisation (MacKerras, 1994).

As a result of economic liberalisation, China now faces real challenges to its integrity. Under such circumstances, the question has been asked: can China hold together over the longer term? There has of course been a long history of predicting the death of China and one must be careful about making rash predictions about the country's future. China after all is not the Soviet Union with its complex mosaic of ethnic groups (of China's 1.34bn inhabitants, 1.043bn are Han Chinese). Moreover, the Chinese state – unlike its late Soviet counterpart – is still capable of taking the toughest of repressive measures. Indeed, there is little doubting the fact that if Beijing was faced with a major threat to its authority, it would not hesitate to use force. But arms alone cannot prevent change, and in an age where unplanned market forces rather than politics are in command, there are good reasons to believe that the centre will either have to renegotiate its relationship with the regions or face major political problems over the long term. The country is clearly not confronting a return to warlordism or even disintegration like the USSR. However, if Beijing continues to assert a degree of formal central control which is no longer consistent with its real power and authority, not to mention economic realities, then there could be dangers ahead (Goodman and Segal, 1994).

Any assessment of the reform process, finally, has to confront the legacy of central planning and, in particular, the position of the 100,000 state-run enterprises which continue to employ over two-thirds of the urban workforce. In this area, paradoxically, the real challenge stems less from the reforms themselves and more from a failure to implement reform. It is quite extraordinary, after all the years of attempting to transform industry and make it more efficient, how little the Chinese leadership has actually achieved. Naturally, there have been some changes, mainly brought about through competition from the growing private sector. But, in general, heavy industry continues to employ about 120 million workers under old-style conditions where the worker's right to work is still given greater weight than the manager's right to hire and fire. This has far-reaching consequences. Most obviously, because the government has felt duty-bound to keep many inefficient industries afloat through massive subsidies, the financial system has been crippled. The pressure upon the government to provide fresh credits to state-run firms has also meant that China remains vulnerable to bouts of inflation. But, most seriously of all, because of the failure to reform the state sector, the country still has a heavy industry which is patently inefficient. According to some sources, a third of all state-owned enterprises were running at a loss in 1992. Others have put the figure as high as 50 per cent (Grant, 1993: 65).

The underlying reason for this impasse has less to do with economics and more with the way in which communist China was constructed in the first place. For while Mao always idealised the peasant, the ultimate stability of his regime depended to a large degree on keeping the ever-growing army of workers in the state sector relatively content. What this meant, in effect, was guaranteeing workers employment and providing for their welfare at the point of production. To all intents and purposes, the same concern about regime stability has guided government policy since 1978. Anxious about creating mass unemployment in the cities, and genuinely fearful of worker discontent (a concern which grew to almost pathological levels at the time of Tiananmen in 1989) the leadership has decided for basically political reasons to keep thousands of sinking firms afloat. Fearing what one Chinese official believed would be 'chaos' and 'social turmoil' if it did carry through far-reaching reforms of the state industrial sector, it has come to the not illogical political conclusion that it is better to leave well alone, at least for the time being.

Government concerns about worker discontent are not without foundation. During the late 1980s, for example, there was a series of strikes, and it would seem that the trend towards industrial action has accelerated in the 1990s. One of the frequent reasons for this has been either late payment or non-payment of wages, and sometimes the threat or even the reality of redundancy. It is significant, however, that the response by the authorities to worker action has not been to wield a big stick but to make concessions. Indeed, where workers have been made redundant or remain unpaid, the government has frequently stepped into the breach with large donations of emergency aid or salary supplements. In some circumstances of course local authorities have taken a more penal approach; and it has been reported that in a number of industrial cities the police have been granted power to arrest 'protesters' who have gathered in groups of five or more. But this has tended to be the exception rather than the rule in dealing with workers who feel both threatened by the new reforms and increasingly alienated from a regime whose commitment to their interests is not as unambiguous as it once seemed to be (Schell, 1994: 419–20).

The new China threat?

China has thus undergone a most peculiar though not necessarily unique form of modernisation in which the elite has maintained a monopoly of political power – made all the more necessary in its own eyes by the destabilising consequences of modernisation itself. The whole process has clearly transformed China in ways we are only barely beginning to glimpse. But it has also had a major and in some ways quite disturbing impact on China's neighbours as well. Coming at a time of great international change when the certainties of the Cold War were beginning to collapse, the economic rise of a country the size of China has already begun to alter the balance of economic power in the Asia-Pacific region. Yet what has made many states especially nervous, paradoxically, is not China's new-found economic strength, but its repressive policies at home. Though no great supporters of liberal reform themselves (indeed many subscribe to the highly dubious and illiberal notion that there exists a distinct set of 'Asian' values which have to be protected from the democratic West) the leaders of the Asian Pacific countries seem to share with the United States the basic assumption that nations which practise good governance at home are more inclined to act in a benign fashion abroad. This does not preclude them trading with China or supporting Beijing in what now looks like its apparently unending struggle with Washington over the issue of human rights. However, resenting US political intrusion in Asian domestic affairs is one thing; being sensitive to the region's geopolitical realities is something else entirely. And the fact remains that China's neighbours are becoming increasingly anxious: the normally diplomatic Japanese; authoritarian states like Indonesia, Singapore and Malaysia with their significant ethnic Chinese populations; and of course Taiwan (Roy, 1994: 149–68).

Such fears cannot be dismissed lightly, especially in an era where the Chinese leadership, having effectively abandoned Marxism as a legitimising ideology, have turned more and more to a form of truculent nationalism to maintain political cohesion at home. Significantly, an increasing number of calls have been made within China for the nation to resist the polluting effects of external influences and to work to make the nation strong and independent. Borrowing the title from a famous Japanese study published in the late 1980s, one Chinese writer has in fact called upon China in the 1990s to say 'No' to the United States and its various efforts to interfere in Chinese internal affairs. The appeal of such a call should not be underestimated. It not only touches a sensitive nerve amongst the Chinese military and the Communist Party, but also amongst ordinary Chinese who are deeply sensitive to what they see as the international wrongs done to China in the past. Moreover, many Chinese are genuinely proud, almost to the point of chauvinism, of the nation's recent economic achievements and the respect that is now being accorded China. Certainly China, in their view, needs no lessons in moral philosophy from nations which in the past have treated it with contempt.

One indication of Beijing's new assertiveness has been seen in its recent relations with Taiwan. Never less than tense since the expelled Guomindang leadership escaped there in 1949, since the early 1990s China has adopted an increasingly tough line towards the island state – in spite of growing economic ties between the two countries. In 1993, for example, Beijing banned all official participation in privately organised meetings to discuss regional security issues. Direct bilateral talks between the two capitals have also been highly acrimonious. In addition, China has engaged in various forms of sabre-rattling in an attempt to remind Taiwan and its people of Beijing's constitutional claim to the island (Crane, 1993: 705–24).

China's assertive stance may in part be understood as an expression of its new hegemonic ambitions in Asia. However, a more likely explanation is a concern that the window for unification may be closing for ever. Chinese hostility also reflects its deep and abiding fear of political pluralism, and, significantly, as Taiwan has moved away from authoritarianism, Chinese leaders have become ever more agitated. This is clearly no coincidence. After all, when Taiwan was a police state, Beijing was happy to score political points by drawing attention to the repressive nature of the island state. This not only helped it discredit the Guomindang regime but the United States as well. But with the passing of the old order, China is no longer able to do this. Even worse, it is now faced with a fairly vibrant democracy on Taiwan and this, it would seem, represents an affront and a threat to Chinese leaders; and will no doubt continue to do so, so long as China denies human rights to its own people. Thus, for the foreseeable future, relations with Taiwan are bound to remain extremely tense. This might not lead to war. On the other hand, the tensions arising out of the China–Taiwan nexus are bound to generate a high degree of regional insecurity, which in turn is likely to stimulate what some predict will be one of the most serious arms races of the post-Cold War era (Klare, 1993: 136–52).

Another expression of what many view as Chinese aggression has been its persistent claims to the Spratley Islands, situated at the southern end of the South China Sea. The islands, though miniscule, are located in rich fishing grounds and sit astride critically important shipping lanes. The sea floors surrounding the Spratleys are also reported to contain vast amounts of oil. According to China, it is only claiming that which has always been Chinese since the Han dynasty. Hence, in its view, it is merely attempting to defend its sovereign rights against the illegitimate claims of others. Naturally enough, this is not how other countries in the region (including the Philippines, Indonesia, Malaysia, Indonesia, Vietnam and Taiwan) see things and have interpreted Chinese moves – in particular its seizure of a number of the Spratley Islands – as a form of blatant aggression. Inevitably, this has led to an impasse. There have been efforts to resolve the problem through talks, and following China's formal seizure of seven of the Spratleys from Vietnam in 1988 there was a series of meetings between the various concerned parties. In 1990, China also offered to set aside its claims to sovereignty in favour of a joint development of the resources of the Spratleys. But all to no avail. Indeed, in May 1992, China took the provocative step of awarding a concession to a US oil company and pledged to defend the Spratleys by force if need be. The following year it then restated its claim to the entire South China Sea by publishing a map which put the whole of the area in its territory. A year later it occupied the Philippines-claimed Mischief Reef.

China's assertiveness certainly points to what some at least see as an inclination to dominate the South China Sea by force rather than negotiate shared control with other claimants to the Spratleys. Yet Chinese moves may turn out to have been in vain. That there is oil around the Spratleys seems likely; but whether or not it can be economically exploited remains unknown. However, even the outside possibility of there being vast oil fields in the South China Sea has proved too tantalising a prize for Beijing to resist; especially in the light of China's known energy needs and particularly now that China perceives itself as the rising power of the Asia-Pacific region (Gallagher, 1994: 169–94).

Those concerned about China's hegemonic ambitions in the region also point to the fact that whereas most countries around the world have been cutting military budgets since the end of the Cold War, China has been using its growing economic wealth to finance a far-reaching military build-up. And however misleading the official figures might be (for instance, they do not include sums spent on weapons procurement or on research and development) it would appear that between 1988 and 1995 the military budget doubled, thus implying that China by the mid-1990s was spending somewhere between $32bn and $36bn per annum on defence. This increase can in part be interpreted as an attempt to pacify important domestic constituencies: notably the People's Liberation Army, whose unequivocal support is necessary to the stability of the regime, and workers in state-owned enterprises whose discontent the government is keen to contain by maintaining full employment. But the rises cannot be explained by domestic politics alone and reflect what some alarmists view as early Chinese preparations for regional war.

The origins of China's military build-up can be traced back to a lengthy debate in the late 1980s and early 1990s which concluded that in a post-Soviet era of high-tech development (dominated in effect by the United States) China had to improve its forces and achieve what the leadership called the 'five breakthroughs': in military thinking, tactics, training, R&D and force structure. A consensus was finally arrived at in 1992 at the party's Central Military Commission to modernise the military so that it could fight a modern war under high-tech conditions. To do this it required new equipment and so turned to the former USSR to purchase, in the first instance, a number of fighter aircraft at knockdown prices. Within a short space of time it had bought 26 SU-27 fighters. It also began negotiating for 79 MiG-31 fighters which would be built in China in a cooperative agreement with Moscow. There were reports moreover that it had acquired air refuelling technology from Pakistan and Iran and had converted some bombers into tanker aircraft in the hope of creating a significant fleet of fighter planes and bombers. It also started to invest a good deal in the training of pilots and crew (Kristof, 1993: 65–8).

According to some analysts, however, the single most important military reform (and an index of China's foreign policy ambitions) has been its determination to develop a 'blue water navy' constructed around an aircraft carrier force. This naval expansion has attracted less attention than the air-force modernisation, but some argue is every bit as significant: and many indeed feel that by the end of the century China will have a viable navy where before it had none. This would not only give China the ability to counter what some see as the threat posed by others (notably the Japanese navy) but would provide it with a set of capabilities diverse enough to secure 'sea control' in China's coastal waters, blockade its adversaries and protect China's maritime territories. More generally, a modernised navy would allow China to project its influence while at the same time providing it with an important status symbol; a statement in effect about its arrival as a serious power on the world stage (Ji, 1991: 137–49).

Those most worried about China's longer-term intentions also believe that there has been and remains a specific cultural propensity amongst its leaders – both past and present – to view the world and the other nations in it in a particularly hostile way. This analysis agrees that there has always been a tradition in China of winning over one's foes through diplomacy and economic incentives. But this, it is felt, has largely been symbolic, and has only been used to justify behaviour in ways culturally acceptable to an elite steeped in a set of Confucian values which lay great stress on restraint and rectitude. In effect, the operational assumptions and policy preferences of Chinese rulers have always been indistinguishable from the *realpolitik* practised by much of the rest of the world. Indeed, many ancient Chinese writers on strategy invariably concluded that the best way to respond to threats (real or imagined) was to eliminate them by force. True, they also called for flexibility; but only as an expedient, until China could be sure of prevailing. Moreover, though negotiations were not unimportant, they were basically a cover for delaying action until the moment was ripe to destroy the enemy.

The degree to which one can 'read' the past into the present (let alone the future) remains open to debate. Some would even question the value of cultural analysis in general, and in this particular instance the somewhat alarmist conclusions which seem to flow from it. Nevertheless, there is enough evidence to support the argument that a belief in raw power continues to influence the thinking of Chinese leaders today as much as it did in the past. This is reflected in a tendency amongst some policymakers to see the world in zero-sum terms in which China as the rising power is engaged in a long struggle for influence with the most obvious obstacle to its ambitions: the United States. Certainly, in Beijing, discussion of Sino-American relations has increasingly tended to focus on the inevitability of estrangement and strategic hostility rather than cooperation. This same discussion, not surprisingly, has taken place in the US, where there still exists a powerful current of strategic thinking formed in the Cold War. And those still steeped in the past – and desperately keen to draw a particular set of realist lessons from it – tend to see the world as a vast Hobbesian arena in which it is quite 'natural' for great powers to compete. Moreover, having convinced themselves that repressive China is a revisionist power whose mission is to translate its new-found wealth into influence and ultimately dominate Asia, these old-style worse case planners preach the virtues of a new containment; not because this is something which they seek or desire as such, but as a logical and necessary response to a geopolitical threat in an area of the international system crucial to the United States (Cox, 1995).

China: the incomplete superpower

Fears about modern China, like those once entertained about the former USSR, are clearly not groundless. China's size, its rapid economic expansion since 1978, the utter indifference of its elite to democratic norms, and its growing military strength, can hardly be ignored. Even its many contemporary admirers who extol its economic virtues and heap praise on those who have managed this minor materialist miracle without the country falling apart, still point to the obvious fact that the new China constitutes a regional problem which has to be dealt with. That said, the question remains whether the new alarmists have overstated the case and by so doing helped prepare the intellectual ground for a costly and avoidable new Cold War.

The case for the 'containment' of China rests in the end upon a particular assessment of Beijing's intentions and capabilities. In this regard, the most obvious argument against those who would advocate a new tough line is that they tend to overestimate the Chinese threat. Thus, while it is quite legitimate for them to point to the speed and extent of the military build-up in the 1990s, it is worth noting that this rise started from an extraordinarily low technical and material base. The twin experiences of the Cultural Revolution and Deng's modernisation programme with its concentrated focus on economics at the expense of everything else (including investment in the Chinese military) left the PLA in a most parlous state. Furthermore, even if one accepted the highest possible estimate of Chinese military spending – somewhere close to $40bn – this remains puny when set alongside that of the United States, which spends close to $275bn per annum on defence. Even Japan, which has an annual defence budget of $50bn, spends more than China on national security. Other states in the region have not been militarily idle over the past few years either. Malaysia, for example, has been busily purchasing advanced equipment from Russia, the US and the UK and as a result will soon possess a sophisticated military machine. Singapore has also been adding to its arsenal. Indonesia has been doing much the same and though its military lacks the technological sophistication of either Malaysia or Singapore, it does have its modern components (Cheung, 1993b: 11).

The limits of Chinese military power are perhaps best illustrated through an examination of its air force. China may indeed have many planes and be acquiring more, but its air force is generally antiquated. For instance, all but a handful of its 4,000 fighters, 40 ground-attack aircraft and 120 bombers are based on 1950s and 1960s technology. The air force has also not been tested in combat since China's disastrous war with Vietnam in the late 1970s, and there are good grounds for thinking that its pilots are inadequately trained. In most critical technologies moreover – avionics, system integration, turbofan engines and composites – the air force is backward. There is also little chance that things will be rectified in the near future. Indeed, the air force will be hampered by a number of serious deficiencies for years ahead. These include: the inability of the Chinese aviation industry to design and produce modern aircraft in large numbers, poor logistical support, rudimentary command and control, a lack of assets to suppress enemy air defences, and a tightly structured political system that stifles initiative and fails to make full use of available resources (Allen, Krumel and Pollack, 1995).

There seems to be little chance therefore of China creating an advanced air force until well into the twenty-first century. This not only limits its global reach but probably also means that it does not even have the capacity to mount a meaningful offensive in the Asia-Pacific region itself. There is certainly little to suggest that it could launch a serious and sustained attack against, let alone an invasion of, Taiwan, given its deficiencies in the air. There have even been grave doubts expressed about the extent to which China could mount a more general defence of its claim to the South China Sea and the Spratleys. The growing wealth and power of its maritime rivals on the one hand, and the enormous logistical problems facing China on the other, together mean that concerns about an imminent military conflict for control of the area may be exaggerated. The fact that Chinese naval forces would be operating far from home without adequate air cover would leave them highly vulnerable. And because Chinese ships have little in the way of modern anti-aircraft missile systems, they would have great difficulty in defending themselves. It is true that China possesses the world's second largest submarine fleet after the United States. However, most of its boats are based on 1950s Soviet designs, which means they are technologically backward and costly to maintain and repair. Apparently, they are also noisy when submerged and would thus be highly vulnerable to modern anti-submarine warfare technology (Cheung, 1993a: 11).

Assessing China's military assets is of course important. But it begs the larger question of whether or not it would actually be in the Chinese interest to threaten its neighbours militarily. There is no easy answer to this. China has used military force in the past to get its way, and there is every likelihood that it will be tempted to do so again. None the less, its leaders still have to make a calculation about benefits and costs, and on balance it seems fairly obvious that China would lose more than it would gain if it mounted a serious military challenge to the balance of power in the region. Such a move would immediately lead to its complete diplomatic isolation in Asia-Pacific. It would also undermine its various efforts to unite the Asian countries. And it would legitimise a permanent US military presence in the region. Furthermore, Chinese aggression would have the most serious economic consequences. Economic interdependence does not always make countries act reasonably abroad, and it would be naïve to suggest that it did. Certainly, it might not be enough to make China moderate its behaviour. On the other hand, the costs to China of breaking the fairly well-established rules of the regional game would be very high indeed given both the level of inward Asian investment into China and the extent of China's dependency on the Asian market.

This brings us back to the issue of economics. China may well be one of the more exciting economies in the world, but as we have already suggested its very vitality has generated a series of contradictions which the Chinese leadership no doubt feel would be best managed in a relatively stable international environment. Equally, though China has achieved much, one must always remember how far it still has to go before it catches up with the more advanced economies. Hovering somewhere between communism and capitalism, it is still in many ways a country in transition between a past it is trying to overcome and a future it has not yet achieved. Nor should we exaggerate its economic power as do some commentators and businessmen. Britain's GDP, for example, is double that of China's, while China's GDP in 1995 was about the same as those of Belgium, Netherlands and Luxemburg combined. A comparison closer to home is even more telling. On the eve of Hong Kong's reversion to the mainland, the 1.34bn people of China produced a total output which was little more than 4 times that generated by the 5.9m people of the British Colony. In per capita terms, Hong Kong's output was 45 times greater in 1995 than that of the mainland. China may be a booming economy, but it still has a long way to go before it becomes an economic superpower (*Financial Times Survey*, 1994).

Towards a new Cold War?

In the last analysis, China's future relations with the outside world in general and the Asia-Pacific region in particular are going to be determined as much by what transpires in the land of the last remaining superpower as by what happens in China itself. This is why China's relationship with the United States remains so critical. Others may invest more in China and criticise it less, but it is what goes on in Washington and not Tokyo or Seoul that concerns the Chinese leadership most. And they are right to be concerned: partly because what other countries say and do in the region is ultimately shaped by decisions taken in the United States; but, more importantly, because the United States has been engaged in an intense debate since Tiananmen Square about what attitude to take towards China. The outcome of that debate will largely determine whether or not there will be a new Cold War with China.

At one level there is no doubting the extent of US concern about China, the most often-discussed one of course being China's fairly appalling record on human rights. But this is only part of a very complex web of factors which have led to increased alienation between the two powers. Other, equally important, issues such as China's policy on weapons exports, its support for the nuclear programmes of both Pakistan and Iran, its growing trade imbalances with the US and its belligerent attitude towards Taiwan, have also caused anxiety in Washington. Some have even speculated that US hostility is a function of an almost pathological need for an enemy in the post-Soviet age. Others have suggested that the deeper cause of US anger is a refusal on its part to accept that this non-white nation has not only succeeded in the short and medium term, but might – over the longer term – challenge what many in the US assume is their right to dominate world politics. In other words, the deeper reason for US concern is less fear of China and more a worry about its own capacity to shape international relations into the twenty-first century.

Yet, in spite of all this, it is evident that the United States neither feels threatened enough nor estranged enough to break with China. Indeed, since 1989 there has been a remarkable consensus in Washington about the necessity of remaining engaged. In fact, at times, so enthusiastic have policy-makers been to reassure Chinese leaders of their benign intentions that they have opened themselves up to the politically damaging charge of appeasement. This argument was made against President Bush when he sent a senior envoy to Beijing very shortly after Tiananmen Square. Later, President Clinton was attacked when he supported the extension of 'most favoured nation' status to China. In the highly charged US political environment, it is still difficult for the foreign policy elite to formulate a China policy which will satisfy everyone.

The reasons for what some see as moral cowardice and others as a higher form of political realism are not difficult to discern. There are, first and foremost, powerful strategic arguments against isolating China. China was for nearly twenty years a useful asset against the USSR, and many in Washington believe it might be an equally useful counterbalance against either Japan or Korea if either attempted to move outside of the US orbit. Moreover, in spite of its indifferent record, China has been and will no doubt remain a critical factor in guaranteeing the Nuclear Non-Proliferation regime. Indeed, without China's diplomatic support, the US would not have been able to manage the crisis occasioned by North Korea's attempt to acquire a nuclear capability in 1994. Nor should we forget (or underestimate) the many ways in which China can help the United States, particularly in the United Nations, where it is a permanent member of the Security Council.

Another equally important reason why the United States wishes to remain on good terms with China is economic. China has over the past decade developed into a major market for US goods. Significantly, by 1995, China had become the United States' fifth largest trading partner, surpassing the United Kingdom and approaching the level of Germany. Total US trade with China that year equalled $57.3bn, up over 20 per cent on 1994. According to official sources, US exports to China by the mid 1990s accounted for over 170,000 US jobs, many of them well paid and highly skilled. Less important perhaps, but none the less not irrelevant, was the growth of US holdings in China. Though a long way behind Hong Kong, Taiwan and Japan, by 1995 the US had acquired a considerable stake in Chinese prosperity by virtue of its $3.1bn investment. This accounted for just under 10 per cent of total foreign investment, and there was every reason to expect this figure to rise as the Chinese economy continued to expand, so long as the US government did not keep raising the delicate issue of human rights.

But the most important reason why a new Cold War with China is unlikely is that it is neither necessary – in so far as China does not represent a serious threat to world order – nor really in the interests of the United States, which has every reason to avoid a costly arms race it cannot afford and a potentially dangerous confrontation which the American people would probably not underwrite in the post-Cold War era. Moreover, the US already has a strategy for dealing with China. This was initially formulated by Nixon back in 1972 and has been endorsed by every US president since; and the strategy, quite simply, is not to seek a permanent confrontation with China but its integration into the world capitalist system. In many ways the policy has already been remarkably successful. It has encouraged economic reform in China itself, made the world a safer place and given China a genuine stake in the international system. Of course this has not made China a democracy. Nor has it transformed China into an obedient dependency of the US. Furthermore, as China has developed economically it has asserted its rights in ways which many other countries in the Asia-Pacific region find extremely uncomfortable. But none of this need lead to a new Cold War, now or in the future. China may not be an easy, or even a particularly humane partner for the West. However, the alternative to a difficult and at times testy partnership would be no partnership at all. And that would be in nobody's interest – least of all China's.

REFERENCES

Allen, Kenneth, Glenn W. Krumel and Jonathan D. Pollack (1995) *China's Air Force Enters the 21st Century* (Santa Monica: Rand).

Barnett, A. Doak (1960) *Communist China and Asia: Challenge to American Policy* (New York: Vintage).

Barnett, A. Doak and Edwin O. Reischauer (1970) *The United States and China: The Next Decade* (London: Pall Mall).

Benewick, Robert and Paul Wingrove (1995) *China in the 1990s* (London: Macmillan).

Cable, Vincent and Peter Ferdinand (1994) 'China as an Economic Giant: Threat or Opportunity?' *International Affairs*, vol. 70(2) (April), 243–62.

Cheung, Tai Ming (1993a) 'Lacking Depth', *The Far Eastern Economic Review* (4 Feb.).

(1993b) 'Instant Navy', *The Far Eastern Economic Review* (18 Feb.).

Congressional Research Service (1994) *China as a Security Concern in Asia: Perceptions, Assessment, and US Options* (Washington, DC: The Library of Congress).

Cox, Michael (1995) *US Foreign Policy after the Cold War: Superpower without a Mission?* (London: Pinter).

Crane, George T. (1993) 'China and Taiwan: Not yet "Greater China"', *International Affairs*, vol. 69(4) (Oct.), 705–24.

Eckstein, Alexander (1997) *China's Economic Revolution* (Cambridge: Cambridge University Press).

Evans, Richard (1995) *Deng Xiaoping and the Making of Modern China* (Harmondsworth: Penguin).

Financial Times Survey (1993) *China*, 18 Nov.
    (1994) *China*, 7 Nov.

Funabashi, Yoichi, Michel Okesneberg and Heinrich Weiss (1994) *The Emerging China in a World of Interdependence: A Report to the Trilateral Commission* (New York: The Trilateral Commission).

Gallagher, Michael G. (1994) 'China's Illusory Threat to the South China Sea', *International Security*, vol. 19(1) (Summer), 169–94

Goodman, David S. G. and Gerald Segal (eds.) (1994) *China Deconstructs* (London: Routledge).

Grant, Richard L. (1993) 'China and its Asian Neighbours: Looking Towards the Twenty-First Century', *The Washington Quarterly*, vol. 17(1) (Summer), 59–70.

Guacong, Huan (1986) 'China's Opening to the World', *Problems of Communism*, vol. 35 (Nov.–Dec.), 59–77.

Harding, Harry (1987) *China's Second Revolution: Reform after Mao* (Washington, DC: Brookings Institution).

Ji, You (1991) 'In Search of Blue Water Power: The PLA Navy's Maritime Strategy in the 1990s', *The Pacific Review*, vol. 4(2), 137–49.

Joint Economic Committee: Congress of the United States (1978) *Chinese Economy Post-Mao* (Washington, DC: Government Printing Office).

Klare, Michael T. (1993) 'The Next Great Arms Race', *Foreign Affairs*, vol. 72(3), 136–52.

Kristof, Nicholas D. (1993) 'The Rise of China', *Foreign Affairs*, vol. 72(5) (Nov.–Dec.).

Kristof, Nicholas D. and Sheryl Wudunn (1994) *China Wakes* (London: Nicholas Brealey Publishing).

Lardy, Nicholas R. (1994) *China in the World Economy* (Washington: Institute for International Economics).

MacKerras, Colin (1994) *China's Minorities: Integration and Modernization in the Twentieth Century* (New York: Oxford University Press).

Roy, Denny (1994) 'Hegemon on the Horizon? China's Threat to East Asian Security', *International Security*, vol. 19(1) (Summer), 149–60.

Schell, Orville (1994) *Mandate of Heaven* (London: Warner Books).

Spence, Jonathan D. (1990) *The Search for Modern China* (London: Hutchinson).

Wheelwright, E. L. and Bruce McFarlane (1973) *The Chinese Road to Socialism* (Harmondsworth: Penguin).

12   Africa: crisis and challenge

Ian G. Hopwood

When Africa is discussed today one often hears reference to 'Afropessi-mism', 'collapsed states', the 'coming anarchy' (Kaplan, 1994; Zartman, 1995). Bloody chaos in Somalia and Liberia, and ethnic slaughter in Rwanda have given powerful justification for this apoca-lyptic vision of Africa's future. Events elsewhere inspire hope. The ending of apartheid in South Africa and the transition to a democratic non-radical political system were something of a miracle, a reminder that sometimes great men do indeed shape the course of history. Decades-old conflicts have also ended in Eritrea, Mozambique and perhaps Angola. Potentially of even greater significance is the move towards political liberalisation, reflecting the continent-wide aspiration for more accountable and democratic systems of government. Which vision gives a better clue to the future? This chapter reviews the economic and political reforms that are the current international prescription for Africa's crisis. It concludes that the weak initial con-ditions, acute internal constraints and unfavourable external environ-ment make for a difficult medium-term scenario. Broader long-term strategies are required, more firmly anchored in jointly agreed inter-national commitments, and better integrated into nationally designed policies that build on the capacities of African communities and take more account of Africa's cultures, values and knowledge systems. Unless otherwise stated, the terms African and Africa refer to sub-Saharan Africa.

Africa marginalised

With the ending of the Cold War, strategic and geopolitical considera-tions no longer compel the major powers to support 'their' African strongmen against perceived threats from the 'other side'. Debates about Africa used to pit internationalists concerned with big-power rivalry against regionalists concerned with African issues who warned of the dangers of making Africa an international battlefield. It is somewhat ironic that now 'the internationalists have declared the game over, the regionalists are desperately searching for a rationale to keep external interest and resources focused on Africa' (Callaghy, 1991: 43). With the reduced involvement of the major powers, space is opening up for the expanded involvement of mid-level powers, both from the region and beyond. Amongst recent examples are Nigeria's leadership role in the Liberian crisis, South Africa's mediation in the Angolan conflict and the involvement of Israel and Iran in shaping new power configurations in the Horn of Africa.

Economically, Africa's traditional importance as a supplier of raw materials (which in many African countries still generate up to 90 per cent of export earnings) has diminished with competition from synthetic substitutes and suppliers in Asia, Latin America and the former Soviet Union; between 1967/8 and 1986/7, Africa's share in world primary product exports declined by half, from 8.3 per cent to 4.2 per cent. The resulting government indebtedness and lack of economic growth have reduced Africa's significance as an export market. Poor economic performance, combined with political instability and deteriorating infrastructure, have discouraged new private investment and lending, and even precipitated some disinvestment (Callaghy, 1991: 41; Gibbon, 1992: 141–2). Africa's marginalisation is such that it is the only region likely to incur net losses (as much as $2.6bn annually up to 2002) under the terms of the GATT Uruguay Round negotiations (Goldin *et al.*, 1993).

At the same time that strategic and business interest has waned, the development coalition for Africa – that traditionally drew support from the voluntary aid agency community, the churches, universities and other socially committed and internationally focused groups – has lost influence in many industrialised countries. Although the public still provides generous support and demands strong government response to acute crises, the frequency and complexity of these disasters may have dulled individual sensitivities and fostered a sense of hopelessness that has weakened commitment to Africa's long-term development and reinforced the retreat from international cooperation. This retreat was already a feature of the 1980s 'conservative revolution' in the major industrial countries which brought to power governments inclined to place (often rather short-term) national interests above international cooperation, and to put their faith in the virtues of world trade and capital market mechanisms over earlier, more interventionist approaches to international cooperation (Killick, 1990: 302). In this world view, other regions were of greater interest, especially political and economic transition in Eastern Europe, and economic opportunities in

Asia and Latin America. In the words of Dr Adedeji, then secretary general of the UN Economic Commission for Africa (ECA), 'Africa has moved from being at the periphery to the periphery of the periphery of the global economy ... the world's basket case' (Young, 1994: 235). What is being done to reverse this economic crisis?

Economic crisis and adjustment

The crisis had its immediate origins in the shocks of the late 1970s and 1980s. Soaring oil prices, drought, rising interest rates and worsening terms of trade, and declining investment precipitated or accelerated a downward spiral of economic deterioration, even in countries which had successfully managed the first years of independence. Very few states could cope as foreign debts became unmanageable, foreign exchange shortfalls curtailed essential imports, public revenues fell and poverty deepened. In the 1980s, of the region's forty-six countries for which data are available, twenty-eight suffered declines in real GDP per capita; the region's economy as a whole shrank by 1.2 per cent annually between 1980 and 1991 while annual population growth was around 3 per cent. In 1991, twenty-one of the thirty poorest countries in the world were African, and the total GNP for sub-Saharan Africa's 500m people (excluding South Africa) was only slightly higher than the GNP of Belgium, with 10m (World Bank, 1993: 238–9).

There has been intense debate about the causes of the crisis and appropriate responses. The Berg Report (World Bank, 1981) greatly influenced donor thinking in the 1980s. It acknowledged some internal 'structural' constraints upon growth – such as underdeveloped human resources, hostile climatic and geographic factors, high population growth – and also pointed to external factors, including stagflation in the industrial North, high energy prices, slow growth of demand in Africa's primary commodities and, for several commodities, adverse terms of trade. However, it identified 'domestic policy deficiencies' and 'administrative constraints' as the chief obstacles that were blocking progress by retarding market efficiency.

Almost a decade later, another major study (World Bank, 1989) adopted what was for many a more constructive tone, with a broader focus on long-term development themes, including human resource development (notably training and basic education, food and nutrition, health, family planning and safe water), poverty alleviation, equitable growth, empowerment, capacity building and, unprecedented for the Bank, strong emphasis on governance and democratisation. However, with regard to the economy, the study recognised external factors, especially falling commodity prices, but again pointed to internal factors, especially the 'declining level and efficiency of investment, compounded by accelerating population growth' as the main causes of falling incomes (ibid.: 3). The UN and the ECA (1989) have given more weight to external factors which, for example, cost Africa $5.6bn from the continuing decline in commodity prices in 1991 alone (UN, 1994: 36). In reality, both sets of factors are important and 'a useful model must capture the complex interconnection of political and economic, and domestic and international factors in economic decline' (Sandbrook, 1993: 12).

The World Bank's conviction that domestic policy weaknesses were the main culprit provided the rationale for the policy based lending of structural adjustment, which assumed that altering these domestic policies – shifting from state led development to market driven approaches – would make a difference. This lending grew rapidly in the 1980s as governments adopted structural adjustment programmes, usually in response to acute foreign exchange shortage; between 1978 and 1990, African countries having agreements with the IMF increased from two to twenty-eight, usually with simultaneous agreements with the World Bank. Definitions of structural adjustment have changed over time and no consensus has emerged as to the 'proper' definition (Killick, 1993: 67). The phrase has been debased by its increasing use to denote whatever policy package a government receiving a 'structural adjustment loan' was being asked to undertake or actually did undertake (Helleiner, 1994a: 5). In principle, distinction should be made between IMF stabilisation policies, aiming to reduce short-term disequilibrium, especially budget and balance of payments deficits and inflation, and World Bank structural adjustment policies, aiming to reorient the structure of the economy for greater efficiency and growth potential in the medium term, which implies more fundamental policy and institutional reforms (Stewart, 1992: 316–18). In practice, this distinction has been blurred because World Bank programmes are almost never implemented without an IMF programme in place. Moreover, despite some tensions between the demand management approach of IMF stabilisation programmes and the supply-oriented thrust of Bank adjustment programmes, the two institutions have increasingly undertaken joint programmes.

The policy prescriptions of the international financial institutions (IFIs – meaning the World Bank and the IMF) have stimulated great controversy regarding their appropriateness and effectiveness. Some non-governmental organisations and church groups in the West have been particularly outspoken, and in Africa the topic has been especially emotive – Lipumba (1994: 32) observes that the dominant opinion among African intellectuals is that structural adjustment programmes are part of the problem rather than part of the solution. There is not even agreement over criteria for evaluation; proponents have tended to focus on aggregate economic indicators, such as GDP, agricultural output, exports, fiscal balances and inflation, whereas critics have questioned the human impact, the weak links to long-term growth and development, and the resulting external indebtedness and dependency. A fundamental problem is that one cannot say what would have happened in the absence of an adjustment programme. Helleiner (1994a) and Lipumba (1994) provide concise and thoughtful summaries of the debate.

The World Bank's most recent assessment reviewed the adjustment experience of twenty-nine countries (1981–91), measuring the extent of changes in macro-economic policy through changes in three main indicators – fiscal, monetary and exchange rate policies. It concludes that for 'the African countries that have undertaken and sustained major policy reforms, adjustment is working' (World Bank, 1994: 1). However, while applauding policy improvements and their positive impact on growth and exports, the assessment notes the policies do not go far enough, and 'the level of per capita growth, even among the countries that have adjusted the most, is still below what is needed for rapid poverty reduction' (ibid.: xi). 'Adjustment alone will not put countries on a sustained, poverty-reducing growth path.' That is the challenge for long-term development and will require not only better economic policies, but also 'more investment in human capital, infrastructure, and institution building, along with better governance' (ibid.: 2). The assessment's findings suggest that IFI supported adjustment programmes help in some degree, but that the results are less than dramatic, at best bringing very modest levels of growth – 0.4 per cent per capita during 1987–91 for all fifteen countries where policies improved (ibid.: 6). They also show that countries have found it difficult to stick with the reform process in all its necessary rigour, with eleven of twenty-six adjusting countries demonstrating a deterioration in policies and one of the six best performers, Nigeria, having since abandoned the measures the Bank argues are most crucial for growth.[1]

Adjustment: some critical weaknesses

Why did adjustment programmes not meet original expectations? While it is impossible here to do full justice to the range and complexity of evidence, major weaknesses can be attributed to: first, a hostile global environment; second, economic policy package design; and, third, relationships between aid agencies and recipient governments (Killick, 1993: 318).

Hostile global environment

Helleiner (1994b: 317) argues that the prime cause of disappointing performance has been the insufficiently supportive external environment. Economic performance of African countries is powerfully influenced by global economic trends, particularly movements in terms of trade, capital flows and world interest rates. All three areas have experienced adverse trends, with terms of trade deteriorating (by an average of 3.3 per cent per year, 1980–9), long-term debt service rising (from $4.8bn or 10.9 per cent of exports in 1980 to $9.4bn or 24.4 per cent of exports in 1990) and real resource flows declining (Stewart, 1992: 329; Helleiner, 1994b: 325-6). Some global trends are probably unavoidable and African economies need to adjust to cope with the consequences. However, the burdens of adjusting are not shared equitably, with a marked discrepancy in the degree of policy rectitude expected of different country groupings. For example, industrialised countries maintain agricultural protectionism and the US runs persistent budgetary and payments deficits without coming under similar international pressure to change policies. Furthermore, there is an imbalance in the world economy in that 'austerity policies in deficit countries [are] unmatched by expansionary policies in persistent surplus countries … with a high proportion of the costs of this [deflationary] bias thrust upon people in developing countries' (Killick, 1993: 301).

Clearly, Africa's adjustment efforts need to be supported by improved international policy coordination and trade and monetary reforms, with an immediate agenda of: (i) strengthening existing compensation schemes to protect against short-term fluctuations in commodity prices, thus giving producers more time to adjust and diversify exports; (ii) reducing tariff and non-tariff barriers against manufactured exports; (iii) increasing concessional resource flows, especially flexible balance of payments support and debt relief. Without supportive action to increase foreign exchange earnings, African countries have little choice other than expand traditional exports, which reinforces a colonial pattern of specialisation, and may even result in reduced export earnings, as expanding production depresses world prices.

Comprehensive measures for debt relief are urgent. Domestic policy changes alone cannot bring recovery when governments devote up to 30–40 per cent of scarce export earnings to debt service, limiting capacity to finance growth generating imports. Even if adjustment related balance of payments support temporarily eases this constraint, the debt overhang still must be reduced. Its existence leads to increased uncertainty and risk, discouraging investment and limiting access to short-term trade credits. It also demands a semi-permanent process of negotiations with creditors that diverts policymakers from more socially productive activities of development-oriented economic decision-making. The most significant official debt relief so far – the so-called Toronto terms – are inadequate. Even the more favourable Trinidad terms (which propose a one-off reduction of the total eligible debt stock by two-thirds, with an initial five-year period of interest capitalisation and an extension of the repayment period from fourteen to twenty-four years for the remaining debt) would still leave fifteen of twenty-one severely indebted African countries with an unsustainable debt service burden (World Bank, 1994: 214). Special measures are needed to ease the significant and growing burden of Africa's multilateral debt (24 per cent of obligations and 40 per cent of debt service payments), owed mainly to the IMF and World Bank, whose statutes prevent the extension of debt relief and require the automatic suspension of disbursements when a country accumulates arrears.

Africa is even more dependent on aid flows in view of the virtual collapse of what Callaghy (1991: 47–8) has called an 'implicit bargain' between the international financial institutions and major Western countries on the one hand, and the Africans on the other. The provisions of the bargain – an 'unwritten contract', in the words of Michael Camdessus, IMF managing director (IMF, 1990: 210–13) – were that if the African countries would reform their economies in collaboration with the IMF and the World Bank, then new international private bank lending and direct foreign investment would be available to sustain these reforms. Although African countries embarked on reform programmes, the IFIs and reforming governments have not been successful in mobilising this increased lending and investment. Adequate medium-term aid flows are therefore essential to help diminish uncertainty and to reinforce sustainability by allowing governments to reduce some of the domestic costs of adjustment, to better protect the vulnerable and to 'buy off' key interest groups.

Cruelly, when Africa's reformers need more aid for development, allocations of development aid have declined under the pressure of donor fatigue and increased support for emergencies, and for Eastern Europe and the former Soviet Union. In spite of the call from the UN's New Agenda for Development in Africa in the 1990s (NADAF) for an increase in official development assistance (ODA) to Africa – from $20bn in 1990 to $30bn in 1992 and thereafter by 4 per cent in real terms annually until 1999 – the UN reports that 1992 ODA had in fact declined to $12.1bn. In response to this declining trend, there have been initiatives to improve aid quality by increasing the share for human development (UNDP, 1994), and by improving the cost effectiveness and coordination of technical assistance, which costs around US$4bn per year (Jaycox, 1993: 8). This raises doubts about the continuity of the required external funding for reforming governments. The sharpened competition for scarce aid inevitably affects power relationships, increasing the World Bank's leverage both as a major funder and as the coordinator of external support through the Consultative Group mechanism.

Design of economic policy packages

The following overview of a few of the many problems encountered underlines that adjustment is an enormously difficult and sensitive task in Africa, where reform is often complicated by other factors – drought, famine, war and AIDS. In this context, government capacity to design programmes is often overstretched, with key policymakers overwhelmed with crisis management and aid negotiations, operating at most within a one year time frame, from one Consultative Group meeting to the next. Capacity problems are further exacerbated by the too rapid turnover amongst IFI staff and/or their government interlocutors (Killick, 1993b: 107). As a result, policy-makers are unable to develop a development vision and most governments have no long-term development policies outside of their adjustment programme, which itself is too often a product of government reactions to external proposals (Lipumba, 1994: 31, 65).

As for the donor agencies, principally the IFIs, they do not always have sufficient in-depth country knowledge to design policy conditions or provide advice tailored to political and social realities and implementation capacities (Nelson and Eglington, 1993: 77–80). The IFIs are highly centralised, with limited country representation. Dialogue with governments is conducted mainly through numerous missions that are usually more interested in producing documents acceptable to their own management and boards than in ensuring they fully reflect African economic and institutional realities (Lipumba, 1994: 62–3). Here it is relevant to recall what Albert Hirschman described as the 'visiting economist syndrome ... the habit of issuing peremptory advice and prescriptions by calling on universally valid economic principles and remedies – be they old or new – after a strictly minimal acquaintance with the "patient"' (quoted in Toye, 1987: 21). The process limits the opportunity for country national decisionmakers to analyse the policy choices, including the all important implementation aspects, and to consider economic policy alternatives (Mkandawire, 1994: 173). 'An almost inevitable result, reinforced by desire to achieve comparability of treatment across countries, is to resort to a more or less standard approach', despite the great diversity among countries (Killick, 1993: 319). Policy packages tend to be complex and overloaded, with a multiplicity of conditions and overly optimistic targets that overstretch the limited technical and administrative capacity of governments. Even with the will and financial resources to undertake change of the scale and complexity proposed, it is doubtful whether many governments anywhere in the world could implement them. Taking Thatcher's Britain as an example, 'despite a government firmly committed to a broad structural adjustment-type programme, with relatively sizable resources, without the pressure of conditionality and with a considerable degree of public support "sectoral" reforms have proceeded only at a highly uneven pace, and were only beginning to reach the health sector, for example, a decade after Thatcher's first election victory' (Gibbon, 1992: 138).

A serious design deficiency has been lack of explicit attention to human resource development in general, and more specifically to the protection of the poor during the economic reform process, a reflection of the weak political organisation of the poor, and of the tendency of programme designers to focus on overall trends and to neglect distributive effects – who are the winners and losers. UNICEF's 'Adjustment with a Human Face' (Cornia *et al.*, 1987) drew attention to the human costs of adjustment and helped influence thinking about programme design. There is now greater consensus on the importance of dealing with the human consequences, not only because of the acute human need, but also out of concern for political sustainability. The 1980s 'IMF riots' in several countries, notably Egypt and Zambia, had shown that even politically unorganised groups may react strongly in the face of deteriorating living standards (Mkandawire, 1992: 309). However, protecting the poor from the costs of adjustment is very difficult, even when there is strong political commitment, which is not always the case. The challenge is to go beyond the social funds and safety net measures, partial responses at best, and to integrate the promotion of poverty reducing growth into the adjustment policy package at the outset. Most analysts seem to concur that those most likely to be affected adversely are the urban poor, land scarce or landless rural poor, and certain not so poor groups, such as government employees threatened with redundancy, with women bearing a disproportionate burden across all these groups. This suggests a strategy based on: (i) promoting the informal sector and labour intensive public works and other employment and income creating activities; (ii) support to small farmers, emphasising expanding access to productive assets and targeting of extension, credit and input distribution services; (iii) increasing public expenditure for basic health and education; (iv) targeted social transfers for the poorest (Killick, 1993: 338–47; Husain, 1994: 16–17; Lipumba, 1994: 49–51, 68). Cornia *et al.* (1992) and Graham (1994) provide extensive analysis and examples of policies and programmes to mitigate the negative impact and measures to protect the poor.

Relationship between aid agencies and aid recipients

Here, there is a major problem of process, what Gibbon (1992: 140) describes as 'conditionally-based muscle-flexing by donors'. Conditionality is usually resented by recipients on at least three grounds: it is regarded as a breach of sovereignty; it implies the donor's priorities and ideas regarding policy design are superior; and it is a constant reminder of power disparities (Nelson, 1992: 31). As most African countries are poor and highly aid dependent, donors in principle can exert great influence, but in practice there appear to be early limits to the policy changes that can be achieved by external leverage (Killick, 1993: 105–7; Helleiner, 1994: 9). There is even evidence that some countries use adjustment funding to buy more time and postpone action (Toye, 1992: 123; Killick, 1993: 313; Nelson and Eglington, 1993: 44). Interestingly, the relevant data in the recent assessment (World Bank, 1994: 258) do not show the expected positive correlation between increased resource flows and macro-economic policy improvement.

If conditionality does not always yield the expected benefits, it also has significant costs, including the tendency of conditionality to undermine national 'ownership' of a reform programme, reinforcing the impression that measures have been imposed upon a reluctant government, even if they are not. 'Without ownership, extensive use of conditions is likely to produce elaborate games of superficial compliance, failure to adopt key supplementary measures to make the reforms effective, or a trail of reform efforts launched and abandoned' (Nelson, 1992: 37).[2] Many times, the manner in which key economic (and other) policy decisions are made – for example, involving stakeholders to help build public understanding and a consensus for implementation – may be as important as their content. Policy decisions most likely to be carried through successfully are probably those that emerge organically through existing political and bureaucratic structures. Conditionality related reforms rarely have these qualities and are thus bound to be fragile, undermined by their crisis-driven nature.[3] To strengthen ownership, the IFIs should reduce the proliferation of conditions, many of which will not be met, and focus more on persuasion and dialogue, backed up by a greater concentration of available funding on programmes prepared by committed reforming governments. This implies saying 'no' to weak reformers, including authoritarian and corrupt regimes which have in the past received support more for political and strategic reasons. The moral issue then is the possible adverse effects of any suppression of external support on the poor and vulnerable groups in those societies.

Finally, the expanding use of conditionality has eroded national sovereignty and made donors active players in the domestic politics of recipient countries, with the danger that they use their influence in ways that have unanticipated political consequences which will have to be borne by others. Many apparently irrational economic policy interventions have a strong political logic, so that external pressure to reverse them could create destabilising political vacuums or ignite ethnic tensions (Killick, 1990: 64; Nelson, 1993: 82–3). Some argue further that the 'brazenly interventionist' mood of the development community undermines the legitimacy and political capacity of African governments, weakening their ability to comply with loan conditions, thus defeating their purpose (Beckman, 1992: 99). Here we turn to such political factors, which have often been underestimated or ignored.

State crisis and response

There was delay in recognising that the origins of the crisis were political as well as economic and that transcending it required political as well as economic reforms. However, by the late 1980s, the strong reciprocal relationship between state decay and economic crisis had been acknowledged, both within and beyond Africa. The Economic Commission for Africa's Khartoum Declaration (1988) stated: 'The political context for promoting healthy human development (in Africa) has been marred for more than two decades by instability, war, intolerance, restrictions on freedom and human rights of individuals and groups as well as the overconcentration of power with attendant restrictions on popular participation in decision making.' The World Bank (1989: 60–1) observed that 'underlying the litany of Africa's development problems is a crisis of governance'.

Convinced that economic failures were linked to repressive and non-representative political systems, and no doubt influenced by the democratic revolution in Eastern Europe, the main bilateral donors had by 1991 made political reforms (human rights, good governance and democracy) major criteria for the allocation of development assistance (Nelson, 1992: 15–17). The IFIs took these concerns on board, but with reservations. They were concerned that multiparty democracy might be incompatible with effective implementation of tough economic reform programmes and, at a time when IFI thinking on conditionality was moving towards 'fewer and simpler', there were doubts about how political conditionality could be designed and monitored and fears of 'conditionality overload' endangering the economic policy agenda (Gibbon, 1992: 142–3; Nelson, 1993: 71–86).

The IFIs and other donors had traditionally supported improved governance as it related to increased honesty and efficiency in the public sector, and other public administration and institutional strengthening activities.[4] Many bilateral donors and NGOs had strongly encouraged participation in development by communities and citizens' groups and some had emphasised human rights, but they had generally avoided directly promoting political reforms to encourage increased competition, as this had been considered an invasion of national sovereignty (Nelson, 1992: 13). This new promotion of competitive democracy seemed to meet with initial success. In autumn 1989, when the Berlin Wall fell, thirty-eight of the forty-five states in Africa were ruled by military junta or one party or one man governments; by autumn 1990, well over half had held, or were moving towards, multiparty elections (*Guardian*, 11 September 1990). Undoubtedly accelerated by donor conditionality, this process was nevertheless strongly rooted in widespread dissatisfaction with corrupt and autocratic regimes – catalysed by sharply declining well-being, especially in urban areas – and a genuine national aspiration for more accountable and effective government. Although progress has slowed or even stalled in cases such as Nigeria, some twenty-five or so multiparty elections took place between October 1990 and June 1994 (Van de Walle, 1994: 1). Of particular interest are cases like Benin, Cape Verde, Malawi and Zambia, where the new multiparty democracy passed the sternest test, the electoral defeat of an incumbent head of state.

Will these fledgling democracies survive in societies with no tradition of multiparty politics and pluralist institutions? To pose this question is not to discount the presence of several democratic strands in most traditional political formations on the continent (Chazan, 1994: 62), and the existence of institutions in many pre-colonial societies that promoted democratic behaviours and ensured public accountability, probity and responsive governance (Schapera, 1970; Smith, 1976;

Vansina, 1978; Chazan, 1994: 61–3). However, they were destroyed or marginalised during the colonial period, and democracy now cannot be applied like 'a patent medicine to be uncorked and poured at will' (Davidson, 1992: 223). Notwithstanding this cautionary note, the political experiment (or gamble) of democratisation is probably as unavoidable as it is indispensable. History has shown that imported models do not flourish; the new political institutions and culture need to evolve through difficult experiment and should be primarily defined from within each country, with firmer roots in Africa's cultural and political heritage than the 'wooden copies of metropolitan institutions' (Young, 1994: 245) of the independence constitutions. Constructive patterns of participation and political competition require careful hand tailoring to fit specific cultural, social and political traditions and circumstances, which suggests donor restraint in the use of conditionality and much greater reliance on dialogue and targeted support (Nelson, 1992: 43–4). Kwesi Botchwey, Ghana's finance minister, aptly summarised:

What is at issue is not whether African countries should democratize or not, for democratization is clearly in the objective interest of African Development. What is at issue is whether it should evolve, or be preserved through essentially internal or endogenous processes with the African people themselves finding their own forms of organization and means of struggle against oppression, or whether it should come about as a condition of external financial assistance and in the form of a checklist of standard institutional arrangements rooted in the alien experience of other countries. (*West Africa*, 25 June–1 July 1990: 1065)

The experience so far points to the complexity of democratisation in a highly volatile situation, characterised by a weak state and civil society, acute economic constraints, high illiteracy and poverty, the lack of a single political culture, and the limited development of a middle class, autonomous from the state (Fatton, 1990; Nelson, 1993; Sandbrook, 1993; Clark, 1994; Rothchild, 1994; Young, 1994). Most analysts urge a long-term approach, some advocating an interim phase of 'limited democracy' or 'minimalist democracy', that emphasises increasing government effectiveness. Some prefer the phrase 'political liberalisation' to 'democratisation' because it expresses an ongoing process of change rather than a move to an (externally defined) fixed end point (Widner, 1994: 8). Possibly in recognition of the uncertain prospects for the new regimes, Western donors do not seem to be insisting as strongly on serious moves towards democracy before authorising aid. Several long-serving autocrats have clung to power, artfully dividing the opposition, making cosmetic constitutional reforms, and even, in a few cases, emerging strengthened by a new electoral mandate (*Washington Post*, 2 January 1995).

Although these political changes are comparatively recent, some preliminary observations can be made about factors conditioning the successful consolidation of democratic rule. The most immediate threat is likely to be the disastrous economic situation, that already contributed to the downfall of the previous governments. New democratic regimes are thus faced with the daunting tasks of consolidating democratic institutions and undertaking urgent economic reform simultaneously. The immediate economic agenda is stabilisation to reduce massive deficits, mobilisation of aid, including debts rescheduling, and initial steps to counter deteriorating living standards and physical infrastructure. Without showing some progress new governments are unlikely to retain power for long, possibly opening the way for renewed authoritarian rule or even state collapse. This latter prospect is always a possibility in a region with recent precedents – Rwanda, Liberia and Somalia – and where other states have experienced political violence, resulting from the failure of political institutions to accommodate competing demands of regional, ethnic and social groups.

Skilful and committed political leadership is important, even more than it would be in less fluid and more institutionalised polities, and can go a long way to mitigate conditions hostile to democracy. To successfully tackle the economic crisis, leadership needs to have an understanding of the acuteness of the crisis and of ways to overcome it. This requires the ability to manage a protracted process of policy change – anticipating political consequences of specific reforms, articulating strategies to counter opposition, mediating conflicts that may arise, negotiating external assistance, and, above all, articulating the new policies in a way that inspires public confidence and permits the building of the broadest possible coalition of support.

Evidence suggests that democracies replacing unpopular and inefficient regimes have the chance of a honeymoon period that the new leadership can use to launch, if not sustain, major economic reform (Callaghy, 1991: 60). A new regime is less likely to be beholden to the vested interests that benefited from past policies and can attract new coalitions around alternative policy directions. The severity of the crisis, the ineffectiveness of past policies, and the knowledge that things are bad or even worse in other countries all contribute to create a climate of opinion that is favourable to radical solutions, not politics as usual. When the situation has seriously deteriorated, people have less to lose from change and are more likely to embrace radical reform.

The extent to which leadership can take advantage of this window of opportunity is significantly influenced by state capacity, eroded by years of crisis and now requiring restoration and adaption to meet many new demands. The complex agenda of economic reform requires of government the institutional capacity and will to design and implement policies concerning prices, trade, banking, finance, foreign investment, public enterprise restructuring and privatisation, and public sector reform, to manage complicated negotiations with donors, and to ensure the political, administrative, infrastructural and legal framework for the satisfactory functioning of markets. Political liberalisation requires enhanced state capacity to respond to more pluralistic societal demands, to allow for channels to represent societal interests and incorporate societal participation in decisionmaking and conflict resolution. In a more politically competitive environment, the state needs mechanisms to successfully contain insistent demands and claims from many groups within the bounds of available resource constraints and the same political arena. Without strengthening the capacity of state institutions to meet this challenge, the reform effort is unlikely to succeed.

A high priority must be reinforcing administrative capacity to collect revenue, enforce laws, deliver basic services and to discharge other core state functions. This capacity has been greatly weakened by the collapse in public sector salaries that has undermined staff morale, encouraged rent seeking behaviour and corruption, and driven some of the best into private employment or emigration. Management systems, remuneration scales and incentive schemes need to be improved in order to re-establish bureaucratic norms and behaviour that will ensure efficiency, impartiality, integrity and predictability (Klitgaard, 1991: 91–113; Sandbrook, 1993: 83–5). Emphasis should be placed on the capacity to design and implement policies and programmes for economic reform and institutional strengthening (Jaycox, 1993).

Evidence of more effective state performance is important to enable the new leadership to maintain popular support and to begin to restore the legitimacy of government and to project a credible societal vision of the future. At present, widespread cynicism and mistrust of government in general, and political leaders in particular, still persists (Sandbrook, 1993: 85, 106–7; Lipumba, 1994: 86–7; Young, 1994: 244). Confidence has to be restored for governments to be able to maintain autonomy from powerful vested interests, and to persevere with reform policies that may encounter resistance. Increased state legitimacy also raises the costs for any groups that may be tempted to seize power and to end the democratic experiment. As economic recovery will take time, improving basic service delivery – vaccinating children, providing basic drugs and school supplies, improving access to water – can clearly demonstrate the increased responsiveness and effectiveness of government.

The government emphasis on redefining the state's role and expanding participation in a more democratic political process has led to a positive reconsideration of decentralisation. Decentralisation and the strengthening of local government capacity can reduce the pressure of demands on the centre, improve state responsiveness to local needs, and broaden participation in local decision-making and in the political process in general. In the past, decentralisation has encountered problems due to local factional power struggles, lack of qualified staff and mismanagement of resources. As centralised approaches have not necessarily been more effective (Wunsch and Onslow, 1990), it may be timely to adopt a decentralised strategy to permit more effective interaction between revitalised local government and the considerable community capacities that have so often been marginalised or undermined by top-down planning (Taylor, 1992; Rahman, 1993).

It is the vitality of the informal sector and the coping skills and ingenuity of ordinary people, especially women, that have enabled households to survive and meet their basic needs. When people's and voluntary organisations have successfully channelled this capacity into community managed programmes, the results have been impressive. For example, the Six-S Movement in Burkina Faso is a particularly successful self-development movement that has evolved into a network of thousands of community based groups – building on traditional mutual cooperation groups for youth and for women – that implement their own development programmes during the eight months of the agriculturally inactive Sahel dry season. Spreading since its foundation in 1976 to neighbouring countries, the movement has brought significant improvements in the areas of rural infrastructure, environmental conservation and household income generation, as well as developing local organisational and technical capacity and reinforcing community confidence and self-esteem (Pradervand, 1989; Rahman, 1993: 123–5). Ruling elites have often been wary of authentic grassroots movements, seeing them as potential threats to national integration and to their own hold on power (Sandbrook, 1993: 144). In turn, grassroots movements have frequently been suspicious of government and have in some cases served as vehicles for dissent and dissatisfaction with the state. In the climate of change towards a more pluralistic society and responsive governance politicians, NGOs and community leaders must learn to cooperate to improve living standards and enhance local control of development.

As economic and political liberalisation push the state out of space it once monopolised, the vacuum will be partly occupied by a variety of actors and interest groups, including the churches, the NGOs and community groups who are already taking advantage of the opportunities for more meaningful participation in public policy. This civil society – defined as the area of organised human activity concerned with the exercise of state authority, which functions in the space between the state and the family (Barkan, 1994: 92) – together with the expanding independent media, can exert countervailing power on state institutions in order to ensure accountable, transparent and responsive governance, and to prevent the personalistic rule and clientelism that were principal factors in the state crisis of the 1980s. An active and vigilant civil society also provides a chance for the next generation of political activists to acquire organisational and leadership skills. At present, the new regimes are relying heavily on 'old war horses, politicians discredited by their previous complicity with the old order' (Bates, 1994: 25–6), and many of the new political parties are still fragile shifting groups, with weak grassroots structures, and unable to play their role fully as intermediaries between the civil society and the state. It is the construction of new, reliable and trusted frameworks of interaction between state and society that is a prime precondition for democratisation (Chazan, 1994: 88).

The focus of this section has been on the period of immediate consolidation of democratic rule, and has not dealt with issues such as ideology, ethnicity, the role of the legislative and the judiciary, which will be of increasing importance in countries where political liberalisation advances to subsequent changes.

Future directions

It is increasingly clear that Africa is not an undifferentiated whole, and that some countries, such as Ghana, South Africa, Zimbabwe and Uganda are more likely to progress, by virtue of multiple factors, including natural resource endowment, leadership capacity, and human and physical infrastructure, while others remain mired in economic crisis, civil strife and social unrest. Even in the best of cases, the daunting problems are of a structural and institutional nature that do not lend themselves to quick fixes. Economic difficulties and widespread poverty still persist, even where structural adjustment economic reform programmes are being implemented. With the emphasis of these adjustment programmes now shifting more to supply expansion, the time horizon gradually lengthening, and the steady addition of new dimensions to the discussion, e.g., poverty reduction, equity in income distribution, environmental sustainability, participatory political forms and improved governance, it has become increasingly difficult to distinguish between 'adjustment' and 'development'. It is therefore appropriate to call a formal end to structural adjustment and to return to development, many would say 'human development' and/or sustainable development, as the central theme of economic policy debate and reform strategies in Africa (Helleiner, 1994a: 5).

Politically, the changes towards more responsive, accountable and ultimately more effective systems of government are advancing unevenly and are likely to yield limited results in the short to medium term, largely due to the weakness of democratic institutions and of the civil society and to the burden of the economic crisis. Earlier, political reforms were not only felt to be intrinsically desirable, but also conducive to economic growth. As countries seek to move from authoritarian to more open polities, and from state guided to more open economies, it is becoming apparent that if pluralist politics and market economics are probably mutually essential in the long run, the processes of moving towards each goal conflict in many ways in the short and medium term (Nelson, 1992: 40). In this context, economic and especially political conditionality can be counter-productive and should be used by donors with great restraint. Instead of insisting on a model of liberal neo-classical political economy which they do not even practise themselves, the donors and IFIs need to allow African countries the time and political space to develop their own unique models (Callaghy, 1994: 213).

Expectations of the reforms have been unrealistically high, and proponents of change have made exaggerated claims for their prescriptions. External agencies, the Bank and the IMF in particular, have been learning by doing and often experimenting without being able to mitigate much of the negative consequences of their efforts. Reform and renewal must be seen as a longer-term process. Change is likely to be slow, incremental, uneven, often contradictory from a given analytical point of view, and dependent on the outcome of unpredictable socio-economic and political struggles. The very depth of the crisis may ultimately bring forth enduring solutions. It has upset existing economic and political forces and has opened up space for new definitions of the state in development, new policy departures, new political coalitions and new scope for political leadership and institutional innovation. Not only governments, but also civil society must be committed to a reform strategy based on a longer-term societal vision that justifies the inevitable sacrifices and hardships and provides a basis for greater social cohesion.

The example of Africa's committed reformers will hopefully inspire the governments and people of industrialised countries to play their part, providing sustained financing, including debt cancellation, and making the necessary adjustments in their domestic and international trade policies that would improve markets for African exports. It would help avoid paternalism, create a stronger sense of partnership and strengthen national ownership, if there was a more genuinely multi-lateral arena where Africa's reform-minded leaders could present their reform agenda, engage donors in an authentic debate over policy options, and negotiate joint reciprocal commitments to which all parties could be held accountable.

A suitable framework for a renewed partnership for Africa could be the commitment to a global ethic that recognises the rights of people, irrespective of race, religion, gender or nationality, to basic standards of living and human dignity. This is morally consistent with the teachings of the main world faiths and builds on the UN's work in establishing international norms through instruments such as the Convention on the Rights of the Child (UNICEF, 1991). The rights and needs of children could be a powerful focus for the mobilisation of statesmen, church leaders, citizens' groups and communities in a global effort that would transcend narrow political agendas in order to reduce death and disease, provide basic services and eliminate discrimination and exploitation. The Declaration and the Plan of Action from the UN's World Summit for Children (UNICEF, 1994) and the follow-up National Programmes of Action provide an initial operational framework, with provisions for international monitoring of progress towards a set of commonly agreed goals, principally in health, education, nutrition, water and sanitation. Although the goals are universal, they would have greatest impact in Africa, where children's needs are most acute. This is not another 'prescription', but rather, a highly visible and relatively uncontroversial focus, that might uniquely contribute to a broader consensus which would progressively lock the international community into an agenda of economic, political and social change towards a more equitable and sustainable pattern of global development.

This could also contribute to a redefinition of development which to many people still has a narrow economic connotation, strongly rooted in Western material values. The classic measures of economic progress do not necessarily reflect improved individual or community well-being, and insufficient consideration is given to privacy, personal security, incidence of drudgery, control over one's life, environmental balance and other culturally or socially defined goals.

By responding to Africa's crisis in a broader and more collaborative spirit, the international community could not only support the efforts of

Africa's governments and peoples, but also rekindle a sense of common purpose and shared humanity that is the essence of planetary survival.

NOTES

1 Data on IMF programmes show that two-thirds of them in the period 1987–90 broke down before the end of their intended life (Killick, 1993: 104).
2 The extent of government ownership predicted the satisfactoriness of adjustment programme outcomes in 75 per cent of cases (World Bank, 1992: ch. 10, Annex 8).
3 Compliance rates are also affected by the extent of the administrative load and the distribution and timing of benefits. Thus, compliance rates seem to be higher for conditions such as adjusting exchange rates or increasing producer prices that offer immediate and widely distributed benefits and can be implemented by a small number of senior technocrats and politicians, and lower for reforms requiring institutional change, such as privatisation or public sector restructuring that often have delayed benefits (Nelson, 1992: 2; Kanbur, 1994: 18–21).
4 The World Bank in principle is restricted to these areas, as its articles of agreement prohibit it from engaging in political activities.

REFERENCES

Barkan, J. D. (1994) 'Restructuring Modernization Theory and the Emergence of Civil Society in Kenya and Nigeria', in D. E. Apter and C. G. Rosberg (eds.), *Political Development and the New Realism in Sub-Saharan Africa* (Charlottesville: University Press of Virginia), pp. 87–116.
Bates, R. (1994) 'The Impulse to Reform in Africa', in Widner (1994), 13–28.
Beckman, B. (1992) 'Empowerment or Repression? The World Bank and the Politics of African Adjustment', in P. Gibbon, Y. Bangura, A. Ofstad (eds.), *Authoritarianism, Democracy and Adjustment* (Uppsala: The Scandinavian Institute of African Studies), pp. 83–105.
Callaghy, T. (1991) 'Africa and the World Economy: Caught Between a Rock and a Hard Place', in J. W. Harbeson and D. Rothchild (eds.), *Africa in World Politics* (Boulder, CO: Westview Press), pp. 39–68.
—— (1994) 'State, Choice, and Context', in D. E. Apter and C. G. Rosberg (eds.), *Political Development and the New Realism in Sub-Saharan Africa* (Charlottesville: University Press of Virginia), pp. 184–219.
Chazan, N. (1994) 'Between Liberalism and Statism: African Political Cultures and Democracy', in L. Diamond (ed.), *Political Culture and Democracy in Developing Countries* (Boulder, CO: Lynne Rienner), pp. 59–97.
Clark, J. F. (1994) 'The Constraints on Democracy in Sub-Saharan Africa: The Case for Limited Democracy', *SAIS Review*, vol. 14(2), 91–108.
Cornia, G. A., R. Jolly and F. Stewart (eds.) (1987) *Adjustment with a Human Face* (Oxford: Clarendon Press), vols. I and II.
Cornia, G. A., R. van der Hoeven and T. Mkandawire (eds.) (1992) *Africa's Recovery in the 1990s* (London: Macmillan).

Davidson, B. (1992) *The Black Man's Burden* (New York: Times Books).

Economic Commission for Africa (1988) 'The Khartoum Declaration. Towards a Human-Focused Approach to Socio Economic Recovery and Development in Africa', in *ECA Annual Report* (New York: United Nations).

(1989) *African Alternative Framework to Structural Adjustment Programmes for Socio-Economic Recovery and Transformation* (Addis Ababa), ECA E/ECA/CM/15/6/Rev. 3.

Fatton, R. (1990) 'Liberal Democracy in Africa', *Political Science Quarterly*, vol. 105(3), 455–73.

Gibbon, P. (1992) 'Structural Adjustment and Pressures Towards Multipartyism in Sub-Saharan Africa', in P. Gibbon, Y. Bangura, A. Ofstad (eds.), *Authoritarianism, Democracy and Adjustment* (Uppsala: The Scandinavian Institute of African Studies), pp. 127–68.

Goldin, I., O. Knudsen and D. van der Mensbrugghe (1993) *Trade Liberalization: Global Economic Implications* (Paris and Washington, DC: OECD/World Bank).

Graham, C. (1994) *Safety Nets, Politics and the Poor* (Washington, DC: The Brookings Institution).

Helleiner, G. K. (1994a) 'From Adjustment to Development in Sub-Saharan Africa: Consensus and Continuing Conflict', in G. A. Cornia and G. K. Helleiner (eds.), *From Adjustment to Development in Africa* (New York: St Martin's Press), pp. 3–24.

(1994b) 'External Resource Flows, Debt Relief and Economic Development in Sub-Saharan Africa', in G. A. Cornia and G. K. Helleiner (eds.), *From Adjustment to Development in Africa* (New York: St Martin's Press), pp. 317–33.

Husain, I. (1994) *The Macroeconomics of Adjustment in Sub-Saharan African Countries*, Policy Research Working Paper 1365 (Washington, DC: World Bank).

IMF (1990) *IMF Survey*, 19(7), 108–11.

Jaycox, E. V. K. (1993) 'Capacity Building: The Missing Link in African Development', Address to 23rd African American Institute Conference (Reston, Virginia), 20 May (mimeo).

Jolly, R. (1988) 'Poverty and Adjustment in the 1990s', in John Lewis (ed.), *Strengthening the Poor: What Have We Learned?* (Washington, DC: Overseas Development Council), pp. 163–75.

Kanbur, R. (1994a) *Welfare Economics, Political Economy, and Policy Reform in Ghana*, Policy Research Working Paper 1381 (Washington, DC: World Bank).

(1994b) 'The Coming Anarchy', *Atlantic Monthly* (Feb.), 44–76.

Killick, T. (1990) *A Reaction Too Far: Economic Theory and the Role of the State in Developing Countries* (London: Overseas Development Institute).

(1993a) *The Adaptive Economy: Adjustment Policies in Small, Low-Income Countries* (Washington, DC: World Bank).

(1993b) 'Improving the Effectiveness of Financial Assistance for Policy Reforms', in *Development Issues, Presentations to the 47th Meeting of the Development Committee* (Washington, DC: World Bank), pp. 103–12.

Klitgaard, R. (1991) *Adjusting to Reality* (San Francisco: International Center for Economic Growth).

Lipumba, Nguyuru (1994) *Africa Beyond Adjustment* (Washington, DC: Overseas Development Council).

Mkandawire, T. (1992) 'The Political Economy of Development with a Democratic Face', in Cornia *et al.* (1992), 296–311.

(1994) 'Adjustment, Political Conditionality and Democratization in Africa', in G. A. Cornia and G. K. Helleiner (eds.), *From Adjustment to Development in Africa* (New York: St Martin's Press), pp. 155–73.

Nelson, J. and S. Eglinton (1992) *Encouraging Democracy: What Role for Conditioned Aid?* (Washington, DC: Overseas Development Council).

(1993) *Global Goals, Contentious Means: Issues of Multiple Aid Conditionality* (Washington, DC: Overseas Development Council).

Pradervand, P. (1989) *Une Afrique en Marche* (Paris: Editions Plon).

Rahman, A. (1993) *People's Self Development* (London: Zed Books).

Rothchild, D. (1994) 'Structuring State-Society Relations in Africa: Towards an Enabling Political Environment', in Widner (1994), pp. 201–29.

Sandbrook, R. (1993) *The Politics of Africa's Economic Recovery* (Cambridge: Cambridge University Press).

Schapera, I. (1970) *A Handbook of Tswana Law and Custom* (London: Frank Cass).

Smith, R. (1976) *Kingdoms of the Yoruba* (London: Methuen).

Stewart, F. (1992) 'Short-Term Policies for Long-Term Development', in G. A. Cornia, R. van der Hoeven and T. Mkandawire (eds.) (1992), pp. 312–33.

Taylor, D. R. F. (1992) 'Development from Within and Survival in Rural Africa', in D. R. F. Taylor and F. Mackenzie (eds.), *Development from Within. Survival in Rural Africa* (London: Routledge), pp. 214–57.

Toye, J. (1987) *Dilemmas of Development* (Oxford: Basil Blackwell).

(1992) 'Interest Group Politics and the Implementation of Adjustment Policies in Sub-Saharan Africa', in P. Gibbon, Y. Bangura, A. Ofstad (eds.), *Authoritarianism, Democracy and Adjustment* (Uppsala: The Scandinavian Institute of African Studies), pp. 106–26.

UN (1994) *Africa Recovery* (New York: United Nations), vol. 7(3/4) (Dec. 93–Mar. 94).

UNDP, UNESCO, UNFPA, UNICEF, WHO (1994) *The 20/20 Initiative* (New York: UNICEF).

UNICEF (1991) 'World Declaration and Plan of Action from the World Summit for Children' and 'Convention on the Rights of the Child', in *State of the World's Children Report* (1991) (New York: UNICEF).

Van de Walle, N. (1994) 'Economic Reform and the Consolidation of Democratic Rule in Africa', Paper presented at African Studies Association meeting (Toronto), November (mimeo).

Vansina, J. (1978) *The Children of Woot: A History of the Kuba Peoples* (Madison: University of Wisconsin Press).

Widner, J. (ed.) (1994) *Economic Change and Political Liberalization in Sub-Saharan Africa* (Baltimore: The Johns Hopkins University Press).

World Bank (1981) *Accelerated Development in Sub-Saharan Africa: An Agenda for Action* (Washington, DC: World Bank).

(1989) *Sub-Saharan Africa: From Crisis to Sustainable Growth* (Washington, DC: World Bank).

(1992) *World Bank Structural and Sectoral Adjustment Operations: The Second OED Overview* (Washington, DC: World Bank).

(1993) *World Development Report, 1993. Investing in Health.* (Washington, DC: World Bank).

(1994) *Adjustment in Africa. Reforms, Results, and the Road Ahead* (New York: Oxford University Press).

Wunsch, J. S. and Dele Olowu (eds.) (1990) *The Failure of the Centralized African State: Institutions and Self-Governance in Africa* (Boulder, CO: Westview).

Young, C. (1994) 'Democratization in Africa: The Contradictions of a Political Imperative', in Widner (1994), pp. 230–50.

Zartman, I. W. (ed.) (1995) *Collapsed States: The Disintegration and Restoration of Legitimate Authority* (Boulder, CO: Lynne Rienner).

13 Of medium powers and middling roles

Denis Stairs

Social scientists who apply their craft to the study of international affairs sometimes display disconcerting habits. One of them comes from their love of conceptual order and their impatience with the untidiness of the real world. Commentators on the roles played by 'middle powers' in world affairs too often exhibit precisely this unrestrained search for relief from eclecticism. Hence they assume, or they try artfully to demonstrate, that patterns exist where in fact they do not, and that causes are simple when they are actually complex.

Generalising about the behaviour of a motley collection of highly differentiated states – operating, as they do, in kaleidoscopic environments with diverse challenges in view and disparate objectives in mind – is risky business. It calls for great care in ensuring that the conclusions reached, and the lessons drawn, do not depend on excessively contorted evidence for such practical import as they are held to possess. It is my purpose, nonetheless, to take the generalising as far as I can, and the task implies a normative as well as descriptive inquiry. The question is not merely what middle powers *can* do (or have done) but what they *should* do, given the world in which we now find ourselves.

What is a 'middle power' and does it really help to know?

The trouble starts with the very idea of a middle power. Part of the problem is that the first of these questions has no 'objective' answer, and hence cannot be disposed of by reference to commonly accepted indicators. But there is also a difficulty with the basic premise upon which the question is founded. That premise is that the place of a given state in the international hierarchy of power is itself a fundamental, if not *the* fundamental, determinant of its international behaviour. The question is thus held to 'matter' because the states that are identified by the answer it generates are expected to behave in similar (but distinctive) ways.

The popularity of this premise can be explained in part as a natural extension of theories of international behaviour that have traditionally (and sometimes usefully) been applied to the security interactions of the 'great', or dominant, powers, and to the 'systemic' patterns that have been attributed to different 'great power' configurations. If it can be shown that the behaviour of *great* powers is a function, in at least some respects, of the relative stores of assets under their control (so that, for example, they are led by the 'structure' of their power relationships to seek to countervail one another), does it not then make sense to hypothesise that *lesser* powers behave in accordance with similarly recurrent, if substantively different, patterns? More succinctly, if 'power' determines behaviour, then middle powers should behave more like one another, and less like either the great powers or the smaller powers. That being so, if we can identify what the middle powers are, we will be in a fine position from which to launch a search for common behaviours. We might even identify among them the performance of a common 'role'.

One of the more obvious difficulties with this premise is that it neglects the possibility that the influence of the hierarchy of power is discontinuous. Perhaps its impact ends with its effect upon the global interactions of the greater states (or their regional, or subsystem, equivalents). It may, in short, be true that great powers (by virtue of their 'power') act similarly and repetitively. But it may also be true that middle powers (in spite of their 'power') do not.

A second, and possibly more significant, difficulty with the premise is that it assumes, or at least it implies, that the patterns of behaviour that we expect to ensue from any specific accumulation of 'power' are patterns of substance, and not merely of tactics. It is assumed, that is, that middle powers will exhibit not only similar tactical repertoires, but also common objectives or purposes. This is an *important* assumption because, unless it can be sustained, we are left with tactical commonalities only, and these are probably trivial. It may well be the case, for example, that middle powers like to do their business in multilateral contexts – whether such contexts be transient and *ad hoc*, or permanently institutionalised. If anarchy occasionally lends opportunity and comfort to the strong, after all, it rarely does much for the weak. The latter, therefore, have a natural preference for the safety of numbers and the security of rule-governed environments. But this is hardly a stunning conclusion. The same reasoning applies to small fish at sea, small boys in a schoolyard and small players in the politics of a university. If the hunt is for power-driven commonalities of no greater interest than this, it is barely worth the blowing of a horn.

Yet, even a brief reminder of the origins of the 'middle power' concept in the contemporary era gives credence to the suspicion that such tactical considerations, at the beginning, at least, were exactly what was at issue. The place to start is at the founding of the United Nations, in reparation for which the middle power concept was propagated most notably by the Canadians and the Australians, and by those others with similar interests who subsequently supported them (Glazebrook, 1947; MacKay, 1969; Eayrs, 1972; Holmes, 1979; Holbraad, 1984; Keating, 1993). The purpose of the propagation was clear and simple: to provide a foundation for the claim of certain states – not great powers, but not pip-squeak powers, either – to an enhancement of their influence within the new United Nations organisation under the terms of its constitutional 'Charter'. This was 'positional politics', and nothing more. The claim itself was based on premises that were identical to those that underlay the claims of the great powers – namely, that power and responsibility go together, and that the new organisation would be effective only if this 'reality' were reflected in the rules governing its decision-making institutions and processes. If it were not, the *institutional* power structure would be so discordant with the *actual* power structure that the organisation itself would fail.

This point - that there was no difference of principle between the advocates of the 'great power' interest on the one hand, and the advocates of the 'middle power' interest on the other – needs emphasis. The supporters of the two sets of claims parted company only in their respective accounts of the international class structure. For the great powers, there were two classes of states: (i) the great powers, and (ii) all the rest. For the middle powers, there were three classes of states: (i) the great powers; (ii) the middle powers; and (iii) all the rest. But this was not a quarrel over fundamentals. Certainly it was not a disagreement of the kind entailed in the competing view (advanced by many of the smaller states) that the institutions of the United Nations ought to be founded, not on practices rooted in the currency of power, but on the principle of state equality.

More significantly for the present discussion, there was nothing in the 'middle power' argument at San Francisco to suggest either a commonality of substantive position, or a sharing of roles. What the middle powers held in common was the view simply that they ought to have more influence in the United Nations than the very small powers, while recognising (with varying degrees of resignation) that they could not reasonably hope to have as much influence as the great powers. How their influence would actually be *used* was a separate matter, and it was not discussed. It could not even be assumed that the middle powers were more keenly 'internationalist' than were the members of the other two classes. Some players in every class might be more sceptical than others, but the basic purpose of the United Nations as a project was presumably one with which *all* of its founders were in at least preliminary agreement.

The thought that the 'middling power' of middle powers may generate a greater commonality of positional and tactical politics than of substantive politics is strengthened as soon as lists of middle powers are drawn up, and their behaviours examined. This making of lists is prone, of course, to idiosyncrasy. If you vary the indicator, you vary the list. You do the same if you toy with the requisite *quantities* of indicator – with the price, that is, of admission. Reality becomes an intellectual artefact. For example, the indicator that many analysts seem to like best is GNP. Technical issues bearing on the reliability and comparability of the data aside, GNP figures are readily available from standard reference sources, appear to 'regress out' a lot of other variables, and provide at least a crude measure of capabilities (actual or potential). But how much GNP is enough to warrant promotion to the middle class? And how much commonality of behaviour do we find when we complete the ranking process and survey the results?

The answer to the first question is that it is up to the analyst. The answer to the second question is, 'Not much'. A couple of examples drawn from the extant literature will illustrate the point, beginning with the widely cited study by Carsten Holbraad (1984). Recognising that the drawing of class boundaries on the basis of GNP alone was an arbitrary exercise at best, Holbraad thought it appropriate to modify the application of the GNP indicator by reference to geopolitical criteria – that is, by considering candidates for admission in the context of their positions within their respective regions. Using 1975 GNP data, he came up with South Africa and Nigeria for Africa; Japan, China, India and Iran for Asia; the Federal Republic of Germany, France, the United Kingdom, Italy, Spain and Poland for Europe; Canada and Mexico for North and Central America; Brazil and Argentina for South America; and Australia and Indonesia for 'Oceania and Indonesia'. On this calculus, the middle power class was then composed of eighteen states – six from Europe, four from Asia, and two from each of the four other geographical areas. But one would be hard put to find among them anything of interest by way of foreign policy behaviours in common. Small wonder that Holbraad concludes 'that any similarity that may be observed in their international conduct and any generalization that may be formulated about their systemic role are likely to flow not so much from a set of inherent characteristics and inclinations shared by such powers as from various external pressures and incentives to which they are exposed' (1984: 91).

A second example can be found in the elegant disquisitions of Bernard Wood. After reviewing some of the intellectual puzzles that are unleashed by the concept of power itself, along with the practical dilemmas that confront the analysts who seek to measure it, he decided, like others before him, to opt for GNP 'as the most acceptable single measure of tangible national capabilities' (Wood, 1988: 17). Using it, he then generated a list that was apparently designed to capture all the states he thought it appropriate to capture (an objective that could be accomplished simply by manipulating the cut-off points). This produced a rank-ordered class of thirty-three, with Italy at the top and Iran at the bottom (Wood, 1988: 18). The list obviously included many of the states that Holbraad had left out (the Low Countries and the Scandinavians among them), but it also omitted Japan and the larger European powers (the Federal Republic of Germany, France and the United Kingdom), all of which Holbraad had effectively demoted to middle-class status.

Like Holbraad, Wood did not expect that his list would allow him to predict directly to common behaviour. His purpose was simply to identify a band of countries that might reasonably be subjected to further comparative analysis. Applying what he called 'behaviour criteria' would have the effect of further qualifying the 'objective rankings' that his GNP indicator had given him, although this would also introduce 'more judgmental and controversial elements' (Wood, 1988: 18).

Indeed it would. Adopting such a procedure amounts, in fact, to conceding that the possession of middling capabilities does not, in itself, count for much as a foreign policy determinant.

Does it count for *anything*? The hint of a reasonable answer to this question is contained in Wood's own procedure, which was to deploy the principal source of power (economic wealth) as a means of limiting his 'scanning range'. In effect, he used his own operational version of the 'middle power' concept to define the universe of states within which the particular types of behaviour in which he was interested were most likely to be found. That immediately left open the possibility that those behaviours could be discovered within the other two categories, as well (that is, among the 'great powers' and 'all the rest'), and that his methodology did not allow him to determine this because it prevented him from having a close look. Still, there is a *prima facie* persuasiveness about his method of attack. Why?

The answer has to do, clearly, with capabilities. Middle powers (however defined) obviously cannot do some of the things that great powers can do. On the other hand, they *can* do things that smaller powers can *not* do. All other causally-pertinent factors being equal, therefore, the list of options (or possibilities) open to middle powers is different from the list available to the great powers and from the list at the disposal of the small powers (although some options will certainly overlap – that is, appear on more than one list). The differences in these 'options lists', moreover, have political consequences. That is, they affect the hopes and fears – which is to say, the expectations – of others, a reality that can have a 'feedback' effect on the options themselves (e.g., by making some of them even more viable than they would have been had the expectations of others been different).

In sum, having middling capabilities determines, not what middle powers states *will* do, but what, in principle, they *can* do (assuming that other factors do not interfere). To put the point another way, in the case of at least some foreign policy behaviours, and certainly in the case of some foreign policy *roles*, having middle power capabilities is a 'necessary' condition, but not a 'sufficient' one. In particular instances, of course, this middle power condition will not be exploited in the way we might normally expect because other factors (other 'sources of foreign policy') intervene. In that event, the middling capabilities are used in other ways (different behaviours are exhibited, different roles are played), or are not used internationally at all. The probability that behaviours will not be standard, but vary widely from case to case, is increased, moreover, by the fact that states that are 'middle powers' globally may be 'great powers' regionally, and act predominantly in accordance with regional opportunities or imperatives.

In the light of these reflections, it is not surprising to discover that those who fabricate assemblages of middle powers and then go in search of the roles they seem to play come up with a polyglot list, or with no consistently characteristic list at all. Bernard Wood, for example, is refreshingly at pains to avoid the trap that comes from thinking of all middle powers as constructively benign, and emerges with a list that includes the roles of (1) 'regional or sub-regional leader'; (2) 'functional leader', that is, being a leader in functional issue-areas in which the middle power happens to have particular strength; (3) 'stabiliser', routinely taking initiatives to separate or counter-balance other powers, or to mediate their disputes; (4) acting 'negatively', as, for example, in 'free-riding', 'fence-sitting', and 'status-seeking'; and (5) performing as a 'good multilateral citizen', by supporting multilateral decisionmaking institutions and processes (1988: 21ff.). Holbraad, similarly entrapped by eclecticism, is drawn into a lengthy and discursive disquisition

(1984). In such an enumeration one looks in vain for pattern, order or taxonomic coherence. States do what states do, which is a lot of different things.

What are the roles we really want to find and where do we really find them?

Having thus demoted (but not completely demolished) the significance of 'middling power' as a determinant of middle power behaviours, and having given appropriate due to the blindingly obvious (not all middle powers behave alike), we are led to shift the analysis, and to ask two rather different questions, the first of them having a heavy normative loading, and the second being essentially, if relaxedly, empirical. The first asks what kinds of behaviours, including *repetitive* behaviours (which are commonly described as 'roles' if they are pursued in relation to the on-going politics of the international system), we are really interested in, and why. The second asks what conditions, over and above the possession of middling capabilities, serve in the real world to encourage the performance of these specific behaviours. What other factors, in short, have to be added to the causal mix to make it work in the way we *want* it to work?

The normative loading of the first of these questions is rooted, of course, in the search for states that can be counted upon to promote the international 'public good'. This is usually defined in terms of cooperative approaches to the maintenance of international peace and security and to the enhancement of such underlying conditions as are thought to make the persistence of peace more (and the recurrence of war less) likely. The focus of the inquiry can thus be rendered more precise by asking exactly which behaviours and roles are thought to serve these purposes.

In Wood's analysis, these roles seem to be the ones that are associated primarily with the third and fifth of his categories – namely, acting as a 'stabiliser' (particularly by separating adversaries and mediating disputes), and displaying leadership in, and commitment to, multilateral institutions and processes. This interpretation would certainly be consistent with the approach taken many years ago by the most influential Canadian analyst of 'middlepowermanship', John W. Holmes, upon whose reflections so much subsequent writing on middle power behaviour has been based. Holmes himself was impatient with compulsive attempts to define precisely what middle powers are and what roles they play, and he knew very well that in any particular case both the middle power status and the middle power behaviour could be fleeting. As he often observed, ambiguity, when calculated, can be constructive. Notwithstanding these hesitations, however, his underlying position was ultimately very clear: from the normative vantage point, 'middlepowermanship' connoted action in 'a middle or mediatory position in conflicts' (Holmes, 1966: 16).

More recently, a triumvirate of Canadian and Australian analysts, in professing their loyalty to the Holmesian tradition, have argued that 'the essence of middle power diplomatic activity is best captured by emphasizing not what this group of countries should be doing but what type of diplomatic behaviour they do, or could, display in common'. Such behaviour is taken specifically to include the 'tendency' of middle powers 'to pursue multilateral solutions to international problems ... to embrace compromise positions in international disputes, and ... to embrace notions of "good international citizenship" to guide their diplomacy' (Cooper et al., 1993: 19). This summary is then refined into a three-part 'itemized pattern of middle power behaviour' entailing performances as 'catalyst' (e.g., triggering initiatives), 'facilitator (e.g., setting agendas and orchestrating processes by which they can be pursued) and 'manager' (e.g., building both institutions and confidence or trust) (Cooper et al., 1993: 24–5).

Similar language crops up in other studies. For example, Peyton V. Lyon and Brian W. Tomlin in 1979 identified the traditional middle power roles (when described, at least, in flattering terms) as those of 'mediator', 'peacekeeper', 'community builder' (or 'organisation maintainer'), and 'moderator' (Lyon and Tomlin, 1979: 12ff.). In a much more recent discussion, Allan K. Henrikson has argued that the 'highest of the middle-power proficiencies ... is the *managerial*', which he has defined as 'the practical ability to control and give positive direction to international undertakings' (Henrikson, 1993: 1). On this account, managerial influence is often exercised through 'mediation' and in the context of 'international institutions' (Henrikson, 1993: 1–2). Mediatory diplomacy in turn takes three principal forms: 'good offices', 'bridge building', and 'planetary management' (Henrikson, 1993: 13–14). Cranford Pratt, among others, goes somewhat farther, in that he seems to require of middle powers that they engage in 'humane internationalism' – that is, that they actively pursue not merely the resolution of third-party conflicts, but the removal of the underlying conditions upon which such conflicts feed, e.g., economic underdevelopment (Pratt, 1989, 1990). Similar preoccupations underlie David Black's comparative work on Australia, Canada and Sweden in relation to Southern Africa, although his findings demonstrate very clearly that 'middle power internationalism' has its roots, not in *one* factor, but in complex *packages* of factors, the specific contents of which may vary from one case to the next (Black, 1992, 1993).

The vocabularies employed in these and other treatments of the subject are unavoidably abstract, but their general thrust is clear enough. Moreover, they overlap, so that it is far from obvious that any useful purpose can be served by muddying the waters with yet more terminological invention. What they all say, almost without exception, is that the behaviour we are interested in (and the behaviour we would like to encourage) is behaviour that (i) strengthens international institutions and processes in a way that promotes the settlement of problems and disputes by orderly political means within rule-governed environments, and (ii) contributes (somewhat more ambitiously) to the removal of the underlying causes of conflict, whatever these causes are assumed to be. In contemporary discussions the list of such 'causes' has lengthened, of course, as the conception of what is meant by 'security' has broadened.

The pursuit of both these purposes requires the deployment of certain tactical repertoires – repertoires that are most commonly associated with a dislike of dogma, a distrust of extremes, a belief in balance, an attachment to compromise, a willingness to give and take and a reluctance to allow the best to become the enemy of the good. These are the attitudinal premises of the inveterate pluralist. They encourage a political praxis that in relation to international affairs is further sustained by the conviction that the alternatives tend either to kill or lead to killing, and that the weak are among those most likely to do the dying.

Such observations bring the focus of the discussion to the second question: what conditions have to pertain (in addition to the possession of middling capabilities) for a state to become wedded to the pursuit of the 'internationalist' objectives thus defined, and to the pragmatically pluralist praxis that it seems to require?

To this inquiry, a taxonomically satisfying response is difficult to devise. The most commonly identified requirements often overlap. Hence, they do not reside in mutually exclusive categories. Nor are they exhaustive. Nor do they represent equal doses of explanatory power. Some are necessary, and some are not. None is sufficient. Among the more obvious of the theoretically enticing 'facilitating attributes', however, are the following points.

First, in principle, and in the vocabulary of the inter-war period, it helps to be a 'status quo', and not a 'revisionist', power. 'Order' is a conservative value, and middle power internationalism is certainly about order. Those who are most likely to cherish it are those who have a vested interest in stability. In relation, therefore, to the existing structure of the state system, the power that aspires to offer benign service needs to be a conservative rather than a radical player, and it has to care more about ensuring that problems are peacefully settled than about the terms upon which the settlements themselves are based.

Second, as a partial corollary of the foregoing, it can be helpful also if the power is free from entanglement in persistent or volatile conflicts within its own region. This is partly a matter of the focus of attention. In the midst of a serious local distraction, any state will have difficulty concentrating on the needs of the broader international environment. It is also, however, a matter of credentials – of the perceptions, that is, of others. From the political, as well as the practical, point of view, states under stress make poor candidates for 'helpful fixer' roles elsewhere in the global system (although there have been occasional exceptions).

Third, it may be reasonable to hypothesise in addition that it helps (although it may not be essential) to have experienced a relatively non-controversial 'foreign policy past'. This, too, is a matter largely of credentials, and what constitutes 'controversy' tends naturally to change with the agenda of international politics itself. When the process of decolonisation was still fresh in the mind, for example, having a history as an imperial power was often a disqualification. For *some* actors, in relation to *some* parts of the world, it still is. There is considerable advantage in being regarded as innocuous. On the other hand, the number of states that in practice are ruled out by this criterion may be decreasing as memories fade and as the pace of change itself accelerates. Political fashions – what is 'in' and what is 'out' – seem now to come and go with dizzying speed, and with them our 'good guy' and 'bad guy' lists.

Fourth, it may sometimes help, as well, not to be seen as the proxy for a greater power. This, too, is about credentials, and reflects among other things the importance of not being regarded as a Trojan Horse. There have been times, of course, when being identified as a great power proxy has actually been a prerequisite for the performance – as in cases where the role has been structured around the troika principle (e.g., in Indo-china). But these were by-products of the politics of Cold War polarisation, and it seems less and less likely in current circumstances that they will recur. The maintenance of a certain distance from the ominous shadows cast by great power – and especially by hegemonic power – ambitions is more commonly preferred.

Fifth, participation may also be encouraged where the player is per capita rich. There are exceptions here, too. India is probably the most prominent example. But if the role is to be habitually pursued, having a high level of per capita income may be as helpful as having a middle-sized aggregate GNP. This is partly because a prosperous populace is less likely to rail against the consignment abroad of resources that might otherwise be expended at home. It is also because such a populace is more likely to be enthusiastic about initiatives that are thought to contribute to the stability of the world at large. A fondness for order is not, after all, uncommon among the possessors of great wealth. This may not, of course, be a salient consideration for helpful fixers who are not inconvenienced by excessively democratic habits at home, and it should probably be noted that at least a few of the world's less-endowed governments appear recently to have been attracted to peacekeeping enterprises by the luminous prospect of hard currency earnings. The mercenary's trade takes more forms than one!

Sixth, finally, it is helpful, perhaps even essential, to bring to the conduct of foreign affairs a conception of politics that is consistent with the tactical repertoires of the pluralist, as already discussed. Although experience of such practices in domestic politics may make it somewhat easier both to warm to the game and to be proficient in pursuing it, this conception need *not* be rooted in a democratic constituency with a liberal pluralist culture. Exposure to the practices and precepts of classical diplomacy can sometimes do the educational job equally well. But whatever the source of the tutelage, it requires at least an understanding that interests and perceptions differ, that most principles are not absolute, and that, in the politics of sovereign states, making deals with the devil may be one of the inescapable requirements of a higher morality. And it is entirely possible that a resigned acceptance of the practical implications of diversity, and a willingness in consequence to work hard at being 'other-conscious', are characteristics that are less common among those who speak for great or imperial powers than among those who represent powers of lesser rank. The latter, after all, cannot avoid taking the former into account, and this experience of subordination is often a spur to empathy. It may be partly for this reason that analysts who have reflected on the politics of international accommodation have thought first of middle powers. In any case, the bottom line is that pragmatism helps. Dogmatism does not.

It will be observed that there is no mention in this list of any unusually virtuous motivation – of the desire, that is, to 'do good' for its own sake. This omission should not be taken to imply that helpful fixers cannot reasonably gain satisfaction from what they do, or that they are unaffected by the politics of compassion among their constituents at home. It means only that the happy conjunction between the national interest on the one hand, and the international service that the performance of the role represents on the other, is due more to fortunate circumstance and geopolitical good luck than to the exercise of a character more noble than others possess. The Phariseean cant that finds it way into the rhetoric of those who take prideful comfort from the contributions of their public servants to the politics of moderation abroad is an apparent hazard of the trade. It is also, however, unattractive and ill-founded, and for that reason is likely to be counterproductive in the end.

Does the foregoing generate a 'middle power' list?

The short answer is, 'Not really'. The problem is that for almost every one of these 'facilitating conditions', there are exceptional cases – examples that defy the expectations or violate the rule. Such exceptions derive from an obvious reality – namely, that different conflicts reflect different political configurations and hence provide opportunities for constructive intervention by different categories of third party. This diversity may have been less evident during the Cold War, when almost every quarrel had a bipolar overlay. The patterns are now more eclectic, and the most dangerous of the disputes arise more frequently within states than between them. In such circumstances, a greater variety of players can often be found to have the political credentials necessary to play the game.

Having said that, it has to be said as well that the reality was untidy even when the Cold War was at its height. As long ago as 1969, the Canadian scholar-diplomat, R. A. MacKay, pointed out in a discussion of precisely this issue that the middle powers had no monopoly in the field of conflict resolution and conflict containment. Using peacekeeping as the classic example of an allegedly middle power role, he observed by way of illustration that of the twenty-nine states that had earlier contributed to the UN operation in the Congo, the majority by far were not middle powers at all, but small powers (MacKay, 1969: 141).

Current realities are even more complex, and may surprise the inattentive. The UN's Office of Peacekeeping Operations, for example, has reported that, as of 1 September 1994, the largest contributor of peacekeeping troops then in the field under UN auspices was Pakistan, just ahead of France, India and the United Kingdom. Canada ranked eighth, *after* Jordan, Bangladesh and Malaysia. Nepal, in eleventh place (following Egypt and Poland), came just before the Netherlands, but was substantially ahead of Norway, Russia, Sweden, Australia and Denmark, and had fielded almost twice as many uniformed personnel as Belgium, which ranked twenty-fifth (Sallot, 1994).

This is a crude measure of constructive performance, and it represents only a snap-shot. If a consistency test were applied as well, with a view to identifying the 'regular' or recurrent performers, the list would become much shorter, and the rankings would be rearranged. And if evidence of repeated cognate behaviours – e.g., conflict resolution *diplomacy* – were also required, it would become shorter still.

Even so, it is increasingly difficult to avoid the conclusion that there is as little satisfaction in moving from the performance of allegedly 'middle power' roles to the identification of middle powers as there is in moving from identified middle powers to allegedly 'middle power' roles. The reality is that middle powers behave in all sorts of different ways, and the roles that have often been associated with them are in fact performed by all sorts of different countries. Facilitating conditions can be identified *a priori*, but there are so many exceptions, and the conditions themselves are surrounded by so many 'ifs', 'ands' and 'buts' that the search for simplifying generalisations is defeated. R. A. MacKay may thus have been right in lending support to Paul Painchaud's argument, some thirty years ago, that the middle power concept was not a 'scientific category' but a foundation for 'an ideology of foreign policy' (Painchaud, 1966: 29–30; MacKay, 1969: 142–3).

Can nothing useful, then, be said, and nothing proposed?

To put such a question is to shift roles, and to move from observer to policymaker. This is an uneasy transition. But the exercise may be worth the risk, if only because the foregoing analysis still leaves behind the nagging sense that a baby has disappeared with the bathwater. The impression that there really are certain powers of secondary rank with similar capabilities and similar minds, and with a similar approach to the maintenance of the international system, seems somehow to survive exposure to the 'real world' observation that things are in fact a jumble. Is there not some sense, for example, in which the Scandinavians, along with the Dutch, Belgians, Irish, Poles, Indians, Canadians and Australians, really have played comparable conflict resolution and containment roles with some regularity? Not all of these, perhaps, are middle powers as measured by conventional indicators, and there is no suggestion that other powers do not also perform from time to time in similar fashion. But for those who can live with tendencies and approximations, and do not require a perfect fit, there may be a *prima facie* commonality about the members of this list – even if the Dutch and the Belgians are inconvenienced in some parts of the world by their imperial past (and the Indians in their own region by a sometimes conflictful present), and even if there are other powers (Mexico and Brazil in Latin America, for example, or Austria in Europe) that alternative observers might think it appropriate to include.

If there is a case to be made for the list as a reasonable, if highly judgemental, first run at the target, it might then be asked, 'Is there something that some, or all, of these powers might now undertake to do in common, and thereby do better?'

In response to this inquiry, one thought comes to mind. It is conceivable that they could act constructively together in preparing for international peacekeeping operations (ranging from peace observation to low-level enforcement), and that they could also consider developing strategies for coordinating their roles in relation to certain peacebuilding initiatives that are aimed at conflict prevention over the longer term. The demand for international services of this kind seems to be escalating rapidly, and the burden has become heavier in response to growing pressures for 'humanitarian intervention'. Even in the short run, more-over, the field operations that now seem to be required have become far more complex than those associated with classical peacekeeping initia-tives (as in Suez in 1956), and are commonly accompanied by signifi-cant investments of non-military personnel (notably development assistance experts, the representatives of NGOs specialising in various forms of humanitarian aid, electoral observers, and – increasingly – police officers). The difficulties, moreover, are gravely compounded where cease-fires have not been fully secured prior to entry, or where the apparatus of state has simply broken down.

Such is the complexity of these new challenges, and so many of them are there, that cries for reform have begun to ring out. Most of them have focused on the United Nations. It is variously argued that the UN's structure should be changed, its Security Council enlarged, its Secre-tariat expanded and transformed, its secretary-general more fully empowered, its Military Staff Committee invigorated, its command and control procedures codified, its financial problems rectified and so on. There are calls as well for the creation of standing armed forces that would be directly under UN control, and for training establishments that would help to professionalise both the performance and the management of UN contingents – however composed – once they are operating in the field.

The problem, of course, is that each of these suggestions challenges a Pandora's Box, the lid of which will spring open at the first sign of serious discussion. There are old hands who think that the challenge of reform is worth a try. But few old hands are confident of the outcome.

In these circumstances, there may well be a case in the medium term for leaving all (or most) of Pandora's boxes firmly shut, and having recourse instead to an indirect line of attack. This *could* entail remedial action by a band of innocuous but reasonably well-equipped powers that would include some or all of those on the foregoing list, together with such others as might be both able and willing to make significant contributions. Their objective would be to coordinate their assets for peacekeeping (and even – in modest measure – for peacebuilding) purposes. They could, for example, engage in joint training activities; develop common understandings with regard to command and control procedures, force structures, and the like; concert their communications practices and technologies; identify specialisations appropriate to their respective capabilities; develop strategies for working effectively with non-military contributors to peacekeeping operations; and work generally to establish a thoroughly professional array of capabilities on a multinational basis. The result would be a small conglomerate of peace-keepers who were cooperatively prepared for international service in much the same way as members of the North Atlantic Alliance were prepared to deal with the possibility of a Soviet attack on Western Europe.

Such an initiative would be clearly consistent with the purposes of the United Nations Charter, and without in any way impinging on the right of individual players to decline in particular cases to serve, it would have the effect of making reliably efficient and effective multinational forces – including both military and non-military components – available to the UN (and possibly to other authorities, as well) as required. In some respects, this would provide a standing 'capacity to work together' not unlike the cooperative operational capacity displayed by the multi-national naval force deployed in the mid-1990s in the Adriatic – a capacity that in that example derives from a long history of practised coordination within NATO.

The advantages of preparing for international 'public service' in this way are several. It obviates the need to tackle the reform of the UN apparatus itself as the prerequisite for progress. The preparations, if necessary, could be initiated more or less independently of the great powers, and even of the UN's internal politics. Since most of the countries involved would have worked closely with one another before (in NATO, in the Commonwealth, in peacekeeping contexts, and so on), and since none has had reason in modern times to quarrel very seriously with any of the others, they would have a head start in dealing with the challenge of working together. In some cases, the initiative would have the effect of providing new benchmarks for making defence policy decisions – benchmarks that are now badly needed as replace-ments for the ones that were regarded as imperatives during the Cold

War. It seems probable, moreover, that it would have a popular reception among the domestic constituents of most, if not all, of the players. Since their interests would not be adversely affected, there is no reason to think that the great powers would take offence, and indeed they would still be expected (even in cases in which they were not themselves peacekeeping 'principals') to provide some of the 'political invisibles' necessary to rapid overseas deployment (transport, supplies, financial assistance, etc.). And, to repeat, it would still remain open to any member of the group to decline a particular invitation to serve. The preparatory work would be aimed at the enhancement of a technical capacity to cooperate in the delivery of an international public service, but not at establishing a firm political commitment. At the same time, there is little doubt that the initiative would generate expectations – both at home and abroad – of a genuine willingness to contribute. Over time, it might also attract other players, thereby giving encouragement to the international 'community building' process.

There is, of course, a 'saints-in-armour' quality to this proposal that non-participating states could find offensive. The participants would be saying, in effect, 'Have guns (together with binoculars, nightsticks, communications equipment, ballot boxes, engineers, police officers, constitutional lawyers, elections experts, etc.), will travel. But only in a just cause.' But most of them are practising as saints-in-armour even now, and the new departure could therefore be explained internationally as no more than the pursuit of an improved level of efficiency. The arrangement would not, in any case, be institutionalised as a 'closed shop'.

It should be recognised that the proposal would not be an entirely new departure. International consultations on peacekeeping have been held by practised peacekeepers before, and an international peace-keeping training centre is being established in Canada. There are other such centres elsewhere. The proposal therefore amounts to a more substantial elaboration of an idea that has already begun to grow.

Whether peacekeeping, as an 'approach to peace', can survive a growing list of unhappy experiences in Somalia, the Balkans, Rwanda and elsewhere, remains, of course, to be seen. Even such powers as are inclined by interest, habit and circumstance alike to volunteer for the task may soon begin to harbour doubts. But doubts have come and gone before, and the fact that peacekeeping initiatives sometimes really do 'help', so that the killing is contained or delayed because of them, makes it highly probable that they will recur. A more systematic attempt to prepare for them in advance might therefore be well-advised.

REFERENCES

Black, David (1992) 'Australian, Canadian, and Swedish Policies Toward Southern Africa: A Comparative Study of "Middle Power Internationalism"' (unpublished Ph.D. dissertation) (Halifax, N.S.: Dalhousie University).

(1993) 'Addressing Apartheid: Lessons from Australian, Canadian, and Swedish Policies in Southern Africa', paper presented at the Conference on Middle Powers in the New World Order (Langdon Hall, Cambridge, Ontario).

Cooper, Andrew F., Richard A. Higgott and Kim Richard Nossal (1993) *Relocating Middle Powers: Australia and Canada in a Changing World Order* (Vancouver: UBC Press).

Eayrs, James (1972) *In Defence of Canada: Peacemaking and Deterrence* (Toronto: University of Toronto Press).

Glazebrook, G. de T. (1947) 'The Middle Powers in the United Nations System', *International Organization*, vol. 1(2), 307–15.

Henrikson, Alan K. (1993) 'Middle Powers As Managers: International Mediation Within, Across, and Outside Institutions', paper presented at the Conference on Middle Powers in the New World Order (Langdon Hall, Cambridge, Ontario).

Holbraad, Carsten (1984) *Middle Powers in International Politics* (New York: St. Martin's Press).

Holmes, John W. (1966) 'Is There a Future for Middlepowermanship?' in J. King Gordon (ed.), *Canada's Role As a Middle Power* (Toronto: Canadian Institute of International Affairs).

(1979) *The Shaping of Peace: Canada and the Search for World Order 1943–1957*, vol. I (Toronto: University of Toronto Press).

Keating, Tom (1993) *Canada and World Order: The Multilateralist Tradition in Canadian Foreign Policy* (Toronto: McClelland and Stewart).

Lyon, Peyton V. and Brian W. Tomlin (1979) *Canada as an International Actor* (Toronto: Macmillan).

MacKay, R. A. (1969) 'The Canadian Doctrine of the Middle Powers', in Harvey L. Dyck and H. Peter Krosby (eds.), *Empire and Nations: Essays in Honour of Federic H. Soward* (Toronto: University of Toronto Press).

Painchaud, Paul (1966) 'Middlepowermanship as an Ideology', in J. King Gordon (ed.), *Canada's Role as a Middle Power* (Toronto: Canadian Institute of International Affairs).

Pratt, Cranford (1990) *Middle Power Internationalism: The North-South Dimension* (Kingston & Montreal: McGill-Queen's University Press).

Pratt, Cranford (ed.) (1989) *The North-South Policies of Canada, the Netherlands, Norway, and Sweden* (Toronto: University of Toronto Press).

Sallot, Jeff (1994) 'Strains on Resources and Political Will Ignite Talk of a United Nations Military Brigade', *Globe and Mail* (Toronto), 8 Oct.

Wood, Bernard (1988) *The Middle Powers and the General Interest* (Ottawa: North-South Institute).

Part 3

Beyond: resistances and reinventions

14 International peace and security in the twenty-first century

Barry M. Blechman

Three opportunities have been presented in the twentieth century to create an effective global system of collective security. The first two followed wars of great bloodshed and human suffering, yet the world's political leaders proved incapable, or unwilling, to take advantage of the revulsion with war to create effective means of containing international conflict. With the end of the Cold War, the paralysis that has crippled the United Nations' collective security system for nearly fifty years has been lifted and a third opportunity presented. So far, however, the world's political leaders again seem unable to transcend the limits of national politics and transform reigning concepts of international security into a paradigm that can keep the peace in the coming century.

Still, there is some reason for optimism about the future. The basic trends in human interactions, both within and across states, point increasingly to fundamental changes in the structure of the world community. Technological trends are particularly important; they not only drive basic economic and political developments, but are creating a truly global community in which shared values can form a lasting basis for a more peaceful world. These changes, eventually, will make possible the creation of more powerful international institutions charged with maintaining world peace and security.

In this chapter, I first describe the trends that are fundamentally transforming the international system. While the overall direction signalled by these changes is positive, this optimistic outlook does not deny the persistence of serious problems in some parts of the world and the inevitable risk of the emergence of national leaders willing to pursue aggressive goals through the use of military force. Consequently, in the final part of the chapter, I describe the changes that are necessary in the United Nations to encourage the creation of an effective global system of collective security.

The international environment

The basic fabric of relations among peoples and institutions, particularly in the industrialised countries, but extending increasingly to many other parts of the globe, clearly points towards more peaceful relations among states.

Economic interdependence. Over the past fifty years, the shift towards greater economic interdependence has given more and more people, in more and more parts of the world, vital stakes in the maintenance of peaceful and cooperative relations with other countries. Today, interdependence means far more than high volumes of trade. The rise of multinational corporations in the 1960s and 1970s was matched in the 1980s by burgeoning investments by national corporations and individuals in foreign countries. The continuing infusion of foreign capital benefits the receiving economies enormously and, politically, the interlinking of national assets and economies in this manner gives citizens of all participating countries greater stakes in one another's well-being.

Interdependence cuts two ways, of course. The greater the number of nations that are integrated into the world economy, the greater the leverage to influence events provided to such economic powers as the United States. By the same token, interdependence means that even the great economic powers are more vulnerable to events over which they have only limited control. Economic distress and political instability in any part of the world's advanced regions resonate in all other countries.

After fifty years of interdependence, people throughout the industrialised world recognise well their stake in stability abroad and the need to support activist policies to help ensure international cooperation and political relations that foster economic growth. People working for giant multinationals have long favoured such policies, of course. But, these days, apprehension for the importance of events abroad for the economic health of one's own country extends to even very small businesses and their employees, many of which are dependent increasingly on foreign markets, or foreign components and materials, or foreign investors – or all three.

Technology diffusion. Technology diffusion is obviously more rapid among the industrial nations, but the lag in the spread of new products and ideas to the more advanced developing countries is diminishing at a breathtaking pace. The spread of advanced technologies is contributing to more rapid economic development in many parts of the world, alleviating sources of international conflict and giving nations incentives to behave cooperatively in order to maintain their access to products, information and technical expertise. The leverage exerted by Western nations over the new countries that emerged from the ashes of the USSR, for example, has as much to do with the latter's hunger for technological know-how and products as with any expectations of the financial support they might be granted. Indeed, the desire of the peoples of Eastern Europe and the former Soviet Union to gain access to the fruits of technology in terms of the quality of their everyday lives seems to have sparked popular discontent with the communist system more than anything else.

The impulse towards the materialistic benefits of technology, and its apparently necessary grounding in Western-style economic, social and educational systems also gives enormous influence to the advanced industrialised countries in the developing world. The global popularity of Western systems of government is based on many disparate elements, but the quality of life made possible by advanced technology is certainly a central element in that appeal.

A global audience. The technological revolution's most visible contribution to the condition of international relations, however, is the greater knowledge and familiarity of peoples with foreign places. Far more people throughout the world have visited foreign countries, or at least have some knowledge of them from television and movies. More broadly, modern technology has turned humanity into a global audience for world events. Knowledge of dramatic occurrences, wherever they happen, and, to an increasing extent, actual images of the events, race around the world, forcing the pace of decision and action in all continents, compressing political processes, stimulating popular movements, necessitating that political leaders act in short order. We all participate in dramatic world events now, and not only in the industrialised nations, but in developing regions as well. When the Czech and Slovak peoples' mass protests brought down the communist government in Prague, the world was their witness, and the revolution spread. Similarly, world condemnation of Saddam Hussein's invasion of Kuwait was so swift, and so widespread, in part, because of the power of the video images resulting from that brutal incursion.

The communications revolution also means that it is virtually impossible for national rulers to deny knowledge of the outside world to their citizens, or to pretend that backward economic or political conditions in their own countries, when they exist, compare well with the situations in other nations. Efforts to seal national borders and create hermetic kingdoms, as mounted by the Burmese and North Koreans, in recent years, and by dozens of dictators before them, are virtually doomed to failure. World protests and condemnations, and the adverse impact of isolation economies, are known to the peoples who suffer under them, making it more difficult, although certainly not impossible, for rulers who flaunt international norms to retain control.

Over the long run, as modern technology diffuses to additional parts of the world, it promises to link more and more people within those countries, into a global network of shared knowledge and mutual interdependence. It promises incentives for peaceful and cooperative behaviour, providing stakes in stability and peaceful intercourse to wider and wider audiences. In the process it leads to the creation of trans-national entities – economically based, professionally based, culturally based, interest-based – which create even closer ties among peoples and institutions in different countries. Eventually, such transnational associations could increasingly overwhelm the ancient sources of conflicts among nations. It is happening already in large parts of the world: North America, Western Europe, East Asia, and in selected countries verging on economic takeoff in other regions. It is, indeed, the foundation for a true and durable international peace.

Value sharing. This closer and more frequent interaction of peoples, their linkage into mutually interdependent networks that cross national boundaries, is bringing a greater sharing of values on a global basis, comparable to that already characterising relations among industrialised nations. It is always dangerous to suggest that the world may be moving towards a shared set of beliefs and values, even of the most general sort, as these trends are far more apparent among some cultures than others, and among urbanised and educated peoples within those cultures than among their less fortunate brethren. Still, there does seem to be some convergence in popular attitudes taking place which is reflected increasingly in the behaviour of national governments.

First, there is a growing common expectation of material rewards – a sense of the correctness that national societies, whether in Bangkok, Cairo, Kiev, Lagos or Lima, should advance materially to a stage in which large portions of the population share in the material comforts of modern life. These expectations may be unrealistic in many places, at least for generations, but that fact makes their impact on world politics no less significant. Moreover, there seems to be spreading recognition that the best way for societies to advance materially is through market economies, modified frequently in one way or another, but clearly more capitalistic than socialistic.

Second, democratic values seem to be gaining widespread adherence – at least the most basic values, such as respect for individual liberties and the benefits of representative government. The strength of the democratic ideal has been particularly apparent in the past few years, as authoritarian governments have fallen in country after country – particularly in Latin America and Eastern Europe. Even the rulers of most remaining repressive regimes feel compelled to kowtow to the democratic ideal now, even as they continue to intimidate their opposition.

Third, and related to the spread of democratic values, there seems to be lessening legitimacy granted to gains achieved through violence or military coercion. The near global unanimity that backed reactivation of the United Nations collective security system to liberate Kuwait may be the most dramatic example of this rejection of military conquest, but it is far from the only one. One clearly cannot carry this impression too far in the face of the continuing survival of such brutalities as the warlords in 'Greater Serbia', but at least these ill-gotten gains seem to be rejected verbally by most of the rest of the world, and nations seem increasingly willing to take actions to record their disapproval. The world may not yet be prepared to act decisively to back up its rejection of gains through violence or coercion, but at least it is not prepared either to sanction the dictum that 'might makes right'.

Related to this rejection of gains through the use of violence is a fourth belief that might now be emerging in many parts of the world: the idea that weapons of mass destruction should never be used and that, if they are not eventually abolished altogether, they should at least be reduced to extremely small numbers. It is far too soon after the end of the Cold War to know how seriously to take the possibility that such a consensus might crystallise, but a number of developments in recent years are encouraging.

Certainly, the alacrity with which President George Bush and President Mikhail Gorbachev retired tens of thousands of tactical nuclear weapons through a series of reciprocated unilateral statements in the fall of 1991 (even before it was clear that the USSR would be dismantled) indicates that the once accepted utility of such devices in warfare is no longer considered seriously. The signing of the Strategic Arms Reduction Treaty by the US and Russia in January 1993, which will eventually reduce US and Soviet nuclear arsenals by roughly 75 per cent from current levels, and the virtual cessation of nuclear production in both countries, is further evidence that neither state sees much of a future in nuclear armaments. The January 1993 signing of the treaty to outlaw chemical weapons by more than 130 nations is another sign of the widespread abhorrence of weapons of mass destruction.

Perhaps more convincing of changing attitudes towards weapons of mass destruction, though, is the higher priority now placed on efforts to contain, and even reverse, proliferation. In developing relations with the new nations that emerged from the Soviet Union, for example, the United States has been making clear that, with the exception of Russia, the relinquishment of all nuclear weapons and related production capabilities on their territories is an essential prerequisite for close ties. Ensuring that only one nuclear power emerges from the USSR is clearly one of the two or three highest priorities of US policy.

More dramatic examples of the new attitude can be seen in the cases of Iraq and North Korea. While the former's situation in the wake of its defeat in the Gulf War is obviously unique, so, too, is the willingness of the world community, including even countries previously vehement about the prerogatives of national sovereignty, to insist that Baghdad yield all mass destruction weapons capabilities and submit to the most intrusive inspection and monitoring procedures to ensure its adherence.

The attitudes expressed and possible actions discussed with respect to the possibility of a North Korean nuclear weapons capability are even more notable, given that Pyongyang had not carried out any transgression of international law, at least not in recent years, and was not the subject of international sanctions. Indeed, the possibility of military action to pre-emptively destroy North Korea's apparent weapons facilities was discussed seriously. And the world's response to the discussion was a far cry from the outrage that greeted Israel's pre-emptive strike on Iraq's nuclear reactor only eleven years earlier.

The infringements on once hallowed principles of national sovereignty implied by the new attitude towards weapons of mass destruction are part of a further relevant change in international values, a more general willingness to challenge the supremacy of national authority within a state's borders. While such challenges are more widely discussed than implemented, and more often by commentators and private citizens than by officials, governments have become more willing to step into civil conflicts, sometimes directly, sometimes through regional organisations or the United Nations. Governments also are evincing tougher attitudes towards governments that are gross violators of basic human rights, as demonstrated by virtually all the world's governments with respect to Haiti. Overall, the number of UN peacekeeping, peace enforcement and good offices missions pertaining to domestic situations has risen from only one or two a year in the 1980s to an average of between ten and twelve a year during the 1990s. Governments have not yet become willing to throw out all tyrants, to be sure, but the unwillingness to accept the legitimacy of repressive governments' rule is certainly a change.

Many other global values that seem to be emerging could be cited, but the point is neither to articulate what those values might be nor to speculate about the pace at which they might be spreading or the extent to which they may be doing so. The important point is much simpler: to the degree that a common ideology might be spreading around the world – consisting of capitalism, democracy, anti-militarism and whatever else – it will help to build, more fundamentally than anything else will, a more cooperative international system. The Cold War was more than a clash of great national powers: it was a clash of ideas. To the degree that the peoples of the world share common values and beliefs, it will make possible a degree of international cooperation in security matters, as in all others, that heretofore was impossible to consider.

The need for collective security

These four unifying trends – economic interdependence, technology diffusion, the global audience and emerging shared values – are leading to a structure of international politics far different from that which characterised the twentieth century.

Of particular importance is the accelerating tendency for countries to work together on international problems, and to build institutional structures and procedures that are making such cooperative behaviour routine. Increasingly, countries seem to prefer to act in concert with nations in their immediate vicinity. This is certainly true with respect to economic and technical matters, where the simple reality is often that problems cannot be solved without the cooperation of countries located near one another.

The interesting element is the degree to which such economic and technical cooperation might lead to consultations, coordination and even common policies in foreign policy and, eventually, security matters. This has already happened among the nations of the European Community, the membership of which will grow sharply during the next ten years. Although the populations of these countries clearly have no wish to relinquish their national sovereignties or cultures, the habit of coordination in foreign policy is by now deeply ingrained and routine.

The die is not nearly so well cast in any other region (excepting North America), but East Asia, at least, has potential to follow suit. Already, the Association of South-east Asian Nations has extended its once strictly economic/technical agenda to foreign policy and security matters. The question is whether the great powers in the region, particularly Japan and China, might eventually join a consultative process that could lead to the kind of close cooperation in East Asia that now characterises European countries.

Other regions remain even farther from collective action on security matters. In these regions, grave problems persist, many of which are leading to civil, and sometimes international, conflicts and to personal deprivation of horrendous proportions.

While much of the world has slowed the growth of its population, high rates of growth continue in Africa, the Middle East and South Asia. Too quickly rising populations aggravate existing problems of economic underdevelopment and place insupportable demands on rudimentary national infrastructures. The unavailability of even basic human services in many nations, the primitive conditions of life, the prevalence of disease and limited life expectancies, and the lack of opportunity for education and economic advancement have created masses of rootless, unemployed and alienated youths – their futures bleak, their expectations marginalised, their susceptibility to blandishments of blame and messianic movements that preach hate and violence, high.

Obviously, the regions suffering from such problems are unlikely candidates for the positive trends noted in the previous section. Such poverty-stricken nations as Bangladesh, Egypt, Haiti and Zaire may be dependent economically on the industrialised world, but they are not interdependent in the positive sense of the transnational networks that link not only the industrialised democracies, but increasing numbers of such developing countries as Israel, Mexico, Singapore and South Korea. Stymied human development and economic stagnation are far more likely to inculcate resentment and alienation than the positive values contributing to a more peaceful world. Underdevelopment makes it difficult for countries to participate fully in the trends towards regional and global cooperation, and certainly impossible for them to receive the benefits of transnational networks based on economic or professional associations.

Nationalism and ethnicity are additional factors tending to fractionate the international community and are perhaps the most visible sources of violence in the contemporary world. The removal of the Red Army and Soviet repression not only from the territories that the USSR occupied during the Second World War, but from lands whose occupation dated back to the 1920s, unleashed a flood of national feelings and aspirations that shocked the world. Although this reborn nationalism has been satisfied in most places with few problems, in others, the fact that patterns of ethnic self-identification do not necessarily coincide with state borders has led to a widening set of stubborn conflicts.

Serious ethnic conflicts exist in other parts of the world, as well. Africa, where for two decades national leaders strove mightily to protect colonial boundaries, no matter how artificially they might have been drawn, precisely in order to avoid a quagmire of ethnic rectification, seems on the verge of a massive escalation of an already high level of violence. The problems elsewhere do not appear nearly so severe, but some major countries, including China, India and Indonesia, are multiethnic states that have experienced serious struggles for autonomy by one group or another, some of which conceivably could be reborn.

Over the long term, if state boundaries can be sorted out in ways acceptable to all relevant parties, and governmental functions decentralised to autonomous local entities, ethnic aspirations can be met without jeopardising peaceful inter-state relations. After all, virtually all states contain diverse groups. The hard technical and economic realities that are causing countries to cooperate increasingly on a regional basis will operate to diminish the tangible consequences of ethnic autonomy, in any event.

There is another aspect of nationalism, however, that will always have the potential to jeopardise continued movement towards more peaceful inter-state relations. This is the temptation for some political leaders to seek fulfilment of nationalistic ideals by playing hegemonic roles in the affairs of their region – or even to seek to conquer neighbouring countries that once constituted parts of ancient empires. Both world wars, of course, can be understood as resulting from attempts by countries to win regional dominance, and the world could certainly again witness such expansionist national policies. Indeed, both the 1980–8 Iran–Iraq War and the 1991 Gulf War resulted from Saddam Hussein's quest for Iraqi dominance in the Gulf. Comparable situations could conceivably arise in other parts of the globe.

In each past case, such potential or actual threats to world peace have required the organisation of effective military opposition. Early recognition of potential aggressors, and a willingness of potential countervailing powers to make clear their resolve to defeat any aggression, prior to its realisation, is of course preferable. It was the recognition by US leaders in the late 1940s of the threat posed to Western Europe by the Soviet Union and the organisation of effective resistance through the North Atlantic Treaty Organization that made possible the defeat of the USSR's regional ambitions without serious violence in Europe. The failure of Western nations to recognise the comparable threat posed by Germany in the early 1930s, on the other hand, meant that Hitler's ambitions could only be stopped through eventual warfare.

The willingness and means to confront emerging regional hegemons will continue to be important in the future. The question is how, in the emerging international environment, such effective deterrence, or, if necessary, defence against aggression, should be organised. In this writer's view, it would be most effective in the future to confront potential aggressors with a determined, well-organised and materially prepared collective security system implemented through the United Nations.

Strengthening the UN collective security system

Most of the leaders of the international community appear to be ambivalent about the United Nations. On the one hand, they argue that the organisation should become more effective in dealing with international security problems, thus relieving states of that task. On the other hand, to the degree that making the United Nations more effective requires yielding power to the organisation, or providing greater resources to it, the goal runs headlong into entrenched beliefs about national sovereignty and the independence of national governments.

Thus, the leaders of the major powers are reluctant to allow the emergence of an independent UN military capability, even if this would enable the organisation to act more effectively in dealing with conflict situations. The leaders of less powerful states are similarly reluctant to support UN intervention against tyrannical regimes in the fear that this would lead to a propensity for the United Nations to intervene in domestic affairs. Even small steps towards empowering the collective security system to act more effectively are resisted by many member states because they fear it could establish a precedent that would further reduce national sovereignty and eventually lead to the creation of a truly supranational organisation.

Nowhere is the ambivalence about the United Nations stronger than in the United States, where a traditional antipathy towards 'entangling alliances' and a fierce sense of national independence both militate against any significant surrender of state prerogatives to international authority. The disappointing record of the United Nations during the Cold War places a special burden on efforts to muster support in the United States for giving more power to the organisation. Moreover, with the disintegration of the Soviet Union having made the United States the world's dominant military power, it takes a certain farsightedness to understand the benefits to US national security of an effective UN collective security system.

When should the UN act? The ambivalence of world leaders about giving the United Nations more power is the most important constraint on the effectiveness of the international security system. A crucial consequence of this ambivalence is a lack of consensus concerning the types of situations in which it is legitimate for the organisation to intervene. Parameters that previously defined limits on UN operations have been pierced in recent years, but no new consensus has yet to emerge concerning the boundaries that should take their place. As a result, great pressures are generated for the United Nations to intervene in virtually all conflicts, and the organisation is being pushed into situations that it would be much wiser to avoid.

For one, as was mentioned, the UN is being asked increasingly to intervene in conflicts that are essentially domestic affairs. The 1994 ouster of the military government in Haiti is perhaps the clearest example of this change. For a second, UN peacekeeping is no longer confined to cooperative situations in which previously warring parties had already decided that they wished to conclude a peace. In recent years, UN peacekeepers have faced hostile adversaries in Bosnia, Cambodia, Croatia and Somalia, to name just a few instances. Indeed, it is uncertain how much longer, and to what degree, the international community and, most importantly, the countries which provide the United Nations with military forces, will be willing to place peace-keepers in harm's way. This blurring of the once-clear line between peacekeeping missions and peace-enforcement operations has significant implications for the kinds of structures and procedures that are required to strengthen the collective security apparatus of the United Nations.

Defining the limits to be placed on the UN security role is a difficult challenge, but it is also an important step towards a more effective international collective security system. If the organisation's role is defined too broadly, in particular, if there is too great a tendency for member states to request UN interventions in domestic conflicts, the organisation may be doomed to failure. The international community is clearly not ready to invest supranational authority in the United Nations. Instances in which the United Nations is asked to intervene against established authority within a single country should clearly be limited to the few, truly egregious cases that involve massive violations of human rights.

Composition of the Security Council. The anachronistic composition of the Security Council is a second fundamental constraint on the effectiveness of the UN collective security system. While the founders' wisdom in establishing a separate body to deal with security questions, and in assigning a special role within that body to the great powers, is even more evident in the 1990s than it was in the 1940s, it is also clear that the states having permanent membership on the Security Council no longer reflect the real distribution of power in the world. The organisational principle behind membership on the Security Council remains sound; the implementation of that principle must be updated to bring the United Nations into the twenty-first century. Any number of proposals have been tabled towards this end. The expedient course is to simply add the obvious claimants, such as Germany, India, Japan and perhaps a few others.

A more far-sighted course would be to shift to a system of regional representation reflecting the increasing tendency of nations to cooperate regionally on foreign policy matters. The world is clearly not yet ready for such a change, but eventually one could foresee a Security Council whose permanent membership included representatives of North and South America, Western and Eastern Europe, West, South and East Asia, and Africa.

Organisational reforms. The management practices and organisational 'culture' of the Secretariat and other UN agencies are a third fundamental constraint on the organisation's effectiveness in security roles. Despite years of pressure, most observers agree that the United Nations continues to be poorly managed, preoccupied with appearance at the expense of accomplishment, and stultified by its own permanent bureaucracy.

There are, of course, thousands of UN employees who work hard, perform brilliantly and conduct themselves with integrity and professionalism in service to the organisation and to the world. Instances of UN employees' dedication far exceeding normal standards, to say nothing of tremendous personal courage, have become commonplace in recent years as the organisation struggles to maintain peace and provide for basic human needs in dozens of difficult situations. Yet, anecdotes describing the inefficiency of the UN bureaucracy are also legion. It is precisely because the UN was considered only a forum for propaganda and political conflict during the Cold War that many of its agencies were permitted to develop inefficient and wasteful procedures, and that some of its employees were able to conduct themselves in an unprofessional, and sometimes even corrupt, manner.

The management problems of the United Nations cause many countries to be wary of investing greater authority and resources in the organisation. Even when national governments are willing to make larger investments in the United Nations, the perception of the organisation as being inefficient, wasteful and sometimes corrupt makes it difficult to persuade legislatures to appropriate the necessary funds. This is a particular problem in democracies that must justify their UN contributions to domestic constituencies. If an effective international security system is going to be created, the UN 'culture' will have to change fundamentally. Many proposals for UN reform have been on the table for years. Among the more important changes would be the following:

First: Appointment of a deputy secretary general to manage the institution and to coordinate the work of its many autonomous agencies. Any organisation the size of the UN requires a full-time manager at the most senior level. As the secretary general himself is far too busy with the organisation's substantive work to give management the time and attention it requires, the appointment of a deputy is an essential step towards a more effective UN collective security system.

Second: Substantial reductions in the number of under and assistant secretary generals and a clear assignment of responsibilities to each of those remaining. The UN currently has more than forty officials at these levels, far too many to be directed by the secretary general, or his new deputy, and the source of much wasted effort and needless bureaucratic procedures and incumbents. A streamlining of the UN Secretariat beginning at this level could be an important source of greater efficiency.

Third: Professionalisation of the UN personnel system. The ideal of a professional international civil service has been eroded over the years as nations have insisted on being able to appoint their nationals to key positions. Criteria for promotions are far from clear, and many have described the UN system as 'cronyism', with accomplishment of the organisation's missions only rarely rewarded, but the right connections and old school ties the key to success. Professionalising the UN personnel system is a crucial step in rebuilding confidence in the organisation.

Financial reforms. Financial problems constitute a fourth fundamental constraint on the UN's effectiveness in security roles. The amount of financial support available to the United Nations for peacekeeping and other military activities is in orders of magnitude smaller than what is deemed necessary for most countries' national defence. As a result, UN peacekeeping operations must routinely get by on limited resources, carrying out their missions with far fewer troops than planners would have preferred, and often sending those forces into the field without the proper equipment, support, or specialised training.

Financial constraints on UN military activities go well beyond the amount of money available – to pay for peacekeeping operations. The procedures that the United Nations currently employs to raise the necessary monies and reimburse the states that contribute to peace-keeping operations evolved during the Cold War period when UN peacekeeping was an *ad hoc* response to the few situations in which the organisation could make a contribution to international peace. Now that UN peacekeepers are being deployed more frequently and are being given broader and more difficult roles, the procedures used to finance UN military operations are proving increasingly insufficient and are constraining the organisation's ability to complete its new missions.

The vast majority of UN peacekeeping missions are budgeted and paid for individually. Every time the Security Council decides that the organisation should undertake a new peacekeeping operation, the member states of the UN must first draw up and authorise its budget. This is accomplished through a complicated and protracted procedure involving mission planners in the Secretariat, representatives of the permanent members of the Security Council (which must approve the mission's mandate), representatives of such other key states as the members of the General Assembly's Advisory Committee on Administrative and Budgetary Questions (which must approve the budget) and those countries directly affected by the operation. As a result, there are frequent delays in getting UN peacekeeping troops deployed, and the forces sent to deal with conflicts are typically much smaller than planners would have preferred. Because missions are budgeted for individually, moreover, funds have not been made available for the various support activities that are necessary for the success of any military operation, such as developing training standards, acquiring common equipment and maintaining a comment centre and planning staff.

The overall financial problems of the United Nations naturally aggravate the problems associated with financing peacekeeping operations. If the secretary general's Working Capital Fund had not already been depleted, for example, resources could be made available from it for special peacekeeper training courses, for acquiring stocks of equipment or for finding ways to reduce the delays in starting operations.

Some relief is in sight; assuming new problems do not emerge, the United Nations's financial problems will ease as the United States continues to pay up its arrears. Additional general financial reforms of the UN system, such as finding a solution to the problem of time-lags between the start of the UN fiscal year and the dates when states actually provide their annual payments, would further ease the situation. Even so, UN military operations would be substantially strengthened by reforms targeted specifically at the methods used to finance peacekeeping.

The most far-reaching solution to the financial problems of the collective security system would be to incorporate all peacekeeping expenses into the regular UN budget. Estimating the financial needs of peacekeeping activities, which are essentially contingency operations, is difficult, but not impossible. In any event, any inaccurate estimates incorporated in a budget can be corrected. Surplus funds resulting from an unusually peaceful year could always be used for related activities (reprogrammed) or returned to members in the form of lower assessments in future years. And there is always the option of asking member states for supplemental appropriations for unforeseen contingencies – essentially the same procedure that is now used for all UN peacekeeping operations.

Integrating the costs of UN military operations into the organisation's regular budget would have the advantage of making it clear that peacekeeping is an essential activity of the United Nations, rather than an *ad hoc* response to unusual circumstances. Such a change would greatly facilitate the establishment of a permanent and widely accepted international security system with some power, both symbolically and in terms of the decision procedures that member states would be forced to adopt. Most importantly, because the financing of each peacekeeping operation is an opportunity for criticism and posturing by national leaders and legislative bodies, the integration of UN military costs with the organisation's regular budget would significantly reduce the problems that are currently encountered when financing for each mission individually must be requested from member states.

Military reforms. Finally, the UN's contribution to international security is hampered by constraints on the conduct of UN military operations. For example, the United Nations has used several methods to secure the military forces that it needs to carry out both peacekeeping and peace-enforcement operations. For the largest and most difficult missions, the organisation typically authorises a member state to either carry out the operation, in effect serving as a kind of sub-contractor to the United Nations, or it asks that state to lead a coalition of members. Under this type of authorisation, the US organised and led the UN enforcement actions in Korea in 1950 and Kuwait in 1990, as well as the second (December 1992) intervention in Somalia. In another example of this approach, the Royal Navy was authorised to enforce the oil sanctions that the United Nations imposed on Rhodesia in 1966–79. In Bosnia, the United Nations has again turned to this approach by using NATO forces to enforce sanctions and other coercive measures. In all these cases, the lead military power operates under the general authority of the United Nations, and in official compliance with guidelines laid down by the Security Council. Nevertheless, the actual authority of the United Nations over tactical decisionmaking is minimal.

In most peacekeeping operations, on the other hand, the Secretariat has assembled an *ad hoc* collection of national military units and individual civilian specialists. Typically, several members contribute infantry battalions, others provide communications units and the necessary transportation, and additional members contribute the various types of civilian personnel (election monitors, police, etc.) that may be required. These assemblages of forces are usually put together quite hastily and, as a result, they leave a lot to be desired in terms of their ability to operate together. In most cases, few of the soldiers have received specialised training for peacekeeping operations or have had any experience in that kind of mission. The officers commanding the operation typically have not had previous opportunities to work together and, in addition, are frequently not familiar with standard UN procedures. Each unit usually brings its own equipment, moreover, making it much more difficult for the national contingents to operate together effectively. With the demand for peacekeeping units rising quickly, these problems are being aggravated as the pool of trained and experienced national contingents is being diluted further by inexperienced units.

The command and control of UN peacekeeping operations represents a special operational problem, and not only because of incompatibilities in communications gear from different nations. The national contingents assigned to a UN operation come under the command of a UN appointed officer, but few countries are currently willing to yield real authority over their soldiers to the United Nations. Indeed, there is often better communication between national contingents and their home capitals than between the UN mission commander and his ostensibly subordinate units. The commanders of national units often consult with their national authorities before carrying out orders from the UN mission commander which they find to be questionable.

Faced with these types of problems, some observers have suggested that the United Nations should organise a quick reaction military force. Sir Brian Urquhart, for example, the former UN under secretary general for Special Political Affairs, called in 1993 for the creation of a standing UN military force composed of individual volunteers, rather than national contingents. The previous year, French President François Mitterrand had proposed that a stand-by 1,000 man force composed of national contingents, which could be available within 48 hours of an alert, be created for the United Nations by member states. Secretary General Boutros Boutros-Ghali seemed to support this proposal in his 1992 report on peacekeeping.

Recommendations like these make many governments uneasy. They fear that the creation of standing or ready capability would give too much power to either the secretary general or the Security Council, or both, and lead to too great a propensity for the UN to intervene in conflicts. The firm rejection of these ideas and others like them by the United States suggests that neither a standing nor a stand-by force are likely to be created in the near future. The ideas deserve careful analysis, however, with an eye towards having viable concepts well understood when such far-reaching departures become more feasible.

In the meantime, each member state should 'earmark' forces that it would be willing to make available to the United Nations for peacekeeping duty under the right circumstances. Each country would then provide those earmarked units with the special training and equipment necessary for them to operate in conjunction with the forces of other UN member states on peacekeeping missions. The earmarked forces would not need to be set aside solely for peacekeeping; member states could also plan to use those forces for national military assignments. Earmarked forces would have to be assigned peacekeeping as a secondary mission, however, so that the special requirements of those UN operations could be incorporated into their training, equipment and composition.

Earmarked forces would not serve at the beck and call of either the Security Council or the secretary general. And creating such a force would not constitute a step towards an independent UN military capability. Earmarking units for possible service in peacekeeping would not mean that they were automatically committed to any specific peacekeeping operation. Member states would reserve the right to review each peacekeeping operation authorised by the Security Council and to decide whether or not to permit their own earmarked forces to participate in that particular mission.

Earmarked forces would create a core force of national military contingents that would be specially configured, trained and equipped for UN peacekeeping duties. UN staff would work with national defence officials to ensure that a balanced mix of different types of forces were earmarked for possible UN duty. UN staff could also work with national military establishments to set training and equipment standards for earmarked forces, to organise staff exercises and planning sessions, and generally to encourage the professionalisation and standardisation of the inventory of forces from which peacekeepers would be drawn in the future.

For this 'earmarked forces approach' to work, it would be necessary to create a far more serious military planning and command capability within the United Nations. This objective could be accomplished in part by breathing life into the Military Staff Committee (MSC), the organisation established by the UN Charter to 'advise and assist the Security Council on all questions relating to military requirements for the maintenance of international peace and security, the employment and command of forces placed at its disposal, the regulation of armaments, and possible disarmament'. According to the Charter, the MSC is to consist of the chiefs of staff of the permanent members of the Security Council, or their representatives.

As professional military advisers to the Security Council, a functioning MSC could provide the expertise and influence required to ensure that the Security Council's decisions on peacekeeping operations were informed authoritatively as to the military requirements of the situation, that member states fully understood the required size and cost of military forces, as well as the types of military activities and rules of engagement that would be necessary to fulfil the mission's political objectives. Such prior clarification of the mandates for peacekeeping operations, including a tough-minded assessment of necessary rules of engagement, could help to avoid UN involvement in situations like Bosnia in 1992/3, when the world community was not prepared to carry out the military actions required to fulfil its ostensible political objectives and for which, therefore, the UN mission was doomed to failure.

In the end, establishment of an effective international collective security system will depend importantly on such a professionalisation of the means available to the world organisation to maintain international peace and security. Even more importantly, placing peacekeeping, like peace-enforcement, clearly under the control of a Security Council whose permanent membership had been altered to more accurately reflect contemporary world power, would eventually give the leading military powers more confidence in the UN system and provide a necessary basis for an effective system of international security.

REFERENCES

There is a rich literature on the issues discussed in this chapter. For further reading on the main issues, see the following:

1. The international environment.
Brown, Seyom (1992) *International Relations in a Changing Global System: Toward a Theory of the World Polity* (Boulder, CO: Westview).
Doyle, Michael (1983) 'Kant, Liberal Legacies and Foreign Affairs', parts 1 and 2, *Philosophy and Public Affairs*, vol. 12 (Summer and Fall), 205–35 and 323–53.
    (1986) 'Liberalism and World Politics', *American Political Science Review*, vol. 80(4), 1151–69.
Goldgeier, James and Michael McFaul (1992) 'A Tale of Two Worlds: Core and Periphery in the Post-Cold War Era', *International Organisation*, vol. 46(2), 467–92.
Jervis, Robert (1991/2) 'The Future of World Politics', *International Security*, vol. 16(3), 39–73.
Keohane, Robert and Joseph S. Nye Jr (1989) *Power and Interdependence: World Politics in Transition*, 2nd edn (Boston: Little Brown).
Milner, Helen (1991) 'The Assumption of Anarchy in International Relations Theory: A Critique', *Review of International Studies*, vol. 17, 67–85.

Mueller, John (1989) *Retreat from Doomsday: The Obsolescence of Major War* (New York: Basic Books).

Rosecrance, Richard (1989) *The Rise of the Trading State: Commerce and Conquest in the Modern World* (New York: Basic Books).

Skolnikoff, Eugene B. (1993) *The Elusive Transformation: Science, Technology, and the Evolution of International Politics* (Princeton: Princeton University Press).

2. UN reform

Berdal, Mats (1993) 'Whither UN Peacekeeping?', *Adelphi Paper 281* (London: Brassey's).

Boutros-Ghali, Boutros (1992/3) 'Empowering the United Nations', *Foreign Affairs*, vol. 70(5), 89–102.

Kassebaum, Nancy L. and Rep. Lee H. Hamilton (1994) *Peacekeeping and the US National Interest* (Washington, DC: The Henry L. Stimson Center).

Ogata, Shijuro and Paul Volcker (co-chairmen) (1993) *Financing an Effective United Nations. A Report of the Independent Advisory Group on UN Financing* (New York: Ford Foundation).

Puchala, Donald J. (1994) 'Outsiders, Insiders, and UN Reform', *Washington Quarterly*, vol. 17(4), 161–74.

Renner, Michael (1993) 'Critical Juncture: The Future of Peacekeeping', *Worldwatch Paper*, no. 114 (Washington, DC: Worldwatch Institute).

Rikhar, Indar Jit., Major General (1992) *Strengthening UN Peacekeeping: New Challenges and Proposals* (Washington, DC: United States Institute of Peace).

United Nations Association of the USA (1992) *A UN Revitalized, A Compilation of UNA–USA Recommendations on Strengthening the Role of the United Nations in Peacemaking, Peacekeeping, and Conflict Prevention* (New York).

Urquhart, Brian and Erskine Childers (1992) *Towards a More Effective United Nations* (Sweden: Dag Hammarskjold Foundation).

15 Affluence, poverty and the idea of a post-scarcity society

Anthony Giddens

My starting point in this discussion is a world that has taken us by surprise. By 'us' I mean not only observing intellectuals and practical policymakers, but the ordinary individual too. In the West at least we are all the legatees of certain strands of Enlightenment thought. The Enlightenment was a complex affair. Various different perspectives of thought were bound up with it and the works of the leading Enlightenment philosophers were often complex and subtle. Yet in general the philosophers of Enlightenment set themselves against tradition, against prejudice and against obscurantism. For them the rise of science, both natural and social, would disclose the reality of things.

Understanding was always itself understood as an unfinished and partial affair – the expansion of knowledge is at the same time an awareness of ignorance, of everything that is not and perhaps will not be known. Nevertheless, knowledge was presumed to be cumulative and presumed also to yield a progressive mastery of the surrounding world. The more we are able to understand ourselves, our own history and the domain of nature, the more we will be able to master them for our own purposes and in our own interests. The underlying theorem, stripped bare, was extremely plausible. The progress of well-founded knowledge is more or less the same as the progressive expansion of human dominion (Giddens, 1990).

Marx brought this view its clearest expression, integrating it with an interpretation of the overall thrust of history itself. In Marx's celebrated aphorism, 'human beings only set themselves such problems as they can resolve'. Understanding our history is the very means of shaping our destiny in the future. Even those thinkers who took a much less optimistic view than Marx did of the likely future for humanity accepted the theorem of increasing control of our circumstances. Consider, for example, the writings of Max Weber. Weber certainly did not see history as leading to human emancipation in the manner envisaged by Marx. For Weber, the likely future was one of 'uncontrolled bureaucratic domination' – we are all destined to live in a 'steel-hard cage' of rationality, expressing the combined influence of bureaucratic organisation and machine technology. We are all due to be tiny cogs in a vast and well-oiled system of rational human power (Weber, 1978).

Each of these visions of the imminent future attracted many adherents. Marxism, of course, shaped the very form of human society for many. Others, perhaps critical of Marxist thought, recoiled before the sombre vision offered by Weber and many others. Marxism, as we all know now, has lost most of its potency as a theoretical perspective on history and change. But Weber's more sombre vision has also lost its hold over us. It does not correspond to the world in which, at the end of the twentieth century, we in fact find ourselves. We do not live in a world which feels increasingly under human control but, rather to the contrary, one which seems to run out of control – in the words of Edmund Leach, a 'runaway world'. Moreover this sensation of living in a world spinning out of our control cannot any longer be said to be simply the result of lack of accumulated knowledge. Instead, its erratic runaway character is somehow bound up with the very accumulation of that knowledge. The uncertainties which face us do not result, as the thinkers of the Enlightenment tended to believe, from our ignorance. They come in some substantial part from our own interventions into history and into the surrounding physical world.

Manufactured uncertainty and external risk

I do not think one could say that the world in which we live today is more uncertain than that of previous generations. I do not see how such a claim could be validated in any case. It is the sources of uncertainty which have changed. We live increasingly in a social and material universe of what I shall call *manufactured uncertainty*. Manufactured uncertainty, or manufactured risk, comes from human involvement in trying to change the course of history or alter the contours of nature. We can separate manufactured risk from *external risk*. External risk refers to sources of uncertainty which came either from unmastered nature or from 'unmastered history', that is, history as lived by taken-for-granted traditions, customs and practices.

The debate about global warming – which is a debate about 'nature that is no longer nature' – offers one among many examples of the advent of manufactured uncertainty. The majority of scientific specialists believe that global warming is occurring, even if all forecasts of its likely consequences are imponderable. Some scientists, however, believe that the whole idea of global warming is a myth, while there is a minority view that what is taking place is actually the reverse – a long-term process of global cooling. The uncertainties which surround the global warming hypothesis do not derive from 'unmastered nature', but precisely from human intervention into nature – from the 'end of nature'. Since we can not be wholly sure whether or not global warming is occurring, it is probably best on a policy level to proceed in an 'as if' manner. As some of the consequences of global warming could be calamitous, it is sensible for nations and the larger world community to take precautionary measures.

Manufactured uncertainty is by no means limited to 'nature which is no longer nature'. It invades most areas of social life too, from local and even personal contexts of action right up to those affecting global institutions. Take as an example the decision to get married today on the part of someone living in a Western society. Fifty years ago, someone who decided to marry knew 'what it was he or she was doing'. Marriage was a relatively fixed division of labour involving a specified status for each member of the married couple. Now no-one quite knows any longer what marriage actually is, save that it is a 'relationship', entered into against the backdrop of profound changes affecting gender relations, the family, sexuality and the emotions.

What explains the increasing dominance of manufactured over external risk? Obviously the origins of this transition are bound up with the advent of modernity as a whole. However, a series of very basic changes sweeping through the world over the past several decades have intensified this transformation of the conditions of uncertainty and risk. Three great sets of changes are sweeping through the industrialised countries and also in some degree affecting most societies across the globe.

The first concerns the effects of *globalisation*. The word globalisation appears almost everywhere these days, but thus far has not been well conceptualised. As I would understand it here, globalisation does not simply refer to the intensifying of world economic competition. Globalisation implies a complicated set of processes operating in several arenas besides the economic. If one wanted to take a technological fix upon the intensifying of globalisation in recent years, it would be the point at which a global satellite communication system was first established. From that point onwards instantaneous communication becomes possible from any part of the globe to any other. The advent of instantaneous global communication both alters the nature of local experience and serves to establish novel institutions. The creation of 24-hour money markets, for instance, a phenomenon that has an impact upon almost all the world's population, became possible only because of the immediacy of satellite communication.

Globalisation is not just an 'out there' phenomenon. It does not refer only to the emergence of large-scale world systems, but to transformations in the very texture of everyday life. It is an 'in here' phenomenon, affecting even intimacies of personal identity. To live in a world where the image of Nelson Mandela is more familar than the face of one's next door neighbour is to move in quite different contexts of social action from those that prevailed previously. Globalisation invades local contexts of action but does not destroy them; on the contrary, new forms of local cultural autonomy, the demand for local cultural identity and self-expression, are causally bound up with globalising processes.

The second major source of social change over recent years is *detraditionalisation* (Beck, 1992). Here again we can distinguish longer processes of transformation from the more intensified changes happening over the past few decades. Modernity, of course, always set itself against tradition – this was one of the very origins of the Enlightenment. Yet during the lengthy period of what Ulrich Beck has called 'simple modernisation' modernity and tradition existed in a sort of symbiosis. Science itself became a kind of tradition – an established authority to which one turned when seeking the answer to puzzles or problems. This symbiosis of modernity and tradition marks the phase of 'simple modernisation' – roughly speaking, the first century and a half or so of industrialisation and modernity.

In the phase of 'reflexive modernisation', which has accelerated over the past several decades, the status of tradition becomes altered. Detraditionalisation does not mean an end to tradition. Rather, traditions in many circumstances become reinvigorated and actively defended. This is the very origin of fundamentalism, a phenomenon which does not have a long history. Fundamentalism can be defined as tradition defended in the traditional way – against the backdrop, however, of a globalising cosmopolitan world which increasingly asks for reasons. The 'reason' of tradition differs from that of discourse. Traditions, of course, can be defended discursively; but the whole point of tradition is that it contains a 'performative notion' of truth, a ritual notion of truth. Truth is exemplified in the performance of the traditional practices and symbols. It is not surprising, therefore, that we should see so many clashes and fracturings today across the world as embattled tradition clashes with a world of much more open life-style choice.

Detraditionalisation is closely linked to the 'end of nature' and indeed the two intertwine very often. 'Nature' disappears in the sense that few aspects of the surrounding material world – and of the body – remain uninfluenced by human intervention. Tradition and nature, as it were, used to be 'landscapes' of human activity, carrying with them a certain fixity of life-style practices. As tradition and nature dissolve, a whole host of new decisions have to be taken (by somebody) in areas which were not 'decisionable' before.

Consider, for example, the field of human reproduction. A variety of aspects of reproduction which were previously 'given' – not open to being influenced by human decisionmaking – now are in principle or in practice malleable. It is possible to have a child without any kind of sexual contact with another adult at all; the sex of a child can become a matter of choice; contraception becomes highly effective, so that the decision to have a child becomes something quite different from when childbearing was more of a 'natural' process. The 'end of nature' in the domain of reproduction, however, integrates closely with the social changes brought about by detraditionalisation. Thus, central to the lowered birth rate in the developed societies today is the series of changes which have promoted the autonomy of women and therefore altered the traditionally given relations between the sexes.

The third great set of changes sweeping through the world concerns those associated with the expansion of *social reflexivity* (Giddens, 1994). This is again not confined to the Western or developed societies, but is bound up with the globalisation of communication. 'Reflexivity' does not mean self-consciousness. It is not a psychological concept, but one concerning circumstances of social life. Reflexivity refers precisely to the condition of living in a detraditionalised social order. In such an order everyone must confront, and deal with, multiple sources of information and knowledge, including fragmented and contested knowledge claims. Everyone in some sense must reflect upon the conditions of her or his life, as a means of living a life at all. Consider as an example the case noted previously – the decision to get married. That decision is taken amid a welter of information about 'relationships', 'commitment', the changing nature of sexuality, of gender relations and of the very institution of marriage itself. Such information or knowledge is not simply a 'background' against which the decision to marry is taken: as remarked earlier, it enters constitutively into the environment of action which it describes.

Living in a highly charged reflexive social environment brings many new rewards and forms of increasing autonomy; at the same time, it brings also new problems and anxieties. As an illustration consider eating disorders and anorexia. As a widespread phenomenon, eating disorders in Western countries are relatively recent, dating only from the past thirty or so years. They are pathologies of a society where everyone is 'on a diet': that is, a diversity of foodstuffs is available, to those who can afford them, at any time of the day, month or year. Diet is no longer given by 'nature' – by the local seasons and by the availability of local produce. In such circumstances individuals have to decide what to eat – in some sense select a diet – in relation to how they want to be. Diet becomes intrinsically bound up with the cultivation of the body – for some people, particularly young women, social pressures to do with bodily appearance can assume a pathological and compulsive form.

When we decide what to eat, and therefore how to be, we know that we are taking decisions relevant to present and future health. A person might resolutely stick to a traditional diet, continue to smoke and so forth, in the face of widely disseminated medical knowledge which indicates these habits to be harmful. Yet he or she cannot do so without being aware of such knowledge claims. Ignoring them is in itself, in effect, a decision.

Institutions under strain

In a globalising world, marked by the swathes of social change just described, pre-established institutions start to come under strain. This is true of areas of social life ranging from personal and intimate social ties right the way through to large-scale global orders. In politics, to take one illustration, the voting population now lives in the same discursive arena as their political leaders. In such a circumstance, political legitimacy starts to come under strain. Deference tends to disintegrate and political activities and procedures which were once acceptable start to be placed widely in question. It is not just happenstance that corruption cases have come to the fore in political life in many countries across the world. Corruption was there previously, although it might not have been treated as such; but in the new conditions of social visibility in which political life operates today, what was once accepted becomes generally seen as illegitimate (although the reverse can also on occasion be true).

Rather than developing the political example, I shall concentrate here upon the question of the welfare state and welfare institutions. Most students of social policy agree that the Western welfare state is in a situation of crisis. That crisis is ordinarily understood in fiscal terms – as part of a 'can't pay, won't pay' mentality on the part of the middle classes. In the more affluent sectors of society, in other words, people increasingly refuse to accept the levels of taxation required to support various groups less fortunate then themselves. Sometimes the fiscal crisis of the welfare state is described, as in Galbraith's phrase, as a 'culture of contentment' (1992): many middle-class people have achieved a comfortable way of life and become protective about it. Others see the situation as more one of anxiety and insecurity; the middle class is no longer exempt from worries which used to concern mainly those in the lower strata of the social order.

I do not mean to say that the thesis of the fiscal crisis of the welfare state, in either of these competing versions, is a wholly mistaken one. It is not. However, one can also look at the problems facing the welfare state in a different way. The crisis of the welfare state, it can be suggested, is in some large part a crisis of *risk management*. The welfare state originated as a 'security state' and was actually called such in some countries. It was the socialised, public counterpart to private insurance. Now the involvement of modernity with insurance makes an interesting and informative story. Modern civilisation on the whole looks towards the future rather than the past, seeking to 'colonise the future'; the future is a 'territory' to be 'occupied'. It is not surprising, therefore, that early industrial enterprise was closely bound up with the emergence of the notion of insurance. What is insurance? Well, it is a means of organising future time. Insurance is a means of protecting against the hazards which might in the future befall individuals or groups in different contexts.

The welfare state, I think it can be said, was an insurance system which was developed in terms of coping with external risk. Certain things could befall the individual: he or she could get ill, become disabled, be divorced or become unemployed. The welfare state would step in to protect those who fell foul of such contingencies. In an era coming to be dominated by manufactured uncertainty, by contrast, welfare institutions based on external risk start to break down. Take as an illustration the changing circumstances of divorce. A half a century or so ago, in most Western countries, only a minority of people got divorced (most of these were cases of men leaving women, because legal and economic circumstances made it difficult for women to extricate themselves from marriage). Where only few divorced, divorce could be treated like a 'hazard of nature' – it might happen to you if you were very unlucky. Where it did take place, divorce happened against the backdrop of gender and family relations which were quite clearly defined and fixed. Today, not only are divorce rates very high compared to what they were; a large proportion of marriages in Western countries are actively broken up by women. In such a situation, reflecting so many other changes in personal and economic life, treating divorce as a 'hazard of nature' makes no sense. Divorce (and remarriage) become part of a much more active series of engagements with the manufactured risks of modern life. Welfare systems cannot simply step in to pick up the pieces;

they have to be redirected and reorganised in such a way as to promote responsible decision-making.

Something parallel applies in the case of health and illness. The medical health care systems of the welfare state were based upon the assumption that falling ill is something which simply happens to people in certain circumstances. In a world of much more actively organised life-styles, where the body is no longer so much of a 'given', this assumption no longer holds good. We all know that how healthy one is tends to be strongly influenced by life-style decisions which one takes, and by alterable states of the surrounding environment. Health care systems come under strain not simply because of the escalating costs of standard medical treatments, but because they still depend too much upon the presumption of illness as external risk.

In recent times critiques of the welfare state have come mostly from the neo-liberal right. Neo-liberals see welfare institutions as promoting dependencies rather than encouraging more responsible life-style practices. The impulse of neo-liberalism has been to cut back upon welfare expenditure and to seek to turn welfare systems into markets wherever possible. In an oblique and negative sort of way, the neo-liberals have had a better grasp of the inadequacies of the welfare state in current social conditions than have most of its defenders. But the relevance of their critiques has been undermined by their fascination with markets. In place of the neo-liberal attack upon welfare institutions, we should seek to provide what I would describe as a *positive critique* of the welfare state, rather than a primarily negative one. A positive critique of the welfare state would aim to restructure welfare institutions so as to bring them more into line with a detraditionalised world of manufactured uncertainty. I believe that many interesting and important issues are raised by such a reorientation, although I shall not pursue these here (Giddens, 1994, ch. 5).

Positive welfare means the active mobilisation of life decisions rather than the passive calculation of risk. We should think in terms of positive welfare, I think, not only when considering the position of the welfare state within the developed societies, but also when approaching the seemingly intractable problem of the divergence between the rich and poor countries globally. There is a shift in political orientations going on today which corresponds in a general way to the shifting circumstances of social life discussed thus far in this chapter. This is a transition from *emancipatory politics to life politics*. By 'emancipatory politics' I mean the pre-given political arena of left liberal political theory and practice. Emancipatory politics is concerned with securing freedom from oppression, with social justice and with the diminishing of socio-economic inequalities. It has been also the defining parameter for conservatism; conservatism arose as a reaction precisely to the left liberal values held first of all in the American and French Revolutions.

Emancipatory politics is a politics of *life chances*. The relevance of emancipatory political problems does not diminish with the advent of life politics; instead, life political issues come to form a new set of contexts of political decision-making. Rather than a politics of life chances, life politics is a politics of life decisions. It comes to the fore to the degree to which the end of tradition combines with the end of nature. In many areas of social life thus detraditionalised, new decisions have to be taken; these decisions are almost always politicised, involving as they do an ethical or value dimension. Crucially, however, issues of life politics cannot be settled by emancipatory political criteria.

The debate surrounding abortion is one example of a life-political issue. Where abortion becomes both easy to obtain and non-dangerous, a whole series of novel questions come to be posed. The issues involved in the abortion controversy, however, do not conform simply and directly to questions of emancipatory politics. The women's movement raised the right to easily available abortion as an emancipatory issue. But the problems posed by abortion cannot just be resolved by such means: they concern questions such as 'at what point is the foetus a "human being"'?

A second illustration of the emerging agendas of life politics is the controversy over the family. In most countries the family has suddenly become politicised, and the discussion of 'family values' intensified. Why should this be? The answer lies in the detraditionalising of family life, something happening not only in Western countries. The discussion going on about the family certainly continues to raise issues of emancipation, but is by no means limited to them. Many issues are raised which are to do instead with the ethics of life decisions. The family is no longer equivalent to a state of nature, but is being reconstructed afresh.

Post-scarcity society

The more life political questions move to the centre of the political agenda, I want to propose, the more it makes sense to think of the emergence of a *post-scarcity society*, particularly within the industrialised countries but to some extent across the world as a whole. The idea of a post-scarcity society has a lengthy history and it is important to distinguish my usage of the term here from others that have been adopted. One sense of the term 'post-scarcity' surfaced in early socialism and also found expression in Marx's youthful writings. In this sense the idea of post-scarcity meant the universalising of abundance. Marx at least hinted at the possibility that industrial society could create so much wealth that everyone might have enough to fulfil all possible needs. Scarcity would more or less disappear. This is not what I mean by the notion; some goods, including especially 'positional goods', will always be in short supply and the world being as it is, there seems no chance of the creation of a social order of superabundance.

In more recent years the idea of post-scarcity has quite often been linked to the so-called 'Inglehart thesis' (1977). On the basis of survey evidence, Ronald Inglehart has proposed that a current of 'post-materialism' is moving through the industrialised countries. People are turning away from the overriding goal of economic growth and orienting their lives towards different values. In so far as it is valid, the Inglehart thesis is certainly relevant to the notion of a post-scarcity society as I use it, but does not offer an exhaustive characterisation of the term. I mean by a post-scarcity society not a distinctive form of social order, but a series of emergent trends. These trends are the following.

First, as mentioned, the increasing involvement of political debate with questions of life politics. Second, the diffusion of circumstances of manufactured risk from which no one can be completely free. Some, but not all, ecological risks are of this type, although ecological hazards are only one form of generalised risk. Third, a decline in *productivism*, where this term is taken to refer to a pre-eminent commitment to economic growth. Productivism sees paid work as the core defining feature of social life. It is this aspect of a post-scarcity society which most closely overlaps with Inglehart's formulations. Fourth, the growing recognition that the problems of modernity cannot necessarily be resolved through more modernity. This refers in effect to a broad consciousness of the importance of manufactured uncertainty. Many examples can be found in the area of technology and technological innovation. The impact and value of technological innovation cannot be itself decided solely in technological terms. For instance, no amount of technical information will show conclusively whether or not a nuclear power plant should be built; such a decision involves an irreducible political element.

In so far as tendencies towards the formation of a post-scarcity society do in fact develop, they are likely to alter the conditions of socio-economic and political bargaining, both within and across societies. There are some positive implications here for issues of poverty and inequality. Grasping these means indicating the relevance of certain kinds of life-political questions for more well-established issues of political emancipation.

Existing prescriptions to do with alleviating inequality tend to be based upon possibilities of the direct transfer of wealth or income from more affluent to poorer groups. I do not suggest that attempts to provide such direct transfers should be abandoned. They have distinct limitations, however, especially insofar as they are bound up with difficulties of the welfare state noted previously. There are some interesting similarities between the critiques of the welfare state which have come from the political right and critiques of welfare aid programmes internationally, most of which have come from the political left. In the context of the welfare state, rightist authors have argued that, for example, the building of large housing estates creates more problems that it resolves. Such estates destroy pre-existing modes of communal life and foster welfare dependency. Those of the left tend to resist such analysis when applied to welfare institutions, but present a quite similar argument when discussing the drawbacks of global aid programmes. Where such aid is used, for instance, to build a large dam, critics argue the result is often the displacement of local forms of interdependence and the creation of new forms of dependency upon the bureaucratic provision of resources.

Thinking laterally about alleviating inequality makes it possible, at least in principle, to escape from such dilemmas. Instead of thinking primarily in terms of direct wealth or income transfers, I want to propose, we should consider the possibilities implied in what I want to term *life-style bargaining*. Life-style bargaining involves the establishing of 'trade-offs' of resources, based upon life-political coalitions between different groups. Four main types of life-style bargaining may be distinguished. Each can in some circumstances be redistributive downwards, although I would stress that in each of these contexts opposite possibilities also exist.

The first form of life-style bargaining depends upon *active risk management*. There are many situations, both within and outside the developed countries, in which the active management of manufactured risk can generate a positive redistribution of resources. An illustration can be taken from the area of health care. There is normally a quite direct correlation between poverty, both relative and absolute, and the risks of contracting various kinds of illnesses. It is not always the actual condition of poverty itself which produces this connection. Rather, the connection comes from certain life-style practices which those in poorer groups tend to follow. Programmes of health education, diet and physical self-care, can quite readily be redistributive downwards. Those who benefit most from such programmes tend to be people in poorer groups, who ordinarily do not have the same access to relevant information and strategies as do more affluent individuals.

A second type of life-style bargaining is *economic life-style bargaining.* In this case there are direct economic trade-offs between groups. A major area of economic life-style bargaining concerns the distribution and nature of paid work. There are powerful trends tending to accentuate inequalities in the domain of work. Some have argued, for example, that there is occurring a generalised lowering of wages of workers in less skilled jobs, because of the impact of global competition – firms have an interest in reducing the costs of labour wherever possible. Moreover, it may be that new technology will eliminate jobs without the creation of new demand which would generate jobs to replace them.

Yet not all changes affecting paid work have such negative implications for equality, and it is readily possible to point to trends and active policies which could move in an opposite direction. In a world where the amount of available work may shrink substantially over the coming twenty years, the distribution of work holds the key to overall social integration. I list here only an example of a situation in which life-style bargaining over work can be redistributive downwards. There is a tendency for people (particularly men) in well-paid jobs to retire much earlier than they used to. Some such early retirement, of course, is involuntary, and the jobs which individuals lose in that case are not necessarily replaced – at least by work of a comparable level. The larger proportion of such early retirement, however, is deliberately chosen. These are people who become 'time pioneers', people who regard the flexible control of their careers as more important than a strict work orientation. In leaving jobs which they could have held on to, they release them for those of a younger generation – with a 'chain of opportunity' effect down the line (Horning, 1995).

The work thereby redistributed may 'filter down' in a patterned way, not altering the distribution of income and wealth very much. Yet if a single job is thus created for a young person, even if that job is relatively poorly paid, the result is likely to be a downwards redistribution of resources. For younger people are disproportionately represented among the 'new poor' and among the unemployed.

A third type of life-style bargaining is *ecological.* As with the other categories, we know that ecological objectives often clash with attempts to produce a downward distribution of resources. Ecologically sensitive policies are sometimes expensive, and may go against the economic interests of power groups. For instance, regulations aimed at limiting industrial pollution can run counter to the maintaining of forms of industrial production which generate employment for poorer people. The ecological news, however, is not by any means all bad – there are many circumstances in which ecological life-style bargaining can be redistributive downwards. This applies both within the developed societies and in more global contexts. The reason is that poorer people by the very nature of their circumstances are often forced to adopt life-style practices which are ecologically damaging. Such is the case in instances ranging from fuel pollution in the developed countries to the cutting back of rain forests in impoverished Third World areas.

As in the other areas of life-style bargaining, there is a diversity of contexts in which more affluent groups share an interest in reducing such ecologically harmful practices. As a minor example, take the policy which has recently been introduced by some European governments of paying a sum of money to the owners of vehicles which are particularly polluting if they trade in those vehicles for newer, less environmentally harmful ones. Since poorer people tend to be the owners of older vehicles, which emit more damaging emissions, this type of policy tends to be redistributive downwards.

The fourth form of life-style bargaining might on the face of things seem much less important that the others, in so far as material inequalities are concerned. This is what I shall describe as *emotional life-style bargaining*. Far from being the least important type, I regard it in some ways as the key to all the others. It refers to negotiation about the emotional conditions of our lives, and these conditions have changed as massively as any of the more formal contexts of social activity in response to the wide social transformations described earlier in this chapter. Particularly important here are the changing relations between the sexes, a phenomenon of world-wide importance and certainly not limited to the economically advanced societies.

Women across the world now stake a claim to forms of autonomy previously denied or unavailable to them. Such a claim plainly has a strong emancipatory element, in so far as a struggle is involved to achieve equal economic and political rights with men. At the same time, however, that claim to autonomy intrudes deeply into the domain of life politics, for it raises issues to do with the very definition of what it is to be a woman, and therefore a man, in detraditionalising societies and cultures. Few things can be more significant world-wide than the possibility of a new social contract between women and men, since sexual divisions affect so many other forms of stratification in societies of all types.

To the degree to which it could be achieved, a new social contract between the sexes would certainly be redistributive downwards. For women are everywhere on average less privileged than men, and again make up a disproportionate proportion of the 'new poor'. Redefinitions of gender and sexuality rebound directly, not only upon the sphere of the family, but upon that of work. Most innovations or changes which improve the working conditions of women reflect back on other inequalities – and the reverse is also true. And what of men? Supposing it became increasingly common for men to redefine the emotional and communicative balance of their lives, moving away from the primacy of paid work and other activities in the public domain? Many consequences tending towards greater economic equality would stem from such circumstances, ramifying through most contexts of social life.

Perhaps all this talk of positive life-style bargaining sounds utopian, given the strength of the influences tending to produce large-scale inequality, social division and even social fragmentation? I do not mean to say, to stress again, that there is any inevitability about the downward redistributive effects of life-style bargaining. Yet whether we like it or not, in conditions of manufactured uncertainty and detraditionalisation such bargaining is likely to become a central feature of formal and less formal political manoeuvring. Within the developed societies, a variety of new pacts, some of which will figure directly in electoral politics, are likely to emerge in the future. One such pact, for instance, might be between older people and the young, for both figure among the more deprived groups in the contemporary world. As always, the currents affecting social life do not have an inexorable character. We always have possibilities of individual and collective choice – this is the very core of life politics in any case. We can try to use whatever choices we have in a fruitful way. Life political mechanisms offer us the possibility of defending some of the emancipatory values which otherwise, paradoxically, are likely to lose their purchase.

I have concentrated my discussion, implicitly at least, mainly upon the industrialised societies, but most of the arguments offered here have a global purchase. None of the major changes analysed in this article are limited to the industrialised world, although they may thus far be most pronounced in their impact there. Globalisation used to mean Westernisation, but does so no longer – not, at least, in blunt fashion. It has become a largely decentred set of processes associated, to be sure, with the global politics in a decentred world, characterised by global risks as well as by emergent global systems. Aid programmes transferring wealth from North to South, of course, can be valuable in attacking global inequalities. Yet, as mentioned, they are subject to some of the same difficulties that have faced welfare systems within the developed countries; and they are in any case quite minimal in terms of the sums involved.

Life-style bargaining is directly relevant to questions of global security. The conjoining of issues of life politics to those of emancipatory politics is today a matter of global scope. Possible trade-offs, for example, exist between ecological outcomes which are in the general interest and downward redistribution. For instance, some forms of agricultural practice which lead to deforestation and to soil erosion are driven by poverty; we all thus have an interest in contesting these. Moreover, processes of detraditionalisation may in some ways be more devastating in a more firmly traditional society than in a more modernised one. Life politics is not a matter only for the more affluent. Some of the poorest groups in the world may have to face a more radically open future than most others – and perhaps all of us might have something to learn from the solutions and life-decisions they come up with (Latouche, 1995).

REFERENCES

Beck, Ulrich (1992) *Risk Society* (London: Sage).
Galbraith, J. K. (1992) *The Culture of Containment* (London: Sinclair-Stevenson).
Giddens, Anthony (1990) *The Consequences of Modernity* (Cambridge: Polity Press).
  (1994) *Beyond Left and Right* (Cambridge: Polity Press).
Horning, Karl, Anette Gerhard and Matthias Michailow (1995) *Time Pioneers* (Cambridge: Polity Press).
Inglehart, Ronald (1977) *The Silent Revolution: Changing Values and Political Styles Among Western Publics* (Princeton: Princeton University Press).
Latouche, Claude (1995) *The Westernization of the World* (Cambridge: Polity Press).
Weber, Max (1978) *Economy and Society*, vol. I (Berkeley, CA: University of California Press).

16 The future of the human past

Philip Allott

There is no escape from yesterday because yesterday has deformed us.
Samuel Beckett, *Proust* (1931)

Human nature. The human condition. Human history

These ideas are the self-forged chains which hold down the soaring human spirit. They exist nowhere but in the human mind, and yet they have made the human mind their prisoner. Humanity will begin to become all that it might be when it frees itself from deformed ideas of what it is.

We rationalise our unfreedom by metaphysicalising our situation. We are not merely what we are; we manifest *human nature*, our species-characteristics. We are not merely what we do; we live *the human condition*, our habitat. We are not merely what we could be; we are the residue of *human history*, our phylogeny.

We fight like caged animals, because to survive is to struggle. We are human predators and human prey, because the animal that hunts survives the jungle. We swarm like termites in social groups, because to survive is to co-operate. We lust like monkeys, because to survive is to multiply; reproduction is our evolutionary purpose and reward. Our *nature* contains such things. Our *condition* imposes such things. Our *history* proves such things. Who could deny a destiny that is written in nature? *We will be what we have been* is all we need to know.

In the human tragi-comedy of the state-system human nature and the human condition and human history are enacted on the grandest stage of all, the great theatre of the world. Until deformed human consciousness is re-formed by human consciousness, there will be war and the infantile rivalries of states, systematic injustice and the countless forms of corrupt and corrupting power.

Human nature

The myth of *human nature* is one of the most ancient, the most widespread, and the most powerful of all myths. It requires us to believe

323

that each of us contains a second self which is a universal self, a self which we share with all other human beings. When we will and act, it is not we, as unique self-determining individuals, who will and act. We are ourselves acted upon as we act, pulled this way and that by a puppet-master whose own behaviour is determined by forces which are far beyond our control.

Our universal self is said to be our *instinctive* self, so gaining a sort of superpsychic prestige. It is the aboriginal self which is the handiwork of millions of years of evolution. It is the *Ur-sich*, to dignify it with a Goethean resonance. It is not even person-like, but rather thing-like, an *Es* (or *Id*), to dignify it with a Freudian resonance.

Or else our universal self is a *biological* self. Evolutionary biologists and socio-biologists invite us to find our natural self in our biological ancestry ('the modified descendant of some pre-existing form', as Charles Darwin described it) (Darwin, 1989: XXI, 9) or in our relationship to non-human animals (with whom we may share a fundamental programme of inclusive-fitness-maximising, as W. D. Hamilton, R. D. Alexander and others tell us). (For a discussion of altruism theory, see Alexander, 1975.) Microbiologists direct our attention to a still more intimate ordering of our physical existence. Sooner or later, no doubt, human nature will be hunted down in the human genome. There will be located a gene for political ambition, probably with a location on the human genome close to the gene for interpersonal violence, and a gene for diplomacy located close to the gene for lying, and a gene for sending-young-men-out-into-battle located close to the genes for preaching and teaching.

And our universal self has long been seen also as our *supernatural* self, made by a special act of creation by the hand that framed our existence. Part of our uniqueness is to share in the knowledge of the nature of our uniqueness. Human nature is then seen as humanity's natural law. We are what we are, and so we should be.

On philosophical grounds, if not on moral or pragmatic grounds, one might have expected that the myth of human nature would by now be leading a marginal and hunted existence. It must be explained why, instead, it is apparently as vigorous and noxious as ever, powerfully conditioning not only mass consciousness but also the minds and the behaviour of the socially and intellectually privileged, up to and including the behaviour of the governments of so-called *states*.

From a philosophical point of view, the idea of human nature faces a complex tradition of critical philosophy which, in the modern world, may be said to extend, chronologically at least, from William of Occam in the fourteenth century to Jacques Derrida in the twentieth. It is a tradition of thought for which universalising and essentialist ideas, such as ideas about human nature, may come to resemble religious idols (to use Francis Bacon's metaphor) or dreams (to use David Hume's metaphor) or nonsense (to use a Benthamite term which was also used by the logical positivists of the twentieth century and their allies) or neurotic projections (to speak in the terms of twentieth century psycho-philosophy).

Fusing the multiple facets of the sceptical-critical philosophical tradition into a single scheme, we may say that ideas about human nature are as intellectually fragile as the six layers of intellectual instability from which they are formed: (1) *the word*; (2) *the idea*; (3) *the meaning*; (4) *the evidence*; (5) *the desire*; (6) *the power*.

(1) The relationship between the visual/aural events of language and all other events is irreducibly obscure. Every day working hypotheses are: (a) the fact that there is a word symbolising a thing or event does not mean that that thing or event has an existence apart from the word or outside human imagination (*unicorn, phlogiston, god, human nature*); (b) the fact that words can appear in equivalent grammatical situations does not mean that there is anything else in common between the things or events they are intended to symbolise (*water is wet; man is selfish; god is love*).

(2) Words in organised clusters (ideas) function by reference to the operational principles (grammar) of a given language (and, perhaps, at a deeper level the operational principles of language in general). But they also function according to operational principles (logic) which discriminate between different organisations of words which are equally possible from a grammatical point of view. Everyday working hypotheses are: (a) grammatical and logical principles cannot guarantee that two similarly organised ideas have the same relationship to non-linguistic things and events (a relationship which used to be identified crudely by the word *truth*); (b) logical (and perhaps even grammatical) principles may be functionally specific, applying differently in different communication situations (politics, law, poetry, religion, science, history; or, to use more abstract Kantian–Weberian terms: in cognitive, normative, or aesthetic discourse).

(3) The communicative effect (meaning, significance) of language-events is the product of an infinity of events within the consciousness of those participating in the communication. Everyday working hypotheses are: (a) (leaving on one side mathematics), there is no single meaning for any single linguistic event; (b) to the extent that linguistic communication is a functionally effective form of human behaviour, there must occur sufficiently coincidental meanings within different consciousnesses.

(4) The functional effectiveness of linguistic communication is increased by the development of procedures which control the assembling of the words and ideas (the evidence) into more complex linguistic events. Everyday working hypotheses are: (a) the more complete the evidentiary rules the more routinely successful the resulting communication (say, natural science versus the human sciences, law versus morality); (b) the fact that a given form of linguistic communication is routinely successful (slogans, creeds) is no guarantee that it has a well-organised evidentiary basis.

(5) Linguistic events take place within individual consciousness which adds powerful inputs (desire) which are unique to the individual consciousness and determinative of ultimate communicative effect. Everyday working hypotheses are: (a) we hear what we want to hear; (b) what we hear is a primary cause of what we do; (c) each person and each society lives in a unique mind-formed reality within which linguistic events have their own meaning.

(6) But linguistic events are also capable of being social events and hence are available to be used in the exercise of social power. What Karl Marx brilliantly identified as the *means of mental production* are a leading feature of a society's productive processes. Everyday working hypotheses are: (a) society can play a major role in forming the content of individual consciousness; (b) society can control social development through the manipulation of consciousness.

Such an apparently arid analysis takes on great practical importance when it is related to ideas which arise as part of the self-constituting of societies. When social power is attached to an idea (*society, state, nation, sovereignty, justice, freedom, equality, self-determination, power, national interest, human nature* ...), it becomes an idea-force capable of generating unlimited and determinative effects in the lives of individuals and societies. In such cases, it becomes as important to call ideas to account as it is important to call to account any other form of social power (political, legal, economic, physical).

The idea of human nature has performed five fundamental functions in the history of human self-constituting.

(1) In the context of religions, ideas about human nature have provided a miscellany of foundational premises for *human self-identifying*: aboriginal goodness or sinfulness, existential dependence or independence in relation to the supernatural, the spark of the divine in human nature (reason, grace, *logos, dharma, bodhi*).

(2) In the context of social philosophy, ideas about human nature have provided miscellaneous explanatory premises for *social self-constituting*: natural sociability or competition, selfishness or altruism,

aggression or cooperation, freedom or subordination, equality or in-equality.

(3) A wide range of ideas about human nature have provided psycho-logical theory with various bases for *personal self-identifying*: ideas of instinct, reason, enlightenment, knowledge, goal-seeking, pleasure-seeking, pain-avoiding, the normal.

(4) In the context of moral philosophy, ideas about human nature have provided initial explanatory premises for *human self-evaluating*: of freedom, choice, responsibility (blame), moral rationality, self-seeking, virtue.

(5) Strangest of all, ideas about human nature have been used in the *(external or inter-se) self-constituting of so-called states*. With vast and tragic consequences, ideas of human nature have been extrapolated to apply to the systematic interaction of the public-realm systems of certain kinds of society. Hypothetical aspects of human nature (selfishness, instincts of self-preservation, instincts of aggression and territoriality, rationality, goal-seeking) have been used to determine, and to understand and evaluate, the *behaviour* of such *states*. In Meinicke's fantasy state-psychology, the *national-state* has a specialised rationality (*Staatsräson*) which guides its pursuit of something called *power*, much as, in Freud's fantasy of human psychology, the human being pursues something called *pleasure* (or, in Adler's version, *power*) (Meinicke, 1924). And all kinds of human foibles and character-defects may then be attributed to the fantasised state – such as the mysticism and brutality against which Troeltsch warned in the precipice year of 1922 (Gay, 1968: 96).

In the wonderful episode in the self-development of human consciousness which we associate with the names of Socrates, Plato and Aristotle, there was articulated and enacted the latent, and devastating, tension which besets all such human self-naturalising. It has been repeatedly re-enacted in the work of the mind-makers of the modern world from Aquinas to Freud.

The tension in question is between the *natural* and the *necessary*. Is the natural a fate or a potentiality? Is virtue a natural inclination to do good or a power to surpass our natural inclinations? Can we be blamed for doing what comes naturally and what is hence, in some sense, necessary? Can we surpass ourselves by our own effort, through contemplation, enlightenment, education, socialisation, psychotherapy? Is the good beyond us but within our grasp? Is human nature a fate or a potentiality?

Religion has, throughout human history, provided ready-made answers to such questions. The religious solution is to say that it is only by transcending the human that humanity can redeem itself. For philosophers, who seek to face the same questions without resort to religion, there have been no simple answers. At least until Freud, the secular modern world has sought to resolve the tension – as Socrates–Plato–Aristotle had powerfully proposed – by seeking the redeeming of the individual in the redemption of *society*. In society human nature is apparently re-formed within a suprahuman process. Our second-self humanity is reconstituted as our second-self citizenship.

The prevalence and the power of the idea of human nature are due to its having been appropriated by social power. It has proved useful as an instrument for the organising of human behaviour by those in command of the formation of social consciousness. It can apparently be socially effective regardless of its specific content, however bizarre and however unsubstantiated by evidence that content may be.

The idea of human nature has been useful because it denies the particularity and the responsibility of each human being. Human nature institutionalises human alienation. Its function is to prevent us from becoming what we might be, by imagining an idea of what we might suppose ourselves to be, and then constituting that idea socially as an idea of what we shall be. It is in this sense that the idea of human nature may be classified as a myth. It relocates human desire and human subjection within an arbitrary reality which is supposedly beyond human control.

In the modern world, the religious manifestation of the myth of human nature faces a powerful secular rival in the making of the modern state and in the modern conceptualising of the social interaction of the so-called states. To seek to rescue humanity from its arbitrary and self-deforming ideas of its self is now to take on as an adversary not only the age-old power of religion but also the mythomania of the modern state and of the modern state-system.

The human condition

It is not difficult to understand why the human species should have become, and continued to be, *a question for itself*, in Saint Augustine's celebrated formula. *Quid ergo sum? What am I? Quae natura sum? What is my nature?* (St Augustine, 1908: 293). It is not surprising that the human race should have persisted in its hopeless search for the nature of human nature, the *hsing* of human beings, as the ancient Chinese philosophers termed it.

More surprising is it that the human race should have persisted in supposing that there might be a natural basis for the *conduct* of human life. *Quid fieri? What are we to become?*

The myth of the *human condition* is, like the myth of human nature, a myth of myths. It is another means of human self-alienation, another means of evading the awful responsibility of being human. And, once again, the myth manifests itself in extremely unstable and incoherent linguistic formulations. The imagining of a human condition gives great opportunities for the abuse of social power. If one is able to propagate successfully a particular formulation of the human condition which makes it possible to determine rather readily and precisely that this or that form of living is natural and therefore inevitable, or natural and therefore intrinsically good, then one may be able to control very many human lives in very general ways. If one were able to extend the acceptance of such ideas far beyond the limits of the culture within which they are generated (say, as in the world religions or in notions of human rights or democracy), or if one were able to extrapolate such ideas to make them applicable to the interactive behaviour of human societies (say, the interactions of so-called states), then it would be possible to control the most general human phenomenon of all, the life of the human species as a whole. It is a large reward for a small effort of linguistic communication.

As in the case of myths of human nature, it has been the historical function of religions to be the primary vehicles for the conveying of myths of the human condition. But from a very early date mythology and non-religious philosophy have sought to achieve similar social effects through appropriately adapted linguistic communication.

In the struggle for survival of communicated ideas, myths about the human condition have selected themselves into patterns which are so familiar to us that they have themselves taken on an aura of naturalness, even inevitability. It now requires a substantial effort, maybe too great an effort, to unthink the routine myths of the human condition.

The most important of all the foundational myths of the human condition is the myth of *exile*, the Prometheus moment in human consciousness. In ancient Israel and ancient Greece, parts of humanity destined to have great power over the development of human conscious-ness chose to found the human condition in an act of defiance by humanity against the divine, and an act of punishment of the human by the divine. By an extraordinary coincidence, in both cases the intricate imaginative idea-structures managed to combine three things which would haunt a large part of humanity ever since: the naturalness of human evil-doing; the curse on human self-surpassing; the degradation of women. The myth-making was prophetic, or self-fulfilling. Evil has been naturalised. Woman has been made by man. Human self-surpassing is called madness. Our natural home is also our place of exile. Our all-powerfulness intimidates us. Our lost paradise is a purgatory. We have internalised, into the depths of our being, fear and hate and shame. Humanity has put a curse on its humanity.

Just as perversely and arbitrarily, we have internalised *conflict* as another foundational myth, the Heraclitus moment in human consciousness. Creative dualities are found in the foundational structures of many cultures: the *prakriti* and the *purusha* of one Hindu tradition; the *yin* and *yang* of Chinese philosophy; the common patterns of duality in other cultures emphasised by Radcliffe-Brown, Lévi-Strauss, Jung and others. In Western culture, the Heraclitan duality has been less benign and more dynamic. In the Judaeo-Christian worldview, the creative dualities flowing from the agonistic relationship of God and Man are closer to the harsh realities of real life than to the ineffable One-seeking (*that are thou; all composite things must pass away*) of some Eastern traditions. From dialectical philosophy to capitalist competition, from the class struggle to Mutual Assured Destruction, we constitute ourselves in conflict. We are conditioned to imagine, with Heraclitus, that *strife is justice*.

A third constitutive sub-myth of the myth of the human condition is the myth of *subjection*, the Antigone moment in human consciousness. As a Confucian philosopher of the third century BC put it: 'the congenital nature of men is evil, the goodness in them acquired' (Fung Yu-lan, 1952: 33). That is to say, social power, laws and customs and government, are necessary to control the unruly nature of human beings. The naturalness and the inevitability of unequally distributed social power, including property-power, the necessity of our slavery for our own good, have been foundational ideas with which, and against which, social philosophies have been constructed ever since.

A fourth form of the arbitrary self-conditioning of human consciousness is the myth of *labour*, the Adam moment in human consciousness. Labour is seen as part of the divine curse laid on mankind. 'With labour I must earn my bread' is God's 'just yoke laid on our necks', as Milton's Adam says (Milton, 1667: lines 1054–5). 'Harsh toil' is one of the evils which escaped from Pandora's jar' (Hesiod, 1988: 39). Once again, the foundational myth was peculiarly prophetic. In the last two centuries the working life of the slave has become the normal life of the citizen. The human race has placed itself on a treadmill of never-ending work ruled by unquenchable desire, rabid neophilia and chronic pleonexia. The tyranny of the division of labour which is capitalism and the tyranny of the division of authority which is democracy have become the ever more efficient means of collective dehumanising, with producing and consuming and voting as tragic parodies of work and desire and reason.

The myth of *happiness* is the Faust moment in human consciousness, desire perpetually frustrated. The discussion of happiness in Socrates–Plato–Aristotle is the discussion of a state of the soul rather than of the mind, an integrative actualising of the good in the living of life. It is close to the idea of holiness in several religious traditions. In the modern world irredeemable loneliness – that which Weber identified in the Calvinist spirit as 'a feeling of unprecedented inner loneliness of the single individual' (Weber, 1958: 104) – has been amalgamated with the relentless socialising of desire, so that the human being seeks happiness in both places, in the mind and in society, and finds it in neither.

It is this that accounts for the effect which Freudianism has had on human self-mythologising. The soul-substitute unconscious turns out to be both isolated and dependent. In the Lacanian version, the formation of the self is a sad and lonely quasi-communicative process of self-constituting through other-constituting. An alienated world is introduced into the depths of the mind, a microcosm of all the myths of the human condition, including even the myth of death. The pursuit of happiness is then nothing but a humble and relentless effort to reduce aggregate tension in our inescapable inner struggle-to-survive-ourselves.

In the myth of *death* humanity has found a peculiarly effective means of self-abasement, the Nemesis moment in human consciousness. Life is given a meaning and a measure by death. The shadow of death is thrown by an uncertain light beyond. Lucretius, writing in the first century BC, must have known that the attempt to demystify death was a wasted intellectual effort. That 'death is nothing to us and no concern of ours'; that nature would not understand all our 'whining and repining' (Lucretius, 1951: 121) are ideas to be feared, because their integration into our consciousness would so alter the content of human self-constituting. And they are ideas to be resisted by those whose social power over other human beings derives from their power over life-after-death.

Exile – conflict – subjection – labour – happiness – death. Prometheus – Heraclitus – Antigone – Adam – Faust – Nemesis.

That humanity must tell itself stories in order to have a framework for living life through consciousness, no one need deny. Different cultures tell themselves different stories at different times. But the myth-structures referred to above have been written into a very substantial part of human consciousness through explicit and implicit acculturation over thousands of years. And, thanks to the profound socialisation and globalisation of consciousness in the modern world, they are ideas which are now haunting all human activity everywhere.

The question is: why does humanity persist in so dismal a view of its own potentiality?

Human history

History is the story we tell ourselves about our past. The myth of history is that we *live* the present but *know* the past. It would be better to say that we endlessly create the past as we make the future. As we suppose ourselves to have been, so we cause ourselves to become. *The picture of time past, which we call Historie* (Ralegh, 1971: 71) is better seen as a distorting mirror in which we see our distorted ideas of ourselves. Myth in, myth out.

Early historians in the Western tradition saw with remarkable clarity that the writing of history is an activity which takes place in some uncertain territory which lies between myth and rhetoric and philosophy and science. Aristotle had been characteristically confident: history describes the thing that has been, poetry a thing that might be (Aristotle, 1982: 35). And Diodorus of Sicily, writing in the first century AD, put into notorious words the brash self-mythologising of supposedly post-mythical historiography. 'For if it be true that the myths which are related about Hades, in spite of the fact that their subject-matter is fictitious, contribute greatly to fostering piety and justice among men, how much more must we assume that history, the prophetess of truth, she who is, as it were, the mother-city of philosophy as a whole, is still more potent to equip men's characters for noble living!' (Diodorus Siculus, 1933: 9).

When Thucydides began to look for *causes* in history, and when Plato proposed the exclusion of the providential fantasy-histories of Homer and Hesiod from the education of the guardians, they articulated a profound human desire to learn from the human past, to discover what Hume called 'the constant and universal principles of human nature' (Hume, 1902: 83). They also laid bare the problems which have beset history-writing ever since.

To invoke one possible typology of history-writing, we may say, for the sake of the present argument, that *providential* history finds god or gods at work in the story of human activity, *rationalising* history finds significant law-like patterns in the story of human activity, *naturalising* history finds relationships of causation in the story of human activity. What all three kinds of history have in common is that they all add something – historical significance – to the mere reassembling of the putative *events* of history, to the king-lists, annals, chronicles, official records and other raw materials.

Providential and rationalising historians are blessed with foresight (through revelation or extrapolation); they are *retrospective prophets* (F. Schlegel, quoted in Cassirer, 1944: 178). When Tertullian wrote, at the end of the second century AD, it must have seemed obvious to a person of optimistic disposition that, 'If you look at the world as whole, you cannot doubt that it has grown progressively more cultivated and populated. Every territory is now accessible, every territory explored, every territory opened to commerce.' Indeed, humanity may have been too successful.

'Most convincing as evidence of populousness, we men have actually become a burden to the earth, the fruit of nature hardly suffice to sustain us, there is a general pressure of scarcity giving rise to complaints, since the earth can no longer support us.' Fortunately plague, famine, warfare and earthquakes will correct overpopulation (Tertullian, *De anima*: xxx, quoted in Cochrane, 1957: 246).

A sanguine Englishman in the late eighteenth century, especially if he were affected by the Enlightenment project of rational human progress, might well believe that the future development of the savage nations would not 'injure ... the system of arts and laws and manners which so advantageously distinguish, above the rest of mankind, the Europeans and their colonies'.

'We may therefore acquiesce in the pleasing conclusion that every age of the world has increased, and still increases, the real wealth, the happiness, the knowledge, and perhaps the virtue, of the human race' (Gibbon, 1901: 169).

Happily, there has always been a more dismal counterpoint to such intoxications, from Hesiod to Spengler and beyond. For the depressive Weber, writing before the Third Reich, what lies ahead of us is 'not summer's bloom ... but rather a polar night of icy darkness and hardness' (in 'Politics as a vocation', 1919, in Gerth and Wright Mills, 1958: 128). (Perhaps he was thinking of Herder's view of history as the story of human 'blossoming'.) And then there are the yea-*and*-naysayers: Nietzsche on his more cheerful days, with the possibility of a new humanity following our present terminal decay (which dates from the time of the Italian Renaissance, according to Toynbee); Hegel, with the troubling idea that we may be living through some sort of logical culmination of all human history, if not of the history of the universe.

As thoughtful historians have always known, we only know the events of history in the form of linguistic communications about those events. Even Oswald Spengler was able to make the almost-post-modern point that there is, for example, no such thing as *Buddhism* which *moved* from India to China. 'Connotations are not transferable ... The same words, the same rites, the same symbol – but two different souls, each going its own way' (Spengler, 1989: II, 57). History is a branch of semiotics. 'To me history is still in a large measure poetry', said the great Swiss historian Burckhardt (Cassirer, 1944: 203).

This may suggest one reason why historians have been so obsessed with war. War seems to be rather unproblematic in terms of semiotics. It seems to be nothing much more than killing and destruction, relatively unambiguous events. Wars make a good story. Lucian, writing in the second century AD, put the point with admirable wit (his allusion is to a familiar saying attributed to Heraclitus), 'very true, it seems, is the saying that "War is the father of all things" since at one stroke it has begotten so many historians . . .' (Lucian, 1959: 5).

War exudes an erotic glamour which affects all those who specialise in war – politicians, diplomats, historians (even international lawyers and international relations specialists). It is very physical, very large, very expensive. Weapons of war ejaculate death rather than life, a greater thrill. War is the game of games for men, sex by other means, male-bonding through mass-murder. And now technology allows us to practise safe war, and television enables us to be voyeurs of war.

The obsession of historians with war is the other face of their obsession with the *state*, the coldest of all cold monsters (Nietzsche, 1964: 75). Politics is civil war by other means, cold war,[1] the game men play in the rest-periods between wars. *Nations* are male fantasies of either or indeterminate gender. *States* are male fantasies of masculinity, of seduction through violence. It seems now that global capitalism may be taking over as the game of games for men: war and politics by other means. And global sport may be war's fourth incarnation (and sex's fifth). War – politics – capitalism – sport: the stuff of ecstatic history-writing.

History-writing experienced a paradoxical Thucydidean–Hesiodian renaissance in the nineteenth century. Hermetic history, by historians for historians, became the task of a new priest class, heirs of those theologians who devoted centuries of intellectual effort to the alle-gorical-anagogical universalising of Judaeo-Christian providential history. And hermetic history begat (or rebegat) historicism: post-religious, post-Enlightenment, post-Romantic *tutti-frutti* history, natur-alising- rationalising-providential, promising various human destinies from the glorious to the awful. But Ranke told historians simply to say 'how things happened' and 'keep to the facts' (from a preface of 1824 and lecture of 1854, in Iggers and von Moltke, 1973: 56, 137), and Dilthey prescribed for scholars 'the law of struggling with the raw material' (Dilthey, 1989: 141), and thereby spoke the doom of genera-tions of pallid research students and arid academics. Such ideas did for professional historians the economic service which positivism and pragmatism did for J. S. Mill's 'moral sciences' (Dilthey's *Geisteswis-senschaften*) in general, legitimising a scholarship-industry located in the monasteries-without-prayer, those temples of misanthropology, the universities. Hippolyte Taine, high-priest among the priests, compared the revolutionary transformation of France to the 'metamorphosis of an insect' (Taine, 1891: iv). The proper study of humanity is human entomology.

The trouble is that, like ideas about human nature and the human condition, hermetic history-writing has a tendency to escape from the library and infect the *popular* and *subconscious* histories which directly affect day-to-day social development. Filtered through the minds of historians, evil and folly and chance can take on the inner logic of a fable or a fairy-tale. For Augustine, Pascal, Lessing, Herder and others human history has been 'the education of the human race'. But history can also be the infantilising or the corrupting or the barbarising of the human race. The human species lives in a human surreality made in the human imagination, an *Umwelt* of the mind (for further discussion of human realities, see Allott, 1992). We cannot by our own effort think beyond our own thinking (our Gödel bind), but, by supposing that human fantasies are superhuman realities, we can make ourselves what we need not have been.

Humanity is *causa sui*, its own creation, made in its own image. There is no human nature, no human condition, no human history. Those ideas are phantom symptoms of humanity's suicidal soul-sickness, the manic depression of a whole species, a species at war with itself, self-exiled in an existential nihilism whose pathogen is humanity's fear of being human and whose products are humanity's excesses of grandeur and misery.

To be human is to be part of the natural universe, but a part that thinks. We are what we choose to be. Humanity's inhumanity is its own creation. We could choose another way, the way of human health and human growth, a new enlightenment. Humanity could take the first step by recognising itself as a society of all human beings which endlessly forms itself in consciousness with a view to its endless self-perfecting, a society whose potentiality is not in its past but in its future (for an attempt to begin again at the beginning, see Allott, 1990).

NOTE

1 The expression *guerra fria* was used by a thirteenth-century Spanish writer to describe the coexistence of Islam and Christendom in Spain (Bozeman, 1960: 426 fn.).

REFERENCES

Alexander, R. D. (1975) 'The Search for a General Theory of Behaviour', *Behavioural Science*, vol. 20.

Allott, P. (1990) *Eunomia – New Order for a New World* (Oxford: Oxford University Press).

—— (1992) 'Reconstituting Humanity – New International Law', *European Journal of International Law*, vol. 3(2).

Aristotle (1982) *Poetics*, W. H. Fyfe (trans.), Loeb Classical Library (Cambridge, MA: Harvard University Press).

St Augustine (1908) *Confessions*, J. Gibb and W. Montgomery (trans.) (Cambridge: Cambridge University Press).

Bozeman, A. B. (1960) *Politics and Culture in International History* (Princeton: Princeton University Press).

Cassirer, E. (1944) *An Essay on Man* (New Haven: Yale University Press).

Cochrane, C. N. (1957) *Christianity and Classical Culture*, 2nd edn (Oxford: Oxford University Press).

Darwin, C. (1989) *The Descent of Man, and Selection in Relation to Sex*, in P. H. Barrett and R. B. Freeman (eds.), *The Works of Charles Darwin* (London: William Pickering).

Dilthey, W. (1989) *Introduction to the Human Sciences*, in R. A. Makkreel and F. Rodi (eds.), *Selected Works*, vol. I (Princeton: Princeton University Press).

Diodorus Siculus (1933) *The Library of History*, C. H. Oldfather (trans.), Loeb Classical Library (Cambridge, MA: Harvard University Press).

Fung Yu-lan (1952) *A History of Chinese Philosophy*, 2nd edn (Princeton: Princeton University Press).

Gay, P. (1968) *Weimar Culture* (New York: Harper & Row).

Gerth, H. H. and C. Wright Mills (trans. and eds.) (1958) *From Max Weber: Essays in Sociology* (New York: Oxford University Press).

Gibbon, E. (1901) *Decline and Fall of the Roman Empire*, J. B. Bury (ed.) (London: Methuen & Co.).

Hesiod (1988) *Work and Days*, M. L. West (trans.) (Oxford: Oxford University Press).

Hume, D. (1902) *Enquiry Concerning Human Understanding*, in *Enquiries*, 2nd edn, L. A. Selby-Bigge (ed.), (Oxford: Oxford University Press).

Iggers, G. G. and K. von Moltke (1973) *The Theory and Practice of History: Leopold von Ranke* (New York: The Bobbs-Merrill Co.).

Lucian (1959) *How to Write History*, K. Kilburn (trans.), Loeb Classical Library (Cambridge, MA: Harvard University Press).

Lucretius (1951) *On the Nature of the Universe*, R. E. Latham (trans.) (Harmondsworth: Penguin).

Meinecke, F. (1924) *Die Idee der Staatsräson in der neueren Geschichte*, D. Scott (trans.), under the title *Machiavellism: The Doctrine of Raison d'état and its Place in Modern History* (1957) (New Haven: Yale University Press).

Milton, J. (1667) *Paradise Lost*.

Nietzsche, F. (1964) *Thus Spake Zarathustra*, R. H. Hollingdale (trans.) (Harmondsworth: Penguin).

Ralegh, W. (1971) *The History of the World*, C. A. Patrides (ed.) (1614) (London: Macmillan).

Spengler, O. (1989) *The Decline of the West*, C. F. Atkinson (trans.) (New York: Alfred A. Knopf).

Taine, H. (1891) *Les origines de la France contemporaine; l'ancien régime*, 16th edn (Paris: Librairie Hachette).

Weber, M. (1958) *The Protestant Ethic and the Spirit of Capitalism*, T. Parsons (trans.) (New York: Charles Scribner's Sons).

Conclusion: security within global transformation?

Ken Booth

So far in the 1990s many of us feel, like Stephen Spender and others at the start of the 1930s, 'hounded by external events' (Hynes, 1976: 65). The speed and confusion of contemporary world politics delay the construction of historical meaning, and make simplification attractive, while coping with the present pushes out planning for the longer-term future. It may of course simply be end-of-century gloom; after all, this is not the first time people have complained about incompetent and visionless governments, the collapse of traditional institutions, widespread social and economic distress, appalling disparities in life chances, racism and hypernationalism, private comfort replacing public ideals, and introspection triumphing over internationalism, corruption over service and helplessness over hope. In terms of mood we have been here before, *but something is new.* The present of world politics is unique in terms of its material conditions: a wired world, a threatened environment, a global population surge, a truly world economy, depleting non-renewable resources, and intercontinental weapons of mass destruction. The mood hints at the meaning: 'Resignation sums up the Distant Past's vision of the future; hopefulness was that of Yesterday; and apprehension is the dominant mood of Today.' These words of Robert Heilbroner (1995: 69–70) neatly encapsulate the cultural, social and political stage in world history in which the chapters of this book are set.

In these confusing times, with contested foundations and visions, a major responsibility for students of International Relations is to try to make sense of events without surrendering complexity, to paint pictures of the future without claiming prediction, and to attempt to devise political forms that offer more hope than presently of delivering peace, security and welfare for more of the earth's population. With these points in mind, this Conclusion discusses the changing context of statecraft and security in this, the first truly global age. The Conclusion of a wide-ranging book such as this cannot easily draw together all the earlier ideas, or answer all the questions posed. Instead it seeks to provide further context for rethinking – resisting and reinventing – in relation to three crucial aspects of global transformation – globalisation, global governance and global moral science.

Globalisation

The context of international relations in the final decades of the twentieth century has changed in a dramatic fashion. This new stage in world history – potentially a step-change in the evolution of human society – cannot easily be reduced to a single word: but to the extent it can, it is encapsulated in the concept of 'globalisation'. This remains a much debated and contested concept, but for me it embraces those changes that have been taking place in politics, society and economy that result in the daily intermeshing and densification of local lives and global processes, and the impact of this on traditional conceptions of time, space, boundaries, culture, identity and politics. This discovery – not always comfortable – of new relationships to distance, time and being is a more fundamental feature of globalisation than the narrowly economic conception that simply equates globalisation with the triumph of capitalism. In short, globalisation is one of those historic step-changes (like the Industrial Revolution) that will revolutionise human society and the world it is shaped by and shapes.

Wherever one looks, there is movement and challenge in material circumstances and social relations. We are living in an era of spectacular change. At the same time there is a pervasive sense that nobody controls the transformations: instead, the transformations control us. It is only necessary to mention the transnational organisation of production, the liberalisation of markets globally, the growth of world cities, advanced information technology, the 24-hour global finance system, changing consumption patterns and expectations, and the pressures on traditional family relationships, local communities, cultural norms and political authority. The changes are eye-catching at the material level but are profound below the surface, at the level of ontology and political philosophy. For students of International Relations, one outcome of the processes of globalisation is that the familiar textbook notion of the sovereign state is called into question. State borders are increasingly open to external penetration on a minute-by-minute basis, to everything except neighbouring armies, as the autonomy of governments declines over economic planning, social ideas and cultural choice. The sovereign state's power to control its own destiny is eroded by globalisation. James Rosenau's term 'post-international politics' becomes everyday more pertinent (1990). This is certainly not to say that governments and states are henceforth unimportant. They are, and will remain influential conduits in the distribution of social, political and economic goods. They regulate the lives of their citizens in manifold ways, but they themselves are more than ever regulated by outside pressures. If the twentieth-century image of the sovereign state has been that of a juggernaut being driven down an *autobahn*, towards prosperity and power, the twenty-first-century metaphor is more likely to see governments as traffic cops, at a busy (probably Asian) intersection, gesticulating wildly while trying to direct the teeming flow of people, traffic and goods – all of which have their own imperatives – as best they can. Governments are busier than ever before, with more functions and pressures, but they have less autonomy.

Globalisation, like other human developments, does not everywhere have uniform effects and is a two-edged sword. It offers the promises of inclusiveness and interdependence, and different and more hopeful visions of the human condition, but as a result of certain ruling ideas, it also magnifies disparities between rich and poor, powerful and powerless, and leaves established political authority structures feeling unable to control the companies and cultural ideas that can exploit the time/space opportunities of a globalising planet. These are the circumstances in which apprehension is the dominant mood. The global market promises wealth and choice, but it threatens protectionism, financial crises, the destruction of nature, unemployment, the marginalisation of welfarism, personal anxiety and other negative social consequences and economic reactions. Levels of insecurity rise, and there is fatalism about human agency. The challenge is therefore to inform globalisation with ideas that can maximise its promise in terms of human community and global welfare and minimise its threats in terms of disparity and dislocation. This is the task for what I later call global moral science.

The political economy of globalisation is one of the most powerful forces shaping our times. At its base is the world capitalist economy. (Expressed differently, this aspect of globalisation can be regarded as an extension of US foreign policy by other means.) Capitalism has been an enormously successful economic system in the way it has provided large numbers of people with goods, but as Robert Heilbroner has argued, persuasively and succinctly, its expansionist nature (marked by unbounded science and technology) intrudes into all aspects of human relationships – with nature and with each other. In Heilbroner's words, 'the commodification of life is not only an intrusion of science and technology into the tissues of sociality, but also the means by which a capitalist economy draws energy from its own environment' (1995: 99). The problem as Heilbroner sees it is that an economy without growth would be 'as incompatible with capitalism as a society without serfdom with feudalism'; it is possible that a static economic society could exist, and possibly be the foundation for 'some kind of humane new social order', but at the same time it may also produce unattractive means of 'handling the inescapable problem of the generation and distribution of income'. For the (historical) moment, Heilbroner concludes, the future is capitalist, with all its 'transient gains and permanent losses', but capitalism will not – cannot – last forever, or even the millennia of some former empires (1995: 100–1). Capitalism, today, is everywhere triumphant, and that might just be its greatest tragedy. For without alternatives, its negative consequences will be allowed free rein, and the prospects indefinitely postponed for the development of a social order that offers a better prospect of reconciling humans with each other and the natural world on which they utterly depend.

The global market produces particular forms of global competition which in turn means that national economies have to compete by the rules, or wither away. Politics within nations is increasingly shaped by economics above nations, and between national economies and the global economy. Consequently, instead of states aiming to become 'local agents of the world common good', to use Hedley Bull's term (1983: 11–12, 14) they have increasingly been coopted to be local agents of the world capitalist good. It was failure in this competition, for example, which sealed the fate of the militarily super-powerful Soviet Union. To be a stagnant post-Stalinist command economy in a burgeoning post-Fordist capitalist world was historically terminal. The Soviet Union did not collapse, it was coopted.

Nowhere are the disciplines of global capitalism better seen than in the belief in advanced capitalist states that levels of taxation (for public spending) must be kept low. We live in the age of the Divine Right of the Consumer. As a result the market threatens the welfare of the powerless and tramples over the natural environment. The claim is heard throughout the advanced industrial world – Galbraith's 'culture of contentment' (1992) – that higher levels of public spending *cannot* be afforded. But what determines the limit is political *choice* not absolute *necessity*. Governments face choices between acting as agents of welfare or agents of the marketplace. Today, 'sovereignty-free' international finance disciplines ostensibly sovereign governments. In the West this could result – because of some competitive disadvantages in global terms – in a loss of material living standards; but this in turn need not result in less fulfilling lives. Those who live on or beyond the periphery of today's islands of prosperity, for example, may have plenty to teach in the twenty-first century about how we might live, since they have already accommodated to modest means. Peripheries of the world unite:

you have nothing to lose but your centres. That said, the peripheries of the global capitalist system do not presently have much to lose, given their position in the global economy, the unhelpful rules of trade under the World Trade Organisation, the structural adjustment programmes of the IMF and World Bank, limited development help (often still tied to politics rather than helping the poor) and punitive debt repayment burdens.

The implications of globalisation, therefore, are not simple or uniformly beneficial. The two-edged effect is also evident in the field of military security. Long-range weapons of increasing destructive potential, range and accuracy have helped to create a global insecurity community. But note that it was out of common insecurity in the Cold War that the idea of common security emerged. The 'new thinking' of the 1980s showed that in the area of international security the negative aspects of global insecurity could be reversed, though the problem of controlling and ultimately eliminating nuclear weapons remains one of the most urgent challenges for statecraft in the post-Cold War era (MccGwire, 1994).

Globalisation's negative effects are not in principle beyond human control. That control – if it is to be in the human interest – will require new expressions of politics. Globalisation is often seen in extreme terms: by some – the ideologists of the market-place – in a very positive light, while by others – anxious about the impact of these forces on people's lives and traditional national control – in very negative ways. The political project of global moral science discussed later must seek to work with the potentially helpful dynamics of globalisation – the consciousness of 'one worldism' – while encouraging resistance to the destructive effects. It should not be assumed that globalisation in all its forms is irresistible, nor should it be assumed that it must mean homogenisation. It is for these reasons that those who have not given in to globo-pessimism have begun to concern themselves with fundamental questions of political theory and practical wisdom in relation to questions of global governance.

Global governance

Global governance concerns the relationships between forms of political authority, and the character of that authority, on a global scale. In other words, global governance refers to those theories and practices which seek to provide legitimised procedures for political activities (and not just those of governments) which are of global relevance. The precise shape(s) of global governance for the medium and long-term future are indistinct, but they will obviously have a profound effect on what we now conceive as international security and key questions of international relations. Clearly what emerges institutionally will be of considerable variety, given the multiple interfaces between the local and the global, but they will be critical to the future of world politics, since it will be the task of these mechanisms to distribute (and redistribute) wealth, accommodate the new and cushion change.

There are presently more questions than answers. How will the interplay of global and local forces be mediated through legitimate political control mechanisms? What will replace the Westphalian international system? What political and economic structures will evolve to cope with the decline of national models of economic development in the face of a globalised economic system? Is the most likely shift in political and economic decision-making power away from the sovereign state to regional economic collectivities grouped around these traditional units? It is difficult to predict how the patterns of global governance will evolve over the next half-century and beyond. It is as difficult as it would have been to predict the Westphalian system before it took shape. What *feels* clear is that something profound is underway, since the sovereign-state system does not work in important ways for the majority of the world's population. The latter's opinion may not yet (or ever) be decisive; more importantly, the ideological underpinnings of state sovereignty and independence are being daily subverted by globalisation, interdependence and regionalisation, while the material conditions of world politics will, short of amazing discoveries, become characterised by the growth of limits. Something profound is taking place, but the post-Westphalian pattern of global governance has yet to be worked out. Whether what evolves produces the cosy image of a global village, or a global Johannesburg (a tense city held together, and apart, by razor wire), or any other urban metaphor for our future remains to be seen. But what seems beyond doubt is the verdict that the rationality of statism – the belief that all decision-making power and loyalty should be focused on the sovereign (for the most part multi-nation) state – has reached its culminating point, and that future patterns of global governance will involve complex decentralisation below the state level, functional organisations above the state level, and a growing network of economic, social and cultural interdependencies at the level of transnational civil society, outside the effective control of governments (for an early vision of this see Falk, 1980). Such multidimensional webs of governance have sometimes been labelled as 'neo-medieval' models of future world politics.

Complexity in forms of governance is likely to be a characteristic of future world politics. As was argued in Chapter 1, the vaunted 'end of history' was not even a pause, still less a finale, and what beckons is not another round of ideological dialectics, but of multilectics about how to run the world, albeit in part rather than in whole. In this cultural babel, the pre-eminence of Western values will be challenged by different voices – some of which will be backed by serious power. The challenge is already present in certain forms of Islam and some so-called Asian values (though the challenge would be better understood and accommodated if the challenge were seen in terms of traditionalist versus modernist values rather than in a cultural essentialist – 'clash of civilisations' – fashion). Cultural essentialism – emphasising cultural continuity, the uniqueness of civilisations, and rejecting the universality of ideas – goes much too far. Most Westerners, for example, would feel more alien in their own traditional cultural past (marked by extreme deference to authority, undemocratic politics and fearful religious orthodoxy) than in the cultural present of today's 'developed' Asian and Islamic worlds. Better Singapore than Salem. Values change. Today's Western values, notably individualism, will not flourish on 'lifeboat earth' if the balance of economic and political power shifts to the authoritarian and anti-Western regions of Asia, and if millions of people continue to be born into wretched lives on the margins of existence. Values are a historical rather than a geographical phenomenon. Today's 'Western' values, in different material conditions, will once again reinvent themselves; this, after all, is in the spirit of Enlightenment.

The spread of the term global governance attests to the inadequacy of the orthodox language of academic International Relations. Terms such as 'international system', 'great powers', 'balance of power' and even 'foreign policy', today sound increasingly marginal if not actually anachronistic. Our words do not work, and so our imaginations are constrained: international relations in this era of rampant globalism and environmental challenge still 'gets said' in the language of textbook statism. Many minds are still in the grip, for example, of a Wightian image of world politics bifurcated between (state-centric) theories of the good life and (inter-state) theories of survival (Wight, 1966). The growth of suprastate regional institutions (the EU, NAFTA, ASEAN, for example) as nodal points for political and economic activity are obvious indicators of the breakdown of Wightian bifurcations. The traditional discipline of International Relations excludes too much for its own good, and certainly for the good of the vast majority of the world's population. Academic International Relations will not be the site for human emancipation in the twenty-first century if it is imprisoned by the concepts and categories of nineteenth-century language.

Those thinking about the structures and processes of global governance for the decades and half-centuries ahead do not think in traditional
global idealist terms – looking towards a world government for example
– but instead contemplate multilayered, overlapping and multifunctional
patterns of legitimate authority. The importance of creating a democratic and law-governed world is central in this project. Among the more
interesting and far-reaching ideas in this respect is the concept of
'cosmopolitan democracy' (Archibugi and Held, 1995). Although the
practical institutional operationalisation of the concept is at a very early
stage of discussion, its advocates seek answers to three questions which
many believe get to the heart of improving the prospects for human
security. How can the international system contribute to the development of democracy inside states? Is it possible to establish democratic
relations among sovereign states? Can decisions which affect the whole
world be taken democratically? The answers are likely to contain familiar
tensions, both at the conceptual and practical levels. There is, for
example, the challenge of creating globally acceptable standards of
behaviour in terms of human rights on the one hand, and the statist
impulse for sovereign particularity on the other.

The sovereign so-called nation-state with which we are now familiar,
and which realists describe (tautologically) as the 'primary actors' in
International Relations (defined in terms of 'relations between states') is
not a fixed entity – the inevitable product of the political nature of
humankind. Sovereign states are historical creations, the product of the
political nature of humankind. And times change. Nevertheless, whatever networks of global governance emerge under conditions of globalisation, some form of 'states' will remain an important part of the jigsaw
of world politics, though they will not be sovereign in the pure
Westphalian sense – any more than they have ever been 'nation states' in
the pure Wilsonian sense. Global governance will have to be truer to
both language and human needs if a serious and persistent level of
violence is to be avoided, and good governance in the human interest is
to be furthered. If the major task in the theory and practice of
international relations during the Cold War was to avoid a superpower
nuclear war, the major task for the post-Cold War era is pre-eminently
that of developing ideas about global governance that will recapture a
sense of the future and of a concept of progress in the interests of human
needs, world community and environmental sustainability. A future
world which is predictably (soon) to be characterised by system overload
has the choice – locally and globally – of being informed by the values of
community or of being driven by multilevel tribal confrontations. Even a
law-governed world will not maximise human security unless those laws

are informed by the values of a just world order. Imagining a politics and ethics on which to build more helpful structures of global governance is the task of what I call global moral science.

Global moral science

Global moral science is not the 'objective' moral science that was attempted by the *philosophes* but is a call to think systematically about how humans can live together, globally, in greater security and hope (Booth, 1995). Global moral science as a label is neutral, but my own preference is for cosmopolitan stories that will help species-identity and improve the prospects for human emancipation. In this sense, it follows a long tradition of those who have wanted to conceive humanity as a whole, rather than according to the divisions created by the interplay of historical circumstances. The main question from this perspective is not 'What will the twenty-first century be *like?*' but 'Who will the twenty-first century be *for?*'

It is possible to present some truly terrifying scenarios for the decades ahead if only 'fairly bad-case' assumptions are extrapolated. The nuclear danger could be back to haunt us, and social stress could lead to Hobbesian nightmares. A world divided, under conditions of globalisation, would be uniquely insecure and deeply inhumane. The signs of such possibilities, fuelled by new cold wars of the mind, are not difficult to find. As the Berlin Wall was being demolished in 1989 – the symbol of the East–West confrontation and a failed monument to an attempt to stop the movement of ideas – many more walls were being built to divide the West from the Rest, in an attempt to stop the movement of peoples. The signs are not encouraging that the governments of the rich world will be able to persuade their voters to reduce their material prospects in the interests of a globally richer life.

Despite the endorsement earlier of Heilbroner's view that apprehension is the dominant mood of today, and the identification of converging global pressures pointing to system-overload, the global future is not inevitably one of permanent and multilevel confrontation. Such a future is likely, however, if the privileged and powerful retreat into lives preoccupied by their private and local needs and wants, and if these fault lines are deepened by ideology. This can only be resisted by the creation of persuasive big pictures of global politics, big pictures that are both inclusive and sensitive to local outlooks. These big pictures are unlikely to be completely new, but rather the result of the refinement and modernisation of earlier exercises in global thinking. Global moral science must seek to reinvent our human future(s) in a manner that is appropriate for tomorrow's crowded and technological world and anchored in a knowledge of all the failed projects and false universalisms of the past, including racism, statism, religious fundamentalism, rampant Westernisation and simple faith in science and technology. At the centre of reconceiving world politics, the success or failure of developing a global human rights culture will be crucial.

One ambitious exercise in global moral science, *Eunomia – New Order for a New World* (1990) was written by one of the contributors to this volume, Philip Allott. A key feature of this book is that it seeks to open up the human future, as opposed to closing it down in the fashion of fatalist realism. Allott's social idealism regards human society as self-constituted. This includes all manifestations of human society, including the games nations play in international politics. The 'reality' of international politics is just one aspect of human-made reality. Society, including international society, exists in a condition of permanent self-constituting. Such construction, reconstruction and occasionally revolutionising of social reality is the result of a society's image of its own self-conceived values and possibilities. These include its ideas of 'the good', which in turn include such self-replicating ideas as 'this is the best of all possible worlds'. Societies change, or not, according to the theories of politics, economics and society that they transmit to each other. For Allott, law is the critical institution for the transmitting of theories into regularised behaviour. The idealist philosophical basis of this set of arguments leads to his important and empowering conclusion, namely that the history of a society, including those phenomena we call 'international relations' and 'international security', is not the result of fate or natural forces. Rather, society and history are constituted by humans; consequently, they can be reconceived and remade, albeit sometimes with great difficulty. The key is human consciousness. Human evolution is the evolution of human consciousness, and theorising is a basic element in that evolution. Theorising embraces both the possibility of theory and the political, economic, social and legal operationalising of theory. For students of International Politics, the challenge laid down by Philip Allott, in terms of inherited self-constituted international phenomena such as 'war', 'sovereignty' and 'nation', is to reconceive, reconstitute and reinvent politics on a global scale. *Eunomia* is one attempt to offer a comprehensive account of human society, a synoptic view of the human sciences, a critical perspective on traditional theory, a philosophical basis for practical theory and an idealist conception of human possibilities. Such an approach constitutes, for me, global moral science at its broadest. It is a start in what is practically ('process utopian') progressive (see, for example, Booth, 1990: esp. 32–4).

Allott's social idealism has to be translated into political practice, and it is here that new social movements are important within and between countries to generate ideas, oppose injustice, and help create new political forms for a world which, within fifty years, will be as unlike today's as today's is from that of two hundred years ago. History has not ended, it has moved into fast forward in this first truly global age. The task of global moral science, in such challenging circumstances, is to infuse globalisation with a reinvented humanity, including its global political expression. The power of ideas in politics can hardly be overestimated, though textbook realism characteristically ignores them in favour of traditionalist and regressive assumptions about human nature, brute power and ethnocentric structures (Garnett, 1987). Ideas make the structures that rule the world, though these ideas may be closely related to material realities. Today, ideas can proliferate rapidly and powerfully, as was evident in 1989, in the Soviet empire and apartheid South Africa. What is at stake for world politics tomorrow is the choice between moralities that divide humanity and moralities that will act as species glue. Will politically authoritative morality always stop at the national frontier, or can it go beyond? Can individual compassion, which can help, be turned into structural compassion, which can solve?

One aspect of global moral science might be described as the exploration of the international political economy of ethics. The problem is not only 'who cares about poverty?' but 'what can be done to change things?' The zeitgeist is hostile, because there seems to be no alternative to the liberal-capitalist hegemony (the expanding market, the shrinking state, privatisation etc.), but the need is pressing, because of the wretched and short lives so many have to suffer. The tragedy of liberal-capitalism's success is that in honouring the individual and trying to evade violence, at the same time it coopts people and institutions in a system that oppresses many and damages nature. Contrary to the West's self-protecting conventional wisdom at the present time, hyper-liberalism is globally more of a threat to more people than hyper-nationalism. The casualties among have-nots in global economic struggles (living marginal lives in shanty-towns or inner cities, or dying of preventable causes before their fifth birthdays) greatly outnumber the casualties in local nationalist struggles (which demand, and get, much more media attention). David Schweickart is one who has criticised the global domination of capitalism on economic and ethical grounds, and has proposed an alternative – what he calls 'Economic Democracy' – that promises more efficiency and rational growth, and more equality, democracy and meaningful work (1993). His is a version of market socialism with decentralised investment planning and work-place democracy. Schweickart sees the creation of an Economic Democracy as part of the struggle to improve the lot of women, to end racism, to achieve a sustainable environment and to bring about world peace: 'To achieve anything, we must struggle for everything' (1993: 356). Reaching the goal is not inevitable, but he considers it a 'rational hope'.

Statecraft and security

The challenge to students and practitioners of International Relations is no less than rethinking global politics – from the top down and the bottom up. What has been explicit in this Conclusion so far has been that global politics are at a crossroads because of the revolutionary material circumstances in which we find ourselves. The choice we (the Haves) face is whether to allow regressive thinking to trap us into a world of private dreams but threatening public nightmares, or whether by resistance and reinvention to seek to build through dialogue, dollars and determination, a human community and global polity on the foundation of the revolutionary material circumstances. Implicit in crossroads is the question of agency. Who will decide? Who will do the resistance and reinvention? Who will take the necessary practical steps?

At this stage of global politics, the empirical answer to these questions of agency is reasonably clear. The engine room for change – if it is to be progressive – will be global social movements committed to world order values such as non-violence, economic justice, environmental sustainability, good governance and human rights (Ekins, 1992; Falk, 1992). But only so much can be achieved without the agency of the state. As was discussed earlier, the role of the state these days is widely challenged, as the limitations of state-centric politics, environmental policy and economics are all too evident. The sovereign state represents neither an edifying transcendent morality nor the rational unit for determining the politics of a global age. Statism – the ideology which focuses all loyalty and decisionmaking power on the sovereign state – was historically the solution to the disorder of the Thirty Years War. In these terms it can be seen as progressive. But it is not unusual in human life to seek to deal with tomorrow's problems with yesterday's solutions. The continuing strength of statism attests to the fact that state elites in particular learned the lessons of their historical moment too well. We have to begin where we are, and pragmatically the governments of sovereign states will remain important actors in world politics and will continue to serve key functions, *inter alia*, in the regulation of violence, the development of law, the direction of social policies and the management of external relations. Statecraft will therefore continue to be of significance. Consequently, even if, in practice, states often behave like 'gangsters' rather than 'guardian angels' (Wheeler, 1996), the 'rational hope' must be that more of them will become what Bull called 'local agents of the world common good'. If the evidence for such an outcome is mixed, there are nevertheless grounds for hope, even in the field of international security.

Global security thinking for the emerging global age seemed to have a false start with the coming to power of Gorbachev in 1985. The ideas he began to operationalise led to the start of a radical shift in Soviet security thinking, and challenged his superpower adversary to follow. Of historic significance was the fact that his policies revealed that a new consciousness – beyond the narrow and militarised power outlooks of the Cold War – could indeed capture the security agenda of a superpower government. The elements of Gorbachev's 'new thinking' were not original. Indeed, some ideas had first been placed on the international agenda at the time of the League of Nations and the first Hague Conference (Wiseman, 1989). More recently, major aspects of his approach were advanced by 'alternative defence' thinkers in the West in the late 1970s and early 1980s. What was novel was the way Gorbachev put these hitherto radical ideas together, and turned them into political practice. Gorbachev's 'new thinking' about security emphasised the importance of common security (security interdependence), an 'all-human' approach to international security, the need to de-ideologise international politics, the political roots of insecurity, a recognition that crises are paths to war, the central importance of arms control and disarmament in security policy, 'reasonable sufficiency' in defence procurement, and defensive defence (MccGwire, 1987, 1991; Meyer, 1988; Allison, 1991). The adoption of such an outlook to international security by all states would not necessarily be synonymous with the end of the war system, but it would represent a radical shift towards what Kenneth Boulding called 'stable peace', that is, a situation in which the dynamics of the security dilemma would have been left behind, and in which war could be considered unlikely not because of the terror induced by mutual threats – the MAD world – but because of mutual satisfaction with the prevailing situation (1979).

Gorbachev was eclipsed in one of the many endings of the Cold War, and what he contributed in the field of international security is now in danger of being dismissed or even forgotten. He transcended the Cold War mindset, and thereby helped to bring it to an end out of choice, not as a result of the defeat or collapse of the Soviet state. The two events – the end of the Cold War and the Soviet collapse – need to be kept separate. Whatever led to the Kremlin's decision to wind down the

Soviet experiment in 1991 should be separated from the Kremlin's earlier decision to end the Cold War. Just as in the late 1940s the problem for the West of learning to live with nuclear weapons became unhelpfully complicated by the problem of learning to cope with the rise of Soviet power (MccGwire, 1985/6), so today the problem of unravelling the meaning of the end of the Cold War has become complicated by the almost simultaneous collapse of Soviet power.

In the winding down of the Cold War in the late 1980s statecraft and security thinking of a high order were displayed by the president of the USSR. But his ideas did not come from nowhere. It goes without saying that they did not emerge out of late-night discussions with the traditionalists of Soviet/Russian strategic culture who had dominated the Kremlin during Gorbachev's rise to power; instead the ideas grew out of the debating within progressive civil society in East and West, which got transmitted and welcomed into the Kremlin. In the process of resisting and reinventing security in Europe (and the Cold War more generally) Gorbachev and the alternative security thinkers were complementary. Civil society and superpower needed each other. A similar complementarity existed between progressive global civil society (in this case those opposing racism) and a growing number of governments in the story of the rise of Nelson Mandela from 'terrorist' to the world's favourite statesman, and the fall of the South African apartheid regime from 'bastion of the West' to global pariah. What these examples show, and others illustrated in earlier chapters, is that choices always exist and that space, however little, can be exploited in the interests of advancing security and emancipation. Rethinking statecraft must be part of reinventing a new metaphysics of security appropriate for the first truly global age, and rethought statecraft must allow space for the cosmopolitan cares of progressive global civil society.

Despite all the warnings, the human sciences have scarcely begun to contemplate the stresses and strains of an overcrowded, overheated planet. In the decades ahead, how much of world politics will resemble what Heilbroner calls 'the rage of the ghetto' (1995: 90)? There is a confident view among some International Relations scholars that international society at the end of the twentieth century is reasonably robust. This is a top down view. Certainly there has not been a major war between the 'great powers' for half a century, and for this we should be thankful. However, when one looks at world politics from the bottom up – from the perspective of the poor, many children, Africa – the picture looks different. Change requires a rejection of the common sense values of the powerful, which have shaped our lives and often depressed our spirits, such as the self-serving homily that 'the poor will always be with us'. The poor are an invention of society. Members of 'primitive societies' have few possessions, but they are not 'poor'. As Marshall Sahlins puts it: 'Poverty is not a certain amount of goods, nor is it just a relationship between means and ends; above all it is a relation between people. Poverty is a social status. As such it is the invention of civilisation' (quoted in Heilbroner, 1995: 28). What we invent, we can reinvent. If such a view is considered utopian and naive, how much more so is the assumption that the human species can survive in good shape in a world dominated by the politics of exclusiveness and the economics of exploitation? But change is obstructed by the historic power of today's ruling ideas about politics and economics, as they have become normalised, naturalised and enshrined as common sense. Ruling ideas always assume their survival, but uncommon sense should warn of the opposite.

To talk of 'beyond' in this Conclusion is not to suppose that there will necessarily be one. 'Humans' as they have evolved may, for a variety of reasons, become extinct as a species, like the Neanderthals. It is in the gap between hope and human achievement (including possible extinction) that this thing called 'international relations' fits, so frustratingly – as a threat and as a promise. Unless, through progress in Global Moral Science, we can develop more rational forms of global governance, then the prospects are, at worst, species elimination, at best a regression into an insecure world of razor wire surrounding one's home and nuclear weapons defending one's country, waiting for catastrophes of greater or lesser magnitude.

For the moment, the progress of human progress has been badly dented. Faith in the future has shrivelled in many societies, although hope for progress remains widespread. The idea of progress has been a powerful force in Western politics, society and economics in the past 250 years. In contrast to the recent past, confidence has declined in both the empirical reality of 'progress' and even sometimes in its desirability. The twentieth century has taught us that progress (at least the type that became compulsive in the previous two centuries) could have a dark side. What gave us better medicines also gave us, through the conventions of international relations, better bombs. It came as a general surprise that progress in knowledge did not translate directly into progress in society, and certainly not in mastery over the future. As animals imprinted with sociality – the capacity to develop complex social relations – it remains for us to *invent* the future, not *discover* it through simply amassing knowledge. The Human Genome Project will reveal some material characteristics of humans, but will not – cannot –

tell us the meaning of life, or of what it might be to be human, except in some biochemical sense. Revealing our biochemistry will tell us no more about the 'meaning of life' than the examination of the chemistry and physics of bricks and wood might tell us about the meaning of a building. Buildings, like humans, comprise material elements, but in both cases it is human consciousness that determines whether the (same) particles constitute a cathedral or a torture-chamber, a divinely ordained queen or a daughter of enlightenment.

We live, I believe, in the early stages of one of the most decisive periods in human history – the first truly global age, with all that implies for reimagining the human implications of a decisive reinvention of time and space, comparable with a small number of such turning-points over the past 100–150,000 years (learning to ride horses, discovering the world is not flat and the Industrial Revolution). The potential evolutionary implications of globalist reimaginings are enormous, not least for politics and economics, including 'international relations'. Natural selection on the African savannah thousands of generations ago created the brains that produced the consciousness that got us here today – a world in which Mutual Assured Destruction and a human rights culture coexist. It remains to be seen whether natural selection in our new material circumstances will accelerate and produce similar two-edged creativity, or a political consciousness dominated by notions of an all-human community. Time is not on our side, and so the task in the human sciences is not – contra Stephen Hawking (1988) – to be distracted by seeking to discover the 'mind of God' (predictably a mirage, a distorted reflection of what exists in the mind of the God-seeker); it is rather the invention of a peaceful and loving humanity through systematic and critical description, understanding, explanation and forecasting. Within this project must be the recovery of hope, a sense of hope, a sense of the future, and confidence in human agency. We have, of course, to begin from where we are. Not all will have the space of a Gorbachev, or the vision of a Mandela. But we all have some. In that regard it is important to remember that the Berlin Wall did not fall: it was pushed. It was thought up, built up, unthought and pulled down. This most symbolic material structure of the Cold War was demolished by people changing their minds. Like the Berlin Wall, the political, social, cultural and economic world in which we live today – nuclear missiles, rat-infested shanty-towns, fundamentalist churches and sweat-shops – are also inventions, susceptible of being thought up, built up, unthought and pulled down.

REFERENCES

Allison, Roy (1991) 'New Thinking about Defence in the Soviet Union', in Ken Booth (ed.), *New Thinking About Strategy and International Security* (London: HarperCollins), pp. 215–43.

Allott, Philip (1990) *Eunomia – New Order for a New World* (Oxford: Oxford University Press).

Archibugi, Daniela and David Held (1995) *Cosmopolitan Democracy, An Agenda for a New World Order* (Cambridge: Polity Press).

Booth, Ken (1990) 'Steps Towards Stable Peace in Europe: A Theory and Practice of Coexistence', *International Affairs*, vol. 66(1), 17–45.

    (1995) 'Human Wrongs and International Relations', *International Affairs*, vol. 71(1), 103–26.

Boulding, Kenneth (1979) *Stable Peace* (Austin, TX: University of Texas Press).

Bull, Hedley (1983) 'Order and Justice in International Relations', *Hagey Lectures* (University of Waterloo).

Ekins, Paul (1992) *A New World Order. Grassroots Movements for Global Change* (London: Routledge).

Falk, Richard (1980) 'Anarchism and World Order', in Richard A. Falk and Samuel S. Kim (eds.), *The War System: An Interdisciplinary Approach* (Boulder, CO: Westview Press), pp. 37–57.

    (1992) *Explorations at the Edge of Time. The Prospects for World Order* (Philadelphia: Temple University Press).

Galbraith, J. K. (1992) *The Culture of Contentment* (London: Sinclair-Stevenson).

Garnett, John (1987) 'Strategic Studies and its Assumptions', in John Baylis *et al.* (eds.), *Contemporary Strategy*, vol. I (New York: Holmes and Meier), pp. 3–29.

Hawking, Stephen (1988) *A Brief History of Time* (New York: Bantam).

Heilbroner, Robert (1995) *Visions of the Future* (New York: Oxford University Press).

Hynes, Samuel (1976) *The Auden Generation. Literature and Politics in England in the 1930s* (London: Faber and Faber).

MccGwire, Michael (1985/6) 'Deterrence: the Problem – Not the Solution', *International Affairs*, vol. 62(1), 55–70.

    (1987) *Military Objectives in Soviet Foreign Policy* (Washington, DC: The Brookings Institution).

    (1991) *Perestroika and Soviet Military Policy* (Washington, DC: The Brookings Institution).

    (1994) 'Is There a Future for Nuclear Weapons?', *International Affairs*, vol. 70(2), 211–28.

Meyer, S. (1988) 'The Sources and Prospects of Gorbachev's New Political Thinking on Security', *International Security*, vol. 13(2), 124–63.

Rosenau, James (1990) *Turbulence in World Politics: A Theory of Change and Continuity* (New York: Harvester Wheatsheaf).

Schweickart, David (1993) *Against Capitalism* (Cambridge: Cambridge University Press).

Wheeler, Nicholas J. (1996) 'Guardian Angel or Global Gangster', *Political Studies*, vol. 44(1).

Wight, Martin (1966) 'Why is There No International Theory?' in Herbert Butterfield and Martin Wight (eds.), *Diplomatic Investigations: Essays in the Theory of International Politics* (London: Allen and Unwin), pp. 17–34.

Wiseman, Geoffrey (1989) *Common Security and Non Provocative Defence: Alternative Approaches to the Security Dilemma* (Canberra: Peace Research Centre).

Index